REBELLION IN THE MOHAWK VALLEY

~

THE ST. LEGER EXPEDITION OF 1777

A careworn and dissolute Brigadier-General Barry St. Leger, ca. 1780
Unknown artist.

REBELLION IN THE MOHAWK VALLEY

THE ST. LEGER EXPEDITION OF 1777

Gavin K. Watt

reasearch assistance by James F. Morrison

THE DUNDURN GROUP
TORONTO · OXFORD

Copy-Editor: Andrea Pruss
Design: Jennifer Scott
Printer: Transcontinental

National Library of Canada Cataloguing in Publication Data

Watt, Gavin K.
    Rebellion in the Mohawk Valley: the St. Leger expedition of 1777

Includes bibliographical references and index.
ISBN 1-55002-376-4

1. Burgoyne's Invasion, 1777. 2. Oriskany (N.Y.), Battle of, 1777. 3. Iroquois Indians — History.
4. Mohawk River Valley (N.Y.) — History. 5. Indians of North America — Canada — Wars —
1763–1814. I. Title.

E233.W38 2002   973.3'33   C2002-901065-9

1   2   3   4   5   06   05   04   03   02

THE CANADA COUNCIL | LE CONSEIL DES ARTS
FOR THE ARTS | DU CANADA
SINCE 1957 | DEPUIS 1957

ONTARIO ARTS COUNCIL
CONSEIL DES ARTS DE L'ONTARIO

We acknowledge the support of the **Canada Council for the Arts** and the **Ontario Arts Council** for our publishing program. We also acknowledge the financial support of the **Government of Canada** through the **Book Publishing Industry Development Program** and **The Association for the Export of Canadian Books**, and the **Government of Ontario** through the **Ontario Book Publishers Tax Credit** program.

Printed and bound in Canada.⊛
Printed on recycled paper.
www.dundurn.com

Dundurn Press
8 Market Street
Suite 200
Toronto, Ontario, Canada
M5E 1M6

Dundurn Press
73 Lime Walk
Headington, Oxford,
England
OX3 7AD

Dundurn Press
2250 Military Road
Tonawanda NY
U.S.A. 14150

Rebellion in the Mohawk Valley

~

The St. Leger Expedition of 1777

To Elizabeth Gillian Robinson

Contents

Acknowledgements   11

Comparative chronology   13

Chapter 1   A Seed Is Sown   21

Chapter 2   1776 — A Year of Manoeuvring   27
             The Ruins of This Once Strong and Beautiful Fort

Chapter 3   The Launch of the Expedition   56
             In Readiness to Embark

Chapter 4   Not Quite as Planned   81
             Fort Ticonderoga. . . Abandoned by the Rebels

Chapter 5   Too Little, Too Late   107
             Rejected with Disdain

Chapter 6   The March of the Tryon County Militia   136
             Rouse Then My Countrymen, Rouse

Chapter 7   Ambuscade at Oriskany   155
             The Indians Rose with a Dreadful Yell

Chapter 8   Tryon County Smiled Through Tears   176
             A Success So Signal

Chapter 9   The Stand-off   195
             Defend This Fort to the Last Extremity

Chapter 10   The Puny Siege   224
              Two or Three Small Popguns

Chapter 11   The Ignominious End of the Siege   240
              Cowardice in Some, Treason in Others

Chapter 12   Retracing Its Steps   262
              An Astonishing Detour

Chapter 13   The Curtain Falls   287
              This Damned Place — Reduced to Ashes

Epilogue   Of Grand Strategy   311

Bibliography   328

Endnotes   342

Index   410

Acknowledgements

This book has been twenty-five years in the making. In that time, I have researched hundreds of books and documents, made many false starts, written in spurts, discarded sections, and begun all over again. Throughout those years, a fellow military re-enactor and historian, James F. Morrison of Gloversville, N.Y., fed me ideas and research. Jim answered specific questions and frequently sent reams of commentary and his transcripts, newsletters, and published monographs and books. Much of the credit for the depth of this study must go to Jim's unflagging interest in the Mohawk region and his wonderful generosity.

Another superb resource has been a major collection of transcripts prepared by William A. Smy, an expert on Butler's Rangers from St. Catharines, Ont. As the late-eighteenth-century world was considerably smaller than today's, Bill's findings reveal a great deal about all the northern regiments, the natives, and the forces of Congress.

An enthusiast who gave wholeheartedly of his time and research was Joseph Robertaccio of Utica, N.Y. Joe took me on a grand tour of several upper Mohawk Valley historic sites — in particular the extensive grounds of the Oriskany battle — and substantially expanded my understanding.

My thanks to Paul Fortier, formerly of the National Archives of Canada, for his invaluable assistance in obtaining photocopies of original documents regarding the Ticonderoga phase of the St. Leger Expedition, and to Leon Warmski, now retired from the Archives of Ontario, for his quietly unassuming direction through the maze of collections held by that institution.

Great thanks to Timothy Dubé, Military Archivist at the National Archives of Canada, for his energetic assistance in straightening out my archival references, and to Paul McIlroy and Sandra Guillaume of the Archives of Ontario for their assistance with this same complex topic.

Assistance has been freely given by a number of re-enactor/historians — Rob Bothwell, Todd Braisted, the late Lew Decker, Peter Ferri,

Steve Gilbert, Noel Levee, Roy Najecki, Larry Ostola, Jeff Paine, Claus Reuter, Rick Sherman, Mike Thompson, and Phil Weaver. A number of historians, writers, genealogists, and archivists also provided help, amongst them DeWitt Bailey, Glenn Forrester, René Chartrand, Christopher Fox, André Gousse, Peter Harrington, John Hayes, Ken Johnson, ObInsp Klingelhöfer, John Merz, Vallena Munro, Denis Robillard, Christine Steenburgh, and Anthony Wayne Tommell.

An amazing resource has been Paul L. Steven's doctoral dissertation "His Majesty's 'Savage' Allies," SUNY, Buffalo, 1984. This is an incredibly detailed and sadly unsung work.

Discussions with the Mohawk historian Okwaho opened my eyes to several facts about Joseph Brant and the Six Nations Confederacy. His observations prevented me from committing several embarrassing errors.

Thanks to the artist-members of the Museum of Applied Military History whose talents add so greatly to our picture of these events.

My thanks to my wife, Gill, who scoured the manuscript and caught so many glitches and unintended mysteries. And a particular note of thanks to my daughter Nancy, who spent many hours applying her professional creative-writing skills to the manuscript.

To all of the many others who have been so helpful and offered continous inspiration, my gratitude.

Gavin K. Watt,
Museum of Applied Military History
King City, Ontario 2001

Comparative Chronology

NOTES

1. It is remarkable that so many primary sources do not agree on the timing of important events. The trouble does not arise over major battles, but over such issues as the day on which Jane McCrae was killed, the day the bridge of boats was destroyed, and so forth. Readers will find variations by a day or two for some events. Nonetheless, the value of the comparative chronology is not greatly impaired by these disagreements.
2. Some personalities jump from one column to the next due to circumstances.

1777	FORT STANWIX, TRYON COUNTY & SCHOHARIE	ST. LEGER EXPEDITION	BURGOYNE EXPEDITION
MAY 03	GANSEVOORT ARRIVES STANWIX		
MAY 05			BURGOYNE ARRIVES QUEBEC
MAY 10	WILLETT ARRIVES STANWIX		
MAY 29		SIR JOHN ARRIVES QUEBEC	
JUN 01		CLAUS ARRIVES QUEBEC	
JUN 06		ORDERS ARRIVE NIAGARA	
JUN 13			LEAVES FT ST JOHN'S
JUN 14	BADLAM SENT TO TRYON		
JUN 20			ISSUES PROCLAMATION
JUN 23		CLAUS LEAVES LACHINE	
JUN 24			BURGOYNE AT CROWN POINT
JUN 25	GREGG SCALPED AT STANWIX	CLAUS SENDS SCOUTS TO STANWIX	
JUN 26		EXP'N LEAVES LACHINE	
JUN 27	UNADILLA CONFERENCE	BRANT AT UNADILLA	
JUN 30	WARNINGS OF ATTACK		BURGOYNE NEAR FORT TICON.
JUL 03	DETAIL ATTACKED AT STANWIX		

1777	FORT STANWIX, TRYON COUNTY & SCHOHARIE	ST. LEGER EXPEDITION	BURGOYNE EXPEDITION
JUL 05		CLAUS QUESTIONS PRISONERS F/STANWIX	
JUL 06			TICONDEROGA FALLS
JUL 07		ST. LEGER IGNORES INTELL'CE	BATTLE OF HUBBARTON
JUL 08		EXP'N AT BUCK ISLAND	FT. ANNE ABANDONED
JUL 09		JAGERS/CDNS ARRIVE	
JUL 12			AT SKENESBOROUGH
JUL 13		BUTLER LEAVES NIAGARA	
JUL 16			FT. EDWARD ABANDONED
JUL 17	HERKIMER'S PROCLAMATION	NEWS OF TICON. RECEIVED	
JUL 19		STL LEAVES BUCK IS.	MAJOR INDIAN COUNCIL
JUL 20		SIR JOHN LEAVES BUCK IS.	
JUL 23		BRANT & CLAUS ARRIVE AT OSWEGO	FT. GEORGE ABANDONED
JUL 25		ST. LEGER GIVES UP ALERT BUTLER ARRIVES OSWEGO JOHN MCD SENT TO RAISE COY	OCCUPIED FT. ANNE

1777	FORT STANWIX, TRYON COUNTY & SCHOHARIE	ST. LEGER EXPEDITION	BURGOYNE EXPEDITION
JUL 26	OBSTRUCT WOOD CK	ST. LEGER LEAVES OSWEGO	JANE MCCRAE KILLED
JUL 27	GIRLS ATTACKED AT STANWIX		BURGOYNE REBUKES NATIVES
JUL 28			OCCUPY FT. GEORGE FT. EDWARD ABANDONED
JUL 29	ONEIDAS ADVISE GANSEVOORT ST. LEGER ON ONONDAGA R.	BIRD SENT AHEAD TO STANWIX	
JUL 30	STANWIX REINFORCED W/200 CONTLS	THREE RIVERS COUNCIL	OCCUPY FTS. EDWARD & MILLER
JUL 31			GATES REPLACES SCHUYLER
AUG 01	CONTINUE OBSTRUCT WOOD CK	INDS AT WOOD CK	
AUG 02	SUPPLIES & 100 CONTLS ARRIVE AT STANWIX	BIRD TOO LATE TO STOP	
AUG 03	HERK CALLS OUT MILITIA FLAG RAISED AT FORT	ST. LEGER HOLDS PARADE & SUMMONS FORT	
AUG 04	MILITIA LEAVE FT. DAYTON		REBELS RETREAT TO STILLWATER
AUG 05	MILITIA ARRIVE ORISKA	INTELL ARRIVES RE MILITIA SIR JOHN SENT OFF TO OPPOSE	INDIANS WISH TO LEAVE PERSUADED TO STAY
AUG 06	MILITIA AMBUSHED. WILLETT RAIDS CAMPS	AMBUSH AT ORISKANY	

1777	FORT STANWIX, TRYON COUNTY & SCHOHARIE	ST. LEGER EXPEDITION	BURGOYNE EXPEDITION
AUG 07	COMMITTEE WRITES SCHUYLER OF DISASTER	ST. LEGER REFUSES REQUEST TO MARCH INTO VALLEY	
AUG 08	WILLETT SENT FOR HELP	FORT SUMMONED AGAIN	
AUG 09	SUMMONS DECLINED LEARNED MARCHES	SIEGE TRENCH OPENED	
AUG 11	WILLETT MEETS LEARNED ON ROAD	STOP FORT'S WATER SUPPLY	
AUG 12			BURG RECEIVES DISPATCH RE ORISKANY
AUG 13	ARNOLD TO LEAD RELIEF	WALT BUTLER SENT ON FLAG SCHOHARIE UPRISING	BENNINGTON EXP'N MARCHES
AUG 14	ORISKA DESTROYED		AT SARATOGA
AUG 15	BUTER'S FLAG CAPTURED	MANY RECRUITS JOIN	AT SCHUYLER'S ESTATE
AUG 16	HERKIMER DIES	HOWITZERS NOT SUCCESS	BENNINGTON DISASTER
AUG 17	RELIEF AT FT DAYTON		
AUG 19	SENT TWO MEN TO VALLEY	SARAH MCGINNIS ARRIVES TRENCH 150 YDS F/FORT	INDIAN COUNCIL HELD
AUG 20	WALT BUTLER SENT'D TO DEATH		MOST INDS WITHDRAW
AUG 21	HONJOST SENT ON RUSE	WORD OF REBEL RELIEF	

1777	FORT STANWIX, TRYON COUNTY & SCHOHARIE	ST. LEGER EXPEDITION	BURGOYNE EXPEDITION
AUG 22	RUSE DELIVERED	STL RETREATS	
AUG 24	ARNOLD ARRIVES FORT		
AUG 26	RELIEF FORCE DEPARTS	ST. L AT OSWEGO. VON K ARRIVES WITH BATT'N	
AUG 28			BRANT ADVISES OF ST. LEGER'S RETREAT & LEAVES
SEP 01			LUNDY CONFIRMS RETREAT
SEP 04		MCDONEL AT OSWEGO	FT. HUNTERS ARRIVE
SEP 07		ST. LEGER DEPARTS OSWEGO	
SEP 14		CARLETON PROMISES TO REBUILD OSWEGO	ONEIDAS & TUSCS TAKE U.S. WAR HATCHET
SEP 15		BUTLER GETS BEATING ORDER FOR RANGERS	DESTROYS BRIDGE OF BOATS OVER HUDSON
SEP 18			ATTACKS ON TICONDEROGA POSTS
SEP 19			BATTLE OF FREEMAN'S FARM
SEP 21			RECEIVES CLINTON'S DISPATCH
SEP 22		EXP'N AT LA PRAIRIE	

1777	FORT STANWIX, TRYON COUNTY & SCHOHARIE	ST. LEGER EXPEDITION	BURGOYNE EXPEDITION
SEP 23		EXP'N MARCH ST JOHN'S	ATTACK ON DIAMOND IS.
SEP 25		ST. LEGER LEAVES FT ST JOHN'S	
SEP 27		ST. LEGER ARRIVES TICON.	COURIER TO CLINTON
SEP 28		MACLEAN ARRIVES TICON.	2ND COURIER TO CLINTON
OCT 03			ARMY'S RATIONS CUT
OCT 04			ONEIDAS & TUSCS JOIN GATES ARMY
OCT 07			BATTLE OF BEMIS HTS
OCT 08			ARMY RETREATS
OCT 14		BUTLER AT BUCK ISLAND	PARLEY W/GATES
OCT 16		FT HUNTERS ARRIVE TICON.	CONVENTION SIGNED
OCT 17		FLAG FALLS AT MT INDEPEND	SURRENDER CEREMONY
OCT 20		WORD OF SURRENDER ARRIVES AT TICON.	
NOV 08		TICON. DESTROY'D & ABAND'D	

CHAPTER ONE

~

A Seed is Sown

On a winter's day in England in 1776, Lieutenant-General John Burgoyne met with Guy Johnson, an exiled colonel of Indian Affairs from the Mohawk Valley. During their discussion, the germ of an idea for an expedition to the Mohawk Valley was first planted.

Smooth, handsome, urbane John Burgoyne was home on leave from America, ostensibly to occupy his seat in Parliament, but in reality to promote his chances for a senior command. By the by, he was enjoying the company of his wife and his love of the theatre — he was also a dramatist — while indulging his distaste for American winters. Never one to doubt his gifts, the ambitious general had observed the debacle at Bunker's Hill and the stalemate at Boston and returned home convinced that only a firm, deft hand (such as his own) could end the rebellion.[1] An accomplished writer, Burgoyne penned a treatise entitled "Reflections upon the War in America,"[2] in which he promoted the concept of dividing the rebelling colonies in half by mounting simultaneous expeditions from the north and south. This idea was not original, but Burgoyne could justly claim the credit for committing it to paper in great detail.

By February of 1776, his efforts had brought him promotion to lieutenant-general and an appointment as second-in-command to Captain-General Guy Carleton, the military commander and Governor-in-Chief of Quebec.[3] Before leaving England, Burgoyne somehow heard of Johnson's whereabouts and arranged a meeting to discuss affairs in Quebec and neighbouring New York province.[4]

Fleshy, gruff, irascible Colonel Guy Johnson was in England to obtain confirmation of his position as Superintendent of Northern Indian Affairs, a role he had inherited from his uncle and father-in-law, the famous Sir William Johnson. The previous June, while at Guy Park, his luxurious Mohawk Valley estate, he received intelligence that a party of New Englanders was going to kill him to prevent his marshalling the Indians against the rebellion.[5] Johnson gathered together 250 Indian Department

John Burgoyne in his youth

Unknown engraver after a painting by
Allan Ramsay, 1755-1756.

employees, tenants, friends, and loyal Mohawks, and, with his wife, Mary, and young children, fled upriver, finally arriving at Oswego. At the old fort, Mary died during a difficult childbirth that had been complicated both by the stress of travel and the abandonment of their lovely estate, Sir William's wedding gift.[6]

Awash with grief and anger, Johnson held a grand council in the crumbling works. He offered the King's hatchet to the fourteen hundred natives who attended and was gratified to have it accepted by many eager warriors. He and his expanded party set off for Montreal to assist the royal administration in preventing a rebel invasion of the province. Guy and his brother-in-law Daniel Claus immediately demonstrated their influence with the Seven Nations of Canada by assembling seventeen hundred of them at a council. The natives readily adopted the Oswego

A Seed is Sown

Fleshy, gruff, irascible Colonel Guy Johnson

Unknown painter.

resolutions of the Six Nations and Detroit Wyandots. Hundreds of war-riors volunteered to serve, but to Johnson's distress, Quebec's Governor Carleton received him coolly and gave his rangers and native volunteers very marginal employment.

Then came the shocking news that the governor had established a separate Indian Department for Quebec and, in the process, deposed Claus as Johnson's Deputy Superintendent of the Canada Indians. This had been a key role of the Six Nations department since the conquest of Canada, so the perfunctory rejection of Claus was a blow against

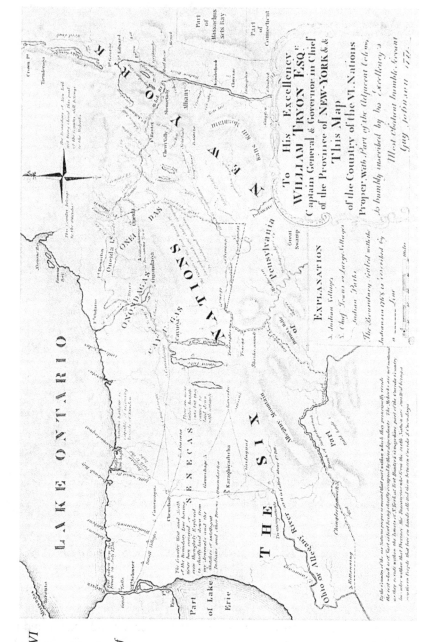

"Map of the Country of the VI Nations" Guy Johnson, 1771

Courtesy of the National Archives of Canada, C-21362.

A Seed is Sown

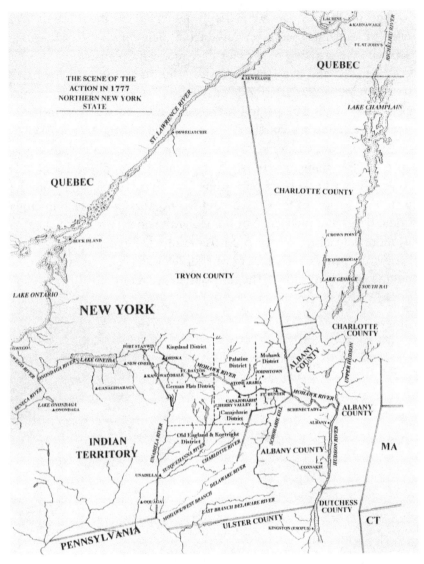

The arena of St. Leger's Expedition in 1777, northern New York State

Gavin K. Watt, 2000.

Johnson himself. For Claus, his removal came particularly hard, as he had been Sir William's first choice for superintendent general, but the old baronet had had second thoughts and decided that the magic of the Johnson name was of critical importance and turned instead to Guy. Sir William had, however, given Claus assurances that he would never want for funds and would have employment for life.[7]

The brothers-in-law were deeply unnerved by these events and sailed to England to lay their case before their superior, Lord George Germain, the secretary of state for the American Colonies.[8]

When General Burgoyne met with Johnson on that damp winter's day, he undoubtedly heard the colonel's vitriolic views on Carleton's misapplication of his officers and natives, but the seed that fell on fertile ground was Johnson's concept for an expedition into the Mohawk Valley.

Johnson painted a very rosy picture. First, there would be the assistance of the many warriors of the fearsome and loyal Iroquois Confederacy, who were simply waiting for a clear call to arms before rising to the support of the Crown. And second, there were the numerous loyal farmers and townsmen of the Mohawk region, who needed nothing more than a firm display of British resolve before taking up arms, in droves, for their sovereign. Burgoyne tucked these gems of information into the back of his mind. The seed was taking root.

CHAPTER TWO

~

1776 — A YEAR OF MANOEUVRING
The Ruins of This Once Strong and Beautiful Fort

Months later, on June 1, 1776, Lieutenant-General John Burgoyne arrived at Quebec City at the head of a large body of British and German reinforcements. The rebels' winter siege of the city had been abandoned only three weeks earlier, and, after the new regiments were integrated, an attack was launched to oust the invaders from the province. Burgoyne commanded the Grand Army's left division, and the rebels were in full rout when his men quietly reoccupied the ruins of Fort Chambly on July 19.[9]

His troops were surprised to see five hundred loyalist partizans approaching along the road from La Prairie. At its head marched Sir John Johnson, the son and heir of Sir William and the most prominent loyalist in the Mohawk Valley.

When his brothers-in-law Guy and Daniel fled the Valley in 1775, Sir John stayed behind to safeguard the family's extensive interests. He had massive estates and numerous tenants of his own to manage, but he quietly assumed the duty of keeping a weather eye on his relatives' properties.

Sir John had replaced his late father as the major general of New York's militia in the Northern District and he had local military affairs to attend to as well.[10] From the days of his youth, the military had been a welcome avocation. During the Pontiac Uprising, Sir John led a detachment of rangers and Iroquois against the fractious Delawares, and later, he was captain of Albany City's mounted militia company. In 1773, he commanded a county regiment of horse.[11]

By 1775, the Johnson faction held many major roles in Tryon County's militia. Sir John acted as the county's brigadier; Guy Johnson was the colonel of a Tryon regiment and the adjutant-general of the New York militia; Daniel Claus was a colonel; and Sir William's old friend, John Butler, was the lieutenant-colonel of Guy's regiment.[12] Many friends

Sir John Johnson —
"a dark insidious traitor"

Oil painting by John Mare, 1772. Courtesy of New York State, Office of Parks, Recreation & Historic Preservation, Johnson Hall State Historic Site.

held field and company commands, and, until Guy Johnson, Claus, and Butler went into exile, the brigade's senior officers had been predominantly loyalists.

With so many of his relatives and associates gone from the Valley, Sir John recognized that he could no longer rely on the loyalty of the militia brigade. Friends in the Valley warned him of the growing support for the sentiments that had led to open warfare in Massachusetts. Vigilance committees, known as committees of safety, created by the local Whigs gradually assumed roles that overlapped those of the royal government's officials. To offset these threats, Sir John decided to secretly recruit a regiment that could be relied upon implicitly. For senior officers, he had a wide variety of choices. Within his social set, which included the Anglican Church and the Masonic Lodge, there were many immigrant half-pay British Regulars and Americans with extensive provincial regimental experience. Amongst his tenants were members of the Scottish Highland gentry, who had brought hundreds of their clansmen to settle on his father's land patents in 1773. These leaders had been officers in the clan regiments and various European armies. Similarly, a great number of veterans and successful farmers, tradesmen, and merchants were available as junior officers and soldiers.

When Sir John received notice of his sister Mary's death in a secret letter from his cousin Guy, his resolve to take action deepened. He fortified Johnson Hall, the handsome Georgian home built by his father and Mary Brant, his Mohawk stepmother. While Sir John mounted Highland guards

Major-General Philip Schuyler, Commander of the United States Northern Department — one of New York State's foremost officers

Engraving after an unknown artist.

round the clock and secretly recruited his regiment, the hounding of local loyalists intensified. Of a sudden, the Tryon County committeemen made two bold moves. First they replaced the militia's absentee officers with men of their own persuasion, and then they disarmed John Butler's tenants. Sir John saw that a confrontation was only a matter of time and decided to seek official support by sharing his plans with the royal governor. In secrecy, he sent a trustworthy Highlander to New York City with a report for Governor Tryon, but details of his dispatch leaked to rebel ears. Soon after, the rebels obtained proof that Sir John was supporting the raising of a full brigade for the Crown in the northern district.[13] Consequently, the Continental Congress instructed Major-General Philip Schuyler, New York's senior officer and a devout revolutionary, to disarm Sir John, his friends, and his tenants.

The forty-three-year-old Schuyler was the scion of one of Albany's most influential and wealthy old Dutch families. He had considerable military experience, having served at the age of twenty-one under Sir William at Lake George and with Bradstreet at Oswego in 1756 and two years later at Fort Frontenac. He ended the Seven Years War as a staff officer in charge of forwarding stores and provisions from Albany to the armies invading French Canada. Schuyler combined a keen mathematical mind with great energy and a flair for organization. His enemies viewed his 1775 appointment to major-general as a sop to "Sweeten, Add to, & keep up the spirit" of New York's conservatives.[14]

To neutralize Sir John, Schuyler assembled four thousand Tryon and Albany County militia, a force large enough to overawe the Mohawks, who were sure to be offended by his armed intrusion into their territory, and to douse all thoughts of Tory armed resistance. In late January 1776, Sir John's men were quietly disarmed and the baronet was required to sign a parole for his future good behaviour.[15]

Sir John reasoned that his bond had been given under duress to men who were traitors to their King and government and he continued recruitment and drew in replacement arms from across the region. Although he and his officers took great care, they were again betrayed.[16]

This time, Congress ordered Schuyler to send the Third New Jersey Continental Regiment (3NJ) under Colonel Elias Dayton to take Sir John prisoner with as many of his "secret" officers as possible; however, their purpose was exposed and several friends warned Sir John. Many of Sir John's recruits, including his designated major, James Gray, were in and about Johnson Hall, and he sent couriers to gather in as many additional men as possible. Reluctantly, Sir John decided to leave behind his pregnant wife, Polly, and two young children.

By May 19, 170[17] men and a handful of women and children had assembled at Johnson Hall with three Fort Hunter Mohawk guides,[18] but several of Sir John's "secret" officers were pursued and detained. John Butler's twenty-year-old son Thomas, an aspiring lieutenant, was betrayed by a family friend while riding to join Sir John and was confined.[19]

Johnson Hall — the family seat of Sir John and Lady Mary Johnson

Unknown engraver after a sketch by Benson J. Lossing, ca. 1851.

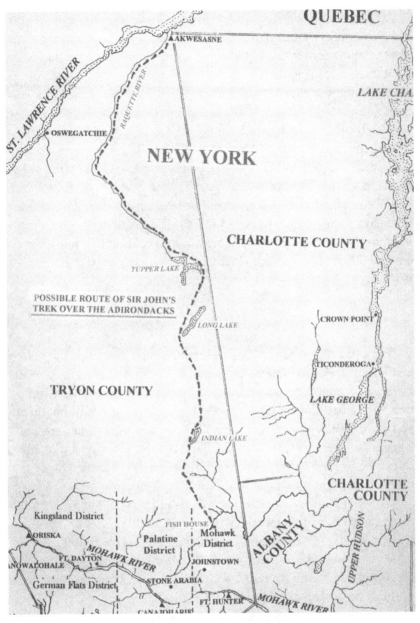

Likely route of Sir John's trek over the Adirondacks

Gavin K. Watt, 2000, after Charles Burton Briggs, "Escape Through the Adirondacks,"
Adirondack Life, Vol. VI, No. 3 (Summer 1975).

The group set off over the Adirondack Mountains towards Quebec on an arduous trek through a wilderness empty of game. On the nineteenth day, the exhausted trekkers were at the point of starvation when some Akwesasnes led them to safety.

Sir John and Gray knew that the prospect of action was a sure tonic for a rapid recovery. While his men recuperated on roasted corn tea laced with maple sugar,[20] Sir John used his tremendous energy and leadership to assemble 350 native and Canadien volunteers, a fieldpiece, and a large number of firelocks. His disparate little army of five hundred set out on June 13 and entered Montreal two days later, only two hours after the 29th Regiment had reoccupied the city. Brooking no delays, he recrossed the river to La Prairie in pursuit of the retreating rebels. He intended to cut them off at Fort St. John's, but when he entered Chambly, he found Governor Carleton there with Burgoyne's division.

What a contrast the baronet and governor made. There was the quietly confident Sir John Johnson dressed like a frontiersman in a wide-brimmed round hat adorned with a rattlesnake band and a fringed deerskin jacket and trousers. A scalping knife hung round his throat, and in his belt was a tomahawk.[21] Sir John was thirty-four, erect and square-shouldered with a long-bridged nose set in an oval face and a thin, well-formed mouth. His dark, intense eyes were framed by natural brown hair swept into a queue.

Guy Carleton was an Irish-born British Regular officer and, at fifty-two, one of the army's most senior generals and the King's representative in Quebec. He was a restrained, forbidding man with rather wooden features, his heavy jaw and prominent nose framed by a fashionable white wig. He was dressed in a scarlet frock coat with gleaming metal buttons, wore a laced cocked hat, and carried a fine sword at his side. An observer would have been hard pressed to recognize that Johnson was the wealthier of the two.

Although Carleton was no supporter of the Johnson faction, he recognized an excellent opportunity and gave Sir John a beating order to raise two battalions of infantry on the frontiers of New York Province. Carleton christened his creation the King's Royal Regiment of New York,[22] often shortened to the "King's Royal Yorkers" or "Sir John's Corps."

In what became his typical, decisive approach, Sir John proposed an immediate thrust into the Mohawk Valley, where he would readily complete his first battalion and get a start on the second. Carleton saw merit in such a venture and sent a dispatch to Captain Forster, 8th Regiment, at Oswegatchie alerting him to a possible movement.[23]

Five days later, at the Church of the Jesuits in Montreal, Carleton held a senior officers' council[24] to plan the campaign against the rebel posts on Lake Champlain. When Sir John's proposal for a flanking attack into the Mohawk Valley was explored, Burgoyne observed that the baronet shared his cousin Guy's opinions. Sir John emphasized the great utility of rallying the Iroquois and confirmed that the region's settlers were avowed loyalists who would rise to a man, or at least were men who could be easily persuaded. Burgoyne enthusiastically embraced the enterprise and Carleton quietly showed interest.

Sir John and Burgoyne parted that day: the baronet trusting that he had an ally for his venture and Burgoyne mulling over this enterprise that had all the signs of being the independent command he so eagerly sought.

In the Valley, the Jersey Continentals, local militia, and committeemen rounded up and jailed more of Sir John's supporters.[25] Less noteworthy offenders were fined and coerced into signing associations for their future good conduct. The iron fist of rebellion menaced all civil liberties in the Mohawk region.

At the same time as Sir John's exiles were recuperating at Akwesasne, Samuel Kirkland, the Congregationalist missionary to the Oneidas at their main castle of Kanawolohale,[26] wrote the letter that prompted the Whigs' first, decisive action at Fort Stanwix. He advised Schuyler that some Oneida leaders had said that "if a party of 500 Men with two or three Rifle Companies were sent to Fort Stanwix," the frontier would be secured.

This was certainly not earth-shattering news, for virtually every man of influence in America knew that the Hudson and Mohawk Rivers formed a water corridor to the Great Lakes and the interior of the conti-

Reverend Samuel Kirkland, Congregationalist minister to the Oneidas and Tuscaroras — "great pains should be taken to prejudice the Indians against him"

Engraving by D.C. Hinman after an unknown artist.

nent, and that a vulnerable portage, formerly guarded by Fort Stanwix and known as the Oneida Carry, lay between the Mohawk River and Lake Oneida. Equally, they knew that the corridor was a possible, indeed likely, route of invasion from the north. Yet, with so many other momentous issues on Congress's agenda, Fort Stanwix and The Carry had simply faded into the background until Schuyler acted on the Oneidas' reminder. Kirkland's letter to the Continental Congress suggested that the Continental Army take post at Stanwix and rebuild the works. His recommendation was immediately adopted. So, entirely unknown to the British command, the rebels had taken a critically important step to prevent an invasion of the Mohawk Valley.

As the first step in the process, the 3NJ marched from Johnstown to the German Flats, where, in conjunction with a company of the Fourth New York (4NY) and a company of militia, the Jerseys built Fort Dayton to protect this vital agricultural settlement.

As instructed, Colonel Dayton sent his senior captain and a Continental Army engineer, Major Nathaniel Hubbell, to inspect the ruins at Stanwix. Captain Bloomfield wrote a wonderfully descriptive account of their findings:

> Took a View of the Ruins of this Once strong and beautiful Fort, which is accounted to lie on the highest ground in all America; as it is the [source?] of the Mohawk-River which runs south to the North [Hudson] River and into the Atlantic Ocean, the head of Wood-Creek which runs directly North into the different Lakes

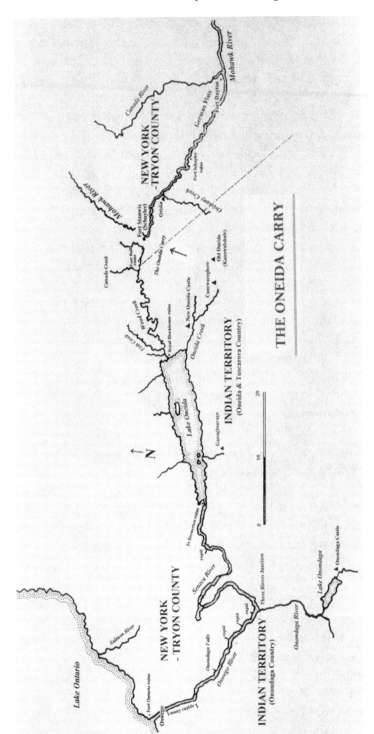

The Oneida Carry

Gavin K. Watt, 2000, after Thomas Mante, "History of the Late War In North America" (Author, 1772).

to St. Lawrence N. by N.E. to the sea, The Oneida-Creek running directly West and the Waters on the East Canada and Fish-Creeks Eastward from the Fort. Fort Stanwix ... is large and well situated haveing a Glacis, Breastwork[,] Ditch a Picket Fort before the Walls which are also well guarded with sharp sticks of Timber [freize] shooting over the walls on which is four Bastions.

The Fort also has a Sally Port[,] Cevort [Covert]-Way, Bridge and Ravelling [Ravelin] before the gate at the entrance. The ruins of five houses and Barracks in the inside built for the Accomodation of the Stores[,] Officers and Soldiery. At about a Mile distance is a Pickquet Fort called Fort Newport built opposite the Dam made over Wood-Creek for the main-guard quartered here for the defence of the Batteaus andc. andc. The Examination of this fortification gave me a better Idea of the strength and Importance of a Fort than any thing I ever before saw or Read.

There are 5 or 6 Families settled in this Rich and beautiful C[h]ampaign Country not a Hill is to be seen around ... Evidence of its being the highest Land in this part of America.[27]

After their reports had been digested at headquarters, Schuyler ordered Dayton to repair and garrison Stanwix, leaving a company behind to complete Fort Dayton at the Flats. On July 12, 320 Jersey Continentals and 140 Tryon militiamen, on supplementary call-up, marched with a company of Lamb's Second Continental Artillery and a bateaux brigade carrying the guns and ammunition.[28] The die had been cast.

In lower Quebec, the weeks dragged on. Enigmatically, Governor Carleton chose not to attack the shattered, smallpox-ridden rebel army. It became clear to the ambitious John Burgoyne that he would accomplish very little cooling his heels with the Grand Army, and he again pressed the case for mounting a Mohawk Valley expedition. He attempted to persuade Carleton by noting that the rebels would be forced to divert resources from Lake Champlain to defend the Valley and re-emphasized the Johnsons' claims about the Six Nations and the waiting loyalists. Burgoyne had visions of cutting a dashing swath through the Valley at the head of a brigade "of three British battalions, with a corps of artillery, some Canadians[,] a large body of Indians" and the Royal Yorkers.[29]

Carleton was perfectly aware of the Iroquois Confederacy's influence over the other native nations. He also recognized the importance of raising Provincial regiments to augment Britain's limited manpower, as much as to illustrate to all Americans the honourable role for loyal men to adopt. Yes, the Mohawk Valley expedition was enticing, but to his deputy's great disappointment, Carleton did not rise to the bait.

Carleton continued to toy with the Valley scheme for more than a month while the preparations to launch his fleet and army onto Lake Champlain ground on. As late as July 19, he warned Lieutenant-Colonel Caldwell at Niagara that part of his regiment and the Indian Agent, Major John Butler, might be required for an expedition. Butler was one of the many prominent loyalists who had withdrawn from the Mohawk Valley with Guy Johnson in 1775. He was fluent in several Iroquoian dialects and had served before the war as a department interpreter.

After Carleton announced the establishment of his own Indian Department, Guy Johnson and Daniel Claus decided they must go to England to seek redress; however, the governor recommended they take post at Fort Niagara, where they could manage the Six Nations' affairs in security. When both men spurned his advice, they earned Carleton's lasting enmity.

Guy Johnson saw the merit of Carleton's recommendation, but the only individual amongst his followers with sufficient seniority and skill to manage at Niagara was John Butler. Johnson approached him reluctantly, as Butler had fallen out with the younger Johnson faction after Sir William's death. Butler, Johnson's elder, was not eager for the assignment. Unlike Johnson and Claus, his family was still in the Valley and he might have declined the posting to Niagara had it not been for fresh intelligence warning him not to return home.[30] As a condition of accepting the challenge, he requested a promotion to Deputy Superintendent or Agent so that he would have more authority with the natives.[31] In some desperation, Johnson granted the request, subject to the confirmation of his own position in England.

Butler arrived at Fort Niagara with a small party of rangers in mid-November 1775. Guy's orders had been crystal clear. The damnable rebellion had touched the very fibre of the superintendent's life. He had been compelled to abandon his home and, in consequence, had lost his wife. Then, Governor Carleton, an old enemy of the Johnson interests, had threatened his unconfirmed commission. Johnson had therefore instructed Butler to bring the Indians into the conflict and wreak havoc on the rebels. However, he was on his way across the ocean to England, and Carleton, who had just been given military responsibility for Fort Niagara, had a radically different agenda, one that entertained hopes for a negotiated settlement to the American grievances. While there was any chance of success, Carleton wanted the Indians to be kept out of direct involvement. At the same time, their unswerving loyalty and willingness for active participation was to be won through treaty obligations and presents. In the face of these conflicting orders, Butler took the measure of his situation and concluded that Carleton held the upper hand. It proved to be a wise decision.

Now, eight months later, Carleton wrote, "I am preparing to follow [the rebels onto Lake Champlain], and shall send a force up [the St. Lawrence River] to Lake Ontario to penetrate that way also into their provinces." He implied that Forster at Oswegatchie would lead the latter effort and ordered Caldwell to "make all preparations . . . and have ready all the force you can collect" while Butler kept "the savages ready . . . and well disposed to act."[32]

At the same time, fears about turning the Iroquois and vengeful loyalists loose in the Valley lurked in Carleton's mind. As an excuse, he threw out a concern about provisioning the force and Burgoyne impatiently offered to personally finance and procure the necessary supplies, but Carleton's scruples prevailed. At the end of July, he ordered the project abandoned.

Fully a year before the Continental Congress issued orders for the refortification of the Oneida Carry, they had recognized the yawning gap in the management of native affairs left by Guy Johnson's exile. Every adult American who had lived through the continent's frequent Indian wars had memories of the terrors and excesses of native warfare. Congress visualized the Mohawk region as a swollen hornet's nest just waiting to be struck, and no congressman wanted to unleash a new tide of bloodshed. To address the United Colonies' lack of an Indian Department, a number of commissioners were appointed to keep the Indians quiet and content. Primary amongst them was General Philip Schuyler.

The Schuyler family had managed Indian affairs for the better part of a century before provincial politics put Sir William Johnson in their place. As well as his intimate knowledge of native life and languages, Schuyler's had his influential Mohawk mistress, Mary Hill, who kept him current with the Iroquios Confederacy's affairs.[33]

In addition to his many military duties, Schuyler accepted this crucial and difficult responsibility. Now, in 1776, several issues demanded attention, such as his decision the previous spring to limit the Indian trade. The Indian Commission feared that the traders' goods would equip hostile forays of native and white partizans, and so Schuyler ordered the traders to go no further than Fort Stanwix and to trade only with pro-Whig castles.[34] Another difficult matter was an explanation for Sir John's flight and the presence in Mohawk territory of uninvited Continental troops. Also, he had to address Congress's pre-emptive decision to refortify the Oneida Carry. When the troops were sent to begin the work, the Confederacy was intentionally ignored in order to avoid the wrangles and delays of native diplomacy. The Whigs' decided friends, the Oneidas and Tuscaroras, were pleased to have the fort's protection, but the other four nations exhibited a discernible coolness.

In the summer of 1776, Schuyler conducted his most successful treaty council at German Flats, attended by seventeen hundred Indians from the Confederacy and the Canada, Lakes, and Ohio Nations. Headmen from the Stockbridges, whose warriors had manned the siege lines at Boston in 1775, took a prominent role in favour of the Whigs. When the council closed, most of the nations had been mollified by Schuyler's explanations and promises and a substantial present of trade goods. A white captive, contentedly living amongst the Senecas, recalled that "The Indians returned to their homes well pleased that they could live on neutral ground, surrounded by the din of war, without being engaged in it."[35]

During the inevitable delay waiting for the Indian nations to gather, a dispatch arrived at the Flats for Schuyler from Colonel Dayton at the Oneida Carry. He reported that he had renamed Stanwix "Fort Schuyler" and added that the works were now "very defensible against almost any Number of Small Arms."[36] Schuyler wrote that same day to

General Washington noting that "Fort Stanwix is repairing and is already so far advanced as to be defensible against light artillery."[37] These accomplishments occurred one year to the day before Barry St. Leger's vanguard arrived on The Carry.

A day or two later, Schuyler received news from Stanwix stating that all the Indians would go to Oswego to meet Guy Johnson on August 10. Johnson would bring two Regular regiments and "sundry Tories and [Canada] Indians" to rebuild Oswego's Fort Ontario. Then he would hold a council and lay siege to Fort Stanwix.[38] As the majority of the nations were already at German Flats, Schuyler discounted the intelligence; however, the news was the first serious indication of a British offensive in the Mohawk Valley.

On September 21, several Oneida sachems and warriors visited Stanwix to announce Sir John's arrival at Oswego with a large army. Alarmingly, the Oneidas announced that they would "take no part in the Quarrel & desired that none of their Young Warriors would be sent any more on any Scout for us."[39] This declaration was a radical departure from the Oneidas' usual position and led to some dismay in the garrison. Dayton sent out a strong patrol towards Oswego. A Jersey officer, Lieutenant Eben Elmer, went with the patrol and wrote a detailed account of the land lying between Stanwix and Lake Oneida, over which St. Leger's army would later approach:

> The Route.' — Course due west — three-quarters of a mile from the Fort, being the usual carrying place, we crossed over the head of Wood Creek, which is a small stream over which is an old bank built for the purpose of raising the water to float the batteaux down the Creek — where there are the banks of an old Fort built for a guard to defend the batteaux, called Fort Newport. Three miles farther are the ruins of an old Fort [Bull] built upon the Creek . . . taken by the French and Indians last war. Four miles farther down is a Creek putting up to the north, called therefore Canada Creek, at the mouth of which was a small fort, now totally destroyed. The land around very good. [A]fter passing this Creek some distance, we

passed through a ridge of barren white and scrubby pine land, exceeding hilly. . . for about 8 miles, when we came into low rich land again, and so upon Fish Creek and down the same until we came to the mouth where it empties into Wood Creek, making in the whole 24 miles, being 1 mile from the Lake.

We arrived at the Forks about 1 o'clock, P.M., where we encamped, falling some few trees, taking the tops to make ourselves bowers to lodge under. Soon after we arrived there, I took the batteaux kept there and a few soldiers and went down to the Lake, which appeared very beautiful, being 10 miles wide and 30 long; and the wind blowing from the west, brought a heavy swell upon this shore, which is a fine shoal sandy shore . . . [We] continued at the Forks. Upon the mouth of this was their Royal Blockhouse.[40]

That same day, the elderly Oneida war captain, Skenandon, came express from Kanowalohale to report that Sir John had left Oswego and "gone over Lake Ontario."[41] The sources for these rumours and counter-rumours are a mystery. Sir John had been nowhere near Oswego; were the Oneidas simply testing the Whigs' resolve?

In the lower Mohawk Valley, action against the local Tories continued apace. A mid-October committee of safety meeting reviewed evidence against two men named McGinnis. Witnesses testified that Robert McGinnis had been heard to "say that the Bostonians were Rebels and Murderers." Richard McGinnis had said that the "New England Provinces were in Actual Rebellion" and that the American cause was unjust. Both men had refused to sign an association, and Robert was "in a passion" at the thought that someone would bring such a paper to him. An informant had heard Richard "Drink King George's health saying Damnation and Confusion to the Congress and all their Adherents . . . a parcel of Rascally Rebels." Their father, William, who had avoided capture, had said that he would never bear arms for the rebellion, as the cause was unjust. The McGinnises' personal arms were confiscated. After swearing "to be Still & quiet they Signed the Association & were Discharged."[42]

On October 20, General Nicholas Herkimer and Colonel Jacob Klock attended a committee meeting to hear the case against William Dillenbach, who had refused to serve in the militia. His captain, Henry Diefendorf, was visiting the malingerer's home and arguing with his wife when her seventeen-year-old son took up a set of tongs to defend his mother. A militiaman threw the lad to the floor and stabbed him in the back. Dillenbach admitted to refusing to appear in arms and lamely stated he was ignorant of Herkimer's order. A witness testified that Dillenbach had declared that he and his brother would be safe "in Case the King should overcome the States." The committee found him "an Enemy to the States of America," fined him "two Shillings Current Money" for not appearing in arms, and confined him "Closely in the Common Goal . . . for thirty Days on his own Expense." When he was released, Dillenbach was to give a bond of "£500 . . . for his future good Behaviour."[43]

The next day, a hearing that perfectly illustrates the social complexities of the rebellion was held at Fort Dayton. The garrison's Continental officers reviewed the case against Han Jost Herkimer, General Nicholas's eldest brother, who had conspired to run off to the enemy with Peter Ten Broeck, Hanjost Schuyler, and thirty Canajoharie Mohawks and had been confined as "a dangerous person[,] disaffected to the Liberties of America."

Peter Ten Broeck was Han Jost Herkimer's son-in-law and a son of General Schuyler's close friend, Abraham Ten Broeck, the Albany County militia brigadier. Hanjost Schuyler, whose activities would be so prominent during the St. Leger Expedition, was a distant relative of General Herkimer. His brother Nicholas came to testify against him.

Two days later, Han Jost Herkimer was interrogated by his brother Nicholas. He told a confusing tale about Ten Broeck, Schuyler, and Sir John's half-blood brother, Quahyocko Brant Johnson,[44] and several other Indians who planned on "going off." He said he had simply been told of the venture, but had not taken part; however, his confession failed to explain why he was found hiding in his cellar. Foolishly, he revealed that he bitterly resented his neighbours' opposition to his nomination as colonel of the local militia regiment. He quoted his son-in-law's comment about the 4th Regiment's second major,[45] that "he would rot before ClapSaddle shoud Rule him, or any such Rascal." Why Han Jost Herkimer believed this revelation would help Ten Broeck's cause is a mystery. Perhaps he hoped to divert attention from himself and reasoned that Ten Broeck was safely out of harm's way;

Captain-General Guy Carleton, the military commander and Governor-in-Chief of Quebec — "one of the most distant, reserved men in the world"

Oil painting by an unknown artist. Courtesy of the National Archives of Canada, C-002833.

however, his dissembling was in vain and he was jailed in Albany as an enemy of the cause.[46]

Investigations such as these were regularly held across the Mohawk region. They illustrate the systematic persecution of Tories, which had replaced the social influence and strong-arm coercion of the Johnson faction. Many folk on both sides of the political spectrum held deep convictions, some visceral, some frivolous, which were later to explode into fury at Oriskany.

Aboard ship on Lake Champlain on October 6, Carleton wrote to the commandant of Fort Niagara with instructions to prepare "all which can be spared of the 8th Regiment & all Indians of your neighbourhood"[47] for service on the Mohawk River in the early spring. Clearly, the Mohawk Valley had fallen off the governor's agenda for the duration of 1776.

When the Carleton's Lake Champlain fleet finally set sail on October 10, the Royal Yorkers remained behind with another Provincial regiment, Lieutenant-Colonel Allan Maclean's Royal Highland Emigrants. The two units were assigned to Lieutenant-Colonel Barry St. Leger, 34th Regt, for patrol duties along the Sorel, Yamaska, and St. Francis Rivers. St. Leger had orders to "seize all Rascals, who may attempt to Steal in or out of the Province . . . or Sculk about from one parish to another, spreading lies."[48]

In a decisive action, Carleton's ships and gunboats destroyed the rebel fleet, which had been built and commanded by Major-General Benedict Arnold. Yet the long period of preparation to challenge Arnold's ships became the major factor of the campaign. After only a brief reconnaissance of rebel-held Ticonderoga, Carleton shocked his army by declaring the season too far advanced to continue operations. He considered it impossible to gather sufficient building materials to rebuild the ruined fort at Crown Point and, on November 2, withdrew his disgruntled troops to winter quarters in Quebec.[49]

The King's Royal Yorkers were sent to the parishes on the island of Montreal, where they would pass the winter working on local fortifications and doing rudimentary training.

Sir John Johnson requested the same bounty for the raising and outfitting of the Royal Yorkers as had been given to Maclean for the Royal Highland Emigrants. His application was referred to Lieutenant-General Burgoyne, who, as his brigade commander, replied in a flowery letter more appropriate to one of his theatrical plays. Its substance was a refusal on the basis that the Royal Yorkers were a fencible regiment, not subject to duties outside America and, only on occasions of great emergency, beyond its own province. The letter concluded, "It is presumed . . . under the influence of so respectable a chief as yourself, the enlistments will be made with little expence,"[50] that is, to the Crown.

This was disappointing news. While Sir John brimmed with confidence that British arms would prevail, he had risked abandoning his family and estates to the vengeance of his enemies without any guarantee that either would be protected or recovered intact. The vast majority of his wealth was in land patents and his income was dependent upon tenants, the majority of whom were in no position to pay their fees, and, in any case, while exiled in Canada he was unable to collect from those who could. In the face of such uncertainties, the heavy expenses required to raise his regiment to full strength and field efficiency represented quite a burden. These expenditures were to be borne as another cost of loyalty. Perhaps this decision was the visible face of Carleton's "private Resentment & pique," which Daniel Claus believed was held against Sir William and his family.[51] On the other hand, perhaps the statement should be taken solely at face value.

In mid-November, Sir John received a warm, personal letter from his friend Ebenezer Jessup with the welcome news that Lady Johnson had delivered a second son, John Jr., while in captivity. Eben was a prominent Yorker landowner from the upper Hudson River who, with his brothers and followers, had joined Carleton at Crown Point. He asked Sir John for permission to raise and command a second battalion of the Royal Yorkers,[52] but it lay entirely outside of Johnson's power to approve a second before completing his first.

Jessup's news about his son's birth focused Johnson's thoughts on the plight of his family. He knew from Polly's secret letters that she was only seventy miles from New York City and so he obtained Carleton's leave to go there to "get my family out of their hands."[53] His second personal mission was to quietly assess whether a decisive action against the Valley might be initiated from General Howe's headquarters in the city.

In early November,[54] General Burgoyne returned to England to sit in Parliament. Carleton had given him instructions to present the plans and requirements for the 1777 campaign to the administration. These included a request for four thousand reinforcements and an increase in the current company establishment from fifty-four to one hundred men for the regiments already in Canada. If these numbers were granted, he planned to detach a large corps to operate in the Mohawk Valley and, perhaps, another to act along the Connecticut River.[55]

Initially, Secretary of State Lord George Germain refused to see Burgoyne, as he was angered with Governor Carleton's abrupt ending of the 1776 campaign.[56] Although previously well disposed towards Burgoyne, he now viewed him with suspicion, thinking he had become one of the governor's sycophants. Germain's poor opinion of Carleton was highly coloured by the governor's sharp impertinence in recent correspondence. As well, Lord George had little understanding of American geography. Unlike the Quebec governor, he was unburdened with hopes of conciliation with the rebels and viewed Carleton's hesitations as lethargy bordering on military incompetence.

Germain's feelings about Carleton were of long standing and his dislike of the man had been nurtured by the opinions of Johnson and Joseph Brant on the misapplication of the Indians in 1775. His dissatisfaction had become so pronounced that, prior to the launch of the 1776 campaign, he sent orders for Carleton's removal as army commander, instructing him to surrender command to Burgoyne once the army crossed into New York. Carleton was to remain in Quebec and re-establish order in the wake of the failed rebel invasion.[57] This dispatch failed to arrive and Carleton continued to lead the army into New York, where he had achieved results far below Germain's expectations.

Several of the governor's actions rankled the secretary — Carleton's conciliatory stance with captive rebel officers; his compliments to their rank and file for their valour; and his soft words encouraging them to return to their former allegiance.[58] Germain viewed such behaviour with suspicion bordering on disdain.

There were other reasons — the secretary had appointed a personal friend to Carleton's staff, but when the man arrived in Quebec, he discovered the governor's brother was in his place. Germain's friend had been icily ignored, and, in retaliation, he had sent a list of Carleton's failings to the Secretary, which included the avoidable delays in building a flotilla on Lake Champlain; poor transport arrangements; the building of unnecessary fortifications; and Carleton's incompetence as an administrator and strategist.[59] Worse, the whole of his pursuit of the beaten rebel army had lacked resolve and vigour and he had failed to maintain an outpost at Crown Point over the winter.[60]

Burgoyne was not dissuaded by Germain's refusal to see him. He was so well connected, well written, and well spoken that, in little time, he deftly broke through Germain's reserve and gained an audience. He may or may not have known of the secretary's earlier decision to give him command of the last campaign, but he soon sensed that an opportunity was in the offing. Whether he had left Canada with the intention of supplanting his superior in the upcoming campaign, or whether he simply found conditions ripe for his ambitions, remains an open question.

Burgoyne dutifully reported Carleton's recommendations while simultaneously courting favour. In the words of one Canadian historian, he "did not

Lady Mary (Polly) Johnson, née Watts

Pencil drawing by Gavin Alexander Watt, 1999, after a pastel by St. Memin, 1797, and a drawing by an unknown artist, Metropolitan Toronto Library.

exactly use intrigue to gain his new post but came very close to it . . . [his] methods . . . did him little credit."[61]

Once again, Germain decided to remove Carleton, but to Burgoyne's hidden alarm, the command was offered to General Sir Henry Clinton. When he declined out of concern for Carleton, the way lay open to Burgoyne.[62]

In America, the rebels had been considering Lady Mary Johnson and her children moral hostages for her husband's good behaviour and, to keep her secure, were moving the family from one control point to another. After a brief recovery from the birth of her son at her aunt's in Albany, Lady Mary had obtained leave to stay at Fishkill, where she planned to plead her case with the Provincial Congress.

Shortly after her arrival, she somehow obtained disguises for herself, her sister Margaret, and the three children and escaped under cover of darkness to Paulus Hook, opposite Manhattan.[63] Legend claims that some Mohawks guided her to Sir John, and the reunited family spent the winter with Polly's parents, the Watts.[64] His first mission accomplished, Sir John and Guy discussed whether New York City, or York City, as it was often called, would be a better launch point than Montreal for the Valley expedition. His cousin's recent experiences with General Howe were not encouraging.

Sir John had just missed seeing his friends Joseph Brant and Gilbert Tice. They had left the city in early November to march overland to Indian Territory. Both men were members of Guy's entourage; Brant was the colonel's Mohawk interpreter[65] and Tice his most senior captain.[66]

Joseph was the brother of Sir William's Mohawk wife, Mary, or, more often, Molly. When his sister chose to live with Sir William, Joseph was taken into the bosom of Johnson's family like a son. He was about the same age as John Johnson and the pair received the same practical training. Although Joseph was a Canajoharie Mohawk, true to tradition, he lived with his Oneida wife's parents at the mixed-nations settlement of Oquaga across the Fort Stanwix Line in Indian Territory.

When Guy Johnson had gone to England the previous winter, he had been eager for Brant to be a part of his appeal to his superiors.

Brant's presence would support Johnson's claims of native allegiance to himself and to the Crown. This suited Joseph, as he and John Hill Oteronyente of Fort Hunter had been chosen by the Iroquois warriors at Montreal to resolve the Six Nations' many land title grievances with the British administration.

During his six months in England, Brant had met the King and many other prominent Britons and had been deeply impressed with the teeming populace, the thriving industry, and the might of the Royal Navy.

Guy Johnson's party returned to America in July 1776, arriving off York City with the fleet bearing Sir William Howe's magnificent army. Brant proved brave and steady in the battle of Long Island and saw the rebels being driven out of York City, but the expected call for the Six Nations' assistance never came.

Brant enjoyed a visit with Governor Tryon while in the city, but inaction unsettled him, and before Howe's Grand Army followed the retreating rebels towards Pennsylvania, he obtained Johnson's permission to travel north. Johnson instructed Joseph to prepare a belt and "speak through it" to the nations,[67] and General Howe entrusted Brant with a message to the Iroquois Confederacy urging them not to "put the least confidence in the rebbles, as he Knew Them to be A Cowardly Deceitfull People."[68]

Captain Gilbert Tice was a veteran Provincial officer of the Seven Years War. In 1775, during the defence of Fort St. John's, he had been grievously wounded leading an Indian party in the first combat action against the rebels. While he was still recovering from his wounds, he accompanied Johnson to England. In quieter times, Tice and his wife had kept an inn in Johnstown. Unbeknownst to himself, while he was with Guy Johnson in England, he had angered the Jersey Continental officers who were using his tavern as an office while they examined Sir John's papers from Johnson Hall. In the midst of their investigation, they were startled to discover that Tice's letter to his wife had arrived secretly from Britain the day before.

Tice and Brant left York City in mid-November and headed for Oquaga.[69] To elude discovery, they travelled only at night and posed as a militiaman and an Oneida on leave from Washington's army. Three weeks later, Brant was joyfully reunited with his wife, Peggie, and their son. The community made him very welcome and gathered to hear his accounts of his audience with the King and Queen, his discussions of grievances with Lord George Germain, and his association and friendship with many other great people. He told war stories of his prowess during the rebel attack on Montreal; his marksmanship when the ship from England fought off a rebel privateer;[70] his daring during Howe's late campaign; and his skills of evasion when travelling through enemy country. These tales stood him in good stead, as it was customary for a warrior to recount his deeds.

Brant was well known throughout the Confederacy as the brother of the renowned Mary Brant, wife of Sir William Johnson. His service during the Seven Years War and the Pontiac Uprising as well as his association with the Johnsons were of note. That he had been chosen to carry messages from Sir William Howe and Guy Johnson added to his lustre.

All of Brant's training at Sir William's knee, coupled with his experiences abroad, had given birth to a burning personal mission. Unable to sit still, he soon assembled a party, which included his Oneida father-in-law, Old Isaac,[71] and Tice. They visited some of the Delaware towns, where his words were well received, then they travelled northwest along the snow- and ice-covered "old Forbidden Path," the backdoor of the Confederacy. At every small hamlet or single dwelling, he delivered his messages from Johnson and Howe. While his words were welcomed, he recognized that the proselytizing of Congress's Indian Commission and the Whig missionaries had taken hold.

Little that occurred amongst the Six Nations missed the watchful Reverend Samuel Kirkland. From his home at Old Oneida Castle, he reported to the Albany committee in mid-December the news of Brant and Tice passing through Oquaga on their way to Niagara.[72]

Meanwhile, in England, General Burgoyne was frustrating Carleton's plan to detach "a large corps" of Regulars to operate in the Mohawk Valley. As the governor expected to command the 1777 campaign, he had honoured his deputy's request of the year before and given him command of this right hook attack;[73] however, once it was apparent to Burgoyne that command of the whole campaign was within his grasp, he maximized the main force and downplayed the Mohawk Valley venture. On February 26, he wrote another treatise, entitled, "Thoughts for conducting the War from the Side of Canada":

I omitted in the beginning of these papers to state the idea of an expedition at the outset of the campaign by the Lake Ontario and Oswego to the Mohawk River, which, as a diversion to facilitate every proposed operation, would be highly desirable, provided the army should be reenforced sufficiently to afford it.

It may at first appear, from a view of the present strength of the army, that it may bear the sort of detachment proposed by myself last year for this purpose; but it is to be considered that at that time the utmost object of the campaign, from the advanced season and unavoidable delay of preparation for the lakes, being the reduction of Crown Point and Ticonderoga, unless the success of my expedition had opened the road to Albany, no greater numbers were necessary than for those first operations. The case in the present year differs; because the season of the year affording a prospect of very extensive operation, and consequently the establishment of many posts, patrols, etc., will become necessary. The army ought to be in a state of numbers to bear those drains, and still remain sufficient to attack anything that probably can be opposed to it.

Nor, to argue from probability, is so much force necessary for this diversion this year, as was required for the last; because we then knew that General Schuyler with a thousand men, was fortified upon the Mohawk. When the different situations of things are considered, viz, the progress of General Howe, the early invasion from Canada, the threatening of the Connecticutt from Rhode Island, etc., it is not to be imagined that any detachment of such force as that of Schuyler can be supplied by the enemy for the Mohawk, I would not therefore propose it of more (and I have great diffidence whether so much can be prudently afforded) than Sir John Johnson's corps, and a hundred British from the second brigade, and a hundred more from the 8th regiment, with four pieces of the lightest artillery, and a body of savages; Sir John Johnson to be with the detachment in person, and an able field officer to command it. I should wish Lieutenant-Colonel St. Leger for that employment.[74]

When all was said and done, Burgoyne had convinced the King and Lord George Germain to reduce the Mohawk Valley expedition to 200 British Regulars, 342 unacclimatized Hessians, and 133 untried Provincials — a comparatively tiny, disparate, and inexperienced force.[75]

Germain ordered that a "proper" detachment of British Artillery be furnished, which, as noted above in Burgoyne's "Thoughts," left scope for his parsimonious interpretation. In another imprecise instruction, Germain called for a "sufficient number of Canadians and Indians" for St. Leger. Although Burgoyne had earlier fantasized about the number of Canadiens he would employ to support his own efforts,[76] he did not record what his expectations were for St. Leger. Yet he was remarkably realistic in predicting that four to five hundred Indians might join St. Leger, likely an estimate from his discussions with the Johnsons. If all went to plan, St. Leger would have between thirteen to sixteen hundred muskets, to which Burgoyne added an artillery detachment of two subalterns and forty rankers.[77]

The year before, he had requested a brigade of British Regulars, fully twenty-four hat companies totalling thirteen hundred all ranks. Now, after a few facile rationalizations, he reduced the Mohawk expedition to a shadow of his original plan. That Schuyler had already sent more than fifteen hundred Continentals into the Valley and had begun to re-fortify the region was either unknown or disregarded.[78] The rebels had deployed a force fifty percent greater than the one thousand men that Burgoyne said had justified Carleton's 1776 recommmendation for "a large corps" and which had excited his own desire to lead a brigade of Regulars. Congress's prudent actions to bolster the Valley's defence countered the pipe dreams that launched the St. Leger expedition.

Brant's small party was well received as it passed through Seneca country. Although his words were carefully attended to, he sensed scant progress and saw that this elder brother nation was committed to neutrality, while drawing presents and compliments from the principal pro-

Major John Butler — the Six Nations Indian Department Deputy Agent at Fort Niagara in the later uniform of Butler's Rangers

Pencil drawing by Scott D. Paterson, 1996.

tagonists. Brant was well aware that the aloof Senecas had a tradition of taking little note of any white faction.

After four frustrating days at Geneseo (Chenussio), he went to Fort Niagara, where he expected to find a warm welcome and ready assistance, but instead he discovered that John Butler received the messages from General Howe and Guy Johnson with a strange reserve. The Mohawk knew nothing of Carleton's contradictory instructions, and it appeared to him that Butler was pursuing a convoluted path with the Iroquois Confederacy, in opposition to his own desire for direct and immediate action. Butler saw that Brant's actions represented a distinct danger to his careful negotiations, and their contradictory goals led to a measure of hostility between the two men, who previously had been on good terms.[79]

Brant wrote to his clan relations at Akwesasne and Kanehsatake in lower Quebec inviting them to an expedition he was planning for the spring. He gave out the ever-popular lure, "you may depend on having your own way of making war," and added a particularly bold comment: "I do not think it right to let my brothers go to war under the command of General Carleton as [he] expects & trys to have the Indians under the same command as the regular Troops."[80]

This message came to the attention of the Quebec Indian Department officers at the two settlements and its contents were quickly transmitted to Carleton.[81] Brant's plan was precisely what Carleton did not want; he construed that Brant intended to conduct "an indiscriminate attack, wherein women and children, aged and infirm, innocent as well as the guilty, will be equally exposed to their fury." In early February, Carleton instructed Butler to thwart the plan, adding: "The force of savages may be employed under proper management to punish effectually when it is necessary and this must answer every end of theirs equally well while it serves so much better the King's cause."[82] It took little for the Quebec officers to dissuade Joseph's clansmen. Spring was a long way off and events would eclipse Brant's plan before then.

Following Guy Johnson's instructions, Brant had a war belt prepared at Niagara and, as was proper and essential, set off for Onondaga to lodge Johnson's belt at the seat of the Iroquois Confederacy's government. On his way through Seneca and Cayuga country, he was again well met.

After he had given the belt and its messages to the Onondaga elders, Brant decided to grasp the nettle and meet with the Oneidas. He travelled to the Tuscarora village of Ganaghsaraga on the edge of Oneida country and sent messages to his Wolf Clan relatives, including Skenandon, to come and share his news.[83] Kirkland immediately interfered, exacting a promise from Brant's clansmen not to respond. He confidently predicted that none of those named by Brant would meet with him,[84] but he was mistaken. Several went to see Brant, and a furious argument ensued over his claim that the King's troops were everywhere victorious. The Oneidas taunted that, if this was so, the King had no need of their help.

Smarting from this sarcastic, albeit logical, retort, Brant set off again for Niagara. On passing through Seneca country, he found his welcome less warm than previously and he chose to blame Butler. More likely, the Senecas were disturbed by this young upstart and recalled that the Mohawks were ever slaves to the will of the English and had been eager participants in the campaign against their Delaware nephews in Pontiac's time.[85] Even Sir William's close friend, their great chief Sayengaraghta, disapproved of young Brant.[86] Disgruntled, he went back to the Cayugas, where he passed some time persuading his mother's kin.

In the midst of this activity, Butler sent two Senecas and a Mohawk as spies to Fort Stanwix "to reconnoiter this garrison, the number of cannon, Strength &c." The Mohawk entered the works for a short period, but under the sharp, distrustful eye of some Oneidas was unable to see much and left.[87] Yet he must have seen or heard from his local clan relations that the works were well advanced and the garrison in substantial numbers. Surely he advised Butler of these facts. Yet somehow the idea persisted at Carleton's headquarters that Stanwix was a trifling, picketed place with a puny sixty-man garrison.

Brant soon grew dissatisfied at Cayuga and returned to Niagara to ask Butler for a substantial supply of powder. Mindful of Carleton's instructions, Butler gave him only enough for a small party, and this stinginess further agitated Brant. He purchased more supplies from the merchants on credit and left.[88] One can imagine Butler's sigh of relief at the sight of his back.

Reverend Kirkland wrote to Schuyler on January 14 advising that he had assembled more than 180 Oneidas and Tuscaroras to hear the news of Washington's exciting victories at Trenton and Princeton. He presented them with Schuyler's gift of six barrels of rum, which proved "very acceptable and [will] do more Service to our Cause than a thousand expended at Treaty." They sent off runners to carry the momentous news "with accuracy and spirit" to their Seneca brothers.

The Reverend reported on Brant's activities:

> [H]e had the War Hatchet from General Howe . . . in the name and Behalf of the King of Britain. This he communicated only to some Tory Indians as he found the Indians in general to be more friendly to the counsel of America than he expected . . . He further observed

the King was very sorry to hear that two nations of the confederacy had forsaken him and joined with those who were in Rebellion and deserved to die.

Kirkland said that Brant's comments "frightened the [Oneidas & Tuscaroras] very much at first hearing." But shortly after, news arrived that many European officers had come to America to offer their services to Congress. A half dozen Oneidas proposed going southwards to see some "French gentlemen or French Vessels . . . by which means they think they shall be able to convince their neighbours of the true state of matters." [89]

CHAPTER THREE

~

The Launch of the Expedition
In Readiness to Embark

Governor Carleton had given Major James Gray of the Royal Yorkers the additional responsibility of organizing intelligence gathering in the Mohawk Valley. On March 4, Gray reported the news brought back by a four-man party under Lieutenent John Hare of the Indian Department, "a man very fitt for the Service,"[90] and, remembering his primary responsibility, submitted a nominal roll of twenty-six Mohawk Valley recruits who had just joined his battalion.[91]

A few days later, the Royal Yorkers began their training in the Manual Exercise, the drill regimen designed to give the men facility and confidence in the use of their firelocks and bayonets and to develop their ability to operate as a team. Gray discovered that some of his officers preferred to keep warm and dry rather than stand in the snow and slush of Montreal. On March 16, he ordered that "all the Officers for the future attend the Exercise of the Men from the hour of Eleven till One in the Afternoon if the Weather Permit."[92]

Carleton received a belated dispatch from Germain, which contained the King's approval for the raising of the Royal Yorkers:

> The report that you received from him of the distressed situation and loyal disposition of the People in that part of the Country from which he came might well induce you to give orders that a Battalion should be raised on that Frontier of your Province for the relief & Protection of his Majesty's faithful Subjects.
>
> The measure as being founded on Wisdom & Humanity is consequently agreeable to His Majesty — As the Services of Sir John Johnson have been such as place him high in the King's good Opinion, His Majesty cannot but approve of your having conferred upon him the command of the said Regiment & trusts that Sir John

has been successful in his Levies and has before this time formed a Corps fit and ready for service.[93]

When Joseph Brant left Niagara and took the path to Oquaga in late winter, he was disillusioned by the lack of progress with his grand mission. His failure with the Oneidas and Tuscaroras was one thing, but the Cayugas and Senecas quite another, and he could not understand why John Butler was conducting Indian affairs entirely at cross-purposes to his personal goals. Butler had not advised Brant of Carleton's pacific instructions; perhaps he felt guilty about his evasion of Guy Johnson's instructions. By the time Joseph left Niagara, the two men had grown further apart.

Brant arrived at Oquaga in late March or early April and began to formulate plans to rescue the Mohawk castles, which he considered were hostages to the whims of the rebel committees of safety. Although the Oquaga settlement was divided between Congregationalist and Anglican adherents, Brant's strong resolve and charismatic personality settled the issue, and he assembled a band of followers, primarily amongst his clansmen. A key member was Sir William's son, the adventurous, hotheaded William of Canajoharie. As a visible sign of the village's loyalty, a Grand Union flag was raised.[94]

In taking these actions, Brant followed the ancient tradition of the rogue warrior who, without the Iroquois Confederacy's sanction, used his family connections and powers of persuasion to build his own party. That he had the support of the substantial Mohawk community and many Oneidas and Mohicans at Oquaga gave him no formal status with the Confederacy at large, but it was his Iroquoian birthright to proceed as he saw fit.

Brant organized the blazing of trails over the Catskills from Esopus to guide loyalist fugitives from Ulster and Orange Counties through the woods to sanctuary at Oquaga.[95] He probably did not expect any of these men to remain with him and thought they would move on to Fort Niagara; however, a number saw him as a man of action and remained to serve under him in the Indian fashion.[96] This growing concentration of red and white loyalists just outside Tryon County's southwestern border caused considerable anxiety across the Mohawk region.

At the end of March, Butler wrote to Carleton asking for confirmation of his rank and pay. He noted that he had served the Crown for upwards of twenty years and for part of that time had ranked as a captain under General Lord Loudoun. He advised that loyalists were arriving daily from the Mohawk River and he had heard from seventy inhabitants of the Susquehanna region who wished to enter "His Majesty's service as Rangers." This news was followed by an application to raise a ranger battalion. He pointed out the rangers' usefulness to the army "as scouts with the Indians" and claimed a battalion could be completed within three months.[97]

Brant's band at Oquaga was only one of the problems that disconcerted the Mohawk region's committees. A Tory named John McDonell Scotus, who lived on the Charlotte River, was recognized as a dangerous leader, a man with energy, compelling charm, and courage. He had been an officer in the Spanish army and had guarded Prince Charles Stuart's treasury in the 1745 Jacobite uprising in Scotland. In Sir John's absence, McDonell had organized friends and relatives from the Kortright, Banyar, Harpersfield, and Stamford patents into a loyal company of militia dubbed "the Highlanders."[98]

Colonel John Harper, who commanded Tryon's recently formed 5th Regiment, wrote that "the peopell of Harpersfield onfortunately fell into the hands of McDanald, who amediatley Swor them not to take arms against the King of Britan."[99] One of the "Highlanders" recalled that the "king's Colours were set up in their settlements,"[100] and Scotus adopted a rebel stratagem when he pressured all those who were slow to embrace loyalty into signing an oath of neutrality.

To the north at Montreal, Major Gray was dealing with the growing pains of his green battalion. He found that a few Royal Yorkers required the strongest form of discipline. For example, on April 4, a corporal was sentenced to the severe punishment of five hundred lashes upon his bare back at the head of his regiment. After receiving his strokes, the man was reduced to the ranks.[101]

An experienced captain from the 31st Foot had been seconded to assist in training the Royal Yorkers. Gray ordered him to take Stephen

Watts's light infantry company and complete it immediately from the battalion. All the old men were to "change their coats with those from the other Companys who shall come in their places; if their Coats do not Answer let the wings be taken off & given to those that come in."[102] Clearly, young Watts had been having trouble weeding out men who were physically or mentally incapable of mastering the rigorous tactical drills required for the company's special roles. Gray's care to perfect the Lights would later deliver solid dividends. Regimental orders continued with the reassignment of some subalterns in the companies and all the officers were scolded with the advice that Sir John had left a list of their seniorities so "that the[re] may be no farther Disputes in Regard to the Officers Ranks."

Captain Richard Lernoult, who was commanding at Niagara after the untimely death of Lieutenant-Colonel Caldwell, wrote to Governor Carleton on April 11 detailing both his and Butler's efforts to persuade the Six Nations to remain quiet until called upon to act with his Majesty's troops. They had cautioned the Indians to "by no means . . . attempt anything by themselves"; however, he noted that exposure of the Mohawk families in the Valley, which was emphasized by the "frequent threats of Schuyler to cut them off, gives the rest of the Nations great uneasiness . . . I am persuaded that should Schuyler attempt to hurt any one of them . . . neither the influence of Colonel Butler has with them now nor any other method . . . will prevent some of the young warriors from taking revenge."

Lernoult also said that six hundred to one thousand Indians had been in council at Niagara for the past three weeks. As well, some twenty "principal people and farmers from the Mohawk River . . . escaped through the woods during the winter to this Fort for protection," and many more were expected shortly. They had "been treated with the greatest hospitality by all the savage Nations on their way hither, except one village (near Fort Stanwix) of the Oneidas, who stopped two or three and carried them back to Schuyler."

Lernoult praised the Mississaugas: "I cannot help but being a little prejudiced in their favour as they have never varied nor required holding Councils to deliberate or would give ear to any one among the number sent . . . to draw them from their allegiance, but remain firm to their first agreement."[103]

On April 17, a detachment of the Third New York Continental Regiment (3NY) reinforced the garrison at Fort Stanwix and commenced that unit's fruitful, but difficult, relationship with the installation.[104] The 3NY's arrival was followed at mid-month by that of a French engineer, Captain B. La Marquisie, with a party of twenty carpenters. He immediately launched his chequered career by dismissing ten of them for incompetence.[105] Schuyler's motives for assigning him to the post are unknown. The general may have decided to give the Six Nations visible proof of French support for the cause, or perhaps he questioned the competence of the garrison's American engineer, Major Hubbell. Schuyler had approved La Marquisie's theoretical plan for altering Stanwix, but why he chose to ignore the recent improvements in favour of a new structure is a mystery. It is clear that Schuyler wanted the fort completed before the opening of the new campaign season, and his sense of urgency was definitely intact as evidenced by his order to the Frenchman to have the men "begin work at daylight and work until sunset, allowing an hour for breakfast and an hour and half for dinner."

The Whigs proved as adroit as the British in spreading rumours to create unease. On April 28, Lernoult reported to Carleton that some Indians claimed that an army of "six thousand Rebels were to take post at Oswego." He warned that Schuyler was "very industrious in spreading such reports which alarm the Six Nations greatly and should he effect such an attempt, I believe it would deter the greatest [number] of the savages from acting with the King's Troops, if not alter their present good disposition towards us."[106]

Colonel Peter Gansevoort, 3NY, took command of Stanwix on May 3. Twenty-eight years old and an ardent patriot, he was intensely loyal to the rebellion. He was well educated and had the background and airs of a patrician, having been born into an old, reputable, moneyed Albany-Dutch family. He was a veteran of the 1775 invasion of Canada and in the following year was second-in-command of Colonel Goose Van Schaick's unnumbered regiment. His portrait shows a firm-jawed, barrel-chested, heavyset man with bright eyes and a pleasantly satisfied demeanour. He stood over six feet, a tall, imposing man.[107]

His personal correspondence reveals that he was exacting, methodical, and sensitive to questions of personal integrity.[108] Despite his stolid appearance, acute sense of honour, and systematic mind, Gansevoort could make fun of himself, often joking that didn't have a single tooth in his head, the truth being that they were arrayed in double rows.[109] He held the affection of his officers[110] and was considerate of his enlisted men, even fatherly, considering his relative youth. Peter Gansevoort would prove to be the ideal man for the chore ahead.[111]

Recognizing Gansevoort's dismay at being relegated to an obscure frontier post, his brother Leonard, an Albany committee of safety member, wrote an encouraging letter. He emphasized that relations with the Six Nations were "an object of the greatest moment not to this state in particular but America in general to maintain Peace and amity with them."[112]

Fort Stanwix's commissary, John Hansen, sent an express letter to the Albany committee on May 13 warning them of Brant's plan to remove all the Canajoharie and Fort Hunter Mohawks to safety in Indian Territory, by force if necessary. He advised that the Mohawk sachems, who were about to attend a council at Albany, intended to pursue this same result by pacific means. They wanted to avoid embroilment in the conflict between the whites and claimed that, regardless of who prevailed, they would return to their castles in the Valley when the contest was over. Hansen was outraged and urged the Indian Commission to send a "Gent'n. of weight and importance" to threaten the Mohawks that if more than twelve Indian families left either castle, their lands would be forfeited to the United States. His sense of opportunism emerged when he wrote:

> The Removal or Desertion of the Indians from fort Hunter may turn out a fine affair to the Corporation of the City of Albany, for I concieve that the Corporation would and ought immediately to Enter the agreeabel fields of Ticonderoga [Tiononderoga] near fort Hunter. Then will be a Blessed Time for it, the annuall Revenue of which might be a Considerable Ease to our fellow Citizens in the Taxes which they will soon be obliged to pay to carry on this Glorious Struggle for Independence.[113]

As land confiscation was the usual penalty levied against inveterate enemies of the rebellion, it is clear that Hansen deeply distrusted the Mohawks. He warned against the anticipated importuning of the sachems and closed with the words, "God forbid that such a Contract should be Entered into in Behalf of this State. I Would rather see the whole Nation Tee Totally D—d."

The balance of the 3NY joined on May 28, except for Captain Thomas DeWitt's company, which was left behind to garrison Fort Dayton. The troops had been led by their colourful deputy commander, Lieutenant-Colonel Marinus Willett, who was accompanied by Surgeon Hunloke Woodruff.[114]

Willett would prove immensely significant in the defence of Stanwix. Born in 1740, he had served in the New York Provincial Regiment during the Seven Years War and, as a Volunteer,[115] was in the disastrous 1758 attack on Ticonderoga. A month later, he experienced Britain's only significant victory of that year, the capture of Fort Frontenac. En route, Bradstreet's expedition had to clear the choked-up creek system on the Oneida Carry,[116] and Willett observed first-hand the effectiveness of the measure. To be sure, this wily colonial soldier retained the memory of the time and effort required to free the obstruction.

At the outset of the rebellion in 1775, the energetic Willett took an active role when he led the opposition to a British attempt to remove military stores from New York City to supply their troops in Boston.[117] Willett seized the small arms that were later issued to the First New York Continental Regiment (1NY), in which he had served as a captain during the invasion of Canada as the commandant of Fort St. John's. He lost his commission the following year when his company fell under-strength;[118] however, in recognition of his devotion to the rebellion, he was promoted to lieutenant-colonel of the 3NY.

Willett was unimpressed by La Marquisie, the French engineer; likely his pragmatic personality and bold ego clashed with the haughty foreigner. He recommended his removal, but Gansevoort was reluctant to take such precipitate action. Two serious errors followed — the erection of new barracks outside the fort's walls and a misplacement of loopholes in the newly installed pickets.[119]

By May, Brant had recruited eighty men at Oquaga.[120] When his provisions were almost exhausted, he led an excursion to the white settlement of Unadilla at the edge of the Fort Stanwix Treaty Line. Two prominent local Whigs were brought to his temporary headquarters and he told them to speak freely, as his own message would be brief. They spoke of the Crown's quarrel with the "Boston people" and said that the colonies were united behind them.[121] They claimed to be friends of the Indians and were worried that Brant had collected an army at Oquaga. Brant replied:

> I am a man for war. I've taken an oath to the King, and will make no treaty with you. I will give these five families eight days to get away, and so long [as they go] they shall be safe. If any among them want to join us, I will protect them and they may stay.[122]

Brant's men gathered provisions and he ingenuously told the "donors" that Butler would pay them when he passed that way. He made it clear that he intended to bring off his people from the Mohawk Valley. As some Canajoharies had been imprisoned, he questioned two prominent local Whigs named Johnston, a minister and his son, why they were "using his Friends ill." He proclaimed "the Mohawks were always warriors — that their agreement with the King was very strong, and they were not such villans as to break the covenant." When the party left the settlement, a white volunteer taunted the Whigs that loyal men had no need to be afraid of rebel troops now.[123]

General Burgoyne arrived at Quebec City on May 5 with dispatches from Lord George Germain. These contained Carleton's first advice that he had been supplanted as commander of the 1777 campaign by his deputy and, adding insult to injury, included the King's expectations that he would retain the role of Quebec's governor and offer every assistance to mount, launch, and sustain Burgoyne. Although he was shocked and miffed, Carleton complied and gave his full support to Burgoyne. He took solace in frequent sarcastic letters to Germain requesting recall from an embarrassing and unrewarding commission.[124] Perhaps with a smidgen of conscience, Burgoyne later confided to one of his brigadiers, "My situation is critical and delicate."[125]

Throughout the winter and early spring, small parties of recruits had arrived at Montreal from the Mohawk, the upper Hudson, and the so-called New Hampshire Grants region. In early May, Major Gray took pleasure in announcing the arrival of a particularly large group from the Mohawk led by Alexander McDonell Aberchalder, his son Hugh, and his cousin John McDonell Leek. The major advised Governor Carleton that "[t]hese gentlemen" had been under arms with Sir John "since the beginning of the troubles" and had been amongst the six prisoners taken by Schuyler in January 1776. At the time, John Leek was ranked as a captain and Alexander Aberchalder, a lieutenant. Gray requested that some funds be granted to these two destitute older men. Leek was worn out from his travails and did not join the Royal Yorkers, but Alexander entered as a lieutenant and Hugh and Donald John McDonell Scotus, the son of Spanish John from the Charlotte River, entered as Gentlemen Volunteers.

The group totalled eighty-two men, of whom seventy-one "took the shilling" in the Royal Yorkers. Forty-five were Scots, "so attached to their chiefs that they can't think of parting with them." Twenty-three had Palatine names, the others Irish and English.[126]

Two days later, Gray put in Regimental Orders the usual reminder to be sure that the men's arms were "in Duty order" and their regimentals clean. He added that the non-commissioned officers were to ensure "their Regt'l hats [were] well Cocked, & their hair Properly Dressed."[127] Under the demanding eyes of Gray and the many other veteran officers, the Royal Yorkers were beginning to take shape. The major was determined his raw Provincials would emulate the appearance and performance of British Regulars, but there was a long way to go.

On May 16, Governor Carleton sent orders to Mason Bolton, the newly ensconced lieutenant-colonel of the 8th Regiment at Fort Niagara. The letter detailed the troops assigned to St. Leger and gave specific instructions for Bolton's action:

> You will accordingly direct that 100 men, with officers in proportion to strength, of the [8th] regiment hold themselves in immediate readiness to march and to obey all orders they shall receive from Lieutenant Colonel St. Leger.

The King having further signified his pleasure that a sufficient number of Indians be joined to this detachment, you will therefore employ every means in your power to assemble as many Indians as you can communicate with and prevail upon them to put themselves with leaders, who will be appointed by Colonel Butler,[128] under the command of Lieutenant Colonel St. Leger, and exert their utmost efforts under his direction of their King and father.

You will consult with Lieutenant Colonel St. Leger in regards of the rendezvous, both of the troops and savages, and give every assistance in your power to promote the service upon which he is employed.

Although it is my wish to give every possible assistance to the commerce of the upper country, yet it cannot be allowed to interfere with the public service. I must desire you will make the Traders who pass your post acquainted that they are not to depend upon the King's shipping for the passage of their goods, arms and ammunition excepted.[129]

Joseph Brant's excursion across the Treaty Line caused many families to flee Unadilla to Cherry Valley and led the fearful inhabitants of nearby Harpersfield to write to General Herkimer on June 10 to request ammunition.[130]

Brant was starved for instructions and sent twenty-four-year-old Robert Land,[131] one of his first white recruits, to New York City across the same perilous regions he and Tice had traversed the previous fall. His message told Guy Johnson of his actions and requested orders about where he should join with General Howe. Johnson advised that the Commander-in-Chief "direct[ed] the Indians to join the first British army on the communications."[132] Before Land returned with this cryptic, minimalist instruction, Brant had heard of Butler's upcoming council at Oswego and decided to proceed there.

On May 22, an entry into Governor Carleton's letter book dealt with intelligence gathered on the upper Hudson River by Lieutenant Patrick Langan of the Six Nations Indian Department. Langan had heard that "Fort Stanwix was to be razed; & a sod fort made in the Room of it with two Redoubts." Obviously, the rebels were waffling over the old installation, and the news contributed to Carleton's confidence that the fort would be a pushover. Yet the lieutenant's other advice should have served as a warning: "The fort to contain 700 men. . . That 3 Regiments was to be Quartered at Fort Stanwix — That they intend if any attempt should be made that way, to cut Trees across Wood Creek to hinder the Batteaus from going up."[133] This intelligence was passed on to St. Leger.

A notice appeared in the Quebec *Gazette*: "On Tuesday [May 27] evening came up the *Nottingham* Indiaman, a transport . . . in which came passengers Sir John Johnson, his Lady and family."[134] Sir John had been recalled from New York City to be deputy commander of the Mohawk Valley expedition, but whether he was privy to the information that General Howe did not intend to coordinate his attack with Burgoyne is unknown. As his cousin Guy was utterly in the dark, it is probable that Sir John was equally uninformed.

Every morning at six o'clock, the Royal Yorkers formed under arms for drill, and every afternoon they fired ball. Major Gray's orders insisted that the officers "be more Particular in Giving the Monthly Returns — Field Returns, Morning Reports, Reports of the Sick, or any other Returns that may be Wanted Relative to Military Duty." His final order was most exciting — the regiment was "to hold itself in Readiness to March to Lachine at an hours Warning," where they would concentrate with the other units of the expedition.[135]

On May 31, Daniel Claus, who was one of the most prominent men to serve under St. Leger, returned to Quebec after two years in England. Claus was a sensitive, intelligent individual who was rather quick to take offence and long to remember it. A contemporary miniature portrait showed a broad forehead with hair pulled back into a queue and fashionable sidecurls. He had wide-set eyes, a mouth curled up at the corners, a moderately aquiline nose, and a firm jaw with a dimpled chin.[136]

When Guy Johnson had failed to regain Claus's role as Deputy Superintendent of the Canada Indians, Claus had struggled to find a position that matched his experience and talents. Finally, he had been given a commission as St. Leger's "Superintendent of the Western Expedition,"[137]

Lieutenant-Colonel Daniel Claus,
Superintendent of the Western Expedition

Unknown artist, a miniature, watercolour on ivory, ca. 1770.
Courtesy of the National Archives of Canada, C-083514.

to act as Guy's surrogate. Although the position was temporary, he was gratified to be sent to Quebec where "a Door was open for me to any Indn. Nation on the Contin[en]t."[138]

At the time of the award, he was told that Sir John would command the expedition,[139] and he found this heartening news, as the two men shared great affection and esteem and both were Americans, one by choice, the other by birth. Exactly when he discovered a British officer had been put over the head of Sir John is unclear. No hint of disappointment has been discovered, but judging from his later acerbic criticism of St. Leger, it is natural to assume a preformed bias.

From his landfall at Quebec City, Claus forwarded his commission to Governor Carleton in Montreal and, a few days later, waited upon him. Claus was totally unaware that a crucially important letter from General Howe for Carleton and Burgoyne had gone astray for ten days[140] and had come into the governor's hands only a scant day or two before Claus's arrival in Montreal. This distressing dispatch contained the commander-in-chief's advice that he would be moving the main army against Philadelphia and would not be "forming a junction" with Burgoyne at Albany. Howe promised to assign a corps to act "upon the lower part of Hudson's River sufficient to open the communications for shipping through the Highlands," but this measure was a far cry from the support that both Carleton and Burgoyne had counted upon for the new campaign. Howe's painful news had not improved Carleton's smouldering temper, for which Claus represented a perfect vent.

When Claus was admitted, Carleton dryly acknowledged the receipt of his commission, but offered no further comment. The governor was extremely aloof, consistent with his belief that Claus had been an absentee manager of the Canada Indians prior to the war and a deserter from the scene of action in 1775 and 1776. He offered no advice or commentary about current affairs, neither regarding the alarming changes to Howe's plans nor of Butler's activities at Niagara. He was deeply disappointed to discover that Claus had been placed over Butler, the man who had served him so well in his time of great need, and he was disgusted that his recent orders to Butler had been countermanded by this development from home.

Carleton's frigid demeanour was not peculiar to his relationship with Claus, for the governor was infamous as "one of the most distant, reserved men in the world."[141] He was said to seek no advice, nor care one whit to please his superiors. When coupled with his readily apparent dislike, his natural reserve froze Claus.

On the last day of May, the Royal Yorkers received this order:

> The Regt to March to La Chine to morrow Morning at
> 6 o'clock — the Officers & Men to carry no more nec-
> essarys with them than what they want for 9 or ten Days
> to Shift themselves with, what Baggage the men Leave
> behind to be put in the Store this Evening at 4 o'clock;
> & every Compy's Baggage by itself — the Quarter
> Master Sergt to see that there is Cloathing taken for the
> use of the Recruits which the Taylors are to make at
> Lachine; what Cloathing is finished to be Given Out to
> the Recruits; Sergt Hillyer to pack what is not finish'd to
> be Carri'd along to Morrow.[142] 1 S[erjeant] 1 C[orporal]
> 12 Old Men to be left behind as Guard for the Stores &
> to Attend the Sick. Surgeons Mate [Joseph Skinner] to
> Remain in Point Clare to take Care of the Sick untill fur-
> ther Orders — the Regt not to fire Ball this After noon.
> A Cart will attend Each Company to Carry the Officers
> Baggage & the Men's Provisions.[143]

The Royal Yorkers return of June 1 showed the addition of Alexander McDonell's company on the battalion strength,[144] indicating that

McDonell had been promoted to captain. That same day, the Royal Yorkers concentrated at Lachine with the two companies of the 34th Regiment, and the Yorkers' tailors were immediately confined to a local garret "to begin Directly to work at the men's Cloathing and to keep Close at them till they are finished."

Beginning June 2, rolls were called twice daily,

> [I]n the morning after guard mounting and in the evening after retreat beating at 7 o'clock — All officers to attend at the head of their Company — all [drum] beats to be taken from the 34th Regt[145] — the troops to be exercised 3 times a day for an hour each time — the commanding officers will observe the kind of Discipline laid down by Colonel St. Leger. The kings royal regiment of New York to fire balls by Divisions till further orders — the hour of exercise will be half after 4 in the morning, at mid Day and at half past 5 in the evening.

Barry St. Leger's presence was first acknowledged in Sir John's orderly book on June 3. As General Burgoyne's personal choice to command the Mohawk Valley expedition, he gave every appearance of being an excellent selection.

Colonel Barry St. Leger was of Huguenot descent, born in Ireland in about 1739. He entered the army in 1756 as an ensign and the next year went with the 28th Regiment to America. By 1758, he had transferred to the 48th, in which he served as a captain in the attack on Louisbourg and at the Plains of Abraham. The 48th was immortalized in Wolfe's dying words when he ordered them forward to cut off the French retreat at the St. Charles River. St. Leger was distinguished by being appointed the brigade-major for the advance on Montreal in 1760. Two years later he was major of the 95th and in May of 1772 he was promoted to lieutenant-colonel in the army. Three years later, he was posted to Canada as the lieutenant-colonel of the 34th.[146]

In his youth, St. Leger had a strong, sharp-chinned face with a small, firm mouth and round, quizzical eyebrows. Rather than fashionable sidecurls, he wore his hair in natural sidewaves with a small queue under a large cocked hat, a style he favoured in later life. At the time of his appointment, he was about forty, and his face had aged con-

A youthful Barry St. Leger

*Engraving after an unknown artist from London
Magazine, 1782.*

siderably, his eyes in particular showing the telltale signs of reckless living.[147]

Here was an officer with North American experience who had received the recognition of a substantive field officer rank. That he had little experience in the American wilderness went unnoticed; that he had no personal experience with natives was ignored.

St. Leger published sage words of advice for his command, many clearly directed towards the inexperienced Royal Yorkers. This counsel indicated the depth of his military knowledge and leadership. A review of his regimental correspondence exhibits great concern for his men, and also shows his strong aversion to what he viewed as insolence, which boded ill for some future relationships.[148] Here are a few examples of his orders:

A Strict and Punctual Adherence to all orders Given, is the life and soul of Military Operations; without it Troops are but confus'd & ungovernable multitudes ever liable to Destruction & sure never to acquire honour to themselves or gain advantage to their Country: therefore Col. St Leger Acquaints the Troops he has the Honour to Command, that the few Necessary Orders he means to give Must Instantly and privately [be] attended to without Descretionary Interpretations whatsoever . . .

Coll: St. Ledger thinks proper to observe to the Kings Royal Regt of New York, That the Surest Method of Making the Noble & honorable zeal they have Lately manifested to their King and Countrys interest take the

Effect they ardently wish for, as well as to Repossess themselves of the peace & property which has been most illegaly wrested from them, is to give a Constant & unwearied attention to the learning of Military Discipline which will give them Superiority over the Confused Rabble they have to deal with.[149]

At Fort Niagara on June 5,[150] Major John Butler received Carleton's dispatch of May 18. As the governor's orders to Colonel Bolton had arrived a few days before, Butler was already well aware of what was expected of him:

> I am therefore to request that you will exert the zeal which has ever distinguished your conduct by now using every means in your power to collect as large a body as possible of the Indians of the Six Nations and any others you can communicate with; and to dispose them to act with all their vigour in concert with His Majesty's Troops under the command of Lieutenant Colonel St. Leger.
>
> The providing and appointing proper leaders (who will have the usual allowances) to this body of Indians is left to your care and judgment, and I hope your health will permit you to accompany this expedition as I know no person so capable of the conducting and management of the Indians.

Butler was instructed to submit a list of his nominated officers with recommendations for their ranks and rates of pay, as well as his own. He was disappointed to read the governor's instruction that the loyalist refugees who had collected at Niagara should join Sir John's regiment, "at least as many as will complete it." They were to be given a bounty of two hundred acres of land for taking up arms till the war's end.[151]

A few days later Daniel Claus revisited Governor Carleton at Montreal to obtain specific orders for the expedition. He asked what rank he was to have during that service. Carleton chose to reply only to the latter, stating "it could not be settled here." When Claus spoke about the equipment required for Indians going on service, he was told that John Butler, "Depy to Col. Johnson," had everything in hand. The style of this reference to Butler stung Claus, as it implied that his own commission as Johnson's deputy was illegitimate.

Unsatisfied, and unaware that Carleton had placed the strictest controls on all Indian goods, Claus inspected the government's storehouses in Montreal and found that there were more than enough goods to meet Burgoyne's needs. Worried that Butler had already disposed of his allotment, he "applied for the most requisite articles" and was affronted when the storekeeper refused his requests and offered the unwelcome opinion that Butler had everything under control. In spite of these trite assurances, Claus obtained some key necessaries on his own credit,[152] a measure that was to prove extremely prudent.

While St. Leger's expedition made its preparations, there were far greater measures underway to concentrate Burgoyne's Grand Army at Chambly. Although not as large as either Burgoyne or Carleton had wished, the army was substantial and of superb quality. Burgoyne's British and German Regular infantry numbered over seven thousand, with an artillery detachment in excess of four hundred men manning a wealth of guns. As the campaign unfolded, the Regulars were joined by one hundred Quebec militia, more than eight hundred loyalists, and nine hundred Lakes and Canada Indians.[153] In the final analysis, Burgoyne fielded well in excess of eighty-five hundred[154] muskets and forty-six fieldpieces.

Frustrated by self-indulgent anger, Governor Carleton took four long days to advise Burgoyne that Howe had no intention of marching north.[155] Remarkably, this thunderbolt caused no alterations to Burgoyne's plans and, seemingly, not even a ripple of consternation.

On June 12, a Royal Yorker Regimental order prohibited the men from wearing their shoes when they went fishing. Only a day later, a General Order was issued with similar warnings:

> As Cleanliness and a Strict Attention to Duty are Indespensable Necessaries in a Soldier, Colonel St Leger Desires the troops Under his Command may be immediately furnished with Necessarys & Each a black stock.

Officers must Inspect their Men Every morning, when they will correct any Man that comes Slovenly to the Parade; they will Likewise Remember that for the future he will impute to their Inattention the un-Soldier Like Parade he Observed this Morning.[156]

Obviously, Royal Yorker morning parades were attended by soldiers with stockings down about their ankles; coattails unhooked; dirty shirt collars askew; wet, scuffed, filthy shoes; and cocked hats flopped. Just as obviously, a proper martial spirit was slow to develop. Undoubtedly, the Regulars were much amused and derisive.

The Royal Yorkers continued to be exposed to the expertise of the two companies of the 34th. During the evening exercises, the regiments primed and loaded and then brigaded together to be exercised by the sure hand of Lieutenant Crofts of the 34th.

Upriver at Oswegatchie, Captain Forster's light company of the 8th was ordered to leave behind an officer and twenty men and send the rest, under Captain-Lieutenant Potts, to Buck Island with the company of Canadien militia when it arrived at their post from Lachine.[157]

St. Leger's General Orders of June 14 increased the artillery detachment by assigning a corporal and five men from the 8th, five men from the 34th, and ten Royal Yorkers. They would assist in serving the expedition's train of two 6-pounders, two 3-pounders, and four 4.4-inch Cohorn mortars.[158]

After Orders for the fifteenth noted that Sir John had promoted John McDonell Scotus Jr. to captain-lieutenant,[159] William Byrne to lieutenant, and Richard Lipscomb to ensign. These three officers would lead the Colonel's Company throughout the campaign. The junior officers of Stephen Watts's specialized light infantry company were Lieutenants Kenneth McDonell and George Singleton and Ensign John McKenzie. Reassignments of subalterns in the other companies were made. Angus McDonell's and Richard Duncan's embryonic companies were without their captains,[160] as they had been unable to join the regiment, and experienced subalterns and NCOs were appointed to manage their affairs.

At Niagara, Major Butler sent messengers to the Iroquois Confederacy's Allegheny and Finger Lakes castles and to the Mississaugas' summer villages on Lake Ontario with word that all were to assemble at Irondequoit Bay prior to joining the army at Oswego. On the Senecas' suggestion, Butler invited the Detroit-area Lakes Indians to send a contingent. On June 15, he sent headquarters a department return listing five captains, nine lieutenants, and seventy-five rangers with their rates of pay, many of whom spoke an Indian dialect. Although his son Walter was not listed, Butler made representation that he should command this body of men. As requested, he gave his opinion on a suitable rank and pay for himself:

> From my long services, the influence I have with the Indians, the rank I have held in Civil, Military and Militia lines, and the interest I possess in the County of Albany and the Mohawk River, I ... hope Your Excellency will not think me unworthy the rank of Lieutenant Colonel, and from the unavoidable expense attending my public station, I humbly hope a Guinea a day will not by Your Excellency be esteemed inadequate.[161]

The Canadiens draughted from the Quebec militia for service with Burgoyne and St. Leger had a chequered history. There was a constant trickle of desertions from the three one-hundred-man fighting companies and the corvées of men assigned to quartermaster and pioneering duties.[162] Discipline in the fighting companies was made worse because the majority of the men who had been selected were bachelors without worldly possessions and unsusceptible to the moral suasion used on the more established, older men. Carleton gave orders to seize all Canadien deserters and assured Burgoyne and St. Leger that once they were apprehended, they would be sent forward so that they could be proceeded against.[163]

At Lachine on June 15, a section of the 34th was issued with hand hatchets to cut boughs to cover the bateaux and prevent them from drying out. St. Leger ordered that no Royal Yorkers were to be assigned to this task, as their attendance at arms drill was more important.[164]

A day later, several appointments to the expedition's staff were announced: as adjutant-general, Captain William Ancrum, assisted by Lieutenant William Crofts, both of the 34th; as quartermaster-general,

Lieutenant James Lundy, Royal Highland Emigrants; Mr. James Kusick as bateaux master; Mr. John Farquharson as commissary; and Mr. Austin Piety as conductor of Artillery, a role he had held for many years in Boston. St. Leger noted that all orders passing through his military secretaries, Lieutenant William Osborne Hamilton and Ensign George Clergis, were to be obeyed as if from himself.[165]

Then came the long-awaited orders "to hold themselves in Readiness to march on the Shortest Notice."[166] On June 19, one year to the exact day that Johnson had received his beating order for the Royal Yorkers, the arrival of a flood of stores indicated that departure was imminent:

> Forty eight Batteaux to be Delivered to the Royal Regt of New York,[167] forty five felling axes & 3 broad axes . . . a number of thole pins — two fishing lines & hooks in proportion to be delivered to each boat. The K.R.R.N.Y. are to take 440 barrels of provision allowing 10 barrels each for 44 Batteaux . . . the rum or brandy delivered out is to be put into the officer's boats for security.

In After Orders it was noted that the Royal Yorkers were to move their craft to the King's stores, where they were

> to be compleated with 14 days provision commencing the 21 June — their boats to be loaded at the Kings stores on Friday . . . brought up to their quarters the same day . . . ready to push off at point of day on Saturday — their [bateaux] Division is to be supplied with three [Canadien] pilots . . . It is expected that the several captains have laid in necessaries for their men for the campaign.[168]

On the same day that the stores and bateaux arrived, the announcement was made of the appointment of Jean-Baptiste-Melchior[169] Hertel de Rouville as the *Capitaine* commanding the company of Canadien militia assigned to the expedition.[170] As a twelve-year-old ensign of French Regulars, Rouville had left Quebec in 1760, served abroad, and returned in 1775 just in time to volunteer for service against the rebels and be captured at the defence of Fort St. John's. After twenty months of captivity, he had been exchanged in the spring of 1777 and returned to Quebec.

The family name Hertel de Rouville was amongst several famous Canadien families who were noteworthy for developing the successful tactics of the *petite guerre*, a blend of European-style discipline with Indian skills and methods.[171] Carleton instructed St. Leger "to declare him in orders at his arrival."[172]

The Canadiens' uniforms were quite different from their British or Provincial counterparts. A Brunswick officer observed a Fort St. John's muster on June 16 and recorded that the men wore brown waistcoats and "very short" jackets with "ungarnished" round hats. Each company's hats and jackets were trimmed in a different colour of lace: red, blue, or green. In contrast, their commissioned officers wore scarlet coats with blue facings.[173]

Joseph Brant's behaviour on Tryon County's southwestern frontier had alarmed General Schuyler. Although Schuyler was swamped in preparations against a major attack from Canada, he addressed this burgeoning threat by dispatching Colonel Goose Van Schaick with a detachment of 150 Massachusetts Continentals to the county. The men were hurriedly scratched together from the three regiments of Brigadier-General Ebenezer Learned's brigade and led by the state's senior major, Ezra Badlam.[174]

Schuyler instructed General Herkimer to call out the Tryon Militia Brigade to confront Brant, and Van Schaick was ordered to join him,

but insufficient provisions prevented the Continentals from marching further than Cherry Valley.[175] Consequently, it was decided the militia alone would have to face the troublesome Mohawk. As Herkimer and Brant

Lieutenant Ignace-Michel-Louis-Antoine d'Irumberry de Salaberry, Hertel de Rouville's Company, Quebec Militia

Unknown artist. Photographer, R. Chartrand. Courtesy of R. Chartrand, Private Collection.

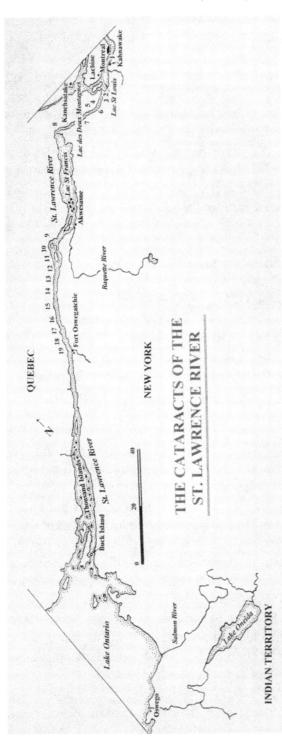

The cataracts of the St. Lawrence River — a major topographical barrier to St. Leger's advance.

Gavin K. Watt, 1999.

1. Sault St. Louis (Lachine Rapids) 2. Les Cascades 3. Sault du Trou 4. Sault du Buisson 5. Pointe au Coulange 6. Le Grand Batture (Les Cedres/The Cedars) 7. Pointe au Diable 8. Coteau du Lac 9. Point Maligne (Sir Wm Johnson's Point) 10. Mille Roches 11. Moulinette 12. Le Batture 13. Long Sault 14. Rapide Plat 15. Pointe aux Iroquois 16. Presqu'ile Pointe 17. Pointe au Cardinal 18. Pointe au Galop (The Lower Galop) 19. The Upper Galop (Pointe de l'Ivrogne?)

had lived three miles apart on the Mohawk River and were Masonic brothers, Schuyler persuaded him that their friendship would ease the meeting.[176]

After inviting Brant to meet with him at Unadilla, Herkimer marched with 380 militiamen and arrived at the settlement on June 19. Brant delayed leaving Oquaga for eight days, waiting for a response to his calls for assistance from the other nations and John Butler, but none arrived. Later, he bitterly recalled that influence from Niagara had prevented help from coming,[177] but more likely, his clansmen had been persuaded by their peers to remain neutral. In any event, Joseph wanted to avoid appearing anxious. The long wait made many of the militiamen very impatient.

At Lachine, the Royal Yorkers' regimental orders read:

> 20th . . . Ens Phillips 1 Sergt. 1 Corl 32 Privates to Be left at Lachine in order to go with the baggage of the K.R.R.N.Y. over Lake Champlain to Crown Point & then proceed after the army under . . . General Burgoyne with the baggage as far as Albany if he should proceed to that place — ten old men to Be left at Point Clair.[178]

Adding together all of the detachments that had been made for various services, the Royal Yorkers' fighting strength had been reduced by sixty-seven, more than the equivalent of a full company.

The last entries written at Lachine in Sir John's orderly book were dated June 21. The Yorkers' bateaux were also to accommodate seven barrels of rum and the provisions and rum barrels were "to be distributed in such proportion as to make room for the Officers & their baggage." Major Gray was advised that the 34th's bateaux would precede his regiment, and he was to assemble his convoy so that his companies were in order of seniority. The boats of the company commanders would lead their units with the older subalterns posted in the rear and the younger in the centre. The boats were to sail abreast where practicable so that the flotilla would not be unnecessarily elongated.

Sir John offered some words of wisdom to his officers, stressing their need for diligence in regulating their men, as so many new companies had been recently created.[179] This advice was much needed, as their first trial was the formidable St. Lawrence River with its numerous cataracts, rapids, and portages. There were sixteen obstructions to be overcome with much effort and fatigue. Canadiens who made their living by working bateaux brigades through or around these hindrances would assist the expedition as pilots. As well, a large corvée of Canadien labourers would handle the craft and assist in portaging the baggage where necessary;[180] however, the troops would be anything but idle spectators. All men were expected to pole and drag the boats, often up to their chests in the icy torrent, and manhandle the awkward baggage. It could be back-breaking, dispiriting work that would try their physical conditioning and discipline.

Les Cascades, the second cataract encountered on the ascent of the St. Lawrence River — boats are mere dots in the tumultuous rush of water

Watercolour by George Heriot. Courtesy of the National Archives of Canada, C-012795.

Daniel Claus had severe doubts about the accuracy of the intelligence about the Oneida Carry that was accepted as valid at Headquarters. Prior to leaving Lachine, he dispatched a scout to Fort Stanwix to determine the true strength of the garrison and the state of the fortification and, if possible, to take prisoners. The party was led by two of Claus's most trustworthy operatives, Captain John Deserontyon and Captain John Hare. At Oswegatchie, they quickly assembled a party of about forty men, including the young Cayuga chief, Schoughyowote, and set off overland for the Mohawk.[181]

When Claus set out on June 23 with Sir John and the Royal Yorkers, the artillery detachment's bateaux were being readied to take aboard the guns. Claus noted that St. Leger would leave the next day.[182] He must have been deeply disappointed that so few Canada Indians chose to join him, considering that he had been their superintendent for well over a decade. It galled him that their refusal gave some credence to Carleton's reasons for replacing him. The governor's Indian officers had obviously done their work well, and when the Seven Nations took to the field, the vast majority attended Burgoyne, not Claus.

CHAPTER FOUR

NOT QUITE AS PLANNED
Fort Ticonderoga ... Abandoned by the Rebels

The correspondence between Colonel Peter Gansevoort and his fiancée, Colonel Goose Van Schaick's sister Catherine, offers some valuable insights into his personality. On June 23, he wrote to "Dear Caty" at her home in Albany, giving her some intelligence about Howe's intentions, as well as some kind words to calm her fears:

> [T]hree French officers taken at sea . . . have since made their escape, they inform that it is the avowed intention of the enemy to carry on their operation to the southward. If this information be true, the Inhabitants at your place are not so much alarmed as they were . . I now flatter myself that you with the rest of the good Citizens will not be driven by the Vile murdering Banditti from your peaceable habitations . . . hence I infer that nothing Threatens from the North and consequently that this campaign will be to me an exceeding inactive one.[183]

There had already been considerable turmoil at Fort Stanwix due to French engineer La Marquisie's errors, but a far more severe jolt upset the garrison's sense of security on June 25. Against Gansevoort's specific instructions, Captain James Gregg and Corporal Samuel Madison went pigeon hunting along The Carry between the ruins of Forts Bull and Newport, where they were attacked and scalped. Madison was killed outright and Gregg was left for dead.[184] Here was a clear signal that lethal danger was close at hand.

The next day, the interpreter James Deane wrote to General Philip Schuyler from Old Oneida about his visit to the Seneca town of Skoiyase, where he had heard that "Colonel Butler only waited for orders to repair to Oswego and that the Indians were to repair to him on [the] firing [of]

Colonel Peter Gansevoort, Third New York Continental Line — the resolute commander of Fort Stanwix

Engraving after a painting by Gilbert C. Stuart, ca. 1783.

a number of cannons . . . Butler has one John Johnson [Lieutenant John Johnston] in a village near where I was . . . who when he heard of my arrival gathered some warriors in order to do me a mischief, but they very much dispised his desire."[185]

Schuyler received this letter two days later and immediately wrote to Governor George Clinton of New York with the conclusion that "an irruption will be made from the westward."[186]

When Joseph Brant finally confronted General Herkimer at Unadilla, he brought a contingent that included an unnamed clan matron, three deputies, and twenty warriors. His key men were William of Canajoharie; the famous Captain Bull, who was a "short dark skinned" Delaware chief; and a curly-headed man of mixed native and black blood named Pool.[187] Herkimer and Colonels Cox, Harper, and Klock sat under a bower and the natives sat on benches.[188] Brant suspiciously eyed the size of Herkimer's party and announced that he had five hundred warriors who could instantly fall upon the militia and destroy them, then mildly added that such action would be unnecessary, as Herkimer was a neighbour and old friend. Schuyler had been right.

The Mohawk was bluffing, he had fewer than two hundred men and only twenty pounds of powder, but Herkimer had no way of knowing. Soothingly, Herkimer said he had simply come to visit with Brant, to which the latter scornfully replied, "And all these have come on a friendly visit too? All want to see the poor Indians; it is very kind." Herkimer described America's difficulties with England, which prompted Brant to reveal his feelings:

The Indians were in concert with the King, as their fathers and grandfathers had been . . . Herkimer and the rest had joined the Boston people against their king . . . That Mr. Schuyler, or General, or what you please to call him, was very smart on the Indians at the treaty at German Flats; but was not at the same time able to afford the smallest article of clothing. That the Indians had formerly made war on the white people all united; and now they were divided, the Indians were not frightened.[189]

These bold, challenging statements provoked an outburst from Ebenezer Cox, which offended Brant. Although he knew Cox well, Brant sarcastically asked if he was George Klock's son-in-law. Cox's father-in-law had been a thorn in the side of the Canajoharie Castle for decades,[190] so he had no difficulty in recognizing Brant's slur and returned a sharp answer. Flushed with anger, Brant and his lieutenants sprang up, hallooed, and ran to their camp to discharge their guns.[191]

Passions were so aroused that the meeting was adjourned until the next day. That evening, in view of Brant's aggressive posture, Herkimer became uneasy with the thought that his men were in danger. He gave Serjeant Joseph Waggoner secret orders to select three

steady men who would keep loaded firelocks at hand and their eyes peeled. If the meeting turned violent,[192] they were to kill Brant and his lieutenants. Should such an action become necessary, it would

The Mohawk, Joseph Brant Thayendanegea — an uncomplimentary image taken during his stay in London

Engraving from the London Magazine of 1776 after an unknown artist. Courtesy of the National Archives of Canada, C-100706.

rob the band of their leadership, probably douse immediate retaliation, and rid the county of four dangerous adversaries. Waggoner chose the general's nephews, George and Abraham Herkimer, and one other — all with steady hands and tight mouths.[193]

When the meeting resumed the following day, Brant reminded Herkimer of his five hundred men who were ready for battle and ominously declared that Herkimer and the militiamen were in his power. To illustrate his point, he signalled and the edge of the woods filled with painted men hallooing and brandishing their arms. Brant said he appreciated Herkimer's reasons for the visit, but it was too late. He and his men would honour the ancient covenant chain with the King, but for now, his old friend Herkimer could go in peace. Joseph would take his men to Oswego for Butler's council.[194]

As the negotiations continued, Herkimer was manoeuvred into lifting the restrictions on the Mohawks' travel between their upper and lower castles and the movements of the Reverend John Stuart and John Butler's wife, Catherine. Further, he promised that the region's loyalists would not be molested.

Other than genuine fear, it is difficult to find another explanation for these concessions.[195] In a further gesture of goodwill, Herkimer gave Brant's men several beeves, which they immediately slaughtered and consumed. The militiamen, who had been on short rations for several days, failed to appreciate Herkimer's gesture.[196] Legend records that when the parties separated, the hitherto bright, sunny sky suddenly darkened, followed by a violent rain and hailstorm — portents of the years to come.[197]

Governor Carleton wrote to Germain on June 26, advising that Burgoyne had

> proceeded on the service allotted to him by your Lordship about the 17th Inst . . . St. Leger has . . . begun his movement taking with him the detachment of the 34th and the Royal Regiment of New York, which is increased to about three hundred men, and a company of Canadians; He will be joined by the detachment of the 8th and the Indians of the six nations with the

Missassauges as he proceeds, about a hundred of the Hanau Chasseurs have since arrived and they are on their way to join him."[198]

At Stanwix, a court martial on June 28 found a soldier guilty of "Cursing the Congress and the Captain [and] for offering to lay a Wager that many more would Desert." He was sentenced to one hundred lashes on his bare back.[199]

On June 30, Schuyler wrote Gansevoort cautioning that

> A report prevails that Sir John Johnson intends to attack your post. You will therefore put yourself in the best posture of defence. Keep out scouts continually towards Oswego, and every other quarter from which the enemy may approach. Be very watchful and alert, that you may not experience the disgrace of surprise. I have written to General Herkimer to support you with the militia, in case you should be attacked.[200]

The scouts were to determine the numbers and identity of the enemy's troops, whether British, Indians, or Canadiens. Memories of the latter's proficiency in previous conflicts continued to haunt the Americans.[201]

Herkimer reported the results of the Unadilla conference to Schuyler on July 2, mentioning Brant's comment that an expedition was preparing to invade the "Western Country" and that his party would join this venture. In anticipation that Schuyler would consider that he had acted beyond his level of authority, he noted that the Tryon committee of safety unanimously approved of his "Proceedings" and considered that he had "acted prudently in our dangerous situation." He further excused his actions by noting that Brant had insisted upon a resolution of his various grievances "upon the spot," and he closed his report with heartfelt and, to an overworked Schuyler, distressing words:

We are yet in a defenceless situation . . . as the Indians
will doubtless make an Incursion into our Settlements,
which it is not very difficult to them to distroy or take
possession thereof. Our Militia cannot be spared and
serve as an Assistance for Fort Schuyler. We want rather
succour ourselves, to save the outward Inhabitants with
their families, I recommend our present dangerous situation to your particular care as we are but few, and the
Enimy will force in as much as possable to put his
friends[,] our runaways[,] in possession of their former
Properties again, if we shall not be expeditiously suc-
coured with Continental Troops I fear the Indians will
make a Ravage of our Frontier Country and . . . will
make an entry in our State from our quarters without
great difficulty.[202]

Gansevoort reported to Schuyler on July 3 that his instructions to avoid
a surprise would be rigidly adhered to, but he had great concerns
regarding his lack of supplies and the inadequacy of his garrison. His
warehouses held 87 barrels of pork and beef, 379 barrels of flour, and a
few more of peas. His supply of rum was reduced to a single barrel. He
respectfully reminded his superior that these goods were insufficient
should the fort be invested, especially as Indian affairs were also being
managed from the fort.[203]

About three-quarters of a mile from Stanwix that same day,
Deserontyon's patrol surprised a sixteen-man work party of the 3NY
that was cutting sod for the fort's repairs. Five men were captured, four
scalps taken, and one of the dead men was left "shockingly butchered."
The detail's commander, Ensign John Spoor, was amongst the captives.[204] Their mission fulfilled, the patrol returned north.

The ritually butchered body of the dead soldier made a strong
impression on the garrison. All were aware of this native practice, but to
see its effects, especially on one of their own, was quite another matter.

On July 4, recognition of the first anniversary of Independence Day
was muted. Gansevoort reported to Schuyler that Captain La Marquisie
was being given every assistance and the troops were worked constantly. Those coming off guard were immediately turned out for fatigues.

He repeated that he simply did not have enough men to complete the work ordered, as, of course, it was necessary to maintain the "internal business of the Garrison." He needed 150 men to block Wood Creek and an equal number to guard the parties cutting and drawing timber. If he dared to pull men from guarding Stanwix and assigned them to those duties, the fort "might . . . be easily surprized by a very contemptible party of the enemy."[205]

Gansevoort noted the increasing number of hostile Indians around Stanwix, illustrating his point by reporting the gruesome details of the attack on Ensign Spoor's party. His litany of woe continued. His salt beef was spoiled and supplies of other meats were reduced by the necessity of making gifts to his native allies. Captain Joseph Savage, his artillery commander, reported that some essential tools for the guns were scarce and many musket balls did not match the bores of the muskets. Moulds of various calibres were requested to correct this latter problem. His powder supply was dangerously low. He pressed Schuyler to address these shortages and to send reinforcements so that he might "by the blessing of God . . . be able to give a good account of any force that will probably come against us."

Gansevoort withheld mentioning that many of his enlisted men drank heavily and were insolent, profane, disobedient, and careless of hygiene. Courts martial were of necessity frequent, as was flogging.[206]

Gansevoort recognized that news of the attack on Spoor's men would soon reach Albany and wrote a calming note to his Caty: "I hope this will not occasion the least uneasiness in you . . . I can assure you that I think myself as safe in this fort as I would in any part of America and shall not expose myself by strolling about the garrison."[207] That same day, Schuyler wrote to General Herkimer:

> I am apprehensive that the agreement you have made with Brandt will not turn out much to our advantage . . . it was prudent not to refuse to let the Mohawks of the Lower Castle go to the Canajoharie Castle, yet permitting Mr. Stewart [Stuart] and Mrs. Butler to reside there, is putting these people in a way to do more mischief than they could have done had they been obliged to remain where they were; and as Brandt informed you that he was going to Butler, and proposed to join in the expedi-

tion . . . against Fort Schuyler, this ought to have prevented every kind of treaty with him; however, as it is
done, we must abide by it. If we act with vigour & spirit,
we have nothing to fear, but if once despondency takes
place, the worst consequences are to be apprehended.[208]

General Schuyler also wrote to the Tryon committee on July 4 quoting
their threat about "the well affected people . . . abandon[ing] their habitations, or submit[ting] to the terms of the friends of Great-Britain." He
chided forcefully, adding a promise that Colonel Van Schaick with Major
Ezra Badlam's contingent of 150 Massachusetts regulars would be left in
the lower county:[209] "You seem to entertain an idea that the enemy are
capable of doing what they please; whereas, in fact, there is great reason
to believe that they will not be able to do much… depend upon it . . .
upon no necessary occasion will you be left without proper support.[210]

On the fifth, Schuyler wrote to the State Congress about the Indian
attack on the pigeon hunters, Gregg and Madison, and the low morale
in Tryon. He expressed concern about his inability to provide adequate
presents for the natives, noting that "the enemy's agents have industri-
ously propagated that we have nothing to give them; that if we get anything, it must come from heaven." He informed them that he had sent
an agent to Boston with ten thousand dollars to obtain additional presents, in particular blankets and strouds, two of the most essential articles.[211] Also, he needed a drove of "fat cattle," as he was short of salt meat
for the Northern Army and "29,000 odd hundred weight [14 1/2 Tons]
has been condemned" at Fort Schuyler.[212]

When Deserontyon's patrol met with Daniel Claus on the St. Lawrence
about sixty-five leagues from Montreal,[213] the superintendent examined
the prisoners separately, giving them no opportunity to develop a common falsehood. By knitting together their information, he gained a picture of the reconstruction at Stanwix, the fort's artillery, and the garrison's strength. Spoor's answers were particularly significant, as he was
privy to details not known to the other ranks.

Particularly alarming was the fact that the garrison was entirely
aware of the expedition, including the numbers and types of troops

assigned and the route they were about to take. Claus sent the prisoners to St. Leger, who was some forty-five miles downriver.

When St. Leger caught up with Claus a few miles from Buck Island, he mused that "if [the rebels] intended to defend themselves in that Fort, our artillery was not sufficient to take it" and added that "He [was] determined to get the truth of these fellows." This offhand comment indicated he doubted their information and implied that Claus's examination had been wanting, which was an unwitting insult to the sensitive loyalist, who was already smarting from Governor Carleton's many slights. Claus reminded him that the prisoners' original interrogation had been conducted separately and their facts were in agreement, but he saw that St. Leger made "little of the prisoners intelligence." He was "full of his Alert," a plan to send light troops and Indians overland to surprise Stanwix with a bold stroke that would unhinge the defence. The prisoners' alarming accounts might have justified a delay to bring up heavier artillery and/or a wait for the rest of the Hessian Jäger battalion, but St. Leger chose to proceed.

To understand St. Leger's reasoning, it should be recalled that Stanwix had lain in ruins for many years and Carleton had apprised him of Lieutenant Langan's May report about the rebels' plans to raze the old works and erect a new fort. In the short time that had elapsed, they could hardly have accomplished much.[214]

St. Leger may have overlaid this misinformation with a typical "old country" opinion that Americans were militarily incompetent. British memories were of sloppy, ill-disciplined, and poorly drilled colonial soldiers officered by farmers, tradesmen, and such ilk. This opinion was nurtured by ignoring any previous military successes attributable to colonial skills. In that distressingly superior British manner, it is entirely possible that St. Leger's prejudice caused him to disregard Claus's advice, no matter how excellent his credentials. After all, Claus was a provincial Indian Department officer and his intelligence had been collected from three dubious sources — Captain Hare, another colonial; Deserontyon, an Indian; and a bunch of rebel prisoners.[215]

Claus' prisoners had provided another gem of information:

> [T]he enemy only expected Sir John Johnson at the head of 5 or 600 undisciplined Tories; reasoning that regular troops would never be given (as they were pleased to style him) to so inexperienced a command-

er, the militia were in high spirits at the thought and would be ready at a call . . . to come and set them up.[216]

As Sir John had as much military experience as most Continental officers, it is obvious that the British were not alone in doubting American abilities. St. Leger seems to have taken no pleasure in this derisive mention of Johnson; however, the rebels' cocksure posturing contributed to his fatal belief that their fort would be easy prey. There was one fact that he should not have ignored — the revelation that the enemy was well aware of the coming expedition, which he, Carleton, and Burgoyne had been at great pains to keep secret.[217]

From the Oneidas' main castle of Kanowalohale, Edward Spencer, brother of the blacksmith, Thomas, wrote to Colonel Gansevoort on July 6. He told him of the British council that was to be held "beside our Town" and hoped that he recognized that the Oneidas were obliged to attend. They had no option; they must, perforce, pass up Schuyler's invitation to Albany. Spencer offered assurances that the Oneidas would remember their many declarations of peace and support for the United States and hinted that the Senecas were of a similar mind.[218]

He also sent a garbled warning that Schuyler's belt inviting the nations to Albany was being returned by the Onondagas as "not proper." This action had every appearance of a convenient excuse. With the British actually on the move in Six Nations country, all the nations were becoming circumspect in their conduct.

Schuyler was constantly bombarded with alarms and demands from every quarter of his widespread command. On July 7, Herkimer wrote from Canajoharie advising that Captain DeWitt, the 3NY commander at Fort Dayton, reported nine armed and painted Indians had been seen nearby. They had halted and questioned a black man about the strength and spirit of his garrison. Herkimer was concerned, noting that Stanwix was unable to supply adequate scouting parties in the direction of Oswego and no friendly Indians were willing to conduct this service.

The next day Schuyler wrote Herkimer from Fort Edward, probably without having received the general's dispatch of July 7:

> The road leading from Fort Dayton to Fort Schuyler is so much incumbered with wood, by the falling of trees across it, that it is rendered impassable for men or carriages. You will therefore please to order two hundred of your militia to be employed in clearing it away, with all the dispatch the nature of the service will admit of, each man bringing an axe with him.
>
> Colonel Gansevoort, who commands at Fort Schuyler, is very pressing for a reinforcement, to carry on the necessary works at that garrison; and as I have it not in my power to send up continental troops for that purpose, I must beg you will order two hundred men of your brigade to his support and assistance. I am, &c.[219]

On July 8, fourteen days after leaving Lachine, the boat brigades and "150 Misisagey and 6 Nation Indians" landed at Buck Island and joined the 8th's Lights and Hertel de Rouville's company.[220] Buck Island is plateau-like and regularly shaped, about a mile in length and somewhat less in width, lying near the junction of the St. Lawrence and Lake Ontario. The next day, Lieutenant John Burnett of the 8th was appointed adjutant of the Regulars.[221] Each corps was ordered to submit a strength return by noon and Captain Potts was to allow the troops an issue of liquor according "to the service they perform."[222]

The Whig chiefs at Oquaga secretly advised Indian Commissioner Volkert Douw that two visitors from Kahnawake had told them that Sir John Johnson was at Oswego and would hold a treaty with the Six Nations. Douw sent Schuyler this news on July 9, adding to the general's concerns by reporting that Sir John would request the Iroquois Confederacy to remain neutral; however, he had one thousand Regulars and was intending to take Fort Stanwix, then to come down the Mohawk River.[223] How Schuyler's head must have spun with rumour and counter-rumour.

The next day, a frustrated Schuyler instructed Gansevoort "to send Capt. Marquisie down & let Major Hubbel superintend the works."[224] La Marquisie's misadventures had gone too far. In another letter, Schuyler ordered the U.S. Northern Army's commissary to "take the most effectual Measures to throw into Fort Schuyler as much provisions as will compleat what is now at that post to a Sufficiency for four hundred men for two months."[225]

Schuyler found the time to write a chiding letter to Herkimer:

> I am sorry, very sorry, that you should be calling upon me for assistance of Continental troops, when I have already spared you all I could . . . For God's sake do not forget that you are an overmatch for any force the enemy can bring against you, if you will act with spirit.[226]

July 10 was a very active day on Buck Island. St. Leger announced his appointment in General Orders "to act as Brigadier General"[227] and the "Vacant" company of Jägers arrived, led by First Lieutenant Philipp Hildebrand.[228] A mixed detachment was ordered to clear ground for the exercising of the army and the various companies were positioned in the cantonment:

> The Kings Regt. and the 34th form one Corps [and] will encamp on the right. The Hessian Chasseurs on the left, and the R.R. of New York in the centre. Lt. Collerten[229] will choose . . . ground on the Right of the Army for his party of Artillery and will begin Immediately to prepare Bark Huts for His Ammunition. The Irregulars [the corvée and Canadien militia?] will be arranged by the Deputy Qr Master Genl. Colonel Close [Claus] will take ground for the Indian Allies.[230]

The regularity of the camp indicates that St. Leger planned a "work-up" period to allow him to assess the merits of his officers and troops and develop their confidence in each other. The stay's duration was geared to Burgoyne's estimated timetable.[231]

On July 11, Lieutenant Crofts, the quartermaster of the 34th, was appointed brigade major, a role that recognized his experience and seniority. Guard mountings were appointed for seven o'clock each morning, for Retreat in the evening at seven o'clock, and Tattoo two hours later. A serjeant and eight privates of de Rouville's were to parade on July 12 and go to Oswegatchie for provisions, and another four were to report to the engineer, Lieutenant Henry Rudyerd,[232] for further instructions. For some unknown reason, Major Gray again tinkered with some of the subalterns' assignments in the Yorkers.

At Niagara on the eleventh, a number of Seneca and forty Lakes Indians[233] arrived, just two days before Butler was to sail to Irondequoit Bay.[234] When he arrived there, the agent was gratified to find a horde of Seneca warriors and chiefs who had answered his call. Many Seneca women, who had not wholeheartedly shared in the declaration for the King the previous fall, had come along to keep the men from falling into a British snare. Immediately, Butler inquired into the needs of the Indians and pointed to a large stock of victuals and many barrels of rum. Beeves were killed and roasted and the natives were encouraged to take what provisions they needed and to partake of the flood of rum. "[T]here seemed to be no limit to the bounty of their father the king. All the Indians were hugely pleased and thoroughly impressed with all this generosity" and the women quite content.[235]

On July 12 at Buck Island, St. Leger officially announced Daniel Claus's commission from the King as the expedition's Indian Department Superintendent, which empowered him to act in his best judgement for his Majesty's service in the management of the Indians. St. Leger privately acknowledged to Claus that he was "an entire stranger thereto."

Claus set about examining the ship that lay offshore with Butler's cargo of Indian goods. Almost every article he had asked for at Montreal was deficient and he congratulated himself on his foresight in purchasing goods "at his own risque," prior to departure. He told St. Leger about the lack of firelocks, and St. Leger procured thirty stands of arms from the artillery stores at Oswegatchie.[236] As natives habitually arrived for service with faulty or no firearms as a ploy to gain a new firelock, this supply was a mere pittance in view of the numbers expected.

Serjeant Killegrew of the 34th was appointed provost martial (with extra pay of 2s.-6d.), and a corporal and four men were ordered as provost guard for the next day. It was noted in orders that "[A]ll prisoners Except those styled officers from the Rebel army to go on all fatigues daily."[237]

On July 15, the Royal Yorkers were ordered to expend all of their serviceable ammunition firing at marks under supervision every morning. Accordingly, the battalion formed up at ten o'clock and fired a miserly two rounds of ball. The next day, the brigade major ordered the Yorkers to send a detachment of one serjeant and twelve "careful" men at eight o'clock that morning to examine the ball ammunition held by the artillery. Sir John's Regimental Orders instructed the officers commanding companies to hold a pay parade "before to morrow night and pay them the Ballance of their accts to the 24th of August Inclusive." The next day, Major Gray instructed the officers to have the men wash their clothing, clean their arms, and examine and report upon the state of their necessaries.

As if in response to Edward Spencer's urgings, General Herkimer wrote to Schuyler on July 15 to advise that Tryon County had responded, albeit reluctantly, and sent two hundred militiamen to Stanwix. Before Schuyler could quite digest this heartening news, the letter continued, saying that the first element of the detachment had been ordered not to march by committee Chairman William Seeber and some other members. It may be tempting to suspect these men of Tory sympathies, but the explanation was far more obvious — they simply were afraid to have their men abandon their farms and families in the face of an Indian war.

Herkimer burned with resentment and had Seeber's order countermanded. New instructions were issued for the detachment to march, but the men were so confused and disturbed that only enough responded to provide a guard for a bateaux brigade, which lay at German Flats laden with ammunition and provisions for Fort Stanwix. To calm fears, these men were sent for only sixteen days of service.

News of the shattering loss of the "impregnable" fortress at Ticonderoga and its mate, Mount Independence, to Burgoyne's advance had swept through Tryon County just days before, and Herkimer reported that many families were planning to leave the frontier. Others were so discouraged that they argued that resistance was pointless and said they would throw in their lot with the enemy when he appeared. Still others voiced concern over the withdrawal of Colonel Van Schaick and the rumours that Badlam's Continentals were about to leave the Valley, which led to the underlying suspicion that the Continental Congress was considering a total abandonment of the region. Of course, the county's Tories were emboldened by these military disasters and crumbling morale and added threats and defiance to the furor. Herkimer advised Schuyler that "no Dependance [can be placed] upon our Militia"[238] and claimed that fifteen hundred Continentals were required to restore confidence amongst the wavering and instill fear in the disaffected.

At Irondequoit Bay, three days of luxurious living elapsed before Butler began the council on July 16. After the opening protocol, he reminded the Senecas of their ancient alliance and requested that they join with him in subduing the King's rebellious children, saying it "was the duty of the British and the Six Nations to support each other when called upon." Butler pointed to the King's riches as evidence that the monarch could and would support the Iroquois Confederacy and its allies and promised that the warriors would be well rewarded. After more of these exhortations, he proffered the hatchet.

His consternation might be imagined when his offer was not immediately accepted, although he took great care to disguise it. The committed warriors of last November's council were wavering, and the old arguments for Seneca neutrality sprang forth. Some speakers reminded their belligerent brothers of the promises made to the United States at several treaties. Others spoke of judging the rights and wrongs of the conflict and the implications of siding with the guilty party.

Butler was confronting three distinct political factions within the Senecas. The inhabitants of the Allegheny and Genesee settlements were the most strongly attached to the Crown. Their old sachems, Sciawa and Serihowane, and their chief warriors, Axe-Carrier, Adongot, and Saweetoa, had received the King's bounty and friendship from Caldwell, Butler, and Lernoult and were committed friends. The Allegheny people, in particular their influential chief Kayashuta, held the view that they had been "deceived or treated ill [by the rebels] at Fort Pitt, and that the Americans intend to cheat them of their lands." It was the Seneca Lake settlements that were closer to the U.S. emissaries and Whig missionaries and they were subject to the admonitions of Oneida and Tuscarora clan members and friends. Their grand chief was the tall, imposing septuagenarian Sayenqueraghta, or Old Smoke. He was a commanding orator, the most prominent of all the Senecas, the senior warrior of the Iroquois Confederacy, and a neutralist.[239]

After lengthy consultation, the nations' headmen announced their decision to remain neutral. In the face of this startling reverse, Butler proved himself a gifted negotiator. Undaunted, he stood before them and, point by point, carefully reviewed all of their previous promises, their alliances, the benefits of supporting the Crown, the immense wealth and generosity of the King — "his rum was as plenty as the water in lake Ontario . . . his men were as numerous as the sands on the lake shore." They retired to reconsider.

Many warriors had been persuaded by Butler's eloquence, but others had not, and the gathering was deeply divided. The controversy was so sharp that even the women were drawn into public discussion, which was a most unusual event. Cornplanter, another prominent Seneca Lake war captain, was amongst those disposed to remain neutral. In the midst of this day and a half of raging debate, the crafty agent injected a gigantic gift of trinkets. Abruptly, the argument ceased. The Indians were dumbfounded. They had never seen such a flood of geegaws — an infinity of coloured beads, bales of dyed ostrich feathers, and, a clincher, hundreds of tinkling bells that delighted the women. As the warrior Blacksnake Dahgayadoh recalled, "the warriors also Never Did see such things." The King was truly rich beyond imagination.

When negotiations reopened, Butler held out two belts that confirmed their ancient alliance with the King. The most significant was the Great Old Covenant Chain. The elders knew it well; the younger men were enthralled as its contents were recited.

Butler would have made Sir William Johnson proud. Both high-minded and base emotions had been appealed to. The honour of the senior, most significant brother of the Iroquois Confederacy was challenged through a display of the ancient belts and a recitation of the Articles of the Covenant, at the same time as a lavish squandering of decorative gifts appealed to their covetousness.

Not Quite as Planned

The shoreline headquarters buildings of the Six Nations Indian Department at the mouth of the Niagara River

Detail from a watercolour by James Peachey, ca. 1784.
Courtesy of the National Archives of Canada, 1989-217-2X.

Again, the sachems met to absorb these new factors. Speeches acknowledging the King's gifts were heard and Butler's repeated proofs of the relative paucity of rebel presents took effect. The Indian Department's officers noted that the natives ceased asking embarrassing questions or making sarcastic comments about the great king begging for assistance to subdue the puny rebels when he was supposedly so all-powerful and had so many men. Their heads were turned with promises of easy victories and much booty. The solemn promises made at Albany and German Flats were ignored and, once again, the confederacy's largest nation opted for war.

At the great celebratory feast that evening, the King made a grand present to every principal warrior of a new suit of clothes, a firelock, ammunition, a tomahawk, a scalping knife, and a brass kettle and, for each war captain, an additional gift of money and the promise of a reward for each prisoner and scalp.[240]

In time-honoured tradition, the Senecas named two principal war captains — Sayenqueraghta/Old Smoke of the Turtle Clan and Gayentwahga/Cornplanter of the Wolf Clan. The former was of such immense stature in the confederacy that he was an obvious selection. The latter, Cornplanter, a robust mixed blood of some forty years, would prove himself an outstanding leader throughout the war.[241]

In the Mohawk region's settlements, Whigs and Tories alike were keenly aware of Burgoyne's expedition on Lake Champlain. Folk of all political stripes had been startled when Ticonderoga fell. Schuyler was par-

Cornplanter Gayentwahga, or Captain Abeel — a Grand War Captain of the British native alliance

After Charles Bird King, engraved by Lehman and Duval, ca. 1836.
Courtesy of the National Archives of Canada, C-040637.

ticularly distraught over the loss of morale in Tryon County and wrote to the Albany committee of safety on July 16: "It is surely not harder on them to turn out the militia, than it is for you and every other county, nor so much so, as they need not go much beyond the inhabited part of their county to defend themselves."[242]

On the seventeenth, the Tryon committee met at Seeber's home to hear the report of three committeemen who had been sent to the principal Oneida castle of Kanowalohale to question Thomas Spencer about the enemy's arrival at Oswego. At the request of General Schuyler, Spencer had just made a visit to the Canada Indians and he gave the committeemen much news,[243] none of it good. On the day he arrived at Akwesasne,[244] he discovered that Daniel Claus and Sir John Johnson were due to speak. Some friends hid him near the council house so that he could hear the speeches. Colonel Claus urged the men to go with him against Stanwix and, with uncanny foreshadowing, predicted the fall of Ticonderoga: "[I am] Sure, that Ticonderoga is mine, This is true, you may depend on, and not one Shot shall be fired." And sure enough, Ticonderoga had fallen, almost as easily as his prediction. Consequently, his next words had a major impact on the committeemen: "The same is with Fort Schuyler [Stanwix,] I am Sure . . . when I come towards that Fort and the commanding officer there shall see me, he shall also not fire one Shot & render the Fort to me."

Spencer advised that Sir John, Claus, and their families were at Oswego with seven hundred Indians and four hundred Regulars and that six hundred Tories were about to join them. Butler was to arrive on July

14 (three full days before the committee's discussion) and conduct a treaty with the Six Nations to offer them the war hatchet. Thomas told the committeemen that the Oneidas were disconcerted that the enemy was allowed to engage Indians "to strike and fight against you" yet General Schuyler would not hear of them taking up arms "in the Country's behalf." He continued:

> Therefore now is your Time, Brothers, to awake, and not to sleep longer, or on the Contrary it shall go with Fort Schuyler, as It went already with Ticonderoga . . .
>
> Brothers, I therefore desire you to be Spirited, and to encourage one another to march on in assistance of Fort Schuyler, Come up, and Shew yourselves as Men, to defend and Save your Country before it is too late. Dispatch yourselves, to clear the Brushes about the Fort, and send a party to cut Trees in the Wood Creek to Stop up the same.
>
> Brothers if you don't come soon without Delay to assist this place, we cannot Stay much Longer on your side, for if you leave this Fort without assistance, and the Enemy shall get possession thereof, we shall Suffer like you in your Settlement and shall be destroyed with you . . .
>
> Brothers, I can assure you, that as soon as Butler's Speech at oswego shall be over, they intend to march down the Country immediately till to Albany; You may judge yourselves, if you don't try to resist, we will be obliged to join them or fly from our Castles — as we cannot hinder them alone.

After digesting Spencer's advice, the committee decided that Major Badlam's men should march to reinforce Stanwix. Badlam was in attendance and replied that his troop's clothing was neither fit for a march nor garrison duties and that their home units were stationed at far-off Fort Edward and could not supply necessaries. Many were barefoot, some had only one shirt, and they were lousy. They had been sent to the Mohawk Valley to scout for Indians and Colonel Van Schaick had not allowed them to take more clothing. [245]

It was a sad litany of legitimate complaints. Badlam's men were poorly equipped and their morale reflected the country's neglect. Yet Badlam had already received Schuyler's orders that he was to repair to Stanwix if and when Gansevoort required his detachment's presence,[246] but for some inexplicable reason he chose not to share this information with the committee. His words were most discouraging to a populace living under the looming shadow of the hatchet.

Despite, or perhaps because of, the prevarication of Major Badlam, Spencer's advice had a substantial effect, and the committee issued a strongly worded and inspiring proclamation over General Herkimer's signature:[247]

> Whereas, it appears certain that the enemy, of about 2000 strong, Christians and savages, are arrived at Oswego with the intention to invade our frontiers, I think it proper and most necessary for the defense of our country, and it shall be ordered by me as soon as the enemy approaches, that every male person, being in health, from 16 to 60 years of age, in this our county, shall, as in duty bound, repair immediately, with arms and accoutrements, to the place to be appointed in my orders, and will then march to oppose the enemy with vigor, as true patriots, for the just defense of their country. And those that are above 60 years, or really unwell and incapable to march, shall then assemble, also armed, at the respective places where women and children will be gathered together, in order for defense against the enemy, if attacked, as much as lies in their power. — But concerning the disaffected, and who will not directly obey such orders, they shall be taken along with their arms, secured under guard, to join the main body. And as such an invasion regards every friend to the country in general, but of this county in particular, to show his zeal and well-affected spirit in actual defense of the same, all the members of the committee, as well as all those who, by former commissions or otherwise, have been exempted from any other military duty, are requested to repair also, when called, to such place as

shall be appointed, and join to repulse the foes. Not doubting that the Almighty Power, upon our humble prayers and sincere trust in him, will then graciously succour our arms in battle, for our just cause, and victory cannot fail on our side.[248]

This spirited address was exactly what the county folk required — a forceful, concerted message from their military and political leaders giving a clear warning of the coming attack on their settlements and providing a course of action for all. The previous confusion of contradictory instructions was gone.

At Buck Island on July 17, St. Leger made a joyful, exhilarating announcement: "St. Leger has the satisfaction to inform the Corps in this expedition that Fort Ticonderoga, a large Quantity of provision & artillery & stores with their whole stock of live cattle were abandoned by the rebels to the grand army the 6th instant; that many prisoners were taken & many killed, and that at the moment the advanced corps of Indians were in hot pursuit." St. Leger was electrified by Burgoyne's easy success and ordered the troops "to hold themselves in readiness to embark on an hours notice" with "40 Days provisions for 500 men." Lieutenant Collerton was to prepare "ammunition For two 6 pounders & 2 Cohorns and 50 ball cartridges per man for 500 men." The 8th and 34th, Watts's and Hertel de Rouville's companies, were ordered to draw their allotment of fifty rounds per man. Bakers were drawn from each corps to prepare bread to feed five hundred men for six days, "well soakt to keep in that time." As an afterthought, "the officers commanding Corps should provide their men with some sort of cases to keep the locks dry through the woods in rainy weather." How this was to be accomplished at the eleventh hour is a mystery.

Obviously, the fall of the legendary Ticonderoga had startled St. Leger into action. Burgoyne's victory must have thrown his timetable to the winds, and he could not dawdle. The event also inflated his confidence. If he had ever contemplated requesting heavier artillery or waiting for the rest of the Jäger battalion, the fall of Ticonderoga flushed it away. The rebels, who had retreated pell-mell from Carleton and from Howe in 1776, had again dispersed in the face of a Crown army. Why would they not run from St. Leger as well? He issued his orders:

> 18th. P. Onondaga. C. Fort Bull.
>
> The Advance guards . . . of all the officers & 80 rank & file of the Kings & 34th Regts, the Tribe of Misisagey Indians, with what is on the Island of the Six Nations, & the officers and rangers will move to morrow at 4 o'clock.[249]

The advanced corps was to carry six days of bread and salt pork "to shut out any possibility of want of provisions from Delays or Disappointments of the K[ing']s vessels."

Although all of the natives on the island were assigned to St. Leger's planned bold stroke, or "Alert," Claus decided to go to Oswego[250] for the more delicate task of greeting the majority of the Six Nations and their allies and sent his juniors, Captains Gilbert Tice, John Hare, and James Wilson, with St. Leger as the natives' officers. De Rouville's and Watts's companies were assigned to accompany the main party. The Canadiens would guard the provisions, and Watts's men would act as the van to prevent insult.

St. Leger's sense of urgency pushed him to risk the ire of the trading companies by diverting their craft "in the interest of the service." The companies had been advised that this measure might be necessary, but that hardly ensured their eager compliance. Their crews were ordered to disembark the trading materials and to load the craft with the expedition's goods, then sail to Oswego and return to Buck Island to reload. Payment was promised for this inconvenience. Captain Potts was instructed to continue the practice until the government's ships returned from Niagara, when their more efficient holds would be used.

The Royal Yorkers had earned an unenviable reputation for various infractions. Major Gray ordered the company commanders to pay the Quartermaster for the work of the Canadiens who had managed the bateaux over the Long Sault cataract. The officers had assumed the exigencies of service would excuse them from paying. The Colonel's Company had lost a bateau and the officers had found it necessary to pay some Indians to recover it. The regiment's troops were careless of their arms and accoutrements, and the battalion was ordered to appear under arms at evening roll call to see what items were missing. All culprits were to be charged. Gray announced grave consequences for such negligence in the future.[251]

Schuyler had not seen the spirited Tryon County proclamation when he wrote a despairing letter to his friend Pierre Cortlandt of the State Council on July 18:

> I am exceedingly chagrined at the pusillanimous spirit which prevails in the county of Tryon. I apprehend much of it is to be attributed to the infidelity of the leading persons of that quarter. If I had one thousand regular troops, in addition to those now above and on the march, I should venture to keep only every third man of the militia, and would send them down [away.][252]

He then wrote to Herkimer advising that he had dispatched some Continental troops to Tryon and stating, "I am extremely sorry to find the people so dispirited as you mention, but I hope you have been misinformed."[253]

The following day, Schuyler wrote from Fort Edward to Van Schaick, ordering him to "forward a ton and a half [of musket ball] with a ton of Powder to the Different posts on the Western Communication." He was to open "all letters from the westward... if they should contain Information that the Enemy are approaching Fort Schuyler or any other part of the Mohawk River, with such a force as to render it necessary that our Troops in that quarter should be reinforced, You will then call upon the Militia of Schohary[,] Duanesburgh[,] Schenectady and Tryon County to march to oppose them, leaving orders at Albany for any Continental Regiment that may arrive there immediately to march to your support."[254]

At Oquaga, Brant's recruiting had slowed to a trickle and his bellicose actions had raised much apprehension. Several senior Oneidas and Cayugas came to remonstrate with him and his followers. On July 19, Indian Commissioner Jelles Fonda reported that their deputation had been successful and Brant would retire into Cayuga country;[255] however, nothing had dissuaded Brant from his chosen course and, before mid-July, he left Oquaga to march north to Oswego.

A court martial sat at Fort Stanwix on the nineteenth to hear a variety of offences. A private of Aorson's company was charged with deserting and enlisting in the artillery. He must have been serving with Captain Savage's detachment right under the nose of his previous company commander. For this brazen act, he was awarded two hundred lashes. A private of Swartwout's company was acquitted of maliciously breaking the cock of his musket. Another man in Tiebout's company was charged with being drunk and leaving his guard post; he was given one hundred lashes. Another private was acquitted of stealing a bayonet.[256] Captain Swartwout arrived with a number of recruits and several lieutenants, including William Colbrath, who kept a superb journal of the events of the siege. Captain Gregg was considerably recovered from his scalping and left for Albany.[257]

At Buck Island, July 19 was again very busy. The departure of St. Leger's "Alert" had been delayed for a day. Now they received orders that the beating of the Troop would signal them to assemble at the shoreline and the Doublings of the Troop would signal them to embark. The detachments of the main party were told to load one bateau with equipment that might be "immediately wanted." These craft would move with the artillery and the provisions for the Stanwix phase of the operation. The balance of the equipage and provisions would stay at Oswego until a "general clearance of that post" was ordered.

Some Canadiens of the bateaux brigade that had conveyed the Hessian Jägers' "Vacant" company upriver had induced eight of Hertel de Rouville's men to desert. As punishment, St. Leger ordered the corvée to assist in transporting the provisions to Oswego and to provide a like number of men to join de Rouville's company as replacements.[258]

The artillerymen, "under the conduct of Lt Collerton," were instructed to carry twenty days' provisions in the bateaux for their own use, and another ten Yorkers were assigned with two of the Yorkers' bateaux to assist them. Three of the prisoners taken by Desertonyon's scout took the oath of allegiance and were assigned as artillery bateauxmen. [259]

The main party's bateaux brigade on Lake Ontario — "the Ensign flown in the bow and a musket fired, all vessels put ashore"

Pencil sketch by Peter Rindlisbacher, 2000.

After Orders of the day described the main party's boat formation. Their craft were to dress in two lines with a vanguard in the lead, followed by Sir John Johnson and the staff. Several signals were specified. When an Ensign was hoisted amidships (probably in the largest merchant ship) and a single musket discharged, all vessels were to set off. If an Ensign was flown in the bow and a musket fired, all vessels were to put ashore. Any craft in distress was to fire three muskets in succession. Each signal was to be relayed by the detachment commanders.

The main party was ordered to sail at four the next morning. That evening, the boats were loaded and bread was baked for the Jägers. Because they had proven negligent, Canadiens were assigned to the Yorkers' boats as steersmen and also, more circumspectly, to the inexperienced Germans.

On July 19 at Irondequoit Bay, Butler received St. Leger's instructions to send one hundred warriors to act in his "Alert" against Stanwix. The agent approached the Senecas and men were dispatched the next day. It is possible that the messenger who brought St. Leger's request delivered Guy Johnson's letter advising Butler that he had been confirmed as Deputy Superintendent of the Six Nations on Sir William Howe's authority.[260]

Such recognition would have been most satisfying and rendered the shock that was to follow all the more biting. After a delay of four days to complete the many complex arrangements, Butler sailed to Oswego.[261]

By the early morning of July 20, only three days after the news of Ticonderoga's capture, all of the troops and Indians had cleared Buck Island. Yet, for all this dispatch, the next phase would neither be as rapid, nor as simple, as St. Leger could have hoped.

~

CHAPTER FIVE

TOO LITTLE, TOO LATE
Rejected with Disdain

When Schuyler vented his spleen over Tryon County in a July 21 letter to the State Congress, he was unaware of General Herkimer's proclamation of July 17. He spoke of Herkimer's "improper agreement" with Joseph Brant and advised that he had ordered Badlam's troops to remain in Tryon and sent Wesson's Massachusetts regiment to join them.[262] He added, "if I may be allowed to judge of the temper of General Herkimer and the committee . . . nothing will satisfy them, unless I march the whole army into that quarter."[263]

Colonel Van Schaick wrote an official and very formal letter from Albany that day to his future brother-in-law. He advised that all troops stationed in Tryon had come under his direction and ordered that all "extraordinaryes" were to be reported promptly, "especially if the enemy should be found to approach towards your post or any other part of Tryon County." He added, "General [Schuyler] desires you to close up wood Creek by falling trees across it in Every part so as to prevent the enemy's sudden approach."[264]

Daniel Claus arrived at Oswego on July 23 and, to his joy and great relief, found Brant was already there with "upwards of 300 men,"[265] including many Fort Hunter and Canajoharie Mohawks. Brant was as close as family, and the two friends spent much time bringing each other up to date. Claus could take satisfaction that Brant was an important ally who recognized his former senior status and would sympathize over his recent setbacks. On Brant's part, he was assured of an influential friend who would support his personal war against the rebels and accept his modus operandi. They displayed all the signs of a formidable team.

Claus's resentment towards Butler, whom he viewed as Carleton's favourite, was already well developed, so he was outraged to hear that the "illiterate interpreter" had refused to adequately equip Brant for service on the frontier.[266] Intrigues against Carleton were obviously doomed to failure, so Butler became an ideal substitute.

Claus was enthused to hear the size of Brant's party. From his perspective, it mattered little that the Mohawk lacked the Iroquois Confederacy's backing when he had such a force at his command. Brant had grown from a warrior to a notable leader, and, in the traditions of the Confederacy, he was a self-made war captain.

Claus listened attentively to the details of the Unadilla meeting with Herkimer. His keen mind committed to memory the names of those who helped or hindered Brant — one list of credits and, ominously, one of long-remembered debits. As Brant's men had been active on the frontiers for two months, their equipment needed replenishing for the coming campaign. Brant was not disappointed; Claus gave orders to immediately re-equip his party, and Brant went to select the goods.

Captain Tice arrived with an express for Claus from St. Leger, ordering him to come immediately to Salmon Creek, twenty miles east of Oswego. He was to bring "what arms and vermilion I had, and . . . [be] prepared for a march thro' the woods." Claus made some quick preparations and was about to set off when Brant interceded, warning him not to leave for fear that the Indians who were coming would "become disgusted, and disperse" in his absence. The expedition was so patently dependent upon native support that such a reaction would precipitate a disaster. Brant suggested sending a note to St. Leger about the danger. His friend's advice should have forewarned Claus that all was not well with the old alliance, but he was quite blinded by his personal grievances.

Further discussion with Tice uncovered the reason for St. Leger's order. He had given the "Alert's" warriors "a quart of rum apiece," hoping to inspire them to greater efforts. Claus knew that so much liquor had made them beyond "the power of man to quiet," and he sent Tice back to St. Leger to report Brant's concerns and recommend a reconcentration at Oswego.

After St. Leger received the message, he asked his Indians to continue with the "Alert," but they were hungover and unwilling and he reluctantly accepted Claus's advice.[267] Before leaving the Salmon River, he dispatched a scout of Mississaugas, Senecas, and six rangers with Captains John Hare and James Wilson to gather fresh intelligence.[268]

On July 25, a contingent of Senecas arrived at Oswego,[269] followed soon after by Butler and forty-seven Wyandot, Ottawa,

Potawatomi, and Chippawa Indians with two Quebec Indian Department rangers.[270] Butler was shocked to discover that Claus was in overall command of the natives. While he was keenly aware of Claus's seniority and proven expertise, being superseded by Claus's commission was hardly a just reward for his dedication. Butler was handed Carleton's letter of July 9, which confirmed Claus's appointment and advised that his own salary would be £200 a year. The governor noted that he could not "with any propriety set you [an] allowance above [Claus's.]"

Amidst this gloomy news came a ray of sunshine: Butler's son Walter was approved as captain-commandant of his ranger company and his ensigncy in the 8th was transferred to his cousin.[271] Then, another splash of cold water: Carleton was shocked by the rangers' rates of pay and pointedly stated that his only comfort was that such excesses applied just for the span of the expedition, a limitation that certainly had not crossed Butler's mind.

Butler was incredulous when Claus decided that the council would not be held at Oswego. Runners were to be sent to intercept parties en route, instructing them to halt at the Three Rivers. As this venue was twenty-four miles closer to Stanwix and more convenient for those coming overland, Butler saw the sense of the change, but he was frustrated to find his instructions altered. He had suffered enough problems with the Senecas without tempting fate.

Butler found that Claus had little idea of the measures he had been forced to employ "to fix the League in the interests of the King," and Claus further strained their relationship by lecturing the older man on the conduct of a campaign. Referring to Butler's treaty at Irondequoit and his plans for another at Oswego, he pompously declared that "Ind[ia]ns on a march upon the Enemy could or did not expect formal meetings and councilling."[272] Butler was dumbfounded; surely Claus did not understand the fragile nature of the present alliance, and obviously he was not receptive to advice.

Butler was unaware that Carleton had not taken Claus into his confidence about the rebels' diplomatic successes in subverting the Six Nations. Without any suspicion of this lack of knowledge, John was offended by Claus's arrogant and simplistic criticisms. The confrontation was not an auspicious launch for a working relationship; however, Butler lacked many of Claus's quirks. He could function well, even as a frustrated deputy.

Sir John Johnson also enjoyed a happy reunion. His friend Spanish John McDonell Scotus,[273] the fiery Scotsman from the Charlotte River, was there to greet him. After an exchange of news, Johnson ordered Scotus to return home, assemble his company and join the expedition on the march.[274] McDonell took leave of his colonel, made his farewells to his newly promoted son, and set off. Unknown to the proud, determined father, this was to be his last view of his eldest son.

St. Leger arrived later in the day. If Carleton's orders regarding the corvée had come, the men who had persuaded de Rouville's militiamen to desert would have been "seized, and sent down [to Quebec] in irons."[275]

St. Leger had fire in his belly. He was distressed and embarrassed that his pet project, the "Alert," had been thwarted, to such a degree that he neglected to mention the event in his later accounts to his superiors.[276] He ordered a general advance the very next day. The expedition would move in two elements, an Advance and a main body. For the Advance, he had

A British officer and three infantrymen of the 1777 campaign

Detail from a watercolour by James Hunter, 1777. Courtesy of the
National Archives of Canada, C-1524.

prepared a detailed description and coloured drawing of the tactical dispositions that would allow maximum speed through the woods while maintaining a posture for instant offensive or defensive response.[277]

His detachments of Regulars would form the main body of the column, marching in two one-hundred-man Indian files,[278] the 8th on the right flank, the 34th on the left. As a screen against surprise, files of warriors marched at one hundred paces from either flank. A transverse line of men connected them to the Regulars.

One hundred yards forward of the Regulars, Watts led an advance guard of thirty Royal Yorker "picked marksmen" in two Indian files. Like the Regulars, they could immediately deploy to left or right, or form to their front or rear. Ahead of Watts by 460 paces were 5 long Indian files of warriors spaced far enough apart to more than mask the width of the column. The scouts' centre file was in communication with Watts by a connecting file spaced at ten-yard intervals. These natives were the young men of the Mississaugas and Six Nations who were not expected to attend the Three Rivers grand council. The rear guard was composed of thirty more Royal Yorker select marksmen, also marching in two Indian files. Each subunit nominated ten marksmen, capable and ready to be rushed to any threatened point of the compass.

If attacked, the column would form "A general Line of Battle." The leading files of natives would form a "line entire" facing their front and the flanking files would face outwards. The Royal Yorkers' advance guard was to front form, the rear guard, rear form. The left wing of the 8th was to form to the front and their right wing face outwards, dressing square with the left wing. Similarly, the right wing of the 34th would front form, the left wing face outwards.[279]

St. Leger had received intelligence about a bateaux brigade coming upriver to Stanwix. Recognizing that his Advance force would be too slow to cut off these boats, he dispatched a fighting patrol of Regular Lights and natives under Lieutenant Henry Bird, 8th, with orders to seize the Lower Landing on the Mohawk River.[280] He had two other hopes: first, that the patrol would prevent the obstruction of the creek system, and second, that its sudden appearance might cause the surrender or an abandonment of the post.

Henry Bird was an enterprising officer who had served with General Thomas Gage's elite 80th Regiment of Light Armed Foot during the Seven Years War. Ensign George Clerges, 34th, one of St. Leger's military

Rebellion in the Mohawk Valley

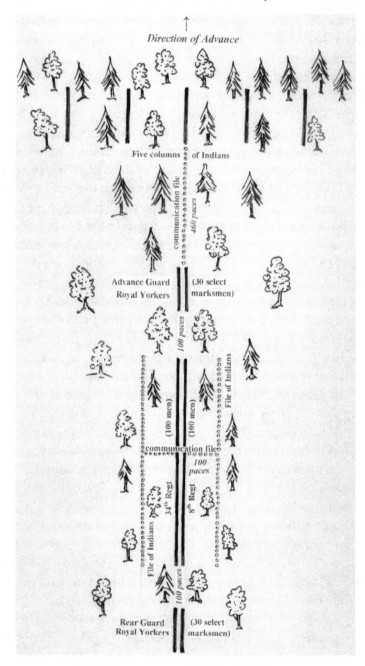

Tactical arrangement of St. Leger's Advance

Gavin K. Watt, 2000. After William L. Stone, Life of Brant, taken from a tinted-ink drawing in St. Leger's escritoire and "St. Leger's Orders for Line of March and Plan of Battle," transcribed in the Military Papers of General Peter Gansevoort.

secretaries, was Bird's deputy. Thirty of Bird's Lights and a squad of the 34th were augmented by Seneca and Mississauga warriors and Captains John Hare and James Wilson of the Indian Department.[281] St. Leger's and Bird's correspondence provides a clear picture of the venture.

At Fort Stanwix on Friday, July 25 a captain, two subalterns, three serjeants, and fifty privates of the 3NY were ordered to assemble three days' cooked provisions and leave at daylight as a guard for the militiamen "Obstructing Wood Creek."[282]

The following day, Gansevoort wrote to Schuyler advising that Herkimer had not supplied two hundred new militiamen, and, as the Tryon men at the fort had orders for only fourteen days of duty, they

would leave in two days. He had heard that Butler was at Oswego with "a number of Indians and Canadians and that Sr. John Johnson was on an Island near Oswego with a number of Tories." As instructed, he had sent a party of 130 men to obstruct Wood Creek; however, he respectfully noted, no provisions or ammunition had been received, "except a few Barrels of Flour."[283]

When Gansevoort wrote to Caty, he revealed, in amazing understatement, a vague

A Continental Line Officer, ca. 1775-76 — United States officers of the Line and militia retained the use of spontoons for much of the war

Watercolour by G.A. Embleton.
Courtesy of Parks Canada.

recognition of his peril. He said that John Butler was kindling a council fire at Oswego and told her "not [to] expect me down till some time in Fall, as I cannot consistent with my Honor and the good of the service leave my post, till we know in what [manner] the treaty will terminate at Oswego."[284]

Startlingly, on July 27, three young farm women were attacked by Indians while picking raspberries only two hundred yards from the fort's walls.[285] Two were scalped; one was killed outright and the other expired in a half-hour. As the third ran from her attackers, two balls passed through her shoulder.[286] The garrison was horrified and enraged. Gansevoort was utterly repelled by this odious deed and wrote to Colonel Van Schaick, "By the best discoveries we have made, there were four Indians who perpetrated these murders. I had four men with arms just passed that place, but these mercenaries of Britain came not to fight, but to lie in wait to murder; and it is equally the same to them, if they can get a scalp, whether it is from a soldier or an innocent babe."

There was little doubt that the time was nigh. In the face of this bold attack, Gansevoort sent the sick, wounded, and mothers with children to the lower valley.[287]

On July 28, Lieutenant Bird advanced two miles and halted to wait for the natives. About two hours later, sixteen Senecas, including the young warrior Blacksnake, joined him. They made for Three Rivers, where they again halted. After a wait of two hours, seventy-five Mississaugas arrived. Bird was unable to persuade the Indians to advance, as they wanted to feast on a pair of oxen the Mississaugas had stolen from the army's drove, so the Regulars left them and continued on for another seven miles, completing nineteen for the day.

The next morning, after waiting for the "savages," Bird despaired and set off without them at six o'clock. He ordered his boats to maintain an interval of seventy rods, half the men with firelocks in hand while the others rowed. If fired upon, the crews were to jump ashore and the other bateaux were to immediately support them. Keeping in mind St. Leger's desire for a rapid advance, the detachment rowed all night and encamped at Nine Mile Point on Lake Oneida.[288]

In Stanwix on July 29, Gansevoort received superb intelligence regarding St. Leger's progress. Thomas Spencer had spoken to an Oneida who had been with Brant at Oquaga and was told that St. Leger's troops were "on this Side Oswego"; some of them were over the falls, and the river above and below was full of boats. Spencer warned that St. Leger expected to "Git to Wood creek before it is Stoped." He would cross Lake Oneida in the night and be at Stanwix in two days. The Oneida told of the treaty to be held at Three Rivers and warned that eighty Indians were to "come crost Fish creek at the fishing Place at the Indian field."[289] Bird's patrol was compromised.

The importance of immediately felling trees into the creek was crystal clear; however, the same day as Spencer's warnings were received, a letter arrived from General Herkimer:

> As the Time of my militia now stationed under your command at Fort Schuyler will be expired this week I beg of you not to detain them longer. The County committee promised them not to stay longer but sixteen days but I prolonged the Time to three weeks from home to home which I assured them under my hand. They will long for the Time in Regard to their Hay — and wheat harvest . . . I hope, therefore, that you'll grant them their Discharge next Thursday that they may reach home at the Three weeks End, especially as one hundred and sixty men Continental Troops are set off to day for Fort Schuyler to reinforce your Garrison. In case of detaining them longer as promised, I really fear that it will cause a Disturbance and an Unwillingness for their future Service when wanted and besides they perhaps would desert from their station to the dishonor of our Country . . .
>
> P.S. Col. Watson [Wesson] as I understand of him is ready and willing to march up with his men to Fort Schuyler as soon as you will Require the same, otherwise he is to stay at Fort Dayton.[290]

On July 30, Captain Hare, nine Mississaugas, and twenty-seven Senecas caught up with Bird. The patrol proceeded fifteen miles to the mouth of

Wood Creek, which they found solidly choked by felled trees. They had failed their first objective. Bird wrote that some warriors who had gone ahead had watched the rebels finish the task without interfering.

With the Tryon militia expecting a release from duty at Stanwix, an addition to the garrison was badly needed if the tasks at hand were to be completed. To Gansevoort's relief, on the thirtieth, DeWitt's company from Fort Dayton and Badlam's 150 Massachusetts men marched into the fort. Orders must have come from headquarters to spur the reluctant New Englander, although there was no indication that the material state of Badlam's troops had improved. Commissary John Hansen returned to Stanwix with news of a flotilla of seven bateaux bound upriver with provisions and artillery ammunition with an escort of one hundred men from Wesson's regiment.[291]

An express from Kanowalohale brought a belt and letter from the sachems of Kahnawake and several neutralists of the Six Nations. Their messages emphasized the deepening rift in the Iroquois Confederacy by giving assurances to the garrison that their nations would remain at peace with their "American Brethern." Less reassuringly, the Oneida runner said "the Enemy were at the Three Rivers near Lake Oneida"[292] and warned that two detachments were to set off ahead of the main body, a party of eight to take prisoners and another of 130 to cut the Communications on the Mohawk River.[293]

On the thirtieth, the Tryon committee of safety received an explicit and accurate dispatch from Thomas Spencer at Kanowalohale:

> At a meeting of the chiefs, they tell me that there is but four days remaining of the time set for the King's troops to come to Fort Schuyler, and they think likely they will be here sooner. The chiefs desire the commanding officers at Fort Schuyler not to make a Ticonderoga of it; but they hope you will be courageous. They desire Gen. Schuyler may have this with speed, and send a good army here; there is nothing to do at New York [City]; we think there is men to be

spared; we expect the road is stopped to the inhabitants by a party through the woods; we shall be surrounded as soon as they come. This may be our last advice, as these soldiers are part of those that are to hold a treaty. Send this to the committee; as soon as they receive it let the militia rise up and come to Fort Schuyler. To-morrow we are a-going to the Three Rivers to the treaty. We expect to meet the warriors, and when we come there and declare we are for peace, we expect to be used with indifference and sent away. Let all the troops that come to Fort Schuyler take care on their march, as there is a party of Indians to stop the road below the Fort, about 80 or 100. We hear they are to bring their cannon up Fish Creek [part of the Wood Creek system]. We hear there is 1000 [militia] going to meet the enemy. We advise not — the [Crown] army is too large for so few men to defend the fort — we send a belt of 8 rows to confirm the truth of what we say.

It looks likely to me the troops are near; hope all friends to liberty, and that love their families, will not be backward, but exert themselves, as one resolute blow would secure the friendship of the Six Nations, and almost free this part of the country from the incursions of the enemy.[294]

After weighing this intelligence, Herkimer issued orders for the Tryon County militia to assemble on August 3 at German Flats and, simultaneously, sent a plea for assistance to the adjacent jurisdictions of Schenectady, Schoharie, and Duanesborough.

On July 31, Bird's Indians said they would go no further in a body, but would instead send out scouts. Bird held a council with their principal men and told them "that if they would accompany me, I should be content; but if they would not go, I should take my white people . . . and proceed myself." Nine Mississaugas declared they would go, but the Senecas protested that he had agreed to take their counsel and they would advance with caution. Bird said that he had agreed to take their advice regarding woods fighting and reminded them that he had spoken of the need to prevent the rebels from "stopping the creek" and also that he had orders to immediately invest the fort.

Nonetheless, Bird recognized that his men alone would be ineffective; he needed his allies and agreed to wait till the next morning, after warning that he must set off at daybreak, with or without them. This pleased the Senecas and they spoke of sending out large scouting parties to prepare the way. True to their word, eighteen to twenty men left that evening; however, as Bird's detachment was now in Oneida territory, three of them secretly went to Old Oneida to warn their Younger Brother that a party was about to attack Stanwix. Of course, the Oneidas already knew this from other informants, but an important protocol had now been observed.

On the last day of July, a personal defeat overtook New York's patrician general, Philip Schuyler. The rather gentlemanly manoeuvring that had marred the relationship between Carleton and Burgoyne was child's play compared to the strain under which Schuyler conducted his command of the Northern Army. A determined party of New England politicians supported his rival, the ex-British officer Horatio Gates, who was viewed by Schuyler's supporters as a vain, ambitious, "sleekit" man. The pro-Gates element saw Schuyler as a dissembling, artful scribe who could compose a good story, but rarely delivered the goods. Schuyler's illness, which had prevented him taking the army into Canada in 1775, was seen as more than ill health, and his evacuation of Crown Point in 1776 raised an immense furor in Congress. The Gates faction steadily plotted to discredit Schuyler, eventually charging him with loyalism. There was scarcely a man of family and substance in America who was not vulnerable through some connection to a loyalist relative or acquaintance, but once the spectre of treachery was raised, defence against innuendo became a major battle.

Throughout all of his rigorous, exhausting activities to manage the Northern Army and his ceaseless efforts to court the Six Nations, Schuyler was under a debilitating personal attack. The Gates faction bided its time in Congress until Schuyler's supporters were absent, then levered him out. It would be weeks before the victor came north to claim his prize, but Schuyler, a man of great honour, remained true to his principles and continued to manage the northern theatre with judiciously applied energy.[295]

At the falls on the Oswego River on July 31, orders were issued that the artillery, the Royal Yorkers, and Hertel de Rouville's company were:

> [T]o take in their loading immediat'ly; each captains boat in the royal Yorkers to carry 4 barrels, 10 lieut['s] boats 5 each, lieutenant[s] Anderson J. [&] Wilkerson [Wilkinson] to carry 4 Barrels each, the privates' boats to carry 6 each, and to hold themselves in readiness to embark at 2 o'clock this afternoon to proceed in the Following order. Royal Artillery. Six Companys of the Kings R.R. of N.Y.[,] Capt Rouvill's Company of Canadians, Lieut Col's Company. The officers commanding companys not to allow their boats to fall back or put ashore without orders or a signal for that purpose.[296]

Several small rapids impeded the river, but the major obstruction was a twelve-foot falls followed by a mile of rapids that required a portage. A pile of stores and provisions at the southern end of that carry was being addressed in the above orders. St. Leger's lightly equipped Advance had negotiated these obstructions with ease, compared to the main party, which was encumbered with the tail of the army.[297]

A Royal Yorker Hatman — one of "King George's men, who are worse than savages"

Pencil and ink drawing by Richard I. Reeves, 2000.

On August 1, an Oneida deputation brought Gansevoort the ominous news that three "Strange Indians" had come to their castle and informed them that one hundred warriors were at the old Royal Blockhouse at the east end of Lake Oneida with the intention to march against Stanwix.[298] Blood ties had proven stronger than loyalty to the King's cause. Fearing for the safety of the approaching bateaux, Gansevoort dispatched one hundred Yorker Continentals under Captain Elias Van Benschoten to augment Wesson's Massachusetts guard.

The garrison was now very much "on the *qui vive*," as Gansevoort believed he had only a matter of hours before an attack. A letter full of sobering and chilling sentiments from his brother Leonard may have stiffened his resolve: "I beg you and depend upon you and your Regiment will not be a disgrace to the New York arms. Your father flatters himself that you will conquer or die."[299]

Willett's orderly book noted:

> August 1, 1777
>
> A Picquet Guard to mount this Evening . . . 1 Capt 3 Sub[alterns] 4 Sergeants, 1 Drummer 80 privates who are in Case of Alarm by the Firing of a Gun to turn out and Man the Bastions, 1 commissioned Officer 1 Sergeant 1 Corporal and 20 privates on each Bastion. And if the Officer Commanding the Picquet shou'd think the Alarm of Sufficient Importance he is immediately to Order the Drum to beat the Alarm, upon which the Garrison is to turn out Immediately and to repair to the Alarm Posts. Major Badlam's Detachment to man the S.E. bastion and adjacent Curtain, Capts. Aorson and Jansen to man the S.W. Bastion, Capts. Benshouten & Tiebout to man the N.W. Bastion, Capts. De Witt, Swartwout and Bleeker to man the N.E. Bastion, Capt. Gregg's Company . . . on the Parade till further orders.

On Saturday, August 2, a frustrated Lieutenant Bird sent word to St. Leger that none of the natives would advance from the mouth of Wood

The gates of Fort Stanwix

Pencil and ink drawing by John W. Moore, 2000, after a view of the 1977 reconstruction by Janice Lang Photography.

Creek except two Iroquois — a Mohawk and an unnamed old acquaintance. Bird was so grateful, he wanted General St. Leger to reward them. He set out with his two supporters and was joined by twelve Mississaugas some three hours along the way. He hoped to meet the Senecas somewhere ahead and invest the fort.

Captain Wilson carried Bird's latest report to St. Leger recommending the ranger's intimate knowledge of the Oneida Carry's creek system and the places where guns and baggage could be landed.[300] Wilson met St. Leger and the Advance at Nine Mile Point later that day. By immediate return, St. Leger approved Bird's "sensible and spirited" operations and advised he had forwarded Brant's volunteers as a willing reinforcement, undoubtedly on Claus's recommendation. His next words offer proof of his hopes for an easy victory and reveal his concerns about possible native excesses:

> You will observe that I will have nothing but an investiture made; and . . . should [the garrison] offer to capitulate, you are to tell them that you are sure I am well disposed to listen to them: this is not to take any honor out of a young soldier's hands, but by the presence of the troops to prevent the barbarity and carnage which will ever obtain where Indians make so

superior a part of a detachment; I shall move from hence at eleven o'clock, and be early in the afternoon at the entrance of the creek.[301]

When Claus left Oswego with the Advance, Butler had been left behind to manage the Grand Council. Claus's absence from such a critical treaty was unwise, especially after his tampering with his deputy's original plans; however, the old ranger was in his stride and conducted affairs in his usual deft manner.

Only the Seneca warrior Blacksnake recorded details of this momentous event and, as he was with Bird at the time, he must have relied upon oral remembrances of the council. Blacksnake said that Brant accepted the war belt on behalf of the Mohawks, but he probably only spoke during the opening ceremonies, as he was at Nine Mile Point on August 2. In any event, there were many official Mohawk captains to receive the belt, such as Deserontyon and the Hill brothers.

The Senecas followed, represented by Old Smoke and Cornplanter. No one seems sure who accepted for the last Older Brother, the Onondagas. It may have been Gahroondenooiya/Lying-Nose, or Oundiaga, who was one of their leading pro-British war captains. The Cayugas, as the first Younger Brother, accepted next, represented by Ojagehte/Fish Carrier. When the Oneidas' and Tuscaroras' turn came to grasp the war belt, most headmen had left and Towawahgahque/Rail-Carrier accepted for the Oneidas and Sheqwoieseh/Dragging-Spear for the Tuscaroras. Both were relatively junior captains who remained faithful to the Crown's cause throughout the war.

As befitted the Keepers of the Fire, the Onondagas were deeply divided over this critical issue. About half their sachems and captains said they would "abide by the antient Covenant made in Albany." Obviously, these men looked upon the recent treaties as extensions of prior agreements. The balance, led by the war captains Teaqwanda and Teyawarunte, stood with the Crown.

The Cayugas were similarly divided. They had suffered equally with the Senecas over the loss of regular trade and were deeply angered by rebel depredations against their kinsmen on the Pennsylvania frontier, yet their internal dissension was sufficiently deep to cause hesitation.

Among the Mohawks, a few of the older Fort Hunter men, who were concerned for the vulnerability of their women, children, and oldsters, clung to their promised neutrality. The sachems of Canajoharie were equally conscious of their castle's exposed position. Unlike Fort Hunter, they named no war captains and their men who chose to fight did so as individuals.

After the treaty fire was covered, the alliance's headmen, in a traditional gesture, cut a large wampum belt into pieces to indicate their separation over the issue of war and their dedication to the continuation of the Iroquois Confederacy.[302] Sadly, the measure accomplished nothing to prevent the outbreak of open hostilities between the nations scant days later.

How Butler managed this council to such a positive conclusion in the face of so many neutralists is a mystery. He had prevailed at Irondequoit, but not without difficulty, and the expedition's pre-emptive march into Six Nations territory was a clear violation of their stated neutrality. All of his diplomatic skills were required to overcome their anger over this severe breach of decorum. Of course, he was assisted by the application of rum and a liberal distribution of presents to a populace starved for trade, and they were also influenced by the pressing example of their young men scant miles away under arms for the Crown's cause.

Blacksnake reported:

> [T]he officers come to us to See what [was] wanted for to support the Indians with Provisions and with the flood of Rum, they are some . . . amongst . . . our warriours made use of this indoxicating Drinks, there was Several Barreal Delivered to us for us to Drinked for the whit man told us to Drinked as much we want of it all free gratis, and the goods if any of us wishes to get for our own use, go and get them, for and from our father gaven to you . . . our chiefs began to think that the great Britain government is very Rich and Powerfull . . . all things a bondantly provided for his people and for us to and Sev[er]al head of cattle been killed for us to Eat and flour the our female Sect was very well please for the Kindness we Receive from our white Brothers.[303]

The Seneca Mary Jemison recalled that Butler cajoled the Indians into going to Stanwix "to sit down, smoke their pipes and look on" while the British taught the rebels a lesson, but this must be overstated.[304] The Seneca headmen were simply too sophisticated to believe that all the Crown's diplomatic efforts and tidal wave of presents had been expended simply to encourage them to be spectators, and Butler's words were far too explicit for such a naive and pacific interpretation. In any case, the Senecas' sachems and captains had taken up the war belt and the die was cast.

While Butler was in the midst of breaking camp at Three Rivers, he became so distressed over Daniel Claus's interference that he wrote a letter to St. Leger requesting clarification about the extent of Daniel's authority. The return message caught him en route to Stanwix, confirming that Claus was "to take the Superintendency" and Butler was to "assist him as much as in your power lies in carrying on the business of this Campaign."[305] There was no latitude in those words. Like the loyal soldier he was, John Butler knuckled under to make the best of a bad situation.

Meantime, the main party led by Sir John Johnson followed behind St. Leger, struggling with guns, ammunition, disassembled wagons, tools, provisions, and tentage.

Father MacKenna busied himself ministering to his variegated flock,

which included the Jägers, as this remarkable priest was also fluent in German. Many of the Hessians were sick from their long sea voyage and the arduous bateaux trip on the river and needed his spiritual comforting.[306]

Although very little is recorded about Lady Polly Johnson and Sir John's sister, Nancy Claus,[307] they

A war captain, stripped for war and carrying a scalp

Drawing by George Townshend, ca. 1759.

undoubtedly travelled with the main party, protected by Royal Yorkers and cared for by servants and the best of bateauxmen. Polly had three children: three-year-old Nancy, born the week before her famous grandfather went to his grave; William, who was less than two years old; and her baby, John Jr., who was only nine months old and who, being sickly, required constant care. They were quite a handful for Lady Johnson, who was four months pregnant.[308]

Polly had bitter memories of her embarrassment at the hands of the rebels to stiffen her resolve, and she yearned to be back in Johnson Hall as the mistress of all about her. For a society belle, she had proven resourceful and tough and was anything but helpless during the expedition.

Nancy Claus, the sheltered elder daughter of Sir William, had two teenaged children. At fourteen, Catherine was of an age to be helpful with her young cousins. William was two years younger, full of the adventure around him and eager to be off with his father and uncle. He may have been a nuisance and difficult to keep occupied, as boys so often can be. Sir John had a great fondness for him and recalled his own tutelage under his father at Lake George in 1755 when he was only a year older than William. When time and affairs allowed, he must have indulged the boy's interest in martial and Indian affairs.[309]

Nothing was recorded about the women who followed the army. Burgoyne's order of May 30 set a ratio of three women per company.[310] The order was directed at the Grand Army's regiments, but as nothing different has come to light about St. Leger's units, the same ratio likely applied. As only three of the seven Royal Yorker companies were at full strength, the number of Yorker women would not have exceeded twenty-one.

It was a mixed blessing for a woman to be accepted for this duty. Camp followers officially received a half ration and, for this largesse, washed and mended the men's clothing, gathered firewood, and nursed sick and injured soldiers. They were not returned on muster rolls and were not enumerated on strength returns. If ever there were nameless ciphers, these women filled the bill.

Provincial followers were most often wives of the soldiers, and their children were allowed to accompany them. The method of selection is somewhat of a mystery. An even disposition, firm attachment to their men, and personal toughness and robustness were prerequisites. At no time were they mollycoddled. They had to be self-reliant and capable of pitching in where another pair of arms or legs was needed to move a burden or clear the way. Nothing was reported of their experiences and their ordeals simply have to be imagined.

While the main party launched its boats onto Lake Oneida and the Advance was at the mouth of Wood Creek, Bird's patrol struck the first blow at the enemy.

The bateaux transporting Stanwix's artillery ammunition and stores arrived the last day of July at the landing below the fort with the two one-hundred-man guards of Wesson's and the 3NY.[311] Everyone was very alert about the Oneidas' warning of "100 strange Indians" lurking in the area, and the troops needed no encouragement to rapidly transfer the stores into the fort.

It was well they moved at speed, as no sooner was the task finished when Bird's Regulars and Indians burst upon the landing, catching the bateauxmen at some last-minute chores. How frustrated Bird must have been to find his quarry so few and his real prize safely in the fort! Now the second goal of his mission had miscarried.

Sentinels in the southwest bastion had been the first to sight the enemy, spotting strange fires in the woods near the ruins of old Fort Newport.[312] The alarm was beat and the troops rushed to their posts. Then men were seen running from the Lower Landing pursued by Bird's detachment, but they made it into the fort. Two were wounded and they advised that Bateaux Captain John Martin and another man had been taken prisoner.[313]

The clamp was on the joint; after a frustrating start, the siege of Stanwix had begun.

Lieutenant-Colonel Willett recalled that the fort had just reached a reasonable state of repair the day before Bird's appearance. A fraise of sharpened horizontal posts had been installed, the parapets were nearly complete, embrasures had been cut into three of the bastions, and pickets had been placed around the covert way.[314] He noted that some tasks were still unfinished because of La Marquisie's incompetence.

With the addition of Lieutenant-Colonel Mellon's one-hundred-man detachment of Wesson's, the garrison stood just short of 750 Continentals. They had six weeks' provisions. Artillery ammunition remained short, with only nine solid shot per gun per day over that same period, but they had small-arms cartridges aplenty.[315]

St. Leger, Claus, and the Advance arrived in the evening of August 2. The main body with the artillery, tents, and baggage were days behind, so the Advance camp was a simple affair.

That same evening, the garrison took further precautions and sent out a thirty-man party covered by a fieldpiece to burn two of the local farmers' barns that stood too near the works. Before venturing out, two guns in the southwest bastion fired canister at the buildings to drive off any Indians who may have been hiding in their cover. The burning was accomplished without incident, as the British and Indians were too preoccupied with settling into their camp.[316]

August 3 was eventful. As the fort was without a flag, the 3NY officers had one made to display their defiance. Lieutenant-Colonel Willett provided a British artillery coat for the blue field, men's shirts supplied white stripes, and various sources, the red. Early that morn, a "Continental Flag" was raised in the southwest bastion and saluted by a gun discharge directed at the British camp. Willett wrote, "the Flagg was sufficiently large and a general Exhilaration of spirits appeared on beholding it Wave."

Later, a patrol ventured from the fort to investigate the bateaux at the landing and found them entirely intact. No doubt Bird had recognized their value to the expedition. A delirious boatman, who had been scalped and left for dead three days before, was discovered with wounds in the brain and right breast. He expired almost as soon as he was carried into the fort.[317]

St. Leger clung to the hope that the garrison would yield, and at three o'clock he paraded his troops. If he had been able to surround the fort on every quarter, this display may have had some impact, but the reality was ineffectual. His men stood out of range of the guns, hundreds of yards from the walls. Even with extended spacing, there were far too few to offer a threat, only 221 Regulars of the 8th and 34th with Watts's 60 Royal Yorkers and a handful of rangers. Apart from Brant's volunteers, the Mississaugas, and some Senecas, the bulk of the Indians were en route from Three Rivers and the main party with 160 artillerymen,

Jägers, Canadiens, and 240 Royal Yorkers was still inching its way up the obstructed creeks.

Certainly, St. Leger had enough soldiers and warriors to seal off the lower Valley, but it was a very dubious exhibition considering the garrison had more than seven hundred men behind strong walls. The display over, St. Leger's men collected hay from the farm fields for bedding. Then a flag of truce appeared at the edge of the woods and advanced towards the fort. The ubiquitous Captain Gilbert Tice was admitted into the fort. He carried messages from St. Leger, including a copy of Burgoyne's proclamation, slightly altered by St. Leger and submitted over his signature.[318]

> By BARRY ST. LEGER, ESQ.,
> Commander-in-chief of a chosen body of troops from the grand army, as well as an extensive corps of Indian allies from all the nations, &c. &c.
>
> The Forces entrusted to my command are designed to act in concert, and upon a common principle, with the numerous Armies and Fleets which already display, in every quarter of America, the power, justice, and, when properly sought, the mercy of the King.
>
> The cause in which the British Arms are thus exerted, applies to the most affecting interest of the human heart, and the military Servants of the Crown, at first called forth for the sole purpose of restoring the rights of the constitution, now combine with love of their Country and duty to their Sovereign, the other extensive incitements which spring from a due sense of the general privileges of Mankind. To the Eyes and Ears of the temperate part of the Public, and to the breast of suffering Thousands in the Provinces, be the melancholly appeal, whether the present unnatural Rebellion has not been made a foundation for the completest system of Tyranny that ever God in his displeasure suffer'd for a time to be exercised over a froward and stubborn Generation. Arbitrary imprisonment, confiscation of property, persecution and torture unprecedented in the inquisitions of the Romish

Church, are among the palpable enormities that verify the affirmative. These are inflicted, (by Assemblies and Committees, who dare to profess themselves friends to Liberty,) upon the most quiet Subjects, without distinction of age or Sex, for the sole crime, often for the sole suspicion, of having adhered in principle to the Government under which they were born and to which by every tye divine and human, they owe allegiance. To consummate these shocking proceedings, the profanation of Religion is added to the most profligate prostitution of common reason; the consciences of Men are set at nought; and multitudes are compelled, not only to bear Arms, but also to swear subjection to an usurpation they abhor.

Animated by these considerations; at the head of Troops in the full powers of health, discipline and Valour, determined to strike when necessary, and anxious to spare when possible; I by these presents invite and exhort all persons, in all places where the progress of this Army may point — and by the blessing of God I will extend it far — to maintain such a conduct as may justify me in protecting their Lands, habitations, and Families. The intention of this address is to hold forth security, not depredation, to the Country.

To those whom spirrit and principle may induce to partake the glorious task of redeeming their Countrymen from Dungeons, and reistablishing the blessings of legal Government, I offer encouragement and employment; and upon the first intelligence of their associations, I will find means to assist their undertakings. The domestic, the industrious, the infirm, and even the timid inhabitants, I am desirous to protect, provided they remain quietly at their Houses; that they do not suffer their Cattle to be removed, nor their Corn or forage to be secreted or destroyed; that they do not break up their Bridges or Roads; nor by any other acts, directly or indirectly, endeavour to obstruct the operations of the King's Troops, or supply or assist those of the Enemy.

Every species of Provision brought to my Camp will be paid for at an equitable rate and in solid Coin. If, notwithstanding these endeavours & sincere inclinations to effect them, the phrenzy of hostility shou'd remain, I trust I shall stand acquitted in the Eyes of God and Man, in denouncing and executing the vengeance of the State against the wilful outcasts. The messengers of justice and of wrath await them in the Field, and devastation, famine, and every concomitant horror that a reluctant but indispensible prosecution of Military duty must occasion, will bar the way to their return.[319]

As instructed, Tice offered the garrison the Crown's protection if they surrendered, which "was Rejected with disdain."[320] His visit had given the garrison its first knowledge that an officer named St. Leger commanded the expedition.[321] Tice was eagerly questioned when he returned to camp. What had he seen and heard? What was the state of the garrison, the preparations of the fort? The questions were mostly in vain, as the rebels had blindfolded him until he was inside a building and again on his return trip to the gate.[322]

Yet Tice had been an excellent choice as emissary. He was well known and, with his reputation as a veteran colonial officer, was politely received by the rebels, although with cool reserve. He had a soldier's eye and the well-practised powers to analyse people as an officer and as a tavern keeper. Approaching the works, he observed the condition of the fortification, the freshness of the materials, the mouths of some guns and embrasures for others. He watched closely the efficiency of the garrison in its guard mountings, how they manned their posts and received his "flag." Inside the fort, he had seen and spoken to several senior officers and measured their resolve. His astute observations shook St. Leger.

The expedition was faltering and operations had scarcely begun. St. Leger's worst fears had come true, for as Claus had predicted, the fort was extremely well prepared. The garrison was in strong numbers and seemed to be efficiently led by men of considerable grit. Their artillery had been witnessed by the firings of the evening before and that morning, and St. Leger certainly recalled Claus's intelligence about the number and weight of the guns. He later reported to Carleton that "The accounts we received in Canada concerning Fort Stanwix were the most erroneous that can be conceived. Instead of the unsuitable and unfinished work we were taught to expect, I found it a respectable fortress strongly garrisoned with 700 men . . . [with] four Bastions fraised and picketted . . . a good ditch with Pickets" and a train of artillery "we were not the masters of."[323]

St. Leger was crestfallen. All thoughts of overawing the fort into submission, followed by a rapid advance down the Valley to Albany, were stillborn. Whether this early reversal of fortune precipitated his excessive drinking is unknown. St. Leger was known to enjoy his bottle, and that reputation, in a time of liberal consumption, is noteworthy. His addiction became common talk amongst his troops and natives. Whether his imbibing was extreme before this initial disappointment or whether it was triggered by it is unclear. His habit would soon be fuelled by many more frustrations.[324]

The next day, St. Leger's troops and Indians built breastworks to protect their camps against sorties by the garrison. Parties of natives and the newly arrived Jägers used the cover of "Bushes, Weeds and Potatoes in the Garden" to creep close to the fort and snipe at men working on the walls. They had considerable success, killing one man and wounding six.[325] The garrison countered with "marksmen . . . immediately placed in different parts of the fortifications to return fire as opportunities might offer."[326]

Mellon's men were to have returned to Fort Dayton that day, which explained the previous day's reconnaissance of the landing; however, St. Leger's parade convinced everyone that the roadway was sealed tight and so the Yankees stayed. At night, a sally was made to burn Johannes Roof's house and barn and bring in two haystacks for forage.[327]

While these minor actions were taking place, the main party was occupied in the creeks and along the Oneida Carry. The Tryon militiamen had blocked the creek system for twenty miles,[328] and it took nine days of back-breaking labour by 110 men under the "diligence and zeal" of Captains Jean-Baptiste-Melchior Hertel de Rouville and Han Jost Herkimer to clear the obstructions.[329] Captain Herkimer was well motivated, as his wife, three sons, and three daughters were being held "prisoners of Congress."[330] For Hertel de Rouville, the task was simply a nasty job to be performed in a professional manner.

While the Quebec militiamen and squads of rangers cleared Wood Creek, the Royal Yorkers and other rangers were assigned to road building, as they were particularly handy with the axe, shovel, and muscle.[331] Both endeavours were noteworthy feats of labour and practical engineering.

The land between Lake Oneida and the Mohawk River was choked with a tangle of creeks, some partly navigable. The primary artery was Wood Creek, which led from the lake to beyond the ruins of Fort Bull.[332] Fish Creek ran into Wood Creek about half a mile from the lake. The former was navigable to Pine Ridge, where the bateaux carrying the disassembled wagons, equipage, and provisions were unloaded for movement along The Carry.

A few miles further up Wood Creek was the junction with Canada Creek. Its waters added to the flow, making Wood Creek navigable below, but above that point, Wood Creek was narrow and frequently very shallow. As the crow flies, the distance from Lake Oneida to Stanwix was fourteen miles, but the "extream serpentine" path of Wood Creek almost doubled the distance.

The creeks' shores were covered in poison ivy and their waters surprisingly noxious, so that travellers carried casks of potable water during their passage through the system. Men who worked in the creeks, struggling to clear obstructions or wrestle with heavily laden bateaux, often fell sick from the exposure and lost the skin off their feet, which later became inflamed.[333]

The Indian path running from Pine Ridge east to Stanwix was too narrow and rough for the haulage of the expedition's stores. A roadway was opened through a tangle of secondary growth and brambles, following a route cleared some seventeen years earlier during the Seven Years War. From the Pine Ridge terminus,[334] Provincials, under the command of Lieutenant James Lundy, cut trees and pulled stumps for eight miles and completed the roadwork in two remarkable days. The men suffered "in the worst of weather,"[335] during a month noted for its oppressive heat and heavy rainstorms. Mortars, ammunition, tents, siege materials, and provisions were brought forward as soon as the road was prepared, pulled by manpower over the raw roadway in the wagons assembled by work parties at Pine Ridge.[336]

Not deigning to wait for the road, the forty-foot artillery bateaux were moved with extreme difficulty through the tortuous upper reaches of Wood Creek, which in places was a mere ten feet wide. The boats frequently jammed between the shores, and the men went into the water to manhandle the craft forward. Upstream, a dam and sluice system that had been used to deepen the creek since Bradstreet's time was employed repeatedly. The men strained to pole and pull the craft against the water's rush for as long as it lasted. With superhuman effort, they moved the three- and six-pounder tubes, their carriages, and ammunition up to the beach at old Fort Bull where, thankfully, a well-used roadway led to Stanwix.[337]

At Schenectady on the lower Mohawk, Colonel Van Schaick wrote to General Schuyler on August 4 to say he had "ordered out one half of the Militia of Schoharie and Schenectady to march immediately to the German Flatts" to assist Herkimer. The Schoharie committee of safety said they had "countermanded [his] Orders to Colo. Vrooman and that none of their Militia can be spared." Equally alarming, his efforts to raise the Schenectady companies were in vain. He had marched from Albany with one hundred men and boys from Learned's Massachusetts brigade under Lieutenant-Colonel John Brooks. When he asked Schuyler whether he was to march into Tryon County with Brooks, he betrayed a typical Regular officer's attitude and pled not to be forced to serve under the militia general. He had a letter from the Tryon committee of safety with the news that Herkimer's brigade was concentrated at German Flats and Fort Schuyler was besieged.[338] A day or so later, Van Schaick was spared the embarrassment of such demeaning service and Brooks marched on alone with his detachment.

At Stanwix at first light on August 5, a sentinel was killed while standing duty in the northwest bastion. All that day, native marksmen kept up an annoying and lethal sniping. In the afternoon, a British detail burned the barracks, which La Marquisie had built some one hundred yards outside the walls, and choking smoke drifted over the garrison.[339] It was a sad waste of labour and materials. Now, burnt-out shells surrounded the fort, giving an unpleasant, threatening outlook for the sentinels.

To add to the garrison's unease, the British threw some bombs from their mortars. Although no casualties resulted, several landed on the fort's parade and walkways between the inner barracks.[340] The Indians were unimpressed with the Cohorn mortars and later observed that their shells were like "Apples that Children were throwing over a Garden Fence."[341]

In the late afternoon of August 5, a startling message arrived for Joseph Brant from his sister Mary at Canajoharie giving advice that between eight and nine hundred men of the Tryon County militia had marched to relieve Stanwix. She warned that the brigade was already at the Oneida village of Oriska, only twelve miles from the British camps,[342] and but a short march away! St. Leger reacted swiftly: "I did not think it prudent to wait for them, and . . . subject myself to be attacked by a sally from the garrison in the rear, while the reinforcement employed me in front.[343] He believed that his Indian allies would best meet the threat. In any event, he had little choice with only 250 troops in camp due to the ongoing pioneering work along the creeks and roadway.

Butler had just come in from Three Rivers,[344] and St. Leger ordered him to collect as many rangers and Indians as possible to block the oncoming militiamen. There was no reluctance amongst the Indians and John quickly gathered twenty rangers to accompany him.

Brant gave Sir John the news, and shortly after St. Leger had issued his orders to Butler, Johnson appeared to press his services as the detachment commander and to recommend that infantrymen were required to bolster the lightly armed Indians.[345] St. Leger acceded and gave Johnson command of the whole. Johnson left immediately, taking Watts's fifty-five-man Light Company, which had been spared the brute work on the road to act as the guard company on the camp.

St. Leger had fresh memories of his misinformed actions that caused the aborting of his "Alert" at Salmon River and chose not to risk having his two senior Indian Department officers away simultaneously, so Claus remained at the camp to deploy the Indians who were continuing to arrive.

Brant was particularly eager for the fray.[346] His men were well equipped and their morale was high;[347] he had no difficulty inserting his volunteers and the Valley Mohawks into the force.

Some five hundred natives were mobilized: two hundred Senecas, Cayugas, and Onondagas,[348] three hundred of Brant's clansmen, Bull's Delawares, a small number of white refugees, the Fort Hunter and Canajoharie Mohawks, and fifty Lakes Indians.[349]

The blocking force set out at five o'clock that evening.[350] That night, they lay in a fireless camp, eating cold rations and suffering from persistent mosquitoes. The senior leaders met in a night council to choose an ambush site, far enough away "to keep the stinking [of] dead bodies off from the tents,"[351] and the force's general dispositions were decided upon, subject to fresh intelligence to be gathered in the morning. The art of ambushing was a native tactical specialty, and Old Smoke and Cornplanter had the principal role in designing the trap with the concurrence of Sir John and Butler.[352] The two officers were content to simply offer observations and advice when required. They were confident in the war captains' capabilities and well schooled in the whites' traditional supporting roles in such affairs.

While these deliberations were underway, the Indians remaining at Stanwix surrounded the fort after dark and "commenced a terrible yelling . . . continued at intervals the greater part of the night."[353] Psychological warfare was another native specialty.

CHAPTER SIX

~

THE MARCH OF THE TRYON COUNTY MILITIA
Rouse Then My Countrymen, Rouse

Despite all the predictions of apathy and widespread disaffection, the Tryon committee of safety's carefully worded proclamation achieved superb results. Their appeal gained further impetus from an impassioned letter written by Colonel Gansevoort about the farm girls murdered at Stanwix:[354]

> Oh! [King] George, the Herod of our day, to what art thee Fallen Like Herod of Old[,] hast thou sent Forth thy Murderers to Slay Innocent Children. Graceous Heaven will thou not take Vengence on these things.
>
> I send you the following particular account . . . to deliver some of the Inhabitants of this oppressed country from that Strange Infatuation which is ever working [th]em up to a persuasion that they have nothing to fear from the Kings murderers... they may Blush when they reflect what a Master they serve — but are there any Americans who will still Continue to subject themselves to this Savage King . . .
>
> Thus to Murder the Innocent Babes of their land... Barbarism itself must stand [amazed] at the supposition, and every Generous heart that is not steeled with Savage Ignorance weep to think that there are such inhumane Monsters who were born and brought up amongst us . . .
>
> One of the Children who was killed & scalped[,] a girl of 13 years of age & daughter of one John Steene who . . . served the King of Great Brittan . . . an old man and unfit for any kind of Service. yet, that King . . . has thus requited him for his former Service. The Girl who received the wound in her shoulder is 16 years of age[,]

the Daughter of one George Reyter . . . a soldier in . . . the 4th Battalion of Royal Americans during the late ware[.] . . . the other is a Servant Girl of . . . Mr Roof the Principal inhabitant of this place . . . The Girl's name is Lenea Stephane Age 20 years . . .

My Countrymen — is the[re] a Man amongst you whose [soul] does not shudder at such Dastardly Bloody business — or is there a pulsinanimous heart which requires Arguments to Urge him to Arms — against the King and Parliment of Brittan, who Disparing of Conquering our country by reducing it to a state [of] wretched vasslage, have declared war against our Poor defenseless Infants. [A]re there still any of you who are . . . indulging yourselves, with the Fancy that you are in no danger, that no harm is intended against you, are you possesed of more innocence than these poor Murdered Children. [H]ave you any right to expect better treatment than they have?, if you fall into the same hands, flatter not yourselves that it is only in this Wilderness where such bloody scenes are to be expected. . . it is true the same kind of Murderers may not overtake you in all your habitations — but the same bloody Tyrant is employing his Murderers of one kind or another throughout your Country — and it is the Vilest Infatuation to suppose your being only [a] looker, will save you from Destruction . . .

Rouse then my Countrymen[,] Rouse[.] It is under God in Your own arms that you are to look for Deliverance and fear not, God is a Righteous God, and in so Righteous an opposition success will most assuredly attend you, to doubt of the assistance of Heaven in such a cause is to Impeach the Justice of Almighty God —

These Indians we are informed are some of those sent out by those D[read]full Emmissaries of Brittan's Tyrant. Sr John Johnson Colonel Classe & Butler.

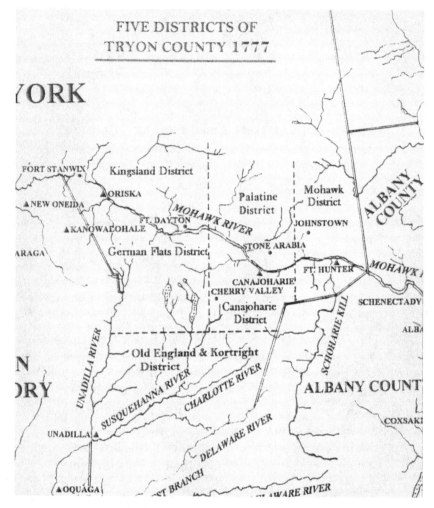

The five districts of Tryon County, 1777

Gavin K. Watt, 2000.

This explosive address was followed by a report from the Albany committee chairman describing the death of a young woman named Jane McCrae, who had been betrothed to a Provincial officer in Burgoyne's Grand Army and was scalped and mutilated by British Indians. Her death was confirmed when the killer flaunted her scalplock in the British camp.[355] The Whigs claimed the event proved the natives' duplicity — they recognized no bond, obeyed no rules, and slaughtered indiscriminately.

The letter further advised that many other Tories, who had been caught between the lines, had been killed by Burgoyne's Indians. The chairman wrote, "What then can those expect who Tamely submit[?] . . . nothing but Murder and Rapine."[356]

Word of these gruesome events spread like wildfire from one farm to the next across the region. The murders of non-combatant innocents struck home, and, as the life of Tryon County was so intimately entwined with the affairs of the fearsome Iroquois Confederacy, the men responded to Herkimer's call to arms in large numbers.

Tryon County's five regiments drew their manpower from individual districts, or precincts. Colonel Ebenezer Cox's First "Canajoharie" Regiment's boundaries were set on the east by a topographical feature on the Mohawk River known as Anthony's Nose, or the Noses; on the north by the river; on the south by the 5th Regiment's district; and on the west by the settlement of Little Falls.

Colonel Jacob Klock's Second Regiment drew from the "Palatine" precinct. This district lay north of the river all the way to the Canadian border and matched the "Canajoharie" district's east and west boundaries. It was a vast region, although active settlement was scarcely more than ten miles north of the river.

The precinct of Colonel Frederick Visscher's Third "Mohawk" Regiments lay east of the Noses on both sides of the river. Its eastern border was Albany County, the northern, the Canadian border, the southern, the 5th Regiment's zone.

Two zones gave a dual name to Colonel Peter Bellinger's Fourth "Kingsland and German Flats" Regiment. Both areas were west of Little Falls; Kingsland lay north of the river and German Flats, south. The upper limit was the border with Canada and the southern, the 5th Regiment's precinct. The western boundary was the Fort Stanwix Treaty Line of 1768, which marked the edge of Indian Territory.

In 1776, a fifth regiment of only three companies was created by the committee to deal with the county's southern regions. The country south of Otsego Lake and bordered on the east by Albany County, the south by the Susquehanna, and the west by the Treaty Line defined the precinct. This mini-regiment was detailed to defend the vulnerable southwest flank and was excused from Herkimer's summons.[357]

Every precinct had its share of the disaffected, but the Mohawk district held the greatest number of Scots immigrants, who, virtually to a man, remained loyal to the Crown. As well, the district was home to the principal Tory exiles, the two Johnsons, John Butler, and Daniel Claus, and many of their properties were still inhabited by loyal retainers.

A colonel commanded each regiment, with a lieutenant-colonel as his deputy, a first and second major as tactical commanders, subalterns as adjutant and quartermaster, and surgeon. In 1777, a regiment comprised nine companies commanded by a captain and assisted by a first and second lieutenant, an ensign, four serjeants, four corporals, and a fifer or drummer. Each regiment flew its own distinctive Colour, as did the brigade headquarters, all espousing some version of the Independence theme.

Prior to 1775, when Guy Johnson was still the adjutant of the Northern New York District, a regiment was directed to have ten companies, including a flank company of grenadiers with bearskin caps and one of light infantry. The latter two companies were to be made up of volunteers from across the precinct. However, the two-flank company system was not in place in 1777, and the militia followed the Continental Line practice in which grenadiers found no favour, but light infantry formations were common.[358]

To draw its complement, each company was given a beat, or population zone. The beat was divided into eight classes, each managed by a regulating officer or NCO. As drafts were called, men were chosen in numerical order so that their time of service was fairly spaced. In dire emergencies, the whole brigade could be called out and all classes went on duty. The system was designed to give each company about fifty-six all ranks, although rolls have been discovered of companies anywhere between twenty-five and eighty rankers.[359]

Prior to hostilities, the classes had a balanced population to draw from and companies had little difficulty building to full strength. Officers and NCOs were men of recognized influence and, preferably, military experience. Of course, once rebellion had taken root, a key factor was their dedication to the cause of independence. Those found wanting were, at a minimum, reduced to the ranks.[360]

Typical of all regular soldiers, the Continentals found the amateurish militia a frequent source of amusement and frustration.[361] They conveniently forgot that they had all at one time been militiamen. Yet the militia was the keystone of the American army, with roots that ran as deep as the original settlements.

When Washington took command outside Boston in 1775, he inherited an army of militia and, from this nucleus, formed the Continental Line.[362] So it was militiamen, not colonial Regulars, who bloodied the British at Breed's Hill and convincingly proved they could be terribly effective soldiers. In fact, the militia was prominent in all American campaigns and was competent when sensibly employed, as John Burgoyne discovered to his chagrin.

The American militia was a military force quite foreign to Britons, as the men brought their own arms when they reported for service. Indeed, the conflict itself "was unique in the memory of the age" as it involved "an armed insurgent population."[363]

The militia of each state had peculiar traditions which developed from its history as a colony.[364] Most of the American colonial militias were based upon a system of mandatory, short-term service by all male citizens/freemen, who were expected to provide arms, ammunition, and accoutrements at their own expense. During the Seven Years War, men were drafted from the militia for active service with the province's para-regular regiments, although volunteers for this type of service were almost always preferred. During the Revolutionary War, this same procedure was used to bolster the Continental Army when required.[365]

New York's earliest military traditions went back to the Dutch West India Company, which supplied protection to its settlers, rather than expecting them to provide their own. The Dutch colony was organized as a commercial enterprise and acquired a "social heterogeneity and attitude toward war that subverted militia organization." When the British took control in 1664 and established their system of militia service, New York's settlement pattern was still fragmented, especially in the frontier regions. Consequently, the colony's defence against New France was dependent upon an alliance with the Iroquois Confederacy as much as, or more than, its own people.[366]

Ninety years after the Dutch were displaced, New York's elderly, crusty lieutenant-governor, the Scottish elitist Cadwallader Colden, wrote:

Our Militia is under no kind of discipline, nor do I think it possible to bring them under any, without being inter-mixt with regular Troops. I had convincing proof of this in . . . 1746 at Albany, when [our] forces . . . against Canada were there. The Officers themselves could not be brought to observe discipline, notwithstanding of their suffering shamefully by want of it, on several occasions. The Inhabitants of the Northern Colonies are all so nearly on a level, and a licentiousness, under the notion of liberty, so generally prevails, that they are impatient under all kind of superiority and authority.[367]

Peter Wraxall, who was the town clerk of Albany and Sir William Johnson's secretary for Indian Affairs as well as captain of one of the province's British Independent Companies, wrote three years later:

The Officers of this Army [primarily from New York] with very few Exceptions are utter Strangers to Military Life and most of them in no Respect superior to the Men they are put over, They are like the heads . . . of a Mob. The Men are raw Country Men. They were flat-tered with an easy & a speedy Conquest; All Arts were used to hide future Difficulties and Dangers from them, and the whole Undertaking in all it's Circumstances smoothed over to their Imaginations.[368]

That year, Yorker militiamen who were called out to Fort William Henry deserted in droves. Many were apprehended at Albany by Lieutenant-Governor DeLancey, who set an example by killing a man who had refused to obey his order to halt.[369]

In 1758, Indians and blacks constituted a high percentage of the three battalions of the para-regular New York Provincial Regiment. While these men could be perfectly competent soldiers, they lacked the spirit of mind of voluntary military obligation which citizen/freeman militia service was based upon. In support of the militia ideal, British General Abercromby wrote that the Provincials could be greatly improved "by drafting them out of the militia, in place of whom they send out at an extravagant premium the rif-raf of the continent."[370]

By 1777, the traditional English colonial militia system was well established in New York, but its efficacy under Whig governance was yet to be tested. Every male from the age of sixteen to fifty was eligible for duty except indentured servants, slaves, Indians, and the halt and lame. Free blacks were expected to serve and slaves were accepted, with the agreement of their owners, often as substitutes for freemen unwilling to face the obligation of service. A few men such as government employees, grist mill and ferry operators, Quakers, and the elderly were granted exemptions.[371] All of these exemptions could be waived during emergencies.

In August 1775, the Provincial Congress instructed that a man who failed to appear "three times successively, or refuse[d] to enlist and do such duty. . . shall be advertised and held up as an enemy to his country." Slackers were fined and the funds generated used to clothe and accoutre poorer men. By 1776, failing to muster had become a litmus test for concealed disaffection to the cause. Such men were not allowed to supply a substitute or simply pay a fine, but were subject to imprisonment or forced service.[372]

By convention, militia mustered for only short, defined terms of service, measured in days or weeks, not months. This restriction limited their utility to the army, as Gansevoort had experienced immediately before St. Leger's arrival when Herkimer's term-expired men went home.[373]

While militia brigades lacked the discipline and training of Regulars, they were still a force to be reckoned with. In Tryon County, the majority of its brigade was composed of Palatine Germans whose unruly history and strange manners left them suspect in many eyes. But if the comments of many Seven Years War British commanders are valid, these Mohawk Valley militiamen were of the old concept — men with an obligation to serve who could be expected to give a good account of themselves.

There is little record of exactly how the Tryon Brigade assembled. Likely individual companies gathered at their usual drill grounds or a well-known landmark on the route to German Flats and then marched to Fort Dayton where the brigade was forming.[374] At each assembly point, records were kept of the absent.

Men like the Empeys of Stone Arabia had long been suspected of Toryism and most of them missed the rendezvous, except for Corporal

Jacob, who was soon to lose his life. It did not take written notes to recall their perfidy; their family would pay a tragic price.

The warning in General Herkimer's proclamation that absentees would receive a fine suggested that such penalties had been often waived in the past. On this occasion, when men failed to show, a difficult decision had to be made whether to march without them. Gossipy comments were made about their politics or their chronic unreliability or timidity, yet everyone was aware that sickness, accident, or failure of notification were possible reasons for truancy. The officers were conscious of time. To march their companies without full complements was undesirable, but to miss the assembly, unforgivable.

Strict regulations stated that each man was to provide a firelock in good working order with a steel ramrod, a cleaning worm, twelve spare flints, and a tool to fix and knap them.[375] There would have been a few decent rifles and smoothbores and many poorer ones; some long, ungainly fowling pieces; a handful of ancient army muskets; and some trade muskets.[376] Many militiamen carried a large cow's horn to contain the mandated amount of coarse, main-charge powder and a smaller one with fine priming powder. These men used a leather bag to carry the prescribed twenty-three musket balls and wadding.[377] Others had the preferred cartridge pouch with prepared paper cartridges,[378] as used by Regulars. All were to bring an edged weapon, either a hanger, a bayonet, or a tomahawk.[379] Each brought a robust container for drinking water, a blanket for bedding, and a haversack containing sufficient rations for three days of marching.

As the brigade was to relieve Stanwix and remain there in garrison, the men had an extra shirt and stockings; a spoon, sheath, or clasp knife; a bowl or plate; and soap and the ubiquitous shaving kit, for this was an era of clean-shaven faces. These items could have been carried in the prescribed knapsack or slung *en banderole* in the blanket.

Only a handful would have been in uniforms from previous service, perhaps from the failed Canadian expedition. Most of the clothing would have indicated the men's occupations, trades, and social stations. The majority was farmers whose shirts, work smocks, waistcoats, jackets, and linsey-woolsey or leather breeches reflected that vocation. They were coloured in earthen hues, rough of cut and cloth, and well-worn. The ever-popular checked shirts may have provided a splash of colour. Some lived by hunting and trapping, or had been with the county's rangers, and would have displayed a woods-wise appearance with smock shirts, trousers, and leggings of wool or leather embellished with a sprinkling of colourful native ornamentation. All men wore some form of headwear — a custom rigidly adhered to.

Major landowners and other men of influence in the community wore more fashionable clothing of fine cloth and cut, perhaps a trifle dated. Most senior officers sported military coats of the approved colour and pattern for New York and rode good horses with quality tack. A handful would have been in worn Continental regimentals. General Herkimer may have embellished his uniform with a fine, brocaded waistcoat.[380]

Like Regulars, each company was divided into two platoons, and there were mess squads within each. One man in each mess carried a cooking kettle or, if fortunate, stuck it onto a wagon. The men's immediate needs would be taken care of by bread, cheese, and cooked or smoke-cured meats brought from home in their haversacks.

When the companies arrived at Fort Dayton, some detachments were given rush assignments. Captain John Breadbake's 5th Company of Klock's Palatine Regiment had marched twenty-five miles to German Flats when an express caught up with them bringing news that Tories were burning farms near the Indian castle at Canajoharie. Such retaliation had been greatly feared by all and, understandably, was a reason for their previous hesitancy. Immediately, a detachment was turned about, but when the men arrived at the settlement, they found that the warning was false. It was reckoned that some Tories had artfully raised the spectre to weaken the brigade.

Captain Christian Howse's 7th Company of Klock's regiment had mustered at Oppenheim, a hamlet lying centrally in its beat, and then marched to Dayton. On arrival, rumours were rampant that Indians were going to attack their settlement, which was being defended by only old men, women and boys. Lieutenant John Zimmerman and ten men were sent back with orders to scout the approach routes and secure known Tory women to prevent them from giving information about the militia to spies. When these duties were complete, they were to rejoin the brigade at Stanwix. Why such a brief scout by a handful of men was considered sufficient to secure the neighbourhood is now a mystery.

In the 3rd Regiment, Private Frederick Sammons of Davis's 2nd Company recorded that John Visscher's 4th Company and some men

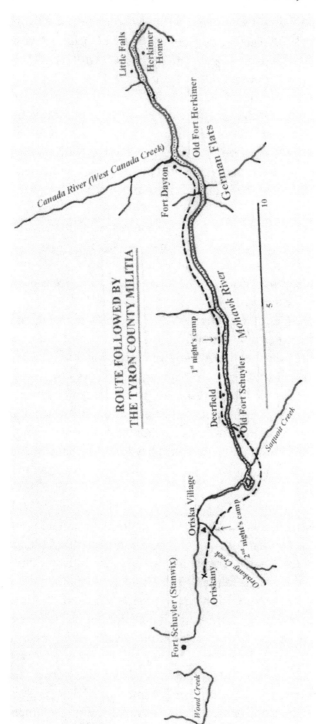

Route followed by the Tryon County Militia Brigade

Gavin K. Watt, 2000.

from his own company received similar orders. Colonel Visscher had word that Indians were going "to fall upon the inhabitants when the men were gone" and returned his brother John's company to Johnstown. Sammons and two others were sent to scout "west and north of the Lake and return by way of Mayfield."

As well, several known and suspected Tories were rounded up and left under guard at Fort Dayton. While Dayton was purpose-built, most of the little forts that gave comfort and protection to the scattered population were simply fortified houses with "Guards . . . consisting of the old men and those not able to march." Even men of the cloth took key roles; the fiery Lutheran minister Johann Daniel Gros acted as the commandant of Fort Plain.[381]

General Herkimer believed he had to arrive at Stanwix before the Crown forces established firm positions around the fort and that meant the sooner, the better. He announced the brigade would leave Fort Dayton on August 4.

There were several tense hours while he and his staff waited to see the response to the summons. The majority of the county's committeemen appeared, but Peter S. Deygert of the Canajoharie district remained behind to defend his community. Ironically, in the coming months, he would be particularly critical of those whom he thought had failed in their duties.

When the morning of August 4 dawned, Brown's company from New Dorlach and part of Whitaker's from Cherry Valley had not yet appeared.[382] Both were from Cox's Canajoharie Regiment. This was of some concern, but overall, the brigade's turnout was excellent, as some one thousand men had assembled.[383]

With memories of Guy and Sir John Johnson's dramatic flights, the coming fighting was obviously going to be rich and easy pickings. Everyone knew that the majority of St. Leger's little army was made up of trembling, no-account Tory refugees. The few militiamen who had fought in the Seven Years War were too old and stodgy to calm these flying spirits, and there were not enough veterans of the Canadian campaign to splash cold water on the rampant enthusiasm. As well, the typical loose discipline of green militia offered little emotional tempering.

Like all such military gatherings of eager young men setting off on an adventure, the muster had the air of a country fair. Some privates brought horses along to ease their march. Samuel Pettingell's 5th Company of Visscher's regiment had arrived at Fort Plank en route to

Dayton with so many horses that their colonel ordered three men back to the settlement of Florida with fourteen of the animals.[384] Visscher's junior officers and men were to march, the senior officers would ride.

This measure was repeated near Fort Dayton when detachments from Nicholas Rechtor's 6th Company, 2nd Regiment, and Jacob Gardinier's 1st Company, 3rd Regiment,[385] were ordered to remain behind to guard the excess horses and baggage that would impede the march.

Many militiamen from remote farms and hamlets had rarely seen such large numbers of folk gathered together, and their boisterousness was infectious. They probably wondered how the British, Tories, and savages could withstand such a grand display of martial ardour.

Very early on the morning of August 4, General Herkimer set off from his home below Little Falls in the German Flats.[386] He rode with some of his senior staff, dispatch riders, and lifeguards and soon joined the brigade at Fort Dayton. There were more rumours of Tory and Indian retaliation, and a handful of men were returned to Herkimer's home to guard his family and their neighbours.[387] The various detachments having been made, about eight hundred men began the march to Stanwix; their column strung out along the narrow, dirt roadway for well over a mile, with spirits high and feet light of step.

Once on the road, the altering the regiments' positions in the column would have been very difficult, so the order of march was set at the very outset. Cox's 1st Regiment led off. The 1st was followed by Klock's 2nd, then Bellinger's 4th, and behind it came five companies of Visscher's 3rd. An ox-drawn "convoy of 15 Waggons of Provisions & Stores"[388] was between them and the rest of the 3rd's companies, which were acting as the rearguard.[389]

The column was a half-mile beyond Fort Dayton when convenient ground was found to call a halt so Herkimer could ride down the ranks on his white horse to offer encouragement. The men stood in silence as Herkimer rode past smiling, sword in hand, addressing each company with words of inspiration. That done, they set off again.[390]

With only periodic stops for rest and refreshment, the column marched through the blistering heat of the day, tramping along the rutted, dirt road in a haze of summer dust. Near sundown, the head of the column halted to camp at Staring Creek, a tributary of the Mohawk named after a prominent local Whig family. Henry Staring was a captain in command of one of Bellinger's companies.[391]

The column was still strung out for well over a mile. Orderly Serjeant John Frank recalled that Ittig's company of the 4th Regiment halted about eight miles from Fort Dayton and camped at Thompson's, a Tory trading post where Guy Johnson had briefly stayed during his flight from the Valley.[392]

Meals were simple and fires were lit to boil up coffee or tea. Keeping warm was of no concern, as the night was hot and sticky, but the swarms of mosquitoes were annoying when dusk fell. Many retired soon after dark, sleeping in their clothing on the road's verges or in the woods.

The younger men stayed awake in nervous agitation, poking the fires, sitting in the smoke to drive off the pests, spinning yarns and singing songs. A few consumed some liquor and boasted of deeds to come. The majority sat with friends and relatives, but some wandered up and down the road looking for acquaintances and a little diversion. Pickets may have been posted to guard the sleeping horde, but no one took that duty too seriously and trusted instead to the false security of a large body of men.

The evening held a different agenda for General Nicholas Herkimer. A council of senior officers and committeemen met to discuss the details of the march. Henry Flanders of Rechtor's company of Klock's regiment was lying sick nearby and overheard their discussion. Herkimer wanted to wait for reinforcements of Schenectady and Albany militia, but the committeemen urged an immediate departure. Frederick Helmer, of the Kingsland and German Flats committee, became abusive, challenging Herkimer that he was afraid to advance. Herkimer became philosophical and pointed out that he could afford to go, as he had no young family, unlike so many in the brigade. His explanations were of no avail, and it was decided to continue the next morning.[393]

This altercation was followed by a heated debate regarding the best route. Herkimer reckoned to cross to the south side of the river at Deerfield, so that the column could avoid risking a river crossing opposed by St. Leger's troops and guns. As the northern route followed high ground and the southern traversed a series of wetlands, several officers argued for the easier advance. Herkimer's logic won, but their agreement was ungraciously given. These arguments indicated a conspicuous lack of trust and solidarity. There was worse to come.

As dawn broke on August 5, the militia awoke and began to breakfast. While all of the men were early risers, many were unused to the demands of military discipline, and the atmosphere of excitement worked against getting the column underway expeditiously. Not too far into their march, the brigade passed through the small Deerfield settlement and soon after crossed to the south side of the river at the ford at Schuyler's Corners. The river bottom churned and softened from the crossing of horses, oxen, wagons, and hundreds of troops. Once across, the column passed a well-known landmark — the lonely ruins of the old Fort Schuyler of the Seven Years War, which some folk called Fort Desolation.

A startlingly brief event occurred while the militia was on the march. For some reason, two men of Klock's regiment were lagging behind the rearguard. Second Lieutenant Jacob Klock of the 2nd Company was mounted and Private John Sponable of the 6th was afoot. Suddenly, Klock's mount shied and snorted at a strange scent. Sensing danger, Klock spurred the animal forward, just as several Indians sprang from the woods and captured Sponable.[394] No information has been found about Klock's reactions.

After twelve gruelling miles, the march ended for the day. The brigade's head stopped at the Oneidas' Oriska village, where two Dutch-style houses and "sundry Indian Huts" sat beside Oriska Creek.[395] The column's tail was about two miles behind at Saquoit Creek. Everyone was tired, and the stimulation that had buoyed their spirits on the first night gave way to genuine fatigue. Soon after eating, the men lay in their crude beds and fell into a deep sleep. Again, there is no record of pickets being set.

Again, Herkimer's day did not end so simply. He was very pleased to welcome a party of some sixty Oneidas who,[396] as promised, had come to join the brigade. Herkimer was aware that many of his officers and men distrusted all natives; at the same time, many other Whigs believed the Oneidas to be the most warlike and competent of the Iroquois.[397] These Indians had made an extremely difficult choice. So many of their brothers had grasped the British war axe at Three Rivers that, by taking up arms against their kin, the Oneidas threatened the ancient Great Peace of the Confederacy.

The March of the Tryon County Militia

*A typical wilderness highway flanked by tall, mature trees and dense under-
growth with deadfall along the verges*

Ink and watercolour by James Pattison Cockburn, ca. 1830. Courtesy of the
National Archives of Canada, C-012632.

Two Oriska war captains were in the party. Honyery Tewahangaraghkan was armed with a rifle, and a sword hung at his side to signify his rank. His wife, Senagena, stood with him, armed with pistols and prepared for battle, as did his son and his brother Honyost Tewahangaraghkan. The second captain was Henry Cornelius Haunnagwasuke. Some others were Blatcop, a principal warrior; the mixed-blood Thomas Spencer, who had already given such timely and eloquent advice to the Whigs, and his brother Henry; James Powless Wakarantharaus; and the half-black Kahnawake, Louis Atayataghronghta, who would later be famous as Colonel Louis, the highest-ranking native in the Continental service.[398]

Herkimer was thankful to receive their intelligence and recommendations. Once again, they warned of Indians blocking the road.

It is not known whether Herkimer developed his next plan based on their information or from his innate sense of caution and military common sense. He reasoned that St. Leger would know of his brigade's march and would oppose its advance, but if a sortie was made from the fort, it would divert his enemy's attention and the column would have a better chance of pushing through. Herkimer decided to send a party to Stanwix with a request for a sortie and chose three local men who knew the terrain intimately. They were First Lieutenant Hans Marcus Demuth, who had been a committeeman in 1775 and was known to Gansevoort, and Privates Adam F. Helmer and Hon Jost Folts,[399] all from the 4th Deerfield Company of Bellinger's regiment. His message advised: "[I have] Arrived at Orisco with 1000 militia in Order to Relieve the Garrison and open the Communication [to the lower Valley] which was then Entirely Blocked up, and that if the Colonel shoud hear a Firing of small Arms [he] desired he wou'd send a party from the Garrison to Reinforce them . . . Colonel [Gansevoort was to] fire three Cannon if the Three Men got safe into the Fort with his Letter."[400]

The three men left before dark and, heeding the warnings about parties of British Indians guarding the road, took trails that skirted through the woods. In so doing, they bypassed Sir John's force.

As dawn broke, the militia awoke and prepared breakfast. The more thoughtful men carefully examined their arms while the brigade's senior officers assembled for another council. Herkimer told them about the Oneidas' advice about hostile Indians on the road and advised that he had sent Lieutenant Demuth to request a sally from the fort to assist the brigade. He stated his firm intention to wait for Gansevoort's signal of three gun discharges indicating that he would comply.[401]

A number of the officers believed that a delay was foolhardy and argued that the sooner the brigade approached the fort, the better their chance of catching St. Leger off guard. Inexplicably, the previous night's acrimony heated up again. With the impetuous Eben Cox as ringleader, Herkimer's senior officers were soon at serious odds, exchanging unguarded, rancorous words within earshot of nearby militiamen. Like a ripple of wind through standing grain, news of the arguments passed down the road from one company to the next.

Cox held a smouldering grudge against Herkimer, who was the employer of some of his family and had embarrassed his father over the tardy payment of a debt.

Klock's second major, Isaac Paris, was a founder of the county's committee and a state representative. Major Paris, Colonel Visscher, and Cox's nephew, Colonel Jacob Klock, with committeemen like Frederick Helmer, supported Cox against the cautious Herkimer. Colonel Bellinger, Herkimer's brother-in-law, and Brigade Major Frey, a distant relative, sided with Herkimer in the unequal exchange.[402]

Herkimer was a stubborn German and held to his position, observing that their security was his trust and he was determined to watch over them like a father. Having failed with persuasion and argument, Cox turned to insults and hinted that Herkimer was a coward. Not content, his taunts turned from insinuation to accusation. The hothead heaped scorn on the older man by reminding the others of Herkimer's apprehensive treatment of Brant at Unadilla as evidence of his unnatural fear.

The stolid Herkimer was not immune to these allegations and his anger smouldered. The insult that finally brushed his caution aside was an accusation of disaffection. His critics muttered about his Tory brother Han Jost and nephew Philip Frey, both of whom had run off to the enemy, and intimated that his reluctance had more to do with Tory sympathies than prudence. These taunts touched Brigade Major John Frey as well, as young Philip was the son of his infamous Tory older brother Hendrick.[403] His other brother, Barent, had left the valley with Guy Johnson and was serving in the British Indian Department with Han Jost Herkimer.[404]

Goaded beyond all patience, Herkimer flared. Glaring about him, he predicted his tormentors would be the first to run when the enemy appeared. In disgust and anger, he ordered the column forward and, calling for his horse, mounted to lead the way.

Even with all his anger, Herkimer heeded his inborn caution and Thomas Spencer's advice, and ordered a van to lead the brigade and flankers to scour the edges of the woods. Although some natives may have been employed as flankers, they were so distrusted that the majority followed behind the 1st or 2nd Regiment.[405]

Rancorous tension hung in the air, sobering many of the officers and men; however, the excitement of the outing still gripped the younger men. Chattering and hawbucking, they eagerly pressed forward in a long column of threes.[406]

~

CHAPTER SEVEN

AMBUSCADE AT ORISKANY
The Indians Rose with a Dreadful Yell

Sir John Johnson's men roused before dawn and ate a simple breakfast, following it by methodically checking their equipment. Any kit that had been previously adjusted for comfortable marching was repositioned for ready access in combat. In typical army fashion, the Royal Yorker serjeants went through the Light Company ensuring that the best of flints were firmly fixed and the cartridge pouches and canteens were full. Every man checked his priming, whether a Light Bob or a self-reliant ranger.[407] Very likely, a depot for storing blankets and knapsacks was established.

Following a tradition not unlike the adjustment of kit and uniforms amongst the white soldiers, the natives refreshed the paint on their faces, torsos, and limbs. They had left their blankets, jewellery, and quillwork finery in the camps at Stanwix and were now stripped to their shirts and breechclouts, or to the clouts alone. Like their allies, they hung their edged weapons ready to hand, and those with firelocks checked the set of their flints and their priming.

Before the morning was an hour old, select native scouts were dispatched to observe the militia column and bring back news of its dispositions, discipline, and morale. One scout found a road-maintenance pit only thirty feet from the roadway and, after laying hemlock branches across the hole, settled inside. He had a long wait before the arguments between the militia officers came to an end and the column began to march, signalled by the creaking and groaning of the wagons. Not too long after, he saw the van and sensed the flankers passing by, then carefully watched the column of troops and wagons. After all had passed, he sped back over an Indian trail to make his report.[408] His mates took similar measures and, unseen, fulfilled their role.

The scouts reported to Johnson's Orders Group of the principal officers. Their findings confirmed Mary Brant's warnings; more than eight hundred men were on the road with a convoy of wagons, supported by a party of Indians that was predominantly Oneida. Whether the scouts had detected any residual bad feeling amongst the officers is unknown, but they certainly sensed the naive ardour of the troops and, most important, described the column's length and structure. In response to this fresh intelligence, the dispositions discussed the night before were adjusted. The meeting then took an unexpected turn that was potentially as divisive as their foes' morning meeting.

Johnson and Butler opened a debate about whether a parlay with the militia might bear fruit. After all, many relatives and friends of the militiamen were in the Royal Yorkers and rangers. On their part, the Seneca leaders were worried about a direct clash with the Oneidas, and they were uncomfortably mindful of the promises of neutrality they had given to the U.S. commissioners. On a purely practical note, they were also concerned about the shortage of firearms amongst the warriors.[409] Taken together, these issues led the chiefs to agree that talk might produce favourable results. Butler proposed to summon the militiamen to lay down their arms and return to their homes.

Brant was incredulous and furious. In the usual native fashion, his face remained impassive, but a thundercloud was just beneath the surface. He argued vehemently that the time for talking had past. He had seen the militia leaders under arms only scant weeks ago; he knew their minds, especially the Klock and Cox faction. These obstinate men needed a hard blow to either set them straight or finish them off. In his opinion, the course was clear.

Joseph became aggressively persuasive; he scornfully stressed the betrayal of the Oneidas and Tuscaroras and pointed out that an approach to the militia would compromise the tactical advantage of

A file of Captain Stephen Watts's company of Royal Yorker Light Infantry

Pen drawing by Gavin K. Watt, 2000, after an album of line drawings attributed to Philip de Loutherberg at Warley Camp, Essex, October 1778. Courtesy of the Anne S.K. Brown Military Collection, Brown University Library.

surprise. His forceful rhetoric and logical arguments demonstrated the leadership qualities that were to become his signature in the later war and earned him a key role in the Canadian Department.

Brant asserted that his men would face the militia alone if necessary.[410] Talk of peace was useless. Sir John was convinced. Remembering the rebels' treatment of his family and inheritance, he signalled to Stephen Watts and the Lights moved off with Brant's volunteers and the Valley Mohawks.

John Butler and his twenty rangers were left behind with the Senecas, Onondagas, Cayugas, Lakes, and Canada warriors.[411] The discussion continued at the usual dignified, solemn pace, but it was uncharacteristically brief. The young Mohawk's words had struck home with both the war captains and the Deputy Superintendent. The Senecas, frequently foremost in such adventures, were dismayed that a junior, self-appointed Mohawk leader had taken the lead, and Sir John's change of heart may have affected them. The talk came to an abrupt end and all marched to join Sir John. When they caught up, it was as if nothing had occurred, and the senior war captains resumed their role as the primary tactical leaders of the force.[412]

The site selected for the ambush was almost ideal. The militia would be trapped on the roadway between two ravines. They would enter the eastern ravine with its swampy bottom and creek and cross over the water on a corduroy causeway.[413] The road then climbed sharply for some one hundred feet and swung southwest to bypass a deep ravine on the right. When that feature was passed, it turned westwards and made a gentle climb through mature woods of giant hemlocks.[414] Swinging slightly northwards, it descended into another ravine and crossed a firm-bottomed creek, then rose upward to continue towards Stanwix.[415]

Dispositions were made based on the scouts' information about the column's length. The brigade would be allowed to enter the stretch of road running between the two ravines. The rearguard would be over the first ravine's corduroy when the vanguard began to climb the western slope of the second ravine. At that moment, the Yorker Lights would spring the ambush by firing a volley down the throats of the van and the First Regiment. This discharge would signal a general engagement and Brant's volunteers and the Mohawks would spring from cover, seal off the corduroy, and close the route of retreat.

The Royal Yorkers were expected to hold firm at the front and stop the brigade's forward movement. This was quite a feat for fifty-five untried youngsters, so their colonel stationed himself with the lads to brace them.

While the column was clamped at each end in the jaws of this vice, the majority of the warriors would attack the main body assisted by the rangers.[416] An instruction might have been issued to target officers and committeemen, or it may simply have been tacitly understood.[417]

Watts probably placed a platoon on either side of the roadway with First Lieutenant George Singleton in charge of one and Second Lieutenant Kenneth McKenzie the other. Johnson and his brother-in-law would have taken a central post with a good view of the roadway. The officers advised the troops of the signal to open fire.

The only serious gap in the plan was the deep ravine, as the Indians were unable to take up positions where it bordered the roadway due to the slope. Otherwise, at all points of the compass, a tight cordon had been created.[418]

Back at Fort Stanwix that morning, the garrison saw some "Indians . . . going off from around the Garrison towards the Landing."[419] Eager latecomers were marching to join their kith and kin in the ambush. They took with them a detachment of Jägers which St. Leger had ordered to assist Sir John. When they arrived at the western ravine, Sir John reinforced his Lights with the Hessians,[420] while the newly arrived Indians moved quickly to join their brothers up ahead.

The natives and rangers had two opposing factors to consider when taking up their positions. They had to be back far enough from the road to be concealed from the militia's flankers, but close enough to rapidly engage the column and immediately reinforce the shock of the opening volley. Aware of the keen vision of the Oneidas, they took extreme care in selecting hiding places.

While native men trained from childhood to stalk game and engage in combat, the younger lads still needed some coaching, as did the inexperienced rangers. Without leaving the smallest sign, the war captains must have walked the roadway, confirming that each man was completely concealed. These observations led to some adjustments, as must the positioning of the latecomers.[421]

A war fever washed over the younger Indians. They had been denied opportunities for the glories of battle that their seniors so often spoke of, but now combat was just ahead, and they would prove themselves as valiant as their older brothers. The war captains and principal warriors knew well how to play on these emotions.

The rising squeal of wagon axles signalled the nearing of the brigade. All the soldiers, white and red, sunk low into their positions. With their oiled skin, the natives were immune to mosquitoes, but the whites were plagued. The air was oppressively hot and humid, dead calm as before a great storm and electric with anticipation.

At about nine o'clock,[422] Brant's men sighted the vanguard. The flankers were seen flitting through the trees. Soon after came mounted men, General Herkimer followed by the staff of the 1st Regiment with Colonel Eben Cox foremost. The Canajoharie Mohawks recognized the brash Cox, the son-in-law of old Jury Klock, their protagonist in so many land disputes. They were greatly satisfied at this turn of events, as vengeance was always foremost in the native mind. The jaws of the keen-eyed observers hardened when they saw their younger brothers, the Oneidas and Tuscaroras. It was a long column — blissfully unaware and stretching beyond sight.

The militiamen were alive with excitement. This was the last day of their long march. Soon they would drive off the Tories and savages and be welcomed into Stanwix as heroes. As they dipped down into the first ravine, the corduroy section lay immediately ahead and the flankers moved in to cross the bog on the logs. Unconscious of being observed, the van negotiated the corduroy and climbed the far slope, passing through an area choked with uprooted trees that had fallen in a vicious windstorm a short time before.[423] Only the roadway itself had been cleared, and all about them was a tangle of fallen trunks. Once past these, the flankers moved back into the edges of the woods. Behind them was a cacophony of sound, an unceasing buzz of voices, the underlying thrum of footfalls and rattling of drums, over which lay the monotonous, creaking squeal of the wagons. The noise and heat numbed their senses.

Once the flankers and van had passed, Brant's men slithered forward, instantly ready to react to the signal. The 1st Regiment passed and the 2nd Regiment came into view. There was Jacob Klock, the son of the persuasive, unprincipled Jury. Then the brigade staff and a party of Oneida and Tuscarora brothers sandwiched between their tail and the staff of the 4th. Was that not Captain Henry Cornelius Haunnagwasuke, the Spencer brothers, and Blatcop? There, on horses, were Captain Honyery Tewahangaraghkan and his wife, Senagena. The

Mohawk watchers felt betrayed: their faces flushed with blood and their eyes glinted in anger.

While most of the natives and rangers hunkered down far from view, a handful of the most trusted were forward to view the passing column. Amongst those were Cayugas and Genesee Senecas who recognized the passing Oneidas. Some Indians and most rangers knew Herkimer, Cox, Klock, and many, many other faces.

At the ambush's western end, the tension amongst the Royal Yorkers and Jägers grew in proportion to the rising sound of the column's advance. In the hot, humid morning, sweat dripped off reddened faces. Slathered hands clutched religious medals to seek strength and solace, and many fervent prayers were murmured by the devout young Scotsmen and Hessians, their Latin, Gaelic, and German phrases absorbed into the heavy foliage.

The staff and leading companies of the 3rd now descended into the first ravine. Behind them came the trundling wagons, the stolid, wet-nosed oxen pulling their burdens, seemingly without effort. The teamsters were worried about the corduroy, as the animals feared the rolling, plunging logs. Then the wagons were on the causeway,[424] some teamsters coaxing, others flogging to encourage the animals to draw the carriages across that treacherous surface. The rearguard companies were about to set foot on the corduroy when, suddenly, there was the sharp crack of musketry.

One of the men on the left side of the van had pre-emptively sprung the trap. No one recorded whether he fired a shot or gave a shout of warning when he saw Indians lying in ambush. There was no exchange of paroles and countersigns, indeed no hesitation. In a blink, the van and flankers were struck down.

The moment that flanker Jacob Casler glimpsed the enemy in the act of firing, he threw himself to the ground. An instant later, there was a crash of gunfire and war halloos resounded in the confinement of the forest. Stark terror was unleashed amongst the startled militia. "After the first fire," [Casler] betook himself to a tree." Somehow, he survived the battle, the only flanker to do so.[425]

Deep in troubled thought, Herkimer was riding alone just ahead of the 1st Regiment.[426] With the first shot, he spun his horse about and spurred towards Cox at the head of the Canajoharie men.

Moses Younglove, the brigade surgeon, was riding with the staff. Thinking the firing was a false alarm, he dismounted, tied his horse to a

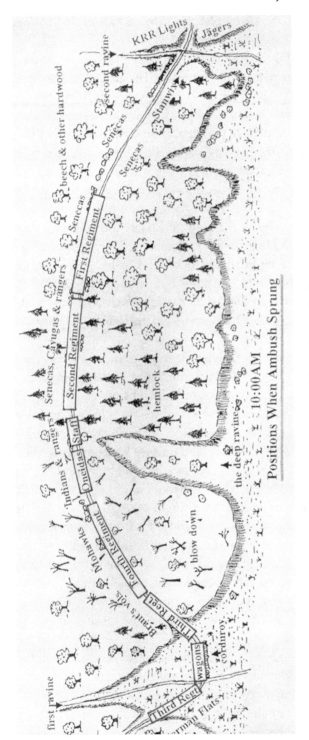

Oriskany — 10:00 A.M. Positions when ambush was sprung

Gavin K. Watt, 2000.

tree, and ran to investigate. He had left his medical bag attached to his saddle. It would never be recovered.[427]

General Herkimer heard Cox's stentorian voice ordering the leading company to form in the roadway to return fire. The general had ordered this very tactic, if the brigade was forced to fight on the road. Cox was having difficulty; the men were in shock, the crack of musketry and shouts of the Indians in terrifying contrast to the almost festive atmosphere they had been enjoying only scant moments before. When some militiamen took flight, Cox warned he would kill the next man to pass him. Instantly, he was forced to fulfil his threat and a hapless victim fell dead in the road.[428]

Herkimer saw that Cox was getting a grip on his regiment and spurred back down the verge of the road to reassure the following regiments. Arriving at Klock's regiment, his prominent figure became a target for a marksman hidden behind a rockpile. A ball hit the general's mare, passed through her body, and came out through Herkimer's leg. The soft lead bullet flattened during its passage and, on exiting, shattered his limb in two places. His horse staggered, then collapsed onto the road, pinning him underneath.

This marksman had already dropped a couple of men who had been standing near Herkimer before Henry Smith,[429] one of the general's lifeguards, was ordered to shoot him. He was a hair's breadth too late, for just as Herkimer was hit, Smith spotted the foe, raised his rifle, and fired. He ran to the rockpile, where he found a wounded man who weakly attempted to defend himself with a tomahawk, and finished him. Smith snatched up the sniper's rifle and horn as trophies and returned to his post.[430]

In the meantime, other men had rushed forward to pull Herkimer from under the stricken beast and carry him to safety in the woods. His wound bled profusely and word was passed for the brigade surgeon, but Younglove was lost in the melee and no professional help came.

At the column's head, the shouting Eben Cox presented an inviting target and he was soon struck. He lurched from the ball's impact and his horse wheeled about, then stampeded into the following company, knocking the men about. Whether his death was by specific aim or by pure chance is unknown.

Beyond the column's head, the Indians, who had lain hidden in the woods, poured onto the roadway to close with the enemy. Many were youths and so eager for glory that they threw caution to the wind. Compelled to set an example, the captains and senior warriors could hardly hold back, even if common sense dictated otherwise. The Indians leapt upon the fallen van members to strip trophies and booty, then rushed towards the 1st Regiment.

This mass of men provided a perfect target for Cox's lead company, which volleyed into them at least once, perhaps twice, sending a smashing weight of lead to hammer into the yelling natives. The militiamen recalled that the Indians were "half drunk" and said they "shewed themselves more openly than has ever been known," but the Senecas were to vehemently deny this claim of drunkenness later.[431]

Not all the Senecas were eager for the fight. A youngster named Red Jacket and three other Genesee youths who were facing their first combat ran off when the firing began and made their way home.[432]

Down the length of Cox's regiment, majors and captains urged the men to close up. Incoming fire came from everywhere; war whoops were at every hand; Indians flitted in and out of the trees. The officers made decisions and, shouting and pushing, faced the companies to where the threat appeared worst, but after their volleys, the men were instantly defenceless. In the act of reloading, they were caught by a storm of hideously painted warriors who eagerly chopped and thrust with hatchets and spears.

Native ardour and tradition drove this surge forward. The blood of the ancestors was pulsing. As became warriors of their race, the majority fought with edged weapons and fell onto the militia, who were struggling to reload, standing in rank and file on the open road fumbling with cartridges, horns, and ball bags, crammed together shoulder to shoulder, arms awry as they cast about their firelocks in an attempt to charge powder and ball into the muzzle. Of necessity, their eyes were averted from the rushing warriors. It was no way to meet this impassioned charge, and the slaughter was horrific. Militiamen fell — hacked, slashed, punctured, and stabbed — onto the roadway. In the gruesome press on the roadway, no quarter was given and none was expected.

Indians with firelocks ran along the sides of the column, giving a point-blank running fire and deftly reloading on the trot. This was a particularly effective tactic, as the militiamen could do little to counter the rush. The companies to their front and rear blocked their view and, of course, their ability to fire.

The rangers roamed the periphery of this struggle, searching out the mounted senior officers, watching for the captains and lieutenants, indeed anyone who demonstrated leadership, and deliberately sniping them.

On the log corduroy, the oxen snorted and heaved in their harness as Brant's men burst onto the road to seal off the retreat. The teamsters were transfixed; there was nowhere to go. They could not move forward into the press of men. It was impossible to reverse, and turning off the causeway led directly into the bog.

Brant's men first crashed into the 3rd's leading companies. They "Ran Down upon the Right and Left of our main Body and kept a Runing fire as they Proceeded."[433] One of Visscher's men remembered the colonel shouting in German, "O Lord God Almighty, run, boys or we are all gone!"[434] The recollection could have been the truth or a malicious lie; however, Visscher may well have shouted something similar in the first shock of the conflict. If so, he quickly recovered and began to stabilize his forward companies.

Serjeant Evert Van Eps of Fonda's exempts was one of the few men who had been allowed to retain his horse. In the opening moments of Brant's onslaught, the animal was shot out from under him and a ball struck him in the left leg. He crawled off the roadway into the bush and survived.[435]

Hacking past the 3rd's men, Brant's volunteers exploded onto the corduroy, swarming over the wagons, tumbling the teamsters into the stamping, struggling terror of the animals' hooves. The wagons turned every which way, and the corduroy became a tangle of dead and dying men with terrified animals strung in their traces. After seeing this horrifying onrush, the 3rd's rearguard companies gave a brief resistance and then recoiled in panic.

According to the native concept of war, an enemy in full rout was an entirely acceptable outcome of an ambush and demanded immediate pursuit. Even so, some warriors could not resist the lure of ready plunder, and they rummaged lustfully amongst the wagons while being shot at by some of Visscher's more composed men. For most of Brant's volunteers and the Fort Hunter Mohawks, the greater enticement was the trophies of hair and weapons to be ripped from the fleeing militiamen. As they gave pursuit, their halloos increased the fugitives' panic. The militiamen were hard pressed to outrun the fleet-footed warriors. Many were slaughtered — tripped up or impaled by a spear, poked by a gun barrel thrust, their heads split open by an axe and their scalps torn off.

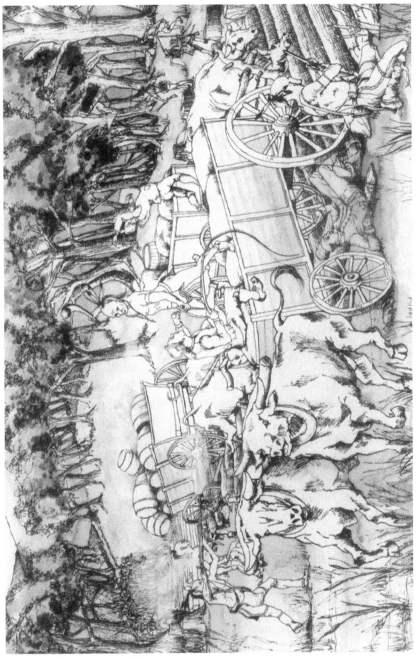

*Brant's
volunteers
swarm the
wagons on
the
corduroy*

*Pencil, ink and
watercolour by
Richard I.
Reeves, 2000.*

Men with their wits about them ran into the woods to escape that road-way of death. Dodging furtively from tree to tree, they reached the river and crossed to sanctuary on the far shore.

At his post at the second ravine, Sir John cursed the ambush's pre-emptive start. The militia van was not even in sight and he quickly ordered the Lights and Jägers to come to grips with the enemy. Watts's Light Bobs and the Jägers advanced swiftly and efficiently; they had trained for precisely such a movement. As they came into range, they commenced firing by files.[436]

With this tactic, each two-man file operated independently, with the men kneeling or standing behind trees or rocks to offer a minimum tar-get for return fire. The first soldier aimed and fired, and when he com-pleted reloading, he signalled to his file partner, who repeated the sequence. The system ensured that no more than half of the men were unloaded at any time. The Light Bobs were chosen marksmen who had recently confirmed their skills firing at marks,[437] which was also true of most Jägers, although it was discovered later that some of them were hampered by inferior firearms.[438]

Normally, deliberate musketry by marksmen was telling, but in this battle their target was a struggling, surging mass of humanity through which their Indian allies were darting in and out. In such a roiling melee, what was aimed at was not necessarily what was struck, and in later years the Senecas complained they were "much annoyed by the Loyalists in the rear keeping up an inconsiderate Fire, — which[,] as they were mixed in combat with the Enemy, did equal injury to both." The Senecas believed that a loyalist ball killed a renowned Squaki war chief, as his corpse was found facing the enemy with a gunshot in his back.[439]

The rebel Oneidas reacted resolutely against their brothers' attack by employing the same running tactic, lashing out with axe, knife, and fire-lock. Blatcop thrice rushed through the field of conflict, striking left and right. Honyery Tewahangaraghkan was said to have killed nine men before taking a ball in the wrist. If so, it was no wonder that British Indian resentment against the rebel Oneidas was later so strong. After his wounding, he stood his ground, striking out with his tomahawk while his wife, Senagena, repeatedly loaded and passed him his firelock.[440]

The rebel Kahnawake, Black Louis Atayataghronghta, spotted a marksman who had shot several militiamen lying in the fork of a fallen tree. Louis risked exposing himself to fire a killing shot and then broke from hiding to take the scalp.[441] The Oneida warrior Blatcop broke the arm of a British Indian with his tomahawk and, assisted by a friend, killed the man.[442]

Of course, the Oneidas' fight was not all one-sided. The mixed-blood brothers, Thomas, Henry, and possibly Edward Spencer, were killed during the combat, but, typically, no record survived of their other casualties.

Some claim the Oneidas stood against this unequal fight till the very end, but there is no mention of them in the later battle.[443] It is more probable that they withdrew through the woods and ravine rather than absorb unnecessary punishment. Whatever the case, their presence and their ardour registered strongly in their brothers' hearts, and an internecine die had been cast in this "Place of Sorrows."[444]

Although the protection of the trees beckoned throughout the opening phase of the battle, much of the brigade followed Herkimer's orders and stood firm in the road. When the Indians fell on them with their hacking, thrusting, running fight, men began to break for cover. Some abandoned their companies to seek refuge in the woods and the deep ravine, carefully working their way northwards to the river and safety.

Private George Walter of Klock's regiment had been severely wounded by a gunshot. While the battle raged about him, he dragged himself down to a small rivulet to slake his thirst, where he was found by a marauding Indian and scalped. With incredible fortitude, George shammed death and survived the battle.

William Merckley and Valentine Fralick of Klock's regiment snuck away from the bloody roadway and were cautiously moving through the trees when William was felled by a ball. Valentine rushed to his assistance, but Merckley told him to "take care of yourself and leave me to my fate." Fralick saw some Indians approaching and hid under a fallen tree. When the warriors left, he returned to his mate and found him tomahawked and scalped. He crept away and survived.[445]

Sergeant Peter Snell of Klock's 7th Company was standing behind a tree when he was startled by a large Indian who ran up on his flank and "snatched his gun from him." The native asked which regiment he belonged to. Without answering, Snell recovered his shock and wrested his gun from the Indian, who bounded off through the trees.[446] The natives were attempting to identify specific targets.

For half an hour, John Duesler and Christopher Eckler of Cox's regiment stood their ground until their officers were killed. John recalled one falling dead in the road. Then they stealthily retreated through the woods to the swamp along the river's shore. After picking their way through the bog, "they ran pretty fast, until they got over the River on the north side" and retreated to Fort Dayton.[447]

The majority of the men held; many were already wounded and dazedly hugged the cover of tree trunks and roots. Indians swarmed everywhere. Once a militiaman fired his musket, he was open to attack from his front, flanks, and rear, but the men were too tempted by the wealth of inviting targets not to fire. Warriors lay in wait, watching for this opportunity, then sprang up and fell upon the militiaman with axe or spear. Others ran through the militia position, counting on their rapid movement to spoil their foes' aim, and boldly rushed at any man who risked firing.

Fighting alone with a muzzleloader was dangerous. A rifle took fifty seconds to reload, a musket at least fifteen, and, except for the most practised, the process required visual concentration. Instead of shooting, simply lying doggo proved the salvation of many militiamen.

Colonels Visscher and Veeder of the 3rd Regiment, both forceful personalities, strove to stabilize their leading companies after they had been mauled by Brant's rush. Some of their men, who had seen the slaughter on the corduroy and the flight of the rear companies, were deeply shaken. Visscher stood in the road shouting at his soldiers to "not . . . run like Cowards . . . stand and fight Like men." He struggled back along the column towards the corduroy, rallying the stunned men, threatening to shoot anyone who ran, and driving them forward towards the 4th Regiment with his sword. During these courageous efforts a ball passed so closely to his head that his queue was severed and a bloody welt raised on his neck. Similarly, Veeder, with sword in hand, braced the men, ordering them to stand their ground.[448]

As Lieutenant Abram Quackenbush of Visscher's 1st Company moved along the edge of the roadway, he was brought up short by the very familiar guttural voice of his boyhood Fort Hunter Mohawk friend, Bronk-a-horse. They had served together under Sir William in the French war, and just before the Indian left with Sir John to go over the Adirondacks in 1776, he visited Abram to offer him a commission in the

Crown's service as requested by the baronet. Bronk-a-horse hoped his friend would serve beside him in the current conflict, as he had in the last, but Abram refused Johnson's offer. Now his Mohawk friend called to him to surrender, warning that no quarter would be given to men taken in arms. Again, Quackenbush refused his friend, and a grim stalking began. Both men were expert marksmen. The Mohawk fired first, planting a ball a scant inch above Abram's head. Seizing his chance, Abram broke cover and drove a ball through the body of his boyhood friend, who moments before risked himself with an offer of safety.[449]

Klock's Palatine regiment was embattled on the roadway midway between the two ravines. Henry J. Walrath recalled the regiment had been "marching through a piece of woods, where the underbrush were very thick" when the "Indians rose & with a dredful yell poured a destructive fire upon [us] . . . three of his companions were shot down at his side." He recalled being "in the hottest of the battle" and "fired nine times & then the Indians rushed up and took him prisoner, tied a cord around his neck & fastened him to a tree."[450]

The brigade was being forced into a concentration. Ahead of the 2nd were the 1st's companies, heavily engaged and slowly being pushed backwards. Behind the 2nd was the 4th and beyond them, just above the first ravine, were the 3rd's lead companies, which Visscher and Veeder were driving up the gentle slope towards the 4th.

Herkimer's tactic of forming on the road had proven ineffective, and the Indians mauled the militiamen. Klock's adjutant, Anthony Van Vechten, became so distraught, he ran amongst the men crying out in Dutch in fear and despair that all was lost — an indiscretion that deepened the panic amongst those within hearing.[451]

When the companies on the road disintegrated and the men took to the trees, they fought as a confusion of individuals, without employing even elementary defensive tactics. After about forty-five bloody minutes, the character of the battle shifted as the men formed into defensive circles. The former commander of the 1st Regiment's 4th Company, Captain Jacob Seeber, who had just returned Continental service in the 4NY, was marching as a volunteer. He understood the value of mutual support and spread the idea amongst Cox's men, and the tactic slowly filtered to the other regiments. Some participants claimed later that this measure was adopted in Klock's regiment through the persuasion of Private Jacob Beeler.[452]

Bellinger's companies advanced to join Klock's men under a punishing fire from both flanks. They drove the Indians from the edge of the higher ground with clubbed muskets and bare hands and, when joined with the 2nd Regiment, formed into defensive circles.

As the realization they were trapped dawned on the militiamen, a grim resignation washed over them. Somewhere, deep inside, they found the will to put up a stiff resistance. In Butler's words, the rebels "recovering themselves, fell back to a more advantageous ground, maintained a running fight."[453]

Some tried ruses to tempt the natives into exposing themselves. Captain Christopher W. Fox of Klock's 3rd Company drew an opponent's fire by raising his hat, but he misjudged the height and a ball punctured his arm.[454]

As the militia drew together behind trees to support each other, more care was taken with loading and some men charged with buck and ball.[455] At short ranges, this load could be devastating, as near misses were converted to hits by the spread of the buckshot. With the militia's newly found resolve, the Indians were threatened with heavy casualties, a punishment they traditionally avoided. As well, their ardour was dampened by the loyalists firing at their backs while they were engaging the rebels in front. Cox's men gained a temporary respite.

The battle's momentum shifted to the Royal Yorkers. With the column's head stubbornly holed up under cover, Sir John judged it was time for the bayonet, and so he turned to Watts's young men. Almost all were Highlanders: six were Grants, five McDonells, four Rosses, three Murchisons, two Camerons, two McPhersons, and many others had Scottish names like McLean, Chisholm, Ferguson, and Urquhart. These youngsters had grown up in the glorious traditions of the clans with stories of charges with the vicious Lochaber axe, the wicked dirk, and the double-edged claymore. The Iroquois had nothing to teach the Scots about close combat with edged weapons. Fresh in their minds was the humiliating "Peacock Expedition," when sneering militiamen scorned their folk and took hostage their honourable leaders. The majority of them had come over the Adirondacks with Sir John and could remember that ordeal as if it were yesterday. Overlaying these thoughts were tales of Highland valour at Killiecrankie, Falkirk, and Prestonpans. Like the Indians, warrior blood pulsed in their veins. The handful of lads who did not share a Highland heritage were inevitably caught up in the heat of passion. No Scotsman would show them up!

Watts, the son of an Edinburgh-born father, passed the word, and the hungry triangular bayonets were drawn from their scabbards and fixed to the muskets with an ominous slithering clank and click as the sockets went home. Led by Watts, Singleton, and McKenzie, each armed with a bayonetted fusil, the company advanced in two ranks in deadly silence. As they closed with the 1st Regiment, they fired a volley at the hidden foe and, giving full throat to a raging Highland shout as terrible as an Iroquoian war halloo, they rushed into the trees.

Many militiamen were without bayonets to counter the charge. Once they discharged their firearm, they faced the charging Lights with clubbed muskets or hatchets and hangers in hand. A few may have thrown their axe, but most were unskilled with this weapon. Some resorted to flight; others stood, dodging the thrusting bayonet and striking at their foe. It was a vicious encounter.

The most resolute of the 1st Regiment held their ground against that charge.[456] One of those was Volunteer Jacob Seeber, the ex-Continental, who took a fatal gunshot wound to his leg. Another was forty-five-year-old Major Samuel Clyde, a veteran of the Seven Years War. Although he was at the forward edge as the charge came in, he missed being bayonetted and was driven to the ground by a blow from a clubbed musket. Recovering, he swept up his firelock, fired at Lieutenant George Singleton, and had the satisfaction of seeing him go down. Later, Major Clyde picked up his victim's fusil as a trophy.[457] But the major was an exception; most men along the edge of the woods scrambled back in disorder or died in place.

No matter how resolutely executed, bayonet charges have limited utility. They depend upon shocking and breaking the thin shell of a defensive line, but the militiamen were in depth amongst the trees and the rush soon petered out. When the Lights pulled back, Singleton was carried to the rear with an ugly wound in his leg, enraged with the passion of the charge and the pain. A number of other youngsters were carried out of the trees with gunshot wounds, slashes, split heads, and broken collarbones.

General Herkimer had been carried to a resting place under a beech tree not far from his fallen mount and propped against his saddle, which had been stripped from his dead mare. The 4th Regiment's surgeon, Doctor Petrie, attended to his wounded leg, but blood continued to seep through the dressing. After calmly filling his pipe, the general lit it with his pocket knife and a flint arrowhead. Of course, Herkimer's purview of the overall battle was extremely limited by the dense woods that surrounded him, but when aides and officers brought messages about the progress of the fight, he was able to respond with a handful of calm, reassuring orders. It was suggested that he should be moved to a place of less danger and he quietly answered, "No, I will here face the enemy."[458] His serene courage inspired all those who were close by him.

Herkimer knew that his companies would be difficult to tackle if they could be properly concentrated and reorganized. He observed that the defensive circles were useful, but insufficient to defeat the wily, agile warriors who rushed in and struck a man as soon as he fired. The men were still uncoordinated. Herkimer ordered the men to operate in pairs, one man firing while the other waited for his partner to reload.

Two veterans of the failed Canadian campaign, who were serving in Captain Hess's 1st Company of Klock's regiment, paired up behind a tree. George Lonis took a shot and stepped back to reload and his mate, Henry Sits, replaced him. When Sits fired, his musket burst. Shaken, but uninjured, Sits searched about for a replacement. Lonis was taking a bead when "the ends of three fingers on his left hand [were] shot off by an Indian and . . . the ball cut his hair above his ear." George would bide his time and get repayment later.[459]

Someone, presumably Herkimer, ordered Colonel Bellinger to lead a party towards the corduroy to bring in the men remaining on the lower ground. The party sortied from the concentration and drew in Visscher's three companies.

While the brigade continued to consolidate on the slightly higher ground between the ravines, single men and small groups still blundered about on the periphery. Many fell to the scalping knife; a few became prisoners. Garret Walrath of Cox's regiment was captured by an Indian who tied his arms and led him away. Garret slyly stumbled against the native's back several times, complaining that his tightly bound arms were making him lose his balance. On one of his staggers, he drew the Indian's knife from its belt-sheath and plunged it into his bowels. Freeing his binding, he rejoined his mates and was quickly rearmed to continue the fight.[460]

Captain Fox of Klock's regiment sent Brigade Surgeon Moses

Tryon County militiamen — "in the hottest of the battle"

Pen and ink drawing by Scott D. Paterson, 2000.

Younglove to retrieve some men he had spotted outside the perimeter. As he drew near, Younglove hailed them in German, but when they responded, he realized they were Hessians and abruptly turned back. The Jägers fired and missed, then moved to cut off his retreat. Younglove escaped, but blundered into some British Indians, who "were scalping and cutting the throats of the wounded." He saw "an Indian sucking the blood from the throat of a white man and passed a white man and Indian both so badly wounded that they could not stand and were fighting with their knives as they lay on the ground." Indians surrounded Younglove and came at him with great fury. He quickly handed his rifle "to a stout elderly looking warrior." When another native tried to pull his watch from its fob, the chain broke. Younglove thrust the watch into the older man's hand and was rewarded with protection from the others' tomahawks.[461] A Royal Yorker serjeant was close by and the aged native gave Younglove to him.[462] The serjeant took Younglove to a depot where several prisoners were being held. Soon, Lieutenant George McGinnis and some other rangers arrived. McGinnis had recently heard that the committee had persecuted his mother, Sarah, by confiscating and selling the family farm. He was in no forgiving mood, and, recognizing the surgeon as an arch rebel, made to tomahawk him. Younglove pled for his life as the rangers stripped the prisoners' breeches' buckles and spurs. Perhaps a few resisted, as Younglove claimed the Tories murdered them, spattering his face with their blood and brains.

Younglove was taken to a place where Johnson, Butler, and the war captains were discussing the battle. Butler demanded to know what cause Younglove was fighting for, and he replied with many strident reasons for opposing the King. Whether Younglove was as provocative as he recalled is an open question, nor is it known whether Butler flared in anger and remarked "he was a damned impudent rebel," or whether the ranger urged some Indians to kill the surgeon. If there had been such a request, it is unlikely it would have been ignored. Still later, the surgeon was seated on a log when other Indians burst upon the scene. In fury, they struck out at him to revenge their losses and he claimed that Sir John shielded him.[463]

Sir John was recognizing a shift in the battle's tempo. Clearly, all forward movement of the column was blunted. With their horrendous casualties, there was no chance the militia would rally sufficiently to resume their advance. Their remnants were compressing into a strong defensive position, which the natives were unwilling to assault. The chiefs were vehemently complaining of their losses, and their desire for revenge would not outweigh such a great and obvious risk.

With most of Brant's men and the Mohawks pursuing the 3rd Tryon's rearguard, the militia outnumbered the men at his disposal. His Lights had attempted the shock of a bayonet charge at considerable cost and, in the process, proven that the militia position had too much depth to employ that tactic again. He had only a small parcel of rangers, a battered company of light infantry, and a Jäger detachment that was ill equipped for in fighting.[464] Such a combination was unlikely to crack Herkimer's defence. To break in and rout the militia, fresh infantry was required.

Sir John decided to return to camp, report to St. Leger that the column was halted, and dispatch reinforcements to finish the chore. He advised the war captains and Butler of his plan and departed, leaving to them the task of keeping the militia bottled up in their lair and wearing down their resistance. Sir John took with him some letters and dispatches that had been discovered in the detritus of the battlefield.

The captured militiaman Henry Walrath was still bound by the neck to a tree when a dozen Lakes Indians came up, loaded with plunder from the wagons. After untying him, they joined with Sir John to return to the camps,[465] where they would store their loot and parade their prisoner.

According to Surgeon Younglove, on the march back, the Irish-born Montrealer George Singleton, whose leg wound may have been playing him hell, betrayed his Celtic roots and urged some passing Indians to kill the surgeon. They demurred, providing yet another mysterious event in Younglove's colourful account. Singleton spoke Mohawk and his request would have been crystal clear, so it seems unlikely that the vengeful Indians would have ignored such a plea. Younglove claimed that the ranger Benjamin Davis, "formerly known in Tryon County on the Mohawk River," perpetrated "frequent scenes of horror and massacre" on the route to the "enemy's head-quarters."[466] The natives had suffered many casualties, so it is possible that Younglove's repeated stories of revenge killings of captives were true; however, it seems miraculous that he survived, surrounded, as he claimed, by so many instances of lethal horror.

The bloody conflict had obscured the darkening atmosphere that hung on every quarter. With the oppressive heat and stultifying humidity of those early August days, the weather had been constantly threatening to break in another great storm, yet when the deluge fell upon the combatants, none were prepared for its remarkable violence. After a few warning patters, the rain coursed down.

John Petrie of the 4th took shelter under a large tree and soon after heard "whooping." Peering out, he saw a party of Indians come together within his range. He had "managed to keep his priming dry" and "instantly drew up his piece and brought down a . . . warrior. The rain prevented their seeing the smoke to determine from whence the bullet came . . . but they took the precaution to change their position. Having reloaded his gun, still unperceived by his foes, he got a deadly aim upon another, but just at that moment a drop of water reached his priming, and his gun gave but the ominous 'click,' hearing which, the rascals fled from that locality."[467]

The pelting shower was particularly refreshing to the hard-pressed militia and equally cooling to the ardour of the skulking Indians and loyalists. The rain fell like an opaque curtain between the opponents, and the clamour of battle abruptly died to be replaced by the thrumming pulse of the downpour.

~

CHAPTER EIGHT

TYRON COUNTY SMILED THROUGH TEARS
A Success So Signal

After an hour, the rain lifted.[468] As a minimum precaution, the Crown's men reset their priming and pricked clear their touch holes.[469] The Royal Yorkers were fortunate that St. Leger had ordered a supply of waterproof covers, and those who were quick off the mark when the storm broke were able to keep their locks dry. The rangers and Jägers probably had similar kit, so there would have been few drowned muskets in the Crown ranks. In any event, special tools were issued to line troops to extract balls and draw wet cartridges,[470] if that degree of maintenance was required.

The militiamen were expected to supply themselves with similar tools, and the experienced and prudent would have done so, but likely many others did not, and drowned firelocks could have been quite a problem. During the break, the militiamen collected cartridges and firearms from the wounded and fallen, but the lack of common bore sizes was an irritation. The militia was rarely well stocked with cartridges, and the supplies in the wagons had been looted or spoiled in the downpour.

General Herkimer had taken advantage of the lull to reorganize a strong defensive position in the blowdown above the corduroy. The Indians recalled that the "remnant of the Enemy retreated in good order to a Pine Wood Thicket, of very difficult access, encumbered with fallen Trees, — where they could not be assailed, but at a great disadvantage." On its east side, the blowdown was bordered by the first ravine with its corduroy bottom and tangle of wagons. The deep ravine was on its west flank, and to the north a slope fell off to a bog, beyond which was the river. The Stanwix road exited the blowdown at its southwestern edge. At almost every compass point, except for the narrow open road, the attackers would have to attack upslope.

Herkimer's saddle had been moved inside the perimeter and the general sat propped against it under a large tree, smoking his pipe and sipping water from his canteen, which a volunteer had filled from a hole at the bottom of a small ravine.[471]

Soon after the rain stopped, the Indians and troops began to creep forward through the drenched undergrowth and rivulets of run-off. A steady, random patter muffled their careful footfalls as drops fell from the leaves overhead. Blacksnake recalled a gruesome picture: "I thought at that time the Blood Shed a Stream Running down on the Decending ground during the afternoon, and yet some living crying for help. But [we] have no mercy . . . for them."[472]

When contact was re-established, the firing was sporadic, the sounds hollow and flat in the drowned forest. In the moisture-laden air, powder smoke hung in tendrils, obscuring everyone's vision. As in the late morning fighting, individuals and small groups attempted to penetrate the perimeter to force a breakdown of the defence.

Evidence suggests the Jägers crept up the western edge of the deep ravine and found "hides" from which they sniped into the position,[473] making movement very dangerous indeed.

Hanau Jägers in action

Ink and wash drawing by Norman J. Agnew, 1999.

In the northwest corner of the perimeter, a tall, lank militiaman of the 1st Company, 3rd Regiment, named Henry Thompson, came to his captain, Jacob Gardinier, to complain of his hunger. Thompson was employed in Gardinier's blacksmith shop, and Jacob was familiar with his odd ways. Thompson was ordered to return to his position, but he pled again and Gardinier told him to eat if he must. Thompson promptly sat on a corpse and ate his fill while enemy balls whirred overhead.[474]

Captain Christopher W. Fox, 3rd Company, 2nd Regiment, who had earlier been shot in the arm while attempting to trick a native marksman, sat amongst his men with his wound partially dressed. He spotted a wounded Indian crawling away and, after calling for cover, stole out of the position with his sword in his good hand. On nearing the Indian, he thought he recognized William of Canajoharie. Fox recalled the Indian asking to be spared, but he took no pity and ran him through. While the thought of a hardened Mohawk warrior pleading for his life strikes a false note, that Fox would not think twice about dispatching William is easy to believe, as that strutting, arrogant Tory was wanted for killing a Whig in a barroom brawl.[475]

When Sir John Johnson arrived at the camps, he reported to St. Leger and gave his opinion that additional troops were needed to finish the job. He received permission to send a reinforcement and ordered Captain-Lieutenant Donald John McDonell to march the Colonel's Company, which appears to have replaced the Light company as the camp guard, with attachments from Gray's, Daly's, and Angus McDonell's. While no specific record has been found, it is probable that no more than seventy men were sent, as so many Royal Yorkers were hard at work building the road across The Carry and manhandling the stores.[476]

The reinforcements may have been a trifle sobered when they saw the wounded men who had been brought from the ambush. No doubt, they heard accounts of the vicious morning combat; however, like most young men entering their first combat, their thoughts were on deeds of valour, not personal vulnerability. Those with previous service were more circumspect.

Most of these men had come away with Sir John in May of 1776, but others had arrived later from the Valley with wrenching tales of the harassment of loyalist families. Some of those stories concerned the families of the men who were about to march with McDonell. These men were motivated.

Lieutenant William Byrne and Ensign Richard Lipscomb were the subalterns of the Colonel's Company. The Irish-born Byrne was from the Kingsborough Patent, north of Johnstown. He had joined the Royal Yorkers in Quebec on the regiment's founding day, so he must have left the Valley with Guy Johnson in 1775 and may have served in the Quebec militia during the defence of Canada. Lipscomb had been a Royal Navy midshipman. He had entered the regiment in September 1776 as a Canadian gentleman volunteer in the Colonel's and by the next May had become its ensign. Both men ended the war as 2nd battalion captains, and as only the most active and deserving officers of the 1st battalion received that recognition, there is little doubt about their leadership abilities.[477]

With Captain-Lieutenant Donald John McDonell at their head, the troops marched briskly towards the Oriskany ambush. Once across the western ravine, they moved through the bullet-torn, bloody, and painted bodies of those overzealous Indians who had charged down the road into the volleys of the 1st Regiment. Then they came upon the scalped dead of the militia van and the mangled corpses of the 1st Regiment, some lying entangled with Indians. The bodies were utterly pathetic, clothes soaked and flesh mangled by scalping and ritual mutilation. Some raw, open wounds seemed to be still seeping blood onto the drenched ground. A few may have recognized faces, perhaps of friends or relatives. Most of the reinforcement would have killed, skinned, and butchered game and domestic animals as a way of life; it was quite another thing to see so many mangled humans. For some, all thoughts of brave deeds sank under a pall of nausea and tingling fear. For a few, there was the strange euphoria of seeing revenge fulfilled. As they continued along the road, they passed more and more bloody corpses.

Major John Butler was the senior white officer on the battlefield. Through prisoner interrogations, he had gained information about Herkimer's request to Colonel Gansevoort for a sortie to assist the column. Over the renewed cracks of musketry, he heard cannon fire from the direction of the fort and deduced that a sortie was underway. He reasoned that if the militia also heard the discharges, they would be eagerly anticipating assistance.[478]

When McDonell's reinforcement marched into view on the heels of the cannon fire from the fort, the crafty ranger had a sudden inspiration. Turning to Stephen Watts, he proposed a simple *ruse de guerre*. Watts concurred and went to instruct McDonell.[479] The troops were halted out of sight of the militia and ordered to reverse their regimentals, turning the off-white linings to the outside. Butler reasoned that the inside-out coats would resemble the linen hunting frocks worn by the Massachusetts troops[480] and hoped that this rudimentary disguise would convince the militiamen that help from Stanwix had arrived.[481] If so, the Royal Yorkers might penetrate the defensive circle. The troops were ordered to attack with bayonets alone so they could stab their way through the outer crust of the defence without alarming the whole perimeter.[482]

McDonell's men quickly complied with these orders. The short respite and activity helped them to regain control of their emotions. When their coats were reversed and put back on, they replaced their accoutrements and donned their hats. Fixing their bayonets, they were now ready for the attempt.

There was one more detail to the masquerade. Following contemporary rebel practice, the men were formed into a column of threes.[483] Then McDonell undoubtedly braced them up with a few choice words of inspiration, perhaps reminding them of their families' and friends' treatment at the hands of the craven rebels who were holed up just down the road. That done, the bogus relief force marched, skirted the deep ravine, and stepped smartly towards the defensive circle.

Lieutenant Jacob Sammons of Visscher's 4th Company was the first to see the marchers, and he shouted enthusiastically to Captain Gardinier the news of an approaching relief. Gardinier was not so easily deceived. Somehow he sensed or saw some indication of perfidy and he roared to his men that the enemy was upon them. They may not have heard, or in their fatigue and excitement failed to give credit to his warning.

Spotting an old friend in the column, a militiaman rushed forward, his hand outstretched in friendship. The innocent was quickly entrapped amongst the advancing troops. Gardinier ran forward to protect his man and, butting and thrusting with his spontoon, parried the captors and recovered his befuddled soldier. A pair of Royal Yorkers pursued Gardinier and he downed both. Eager to stop him before he exposed the thin disguise, Captain-Lieutenant McDonell and two of his

John Butler's ruse de guerre — men of the Royal Yorker reinforcement reverse their coats

Ink drawing by Roger E. Roy, 2000.

men grappled with the muscular blacksmith, who demonstrated the usual strength of his trade, well fortified with deadly desperation.

One of Gardinier's spurs became entangled in his enemy's clothing. He tumbled to the ground and was pinioned by a bayonet through each thigh. McDonell made to finish him with a bayonet thrust to the chest, but Gardinier grasped the plunging blade with his bare hand, deflecting it. The momentum of his lunge carried McDonell forward, and Gardinier clutched him in a bear hug, using his body as a shield.[484]

Adam Miller, one of Sammons's privates,[485] who had earlier been taken captive and escaped, awakened to the danger and rushed to the rescue, felling one of the Tories who was bayonetting Gardinier. Young Donald John McDonell was no mean man in his own right, and, with the strength of his father's fiery disposition, wrenched himself free of Gardinier and sprang up to attack Miller. The agile blacksmith saw his opportunity, snatched up his spontoon, and, rising up on his buttocks, thrust the spear-tip into McDonell's throat, killing him outright. In the affray, Miller escaped with a wound to his right hand.[486]

A few of Gardinier's men rushed to assist him, but most were still incredulous and shouted that he was killing friends. Gardinier bellowed that they were wrong; the enemy was amongst them! "Fire away!" he commanded. At last, some responded and opened fire at the Tories in their midst.

The Royal Yorkers saw the game was up and charged forward with their bayonets and, with the tactical advantage of concentration, broke through the defensive skin. Butler and Watts had anticipated this success, and word was quickly spread to tighten the cordon around the perimeter.

The early battle had been shockingly fierce, but now it took a different twist. In the reinforcement were well-known tradesmen and artificers from Sir John's estates and the brothers, uncles, cousins, in-laws, neighbours, and church and school chums of the militiamen — men of the same diverse ethnic mix, Palatines, Dutch, Irish, Scots-Irish, and English sprinkled with more Highlanders. No love was lost between the militia and these Tory refugees. The fear and anger of the ambush and the passions of opposing loyalties boiled over. Some militiamen rose to meet their enemies, "rushing from behind their covers, attacked them with their bayonets, and those who had none, with the butt of their muskets."[487]

Miraculously, Gardinier escaped from his grim struggle and severe wounding. Not stopping to rest or have his wounds dressed, he crept

Tryon County Smiled Through Tears

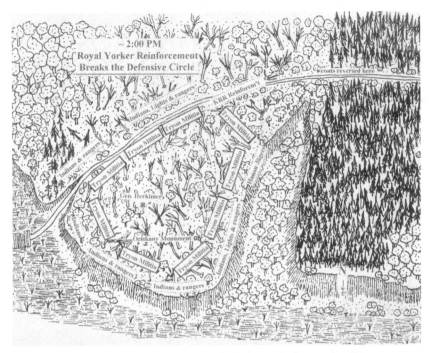

*Oriskany — 2:00 P.M., Royal Yorker reinforcement breaks
the defensive circle*

Gavin K. Watt, 2000.

into a cavity in the base of a tree and called to his waiter to collect the firearms of the fallen. The lad loaded them one after the other and passed them to Gardinier, who used them to good effect.[488]

Inside the tangle of the defensive position, the twice-wounded George Walter of Klock's regiment lay beside General Herkimer and watched three Royal Yorkers rush at Captain Andrew Dillenback of the 2nd Regiment to take him prisoner. Dillenback had boasted he would never be taken alive and fought like a wildcat. One Tory seized Dillenback's musket; Dillenback wrestled it free, reversed the butt, and drove it into his attacker's face. Then he shot the second man and bayonetted the third. As Dillenback stood victorious, a ball hit him in the head and killed him. That this fracas occurred within sight of Herkimer's position on the east side of the blowdown illustrated the depth of the Royal Yorkers' penetration.[489]

The snarled tree trunks formed a latticework. Where two or more trees overlaid each other, men created strongpoints, but their sight lines

Wounded General Herkimer calmly smoking and issuing orders while propped against a beech tree — this famous interpretation makes Herkimer look older than his forty-nine years

Engraving by James C. Bear after an unknown artist.

were very limited and it was possible for the enemy to overrun a neighbouring position without it being obvious. Somewhere inside the circle, Captain Henry Diefendorf, commander of the 1st Regiment's 5th Company, grappled with an Indian, bore him down, and ran him through with his sword. Diefendorf then dodged behind a standing tree as a second assailant came at him. George Casler, one of his privates, saw the charging Indian and shouted a warning to his mate, William Cox. Hearing the yell, Diefendorf bobbed out for a glimpse and took a ball in the chest. Just then Cox fired and the native veered off, bounded into the air, then collapsed to the ground. Cox reloaded and ran to investigate. He found the Indian had a broken leg. The warrior threw up his hand and shouted what sounded like "you-ker! you-ker!" Cox supposed this was a plea for quarter, but he paid no heed and fired a ball into his head.

Diefendorf lay on the ground, every breath causing his shirt to flutter around the hole in his chest. In a faint voice, he begged for a drink. Henry Sanders stamped his heel into the boggy ground, and when dirty water seeped into the depression he ladled it into his shoe and gave his captain this small relief. Diefendorf expired shortly afterwards.[490]

Steady pressure around the perimeter coupled with the penetration into the northwest wall collapsed much of the defence. Butler reported, "At length the Indians with a detachment of the Yorkers and rangers, pursuing that [opening] blow, utterly defeated them with the loss of 500 killed, wounded [and] taken."[491] Adam Miller recalled that "[t]he enemy appeared to be the strongest party and succeeded in taking a number of arms from the American army."[492] For the Royal Yorkers, this success had a cost. As well as McDonell's death and several men wounded, the "gallant" Stephen Watts, "whose amiable qualities deserved a better fate," was lost somewhere on the bloody field with three wounds, including a massive opening in his leg and a bayonet puncture through his throat.[493]

Watts had spotted Colonel Peter Bellinger, commander of the 4th Regiment, and was stalking through the tangle of trunks to position himself for the kill when Private John Leathers stepped from behind a tree and shot him down. The fallen captain was attacked by some militiamen who slashed at him, stuck a bayonet into his throat, and left him for dead.[494]

The mopping up of the most stubborn militiamen was underway when sounds of heavy firing were heard from the direction of the fort. An Indian runner arrived and advised that a sortie from the fort had struck the undefended camps. The cry "Omenh!" — the Iroquoian signal to withdraw — was raised, and most of the Indians departed the bloody field to save their women and possessions.[495]

The Jägers, rangers, and Yorkers, the latter very aware of how sparse the guard had been in the camps, broke off contact and, collecting what wounded and dead they could find, followed their native allies. It was about three o'clock. Including the break for the storm, the battle had raged for six brutal hours.[496]

The relief of the survivors of that final onslaught might readily be imagined. They could scarcely credit their good fortune. One participant reported that "[O]ne hundred and thirty men were left fit for duty" out of the eight hundred who had marched in the column. A few days later, a committeeman wrote that 150 had "stood the field," and the heroic poem about their deeds read, "Not one Hundred Fifty Remained on the field who forming in a circle determin'd not to yield."[497]

After seeing the enemy retire, the survivors cautiously emerged from cover. Ensign Putman, who had shared a tree with Captain John James Davis, commented that the Indians "have pretty much all left us." Davis had just replied that "some of them are lurking about here yet," when a ball passed through his throat, killing him instantly. Putman saw the sniper break cover and sent a shot after him. The Indian ran on at full tilt, then suddenly staggered and fell. Putman found him dead and rifled his possessions, keeping a small compass as a trophy.[498]

Davis's death was quickly followed by the capture of Adam Miller by a party led by the ranger captain, John Hare. Colonel Bellinger spotted

Hare's men spiriting Miller away and ordered his men to fire. Fortunately for Miller, their aim was true, and in the confusion he escaped and Hare was killed. Also slain was ranger captain James Wilson, but whether in this same action or not is unknown.[499]

The militia had no thought of continuing the march to Stanwix; their bodies and spirits were exhausted, to say nothing of their ammunition. They collected their wounded and set about building litters.

A coterie of devoted men gently lifted General Herkimer from his blood-sodden station and placed him on a stretcher of poles and blankets. Three Indians, who had patiently lain in wait for just this moment, rushed at the general to finish him. Alert guards saw them and a fusillade took the assailants down. Some veterans of the action recalled these shots were the last of the battle.[500]

George Lonis, who had earlier lost some fingers to a gunshot, was a tough bird. Two winters before, he had frozen his feet during the invasion of Canada. Somehow, in the confusion of the aftermath, he had the wits to collect a Tory prisoner and find an enemy officer's horse complete with a portmanteau containing a uniform coat, some linen, and a pewter teapot tied to its tack. George made six dollars when he sold the coat and more money later when he sold the horse. His family had the joy of the teapot.[501]

Derick Van Vechten, who later became an ensign, was also thinking ahead, but in a more selfless, practical vein, when he retrieved and carried off seven firelocks.[502] George and Dereck were exceptions; most survivors were physically drained and devoid of much initiative.

Some men searched for relatives. A friend asked a survivor named Fox if he had seen his brother. He replied "no" and then asked if the friend had seen his brother. "No" was the answer. Fox moved through the fallen turning the scalped corpses over to search their gory faces. He had no success.[503]

Those who were physically able were instructed to hoist the litters and carry the bleeding and groaning wounded down the slope and across the choked causeway. About fifty wounded were all that could be borne, and that was possible only with the assistance of Captain Whitaker's men, who, having missed the rendezvous at Fort Dayton, had just arrived to join the brigade. Of course, the walking wounded made their own way out.[504]

What a terrible sight greeted the men as they began their retreat. The bodies of their fellows were strewn under trees and in the roadway, mingled with those of the foe. There was shock and anguish when they saw dead relatives and friends. Equally, there was also joy and relief when they discovered close friends and relatives whom they had given up for lost.

The Royal Yorker captain Stephen Watts was found with his leg and throat torn open. He had bled profusely and was almost unable to speak. Even after the horror of his experience, Private Henry N. Failing of Cox's regiment found pity and carried Watts to a nearby creek so he could quench his thirst. In gratitude, Watts gave his helper his silver, hunter-cased "bulls-eye" watch. Legend says that his woven silk officer's sash was taken as a souvenir by a man named Sanders who may have assisted Failing.[505]

Once onto the corduroy, the survivors threaded through the tangle of animal and human corpses, harness and wagons, and struggled up the eastern slope, out of that horrid place of death with its stench of gunpowder, blood, and drowned vegetation. They had seen more than enough carnage, but there was more, for all along the road to the Oneida village was the bloody evidence of the rearguard's punishment.

As the survivors struggled along the road somewhere west of Oriska, they were met by the platoon of Rechtor's company of the 2nd Regiment, who had been left behind to guard the baggage. Rechtor's men had been greatly alarmed by some fugitives' tales of disaster, and he and his subalterns decided it was more important to reinforce the brigade than guard baggage.[506] The fresh manpower provided a welcome relief for those burdened with the awkward litters.

Abraham Quackenboss, one of Gardinier's privates, took similar action. He had also been assigned to guard the baggage and horses, but when word drifted back of Gardinier's grave wounds, Quackenboss "took one of the Horses belonging to the Army . . . and went in search of his Captain."[507] The heroic blacksmith welcomed this succour.

When the mournful march reached the Indian settlement, Colonels Visscher and Veeder wearily organized the care of the wounded. A carriage was found and made ready for General Herkimer, and he travelled on. Most of the survivors continued to straggle after him, and only a handful remained behind, so the colonels sent a runner to ask the general to persuade some men to return. Visscher and Veeder struggled on with the help of those who came back, but it was almost dark before most of the wounded were carried over the big hill east of Oriska.[508]

Some exhausted men were unable to help. Jacob J. Failing and three others, who had carried out their wounded subaltern, Ensign Henry

Timmerman, fell to the ground and slept as if dead. Conrad Kilts and three friends had borne their neighbour, John Snell, the four long miles to the castle and laid him in a building beside three other men before collapsing into a deep sleep.[509]

Most of the brigade straggled on a further eight miles to the ruins of Old Fort Schuyler, where many wounded lay all night without medical attention.[510] Whitaker's and Rechtor's men did their best to offer comfort, as did a handful of local women who had rushed up the road to meet the returning men.

There were varied reactions in the Valley to the news of the ambush. The detachment under Lieutenant John Zimmerman, which had been sent home to prevent an Indian attack, discovered the alarm was false and marched to rejoin the brigade. On the road, they met some of the rearguard "who informed that all was Lost." Convinced that a horde of victorious Indians was close behind, Zimmerman turned about again and marched for home.[511]

Honyery Tewahangaraghkan's wife, Senagena, rode express to the lower settlements to bring news of the battle and the need for assistance.[512] People brought boats to the ford near Old Fort Schuyler and the worst of the wounded were boarded. Herkimer was one and Jacob Seeber, the ex-captain of Continentals, another. Seeber was put ashore at Fort Herkimer, where his shattered leg was amputated, but the surgeon was unable to stem the flow of blood and he slipped away. The general was taken to the landing below Little Falls and then to his home.[513]

Some veterans recalled that when the ragged column arrived at Fort Dayton, Lieutenant Colonel Campbell and First Major Clyde of the Canajoharie Regiment dismissed the remnants.[514]

The exhausted litter parties, who had collapsed at Oriska, struggled awake the next morning. Kilts and his friends discovered that their neighbour Snell and the other three wounded had died overnight and they struck off for home.[515] Ensign Timmerman had survived, and Failing's group rested till evening, then set out with his litter.[516]

The despondency across the Mohawk region can be readily imagined. When families and friends reunited, the shock of missing faces was keenly felt. In some families, no men returned. The devoutly religious inhabitants were greatly distressed that the bodies of their fallen had been left on the field, yet the fear of the Indians was too great to allow retrieval. Except for a handful, the dead were left to decay in the ravines and woods.

What had been happening at Stanwix during the bloody engagement? It must be remembered that General Herkimer had dispatched three men to the fort on the evening of August 5 with two requests for Colonel Gansevoort. The general advised that he would wait to hear a signal of three cannon discharges before the brigade marched from Oriska and, when the garrison heard small arms fire, he wanted them to sally out to assist the brigade to break through the siege lines. Of course, these plans were disrupted when some of Herkimer's officers forced him to march without waiting for the signal.

Dawn broke over the fort on August 6 after a long night that rang with savage Indian yells. Great alarm ensued when a second sentry in the northwest bastion fell to a sniper's bullet. After that shock, the garrison found the morning's silence ominous and the officers grew uneasy.[517] When they saw parties of Indians leaving the siege lines, they grew suspicious that the expedition was bypassing the fort. If so, the Tories would circulate rumours that the garrison had succumbed and cause wholesale defections throughout the region.[518] Action had to be taken and First Lieutenant Henry Diefendorf,[519] 1st Company, 3NY, "was Ordered to get Ready to set of[f] for Albany this Evening to Inform Genl Schuyler of our Situation."

After several unsuccessful attempts to infiltrate through the British Indian outposts, Herkimer's messengers managed to struggle through an impenetrable swamp and entered the fort in mid-morning.[520] By that time, the brigade was heavily engaged in battle at Oriskany.

Gansevoort received them immediately and, after absorbing Herkimer's message, gave orders to fire the requested signal of three guns. This was quickly done and the garrison gave three cheers to celebrate the militia's march. Now, the morning's silence and the Indians' movements were explained and Diefendorf's mission was cancelled.

The messengers had arrived much later than expected, and although no one recorded whether or not the garrison heard the sounds of small arms fire from the battle raging at Oriskany, a sortie was immediately assembled under the command of Lieutenant-Colonel Willett. His force of 250 men was fully a third of the garrison, drawn equally from the New York and Massachusetts Continentals with an iron 3-pounder fieldpiece and a crew commanded by Captain-Lieutenant Joseph Savage.[521] Willett recorded that

> The men were instantly paraded, and I ordered the following disposition to be made; thirty men for the advance guard, to be commanded by Capt. Van Benscouton [1st Coy, 3NY], and Lieutenant Stockwell [1Lt 3rd Coy, 3NY]; thirty for the rear guard under the command of Captain [Jacob] Allen, of Massachusetts troops, and Lieutenant Deuffendorf [1Lt Diefendorf, 1st Coy, 3NY]; thirty for flank guards, to be commanded by Captain —, from Massachusetts, and Ensign [Joshua] Chase. The main body formed into eight subdivisions commanded by Captain Blacker [Bleecker, 8th Coy, 3NY], Lieutenants Comine [Conine, 4th Coy, 3NY], Bogardus [1Lt, 8th Coy, 3NY], McClenner [McClellan, 7th Coy, 3NY], Coffraunder [2Lt Ostrander, 1st Coy, 3NY]; Ensigns Begley [Bagley, 3rd Coy, 3NY], Lewis [4th Coy, 3NY], Dennison [Denniston, 2nd Coy, 3NY]; Lieutenant Ball [1Lt, 5th Coy, 3NY], the only supernumary officer, to march with me. Captain Jansen [3rd Coy, 3NY] to bring up the rear of the main body. Captain Swartwoudt [Swartwout, 4th Coy, 3NY], with Ensigns Magee [1st Coy, 3NY], Ament [5th Coy, 3NY], and 50 men, to guard the field piece, which was under the direction of Major Bedlow [Ezra Badlam, MA].[522]

As the whole garrison was on an alarm status, the force was quickly formed-up, but a sudden downpour swept over the fort and everyone was dispersed to the barracks.[523]

The rain abated after an hour and the drums beat assembly. The sortie marched out and its elements took up their assigned roles on every quarter. Remarkably, their exit and march were entirely unopposed; not a single Hessian or Indian sniped at the column. The troops marched along the old military road to the Upper Landing, where the roadway lay within fifty yards of the opposite shore. With sensible foresight, Willett detached Major Badlam with Savage's fieldpiece and

Swartwout's infantry guard at the Landing to cover his route of withdrawal in case of a British counter attack.[524] He then resumed the march towards the Lower Landing.

Prior to Willett's approach, an Indian arrived at the Lower Landing and told Lieutenant Bird that Sir John was "pressed." Unaware that Johnson had returned to camp, Bird pulled his company from its post and briskly set off to reinforce the ambush.[525]

The appearance of this mysterious Indian, who so fortuitously caused Bird to vacate his post, suggests that the camps had been carefully scouted prior to the sortie leaving the fort. From the scouts' intelligence, Willett knew that the only serious opposition to his foray would be Bird's company, and he sent one of the garrison's Oneida scouts with a message designed to lure Bird away.[526] If this is so, the sortie was executed with cunning, rather than the headlong, opportunistic fervour suggested in Johnson's account. Further, it argues that his intention from the outset was to raid the denuded camps, not to assist Herkimer directly.[527] No matter, there was a need to divert British attention from the militia relief column, and a raid on the camps would achieve that result.

Willett's force travelled the road for a half-mile towards the Lower Landing when it came upon the Royal Yorkers' main camp. The obvious lack of activity in the tent lines was like a magnet. Captain Van Benscouten's advance guard attacked so rapidly that Willett later reported "his extraordinary spirit." The tiny Yorkers' quarter guard was easily driven off, but not before giving the alarm to Sir John, who was in his tent talking with the wounded Lieutenant Singleton.[528]

There is no contemporary record of what happened next, but Sir John must have abandoned Singleton and rushed to his family. The baronet would not risk his wife and children to the vengeance of his enemies for a second time, especially with such vivid memories of the scenes in the ravine.[529] With so few troops at hand, resistance was impossible, and the baronet, his family, and their guards fled to the riverbank with Willett's troops giving a "fair firing . . . while they were crossing the river."[530] Willett may have detached his Oneida scouts to chase down Sir John, as they later reported his probable death.[531]

Flankers were pushed out on every quarter to see if any opposition was close at hand, an as there was none, the camp was thoroughly plundered. Sir John's personal papers, his orderly book, and some dispatch-

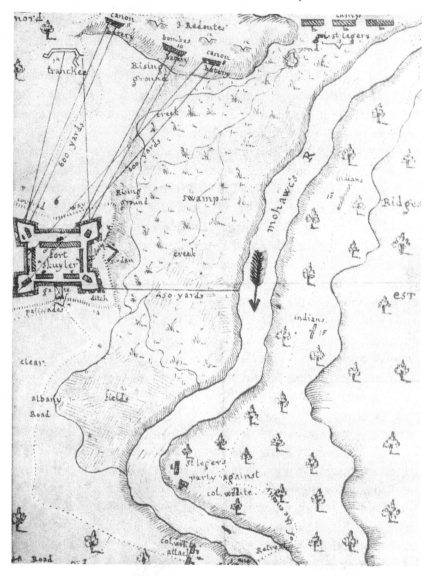

Willett's sortie and St. Leger's deployment in response
Detail from a sketch by Capt. François Louis Teisseidre de Fleury, 1777

Courtesy of the Emmet Collection, New York Public Library.

es and the letters taken from the militia at the ambush were carried off with a Grand Union flag and four camp colours. Goods that were too cumbersome were destroyed or thrown into latrines and offal pits.[532]

The sortie next moved against a large Six Nations camp nearby where militia major Isaac Paris was being held captive. Paris had been spared death by Sir John's intervention at Oriskany, but his luck had run dry. Claus reported that "The few Indns... were oblidged to fly for it, & either leave the Prisr. to the Rebels or destroy him, wch. they did, & always do."[533] That done, the men, women, and children ran for the nearby woods and swamp. Two sick Indians who had been left behind were killed by the troops. The Continentals collected kettles, arms, blankets, a rich haul of Indian finery, "cloaths, wampum & silver work," including the medicine bundle of the Senecas' Little Warriors' Society.[534]

During their rampage through the two camps, the troops discovered six corpses and captured Singleton and three other wounded whites. Willett anticipated retaliation and wasted no time. The detachment reformed and, loaded down with booty, began its return march.[535]

St. Leger reported that he had expected just such a movement, and when word came that a sortie had exited the fort, he ordered Captain Robert Hoyes to take his two companies of the 34th and "immediately . . . cut in upon [its] rear, while they engaged the Lieutenant."[536] But, of course, Lieutenant Bird had already been drawn off and St. Leger's descriptive word "immediately" was quite an exaggeration.

If a damning letter written by St. Leger's regimental chaplain, Reverend Scott, is to be believed, when the warning about the foray reached St. Leger, he was celebrating the Oriskany ambush in the company of Nancy Bowen, one of the loyalist ladies. This little party may have been in progress earlier when some Indians brought militiaman Henry Walrath to St. Leger's tent. Magnanimously, St. Leger had given the prisoner some victuals before he was led away to his captors' camp.[537]

At some point in the get-together, St. Leger called out to his "favourite . . . Come, kiss me Dear Nancy, I have gained the greatest Battle that has been fought this war." Supposedly, she offered the tart rejoinder, "You Sir? Lord, I thought it was the great Sir John Johnson and it was miles from us." Annoyed, St. Leger snapped, "Hold your tongue, you B____. It was my command."[538]

As Reverend Scott held a deep grudge against St. Leger, his highly descriptive account is questionable; however, if such a party was in progress and several glasses had been consumed, a sortie from the fort was probably the last thing on St. Leger's satisfied mind. Captain Hoyes may have made some preparations, but, in view of what occurred, an "immediate" reaction time by any of the British officers is improbable.

Hoyes was no sooner dispatched than St. Leger received the message that Bird had "quitted his post" to assist Sir John at the ambush. St. Leger now grasped the depth of the danger and acted quickly, assembling the hatmen of the 8th and setting off at their head to assist Hoyes.[539]

Hoyes's companies forded the Mohawk to the east side so they could approach the Upper Landing shielded by the trees that lined the bank. This cover proved inadequate and the "Lobsters" were engaged by the fort's guns as they passed in front of the east wall. As they began to form up in a thicket across from the Upper Landing, Badlam ordered Savage to smack them with canister and Swartwoudt's guard to deliver a "smart Discharge of Small Arms." As well, a gun in the fort's southeast bastion added its weight.[540]

The 34th returned fire under this fierce response, but their musketry was "very wild"[541] and they soon panicked and "scamper[ed] off,"[542] which allowed the sortie to re-enter the fort with all its plunder.

St. Leger reported a quite different version of events. He claimed that Hoyes's detachment "with executive fire" immediately drove the enemy into the fort, "without any farther advantage than frightening some squaws, and pilfering the packs of the warriors."[543] Judging from these glib, dismissive words, St. Leger and the 8th's hatmen arrived too late to participate.

Willett's men marched through the fort's gate at about four o'clock with "not one Man being killed or wounded." What an accomplishment — classic planning and execution with the maximum accomplished at little risk.

The five captured colours were raised on the flagstaff to fly under the Continental flag as "Trophies of Victory,"[544] and the men mounted the fort's ramparts to give three lusty cheers.

~

CHAPTER NINE

THE STAND-OFF
Defend This Fort to the Last Extremity

When the Royal Yorkers and Indians arrived back at the siege lines, they were enraged to find their camps thoroughly plundered. To add insult to injury, the Royal Yorkers could see their Union flag and camp colours flying gaily under the fort's Continental flag. The day's great exertions were further soured by the need to put order to the chaos. In the Hessian riflemen's camp, two Jägers were reported missing after the battle.[545] Major John Butler made a quick assessment and determined that two officers and one ranger were dead of the twenty men who had been in the battle and one or two others were missing. The taking of the Royal Yorker roll call was considerably more difficult, as the reinforcement had been so quickly assembled from different companies. In the final analysis, it was found that two men were dead and eighteen were either wounded, captured, or missing in the action.[546] Surgeon Charles Austin was a very busy man.

In the Indian camps, a grim accounting was taken of their casualties. Sixty-five of the 450 men engaged were casualties, a staggering ratio from their perspective. Their grief was manifested in traditional "Doleful yells, shrieks and howlings."[547] The Senecas had been in the forefront of the opening attack and had suffered the worst, losing seventeen dead and sixteen wounded, "of their favourite chiefs and confidential warriors." The Cayugas were almost as unfortunate and later harboured a deep resentment. Old Smoke's son Tocenando, the first prominent Seneca war captain to declare for the Crown, had been killed. In all, nine of the British alliance's war captains were dead.[548]

Their anger was heightened by the women's accounts of being driven off by the sortie and the thievery that followed of their silver, fine clothing, and wampum bundles. Their bark shelters had been burned and scattered and their blankets stolen. Without them, "they had nothing to cover themselves at night, or against the weather, and nothing

[was] in Camp to supply them."[549] Resentment smouldered, and their militia prisoners sensed the depth of their displeasure.

That night, for the first time in the Iroquois Confederacy's history, a council of senior headmen settled a primary piece of diplomatic business by deciding to send a "bloody hatchet" to the Oneidas to give warning that they were now considered an enemy.[550]

In contrast, the day invigorated St. Leger. He ordered Lieutenant Glennie[551] to "complete a two-gun battery and mortar-beds, with three strong redoubts in the rear, to enable me, in case of another attempt to relieve the garrison by their regimented troops, to march out a larger body of the King's troops."[552]

The evening in the fort saw the posting of an exciting order that was even more stimulating than running the Tories' captured colours up the flagstaff. It read "All the plunder taken . . . this afternoon is . . . to be delivered to Adjutant [George] Sytez [so] that an equal division may be made among the party that went out under the command of Col. Willett."[553]

The unopened bundle of letters addressed to members of the garrison and Johnson's papers were found "of some service."[554] Colbrath listed the loot: "Blanketts, Brass Kettles, Powder and Ball, a Variety of Clothes, and Indian Trinketts and hard Cash together with four Scalps" two of which were "neatly Dressed and . . . platted" and "[s]upposed to be those of the Girls" who had been attacked while berry picking.

An interrogation of the Tory prisoners and a review of Sir John's papers revealed that St. Leger's force was "1210 strong [including] 250 Brittish Regulars . . . they are all Arrived and have with them 2 Six pounders, 2 three pounders, and 4 Royals." A note revealed that Captain Watts was suspected dead and that "among the Enemy [was] a Tory named Harkeman, brother to the General."[555]

Of personal importance to Colonel Peter Gansevoort was a letter from his betrothed acknowledging his letter of July 26, in which he had given her strong reassurances of his safety. Caty said his words were like a "Cordial to a Faint Heart," but shortly thereafter, she had an express from Stanwix saying that three thousand Regulars, Canadiens, and Indians were at Oswego and she became very anxious. As this intelligence had been obtained from Indians, she gave Peter some advice: "I hope you not put much trust on Our Indians. They are a Sett of people not to be trusted on. All my fear is that you will be blocked up in the

Fort and will be forced to Surrender for want of provisions and left to the Mercy of those brutes."[556]

That evening, a wounded Tory from the camps died and a Tryon militiaman crept through the cordon around the fort bringing further word of the ambush. Inexplicably, he slandered Herkimer, claiming that "[I]n the Battle he hid himself in the Mud and Grass, and that General Harkeman and a Number of Regular Officers and Indians passed him in Conversation." Colbrath thought that "This was a Lye"[557] and, as the tension of the siege mounted, the accusations were forgotten.

That night, two senior militia prisoners underwent yet another ordeal. Lieutenant-Colonel Frederick Bellinger of the 4th and wounded Brigade Major John Frey were persuaded to pen a despairing letter to Gansevoort. Sir John Johnson, Daniel Claus, and Major John Butler probably had a hand in this affair, as they were well acquainted with both men. Most of the letter's bare facts were accurate; however, their recommendation that Gansevoort surrender his post suggests the exhausted and distraught pair were subjected to considerable coercion. By half past nine that evening, the letter was finished.[558]

The prisoners already in Provost-Serjeant Killegrew's custody were fortunate, as several attempts to gain release of the four militia officers held by the Indians were rebuffed. Butler later reported their death with the chilling words, they "were conformable to the Indian custom afterwards killed."[559] It was a native tradition to test a captive's courage by taunting him about his coming fate. Undoubtedly, the prisoners received their share of this baiting and spent a chilled night of dreadful anticipation, stripped to their shirts and drawers.

On the night of August 6, there had been some difficulty selecting a man for the dreaded northwest bastion's sentry post where the sentinel had been killed at dawn on the last two mornings. Everyone was astonished when a volunteer stepped forward. In the dark before dawn, the fellow erected a scarecrow sentinel with a hat, watch-coat, and musket propped at the support. He then crouched behind the parapet and peeped through an embrasure.

While this ruse was in preparation, the native marksman, who had been successful two days running, climbed a black oak tree standing some 165 yards from the bastion and waited for first light. As dawn broke, the familiar rifle barked and the crouching sentry saw a telltale puff of smoke rise above the tree. He informed the Serjeant of the Guard and the morning gun was aimed and discharged a round of canister. To the joy of the garrison, the sniper was blown off his perch. An examination of the dummy sentinel revealed the Indian's unerring aim. Had the target been a live man, King George would have had one less enemy that morning.[560]

The southwest flag bastion of Fort Stanwix — each of the four bastions had exposed sentry boxes; however, in fair weather, the sentinels stood in the open for improved observation

An ink and wash drawing by John W. Moore, 2000, after a view of the 1977 reconstruction by Janice Lang Photography.

As the sun was rising in the Senecas' camp, the four militia officers were led out to run the gauntlet. Often, the fleet of foot survived this vicious ordeal with a few lacerations and bruises, but not these unfortunates. The Senecas were in no mood to be charitable, and revenge in full was exacted on the hapless victims.[561]

If we are to believe any of Surgeon Moses Younglove's lurid accounts, the death of Captain Robert Crouse, 4th Company, 1st Regiment, was extremely ugly. It was said that Crouse was the tallest and strongest man in the Valley, and great note had been made of his effortless flourishing of the brigade's Colour during the parade on the frozen Mohawk River in January 1776. Crouse may have given particular offence to the Indians, or his immense stature challenged their dark craving for vengeance. Younglove claimed they hacked off his legs at the knees and forced him to walk on the stumps while they jeered he was no taller than they were. As his life ebbed from his wounds, he suffered other painful indignities, and when dead, they tore off his scalp.[562]

After his visit with St. Leger the previous afternoon, Henry Walrath had been taken to the Lakes Nation's camp where he was pegged-out on the ground overnight. "[T]he musketoes bit him so bad that on the next morning his face was so swelled that he could scarcely see."[563]

The artillerymen, Royal Yorker artificers, and the 34th's infantrymen worked vigorously to build the 6-pounder battery and the three defensive redoubts sited behind it. Captain Lernoult of the 8th was ordered to construct and man a second set of redoubts sited beside the military road near the Lower Landing. He was given the 110 troops of the 8th and a party of artillery for the task and "established himself with great judgement and strength, having an enclosed battery of a three-pounder opposed to any sally from the fort, and another to the side of the country where a relief must approach; and the body of his camp [was] deeply entrenched and abbatised."[564] All well conceived and executed, but a couple of days too late.

Many Indians took advantage of the lull to revisit the ambush site. They completed the collection of their wounded and dead and, in the process, lifted rebel scalps and looted valuables, clothing, arms, and accoutrements. They ranged over the battlefield and no doubt marvelled that along the mile of roadway between the two ravines the trees were scarred by bullet strikes from their roots to almost thirty feet above the ground.[565] No one opposed their foraging, not even the Oneidas. It is not known how many lonely, wounded militiamen were dispatched, but every wounded warrior or corpse brought back to the camp deepened their thirst for revenge.

Claus noted that "The number of the [Indian] Wounded being very great, & the Villages of the confederates at a small Distance, (the most remote three or four Days Journey,) — they began to move them there, where they might be better taken care of, without incommoding their operations."[566]

John Sponable, who had been captured the day before the battle whilst lagging behind the column, was taken away to Canada by a Mississauga party. On the first night, the Indians bundled in blankets around the fire and commenced "a most piteous lamentation" over their losses. Sponable was feeling equally grim about his fate and joined in the howling. One after the other, the natives stopped to listen. After that strange event, John was treated with great kindness, as the Indians believed he had shared their grief.[567]

The expedition lost a most significant opportunity for success on August 7. Old Smoke and Joseph Brant came to Johnson and Claus with a proposal to "pursue the Blow" delivered at Oriskany. This teaming up of the native alliance's senior war captain with the Mohawk upstart was rather remarkable, but clearly Joseph had proven his worth. The two natives reasoned that morale in the Valley would be at a low point because of the militia's heavy casualties, especially as so many political and military leaders had been killed. They believed that an immediate foray would finish the rebellion in the region. The two white officers agreed and Johnson went to St. Leger to obtain permission to "march down the country with about 200 men," Claus, and "a sufficient body of Inds."[568]

St. Leger refused, claiming there were insufficient troops to prosecute the siege. Johnson may have suggested that the Indians be sent on their own; however, St. Leger feared giving full rein to either loyalist or native vengeance, especially after hearing reports of the vicious fighting in the ambush and the brutal, ritualistic killings in the camps. He ignored the obvious strategic advantage that would accrue to himself and Burgoyne by dropping a nest of rattlesnakes in Schuyler's rear. It was a costly oversight, for, as Claus later wrote, "The inhabitants in general were ready . . . to submit and come in."[569]

Protocol demanded that St. Leger hold a council to explain his decision, so he instructed Claus to gather the principal men together that afternoon. When the council convened, the commander repeated the same simplistic explanation given to Sir John and assured the chiefs that, with their continued support, his soldiers would quickly subdue the fort. If the natives promised to refrain from seeking vengeance on the garrison when Stanwix fell, all the public stores would be theirs. The council adjourned and the chiefs discussed this tempting offer till long past sunset before reaching a common accord.[570]

The depth of despair in the lower Valley was dramatic. Herkimer's former brother-in-law,[571] committeeman Peter S. Deygart, thoroughly
alarmed Schuyler by writing:

> [O]n Wednesday the 5th [sic] between Arisko
> [Oriska] and the Fort, the Militia were attacked and
> according to what information I have as yet received,
> the Militia are entirely cut to Pieces; the General is
> killed and with most of the Field Officers… there-
> fore hope you will immediately send assistance or
> this Quarter must of course fall into the Enemie's
> Hands, as the whole of the Militia was in the
> Engagement except a few Guards that were stationed
> in different Places in the County consisting of old
> men and those not able to march, so that we cannot
> if the accounts received be true, (which there is too
> much Ground for) raise another Force to make any
> Stand with.[572]

At midnight, Herkimer's three messengers, Demuth, Helmer, and
Folts, slipped out of the fort to advise the lower Valley of the garrison's
resolve to hold out. In the bustle of activity, two men managed to desert.[573]

At six o'clock in the morning of August 8, an express arrived at
Albany carrying Peter Deygart's letter. General Schuyler digested the
terrible news and testily reported to Congress that he had "not had a
line from any one else on the subject." He assured his political superiors that Stanwix was well supplied with flour, salt provisions,
pease, and cattle on the hoof, implying that the militia's failure to
make a relief would not precipitate an immediate collapse of the
garrison. Nonetheless, he recognized that something had to be
done and immediately set about "to procure a body of men to march
to its relief."[574]

At St. Leger's camp on the morning of the eighth, the Indian council reconvened. The chiefs advised St. Leger that, due to his promise of plunder, they would comply with his request, providing the rebels did no more injury to their people. However, should the rebels continue to resist and cause more native casualties, they would exact a terrible retribution on the garrison and carry death and destruction to the inhabitants in the Valley below.

Meanwhile, at the village of Caughnawaga in the lower Valley, the county committee wrote to their peers at Schenectady:

> We herein transmit you the best Intelligence we could learn from sundry persons who have been in a Battle . . . at Oneida Creek halfway between Oriska and Fort Schulor, between a party of the Indians and our Militia, the dead and wounded as far as we can learn is hereunto annexed; we have received a letter wrote by order of Genl Harkemer; to send up all the militia and other forces we can to their immediate assistance; as the greatest part of those we have already sent are cut off; we therefore expect you will send up to us immediately all the forces you can, and you will please send the like directions to the committee in Albany for like purpose, [so] that we may be enabled to stand [against] our Enemies; Fort Schuyler is still attacked and a smart fire kept up on both sides, God only knows the event.[575]

The annexed list of dead and wounded was sparse and inaccurate; however, Caughnawaga was a long way from Fort Dayton, and the local militiamen were just arriving home from the battle. Herkimer hoped to goad the committees into a patriotic fervour by urging a call-up of the Schenectady and Albany militia, but more likely, he scared them out of their wits by revealing the nakedness of their western border.

In mid-Valley near the Mohawks' upper castle of Canajoharie, a party of warriors, fresh from the Oriskany bloodbath, visited the home of

The audacious Lieutenant-Colonel Marinus Willett, shown wearing the presentation sword given to him by the Continental Congress in recognition of his significant role in the defence of Fort Stanwix

Oil painting by Ralph Earl, ca. 1790. Courtesy of the Metropolitan Museum of Art, Bequest of George Willett Van Nest, 1917. [17.87.1]

their trusted loyalist friend, Hendrick Frey, the eldest brother of the Herkimer's brigade major. The Indians were on their way home and knew that he would want news of their victory over the rebels. Hendrick's sister served refreshments while the men sat round a table, and she was shocked to see that a Mohawk wore her brother John's shirt. One arm was very bloody and perforated by a ball. She rushed to Hendrick and whispered what she had discovered. He reassured her that the garment belonged to someone else, but she knew better, as she had made it herself. Knowing well the native character, Hendrick calmed his sister.

When the Indians had their fill, they took their leave, and Hendrick followed, quietly taking aside the man with the shirt to ask how he came by it. The warrior said he had wounded and captured a rebel officer and, after stripping what he wanted, sold him to a British officer. Reassured that John was alive, Frey returned home to tell his sister.[576] John's plight had obviously softened Hendrick's heart, as not long before, he had publically exclaimed, "With my Brother John . . . I never will make up, but with the Sword."[577]

The expedition's native strength continued to dwindle. The Lakes warriors who had captured Henry Walrath decamped and left for the west taking Walrath, a second prisoner, and a great deal of booty from the militia's wagons.[578]

These defections may not have registered on St. Leger's consciousness, as there were more pressing problems. He reported that "by the unabating labour of officers and men, (the smallness of our numbers never admitting of a relief, or above three hours sleep or cooking,) the batteries and redoubts were finished." These tasks were just complete when Lieutenant Glennie gave a startling report advising that the 6-pounder carriages were "rotten and unserviceable." Serjeant Young's Royal Yorker artificers and the artillerymen were immediately put to work fabricating "new cheeks & axle-trees."[579]

St. Leger decided to summons the garrison a second time. Now he had material with which to cow them — the agreement with his native allies and their dire threats and the letter from Bellinger and Frey about the militia brigade's defeat. As well, it would be useful to have a lull while the 6-pounder artillery carriages were rebuilt.

That afternoon, a party of Indians returned from roaming the battlefield carrying Captain Watts in a litter.[580] Somehow, Watts had managed to staunch his bleeding, and for two days and nights he lay beside the stream where Failing had left him. He was almost delirious, weak from pain and loss of blood from his several, fly-blown wounds. The Indians had taken great care to bring him such a distance and Sir John rewarded them with many traditional words of thanks and gifts.

Sir John prevailed upon Surgeon Austin to do his very best. Watts's shattered leg was removed and his other wounds reopened and cleaned, with special care taken of the throat laceration. Although Watts was a fit young man, it is clear that Austin's care was exceptional, as his patient later served as a one-legged captain of the 8th Regiment, got married, and sired several children.[581] His opponents, Captain Seeber and General Herkimer, were not so fortunate.

With the wasted image of his wife's brother fresh in his mind, Johnson persuaded St. Leger to send Austin with the Flag so that Lieutenant Singleton and the other captured soldiers could be examined.[582]

At the Continental Army's northern headquarters, General Schuyler was fully conscious of the nature of the warfare that threatened to engulf the Mohawk Valley. As the Albany County militia had refused to march to Stanwix's relief, he was forced to weaken the core of his main army by sending more of his scarce Continental troops. Several elements of Learned's Massachusetts brigade were already in the Valley; Badlam's 150-man detachment and part of Wesson's regiment were at Stanwix and Dayton, and, on the sixth, Schuyler had sent Lieutenant-Colonel John Brooks with a detachment of one hundred raw men and boys of Jackson's regiment from Schenectady.[583] He continued the brigade's deployment and ordered Bailey's regiment, the balance of Wesson's and Jackson's, and the 1NY under Lieutenant-Colonel Van Dyck into the Mohawk. This grouping marched from Stillwater with two brass pieces of field artillery.[584] Several days of heavy marching would see them at German Flats.

At Stanwix at midday on the eighth, the British artillery "threw a parcel of [mortar] shells . . . none of which did any execution" and the garrison returned the compliment with a salute of solid shot. In the late afternoon, a British duty drummer stepped out from the siege lines and beat a chamade and a flag of truce was shown. Colbrath recorded, "About 5 o'Clock this evening Colonel Butler with a British Captain & a Doctor from the Enemy came to the Garrison with a Flagg."[585]

Seeking a parley — a British drummer beats a chamade

Ink drawing by Don Lux, ca. 1983. Courtesy of Eastern National Park and Monument Association.

Willett recalled that the emissaries were led blindfolded into Gansevoort's dining room. The windows were shut, candles lit, and the table spread with a serving of cheese, crackers, and wine. The guests were seated at one end of the table and Colonels Gansevoort, Mellon, and Willett sat at the other. The room was filled with Massachusetts and Yorker officers, as it was thought "desirable, that the officers in general should be witnesses to all that might take place."

After "a few common-place compliments" and the passing of cheese and decanting of wine, St. Leger's adjutant-general, Captain William Ancrum, spoke to the purpose of the flag. He presented Gansevoort with a copy of the Bellinger/Frey letter, which the Whig officers immediately viewed with great suspicion. Ancrum advised that

> General St. Leger had with much difficulty, prevailed on the Indians to agree, that if the garrison, without further resistance, shall be delivered up, with the public stores belonging to it, to the investing army, the officers and soldiers shall have all their baggage and private property secured to them. And in order, that the garrison may have a sufficient pledge to this effect, Colonel Butler accompanies me to assure them, that not a hair of the head of any one of them shall be hurt.

Ancrum turned to Butler and asked, "That, I think, was the expression they made use of, was it not?" Butler agreed and he continued:

> I am likewise directed to remind the commandant, that the defeat of General Herkimer must deprive the garrison of all hopes of relief, especially as General Burgoyne is now in Albany . . . sooner or later, the fort must fall into our hands. Colonel St. Leger, from an earnest desire to prevent further bloodshed, hopes these terms will not be refused; as in this case, it will be out of his power to make them again. It was with great difficulty the Indians consented to the present arrangement, as it will deprive them of that plunder which they always calculate upon, on similar occasions. Should,

then, the present terms be rejected, it will be out of the power of the colonel to restrain the Indians, who are very numerous, and much exasperated, not only from plundering the property, but destroying the lives of, probably, the greater part of the garrison. Indeed the Indians are so exceedingly provoked, and mortified by the losses they have sustained, in the late actions, having had several of their favourite chiefs killed, that they threaten . . . to march down the country, and destroy the settlement, with its inhabitants. In this case, not only men, but women and children, will experience the sad effects of their vengeance. These considerations, it is ardently hoped, will produce a proper effect, and induce the commandant, by complying with the terms now offered, to save himself from future regret, when it will be too late.[586]

Willett recorded the answer given to St. Leger's proposal: "[S]hould this be the case, the blood of those inhabitants would be upon the heads of Mr. Butler and his employers, not upon us, and that such proceedings would ever remain a stigma upon the name of Britain; but for our parts we were determined to defend the fort."[587]

The threatening nature of the summons was immediately and openly derided as unbecoming of British officers. Gansevoort proposed a cessation of arms until the morrow at nine o'clock, ostensibly to consider the terms.[588] Clearly, Gansevoort's request had been anticipated, as Ancrum agreed to it without consulting St. Leger. Of course, Gansevoort was happy to make this proposal, as it would consume time, which, within reason, was in his favour.[589]

Ancrum received permission for Austin to visit the wounded prisoners and Dr. Hunloke Woodruff, the garrison's surgeon, accompanied him.[590] When they were finished, the emissaries were again blindfolded and led to the gate.

Late that evening, the garrison sent out a water party and an escort to the river. One of the guards deserted, leaving his firelock behind, and, almost immediately, a British sentinel fired at him. As he stumbled about, another, and then another, sentinel shot at him.[591] This desertion conveniently located the enemy's posts and tested their vigilance, information that was of prime importance to the events that followed.

Despite the officers' bravado in front of the British truce team, their confidence was not so buoyant that they ignored their peril. In an evening meeting, the field officers decided to have Lieutenant-Colonel Willett and Lieutenant Levi Stockwell, "a good woodsman," steal through the siege lines and "get down into the country" where they would give "a proper representation of our affairs" and persuade the Tryon militia into a second effort. They gave no credence to the Bellinger/Frey letter and little to Ancrum and Butler. This was just as well, as other than the fraudulent claim that Burgoyne was in Albany, the information was quite accurate.[592]

As was the case with the three militiamen the night before, this was a bold venture and entirely characteristic of Willett's dedication and spirit. At 1:00 A.M.,[593] the pair slipped "privately through the sally port of the fort" armed only with eight-foot spontoons. They knew that breaking through the thin crust of the siege lines and avoiding the native patrols was a particularly hazardous phase of their journey. They moved silently into the marsh, which lay to the east of the fort, and, reaching the river's shore, "crossed over a log unperceived by the enemy's sentinels, who were not many yards from them." Once across, "they advanced cautiously into a swampy wood" only to find that the night was so black they could not "keep a straight course." Floundering about, "they were alarmed by the barking of a dog," which they thought belonged to the Indians, who had relocated their camp to that side. They decided to wait for sufficient light and leant against a large tree trunk. After several hours, the morning star appeared and they set a northerly course. Having trudged a few miles, they again struck the river, which had curled back to the northeast.

To foil pursuit, they walked in and out of the water, using their spontoons as staves, and sometimes crossed to the other side and walked on that shore. At dawn, they hit upon an expanse of flat rock where they stepped out rapidly, confident that their tracks were concealed.[594]

Willett had foreseen that his disappearance in the dead of night would unsettle the garrison, and he left an address, which was read to the troops at the morning parade on August 9:

My secret and unexpected Departure from the Garrison, by order of Col. Gansevoort will Undoubtedly Surprise you and I dont doubt you will belive me when I Assure you that the thought of parting with you tho but for a few days afflicts me greviously . . .

Let no man's heart fail him, tho he is surrounded with a sett of Cruel Savage Enemies; there Cruelty & Vengence should cause us to double our Fortitude & Diligence. The Enemies we have to encounter with [are] by no means as powerful as they are cruel, and there Cruelty ought undoubtedly to make us the more determined, nor is there any Reason to fear that with the Blessing of Heaven, you will in a very few days be delivered from those direfull enemies with which you are now Surrounded.

You will Easyly perceive the Propriety of my keeping my design a secret from you as it is impossible to Mention it without being in danger of being Counteracted in it by its coming to the knowledge of the Enemy. — for Maloncholy as the Consideration is, it is true that there have been Villains among you, Wretches who void of the obligations they are under to there God and there Countrey have basely deserted to our Cruel and Unatural Enemies.

May God almighty preserve any more of you from this shamefull and Abandoned Crime. — For my own part I assure that not a step that it is possible for me to take for your speedy deliverance shall be omitted nor am I without the most sanguine hopes that I shall soon enjoy the pleasing sight of seeing you again on this parade, & Gloriously Congratulating you on a Glorious Deliverance from your Present Enemies, and in assisting you to divide their spoils among you.

In the mean time I beseech you by all the love and regard you have for yourselves and your Countrey, and all the regard you have for me to persevere in doing your Duty like good Soldiers. Dont be afraid of your Enemies. They are truly a Contemptable pack, — Their designs are of the most barbarious kind, but their power is not sufficient to put there Diabolical purposes into execution — do your duty and fear not, but God Almighty will bless you with success eaqual to your most Sanguin hopes. I am my Dr. Bro. officers & Soldiers

  Yours Most Affectionately, M. Willett[595]

This much-needed, spirited address was received with apparent satisfaction. It represented a superb example of how a dedicated officer could inspire his peers and subordinates.

At Albany, General Schuyler wrote to Colonel Wesson advising that elements of his regiment had marched for Fort Dayton two or three days before. He instructed that, if General Herkimer had returned to German Flats, Wesson was to march to his aid "leaving two Officers and thirty men in Fort Dayton." Or, if the general held "his Ground at Orisko or any where above your post you will also join him, sending me frequent intelligence of what passes in that Quarter and try to get information from Fort Schuyler and let me have it by express."[596] By the time these orders arrived, Wesson knew the details of the disastrous ambush and he kept his troops at Dayton to defend the post against the expected onslaught.

Gansevoort proved a fox of the first water when he gave his answer to St. Leger on the morning of August 9 in words that reflected the garrison's growing confidence that the British lacked the wherewithal to force the fort.[597] The commandant toyed with St. Leger, "Requesting him to send his Demands in writing."[598] St. Leger's reply was a mite testy:

> I have the honor to give you, on paper, the message of yesterday; though I cannot conceive, explicit and humane as it was, how it could admit of more than one construction. After the defeat of the reinforcement, and the fate of all your principal leaders, on which naturally you built your hopes, and having the strongest reason, from verbal intelligence, and the matter contained in the letters that fell into my hands, and knowing thor-

oughly the situation of Gen. Burgoyne's army, to be confident that you are without resource.[599]

St. Leger had been stung when Ancrum repeated the rebel officers' retorts, so he restated the conditions imposed by the Indians and added some comments:

> [A]fter a consultation with each nation that evening, at their fire-places . . . [t]heir answer, in its fullest extent, they insisted should be carried by Col. Butler: which he has given you . . . You are well acquainted that Indians never send messages without accompanying them with menaces on non-compliance, that a civilized enemy would never think of doing. You may rest assured, therefore, that no insult was meant to be offered to your situation by the king's servants in the message peremptorily demanded to be carried by Col. Butler; I am now to repeat what has been told you by my adjutant general.[600]

St. Leger confirmed his bond that the garrison would be well treated if the fort was immediately surrendered. He added that he expected an immediate answer and absolved himself of the consequences to the lower Valley if Gansevoort failed to comply. The message was very much the carrot-and-stick approach, so often successful in this and previous wars.

It is extremely doubtful that Peter Gansevoort suffered a moment's hesitation over "the General's tender and Compassion'd Letter."[601] He had the examples of the infamous Whig defeats at Ticonderoga and The Cedars. Then, there were his family's and sweetheart's expectations that he should stand firm and the Oneidas' urgings to be courageous. Peter was true to the renowned stubbornness of his Dutch origins and sent a brief reply early that same day: "[I]t is my Determined resolution . . . to defend this Fort to the last Extremity in behalf of the United American States, who have placed me here to Defend it against all their Enemies."[602]

Thrice rebuffed, a frustrated St. Leger ordered an immediate resumption of hostilities. His guns discharged "a Number of Shott"[603] and the snipers went to work. The garrison replied in kind. St. Leger also ordered work to begin on a siege trench and, to the dissatisfaction of Capitaine

Hertel de Rouville, the Canadiens, who were more trusted as pioneers than infantry, were assigned to the digging. Serjeant Andrew Young's party of Royal Yorker artificers were kept busy helving entrenching tools.[604]

When the British mortars concentrated on destroying the barracks, Gansevoort became concerned for the provisions and ordered their transfer onto the fort's parade. He also instructed that the "public papers and money in the Hands of Mr. Hanson & the papers in the Hands of Mr. Van Veghten belonging to the Paymaster… be lodged in the Bomb proof in the S.W. Bastion." The shelling during the day produced little result; however, at "half past 10" in the evening, the British commenced a second bombardment that "continued till daylight. Their Shells were very well Directed. They killed one Man and wound'd another, both of our Regiment."[605]

Downriver in the hub city of Albany, precious little was known of the state of the western frontier. The shocking loss of Ticonderoga and St. Leger's arrival at Stanwix had developed cracks in the citizens' previous brave resolve, and from late July through early August the Albany County committee of safety's minutes recorded a litany of the menacing misdeeds perpetrated by local Tories. Then, on August 9, dreadful rumours arrived about the slaughter of Tryon's militia and the committee wrote to the State Council at Kingston advising that their Schenectady peers had requested a reinforcement of militia to protect the town from the expected onslaught by lurking Tories. They had been compelled to say they were unable to offer assistance due to more pressing concerns. With alarm, they added: "A Capt. Mann, of the Militia of Schoharry has collected a number of Indians & Tories; declares himself a Friend to King George, & threatens destruction to all who do not lay down their arms or take protection from our Enemies."[606]

General Schuyler had already advised the State Council that Albany County brigadier Abraham Ten Broeck had ordered his brigade to muster for service against Burgoyne and that neither the Schenectady nor the Schoharie companies would turn out for fear of denuding their communities.[607] The companies that did assemble were dispatched north to counter Burgoyne's advance, and Schuyler wrote that their departure stripped the lower county. Obviously, a great crisis was developing.

By dawn of August 9, Willett and Stockwell were trudging through dense woods. They kept on for all the daylight hours, taking only a few small breaks. By nightfall, they thought themselves free from pursuit and, after a sparse meal of cheese and crackers washed down from a canteen of spirits, they lay down to sleep. Although the days were blistering hot, the nights were chill and, having no blankets, they huddled together and slept fitfully.[608]

The morning of the ninth, Demuth and Helmer, two of Herkimer's scouts who had exfiltrated from Stanwix, arrived at German Flats to bring the first news from inside the fort. Peter Deygart, who had assumed the mantle of chairman of the Tryon committee,[609] immediately wrote to the State Council at Kingston:

> Just arrived Capt. Demuth and John Adam Helmer...
> Concerning the battle on our side, all accounts agree
> that a great Number of the Enemy is killed. The Flower
> of our Militia either killed or wounded except 150 who
> stood the Field and forced the enemy to retreat. The
> wounded are brought off by these brave men; the dead
> they left on the Field for want of a proper support. We
> will not take upon us to tell of the behaviour of the
> rear; so far as we know, they took to flight, the first fir-
> ing... We are surrounded by Tories a party of 100 of
> whom is now on their march through the woods...
> Major Watts [o]f the Enemy is killed[,] Joseph Brandt,
> William Johnson, several known Tories and a number
> of Indians. Gentlemen, we pray you will send us suc-
> cors. By the Death of the most part of our committee
> members, the Field Officers, and several being wound-
> ed, every thing is out of order, the people Intirely
> dispirited, our County at Esopus [Kingston] unrepre-
> sented, that we cannot hope to stand it any longer with-
> out your aid. We will not mention the shocking aspect
> our Fields do shew.[610]

This letter, written only three days after the battle, paints a vivid picture of the county's anguish. Deygart's inaccurate claims for the enemy's casualties showed more invention than hard facts, and the critically significant deaths of so many anonymous war captains and warriors received scant notice.

After a miserably cold night, Willett awoke at first light on August 10 with a painful rheumatic attack in his knee. Undaunted, he and Stockwell set off to the south towards German Flats, but their going was slow as Willett limped for several hours until the exercise and sunshine warmed the joint. Their meagre supply of food was exhausted and only the liquor sustained them as they moved south through dense forest. At nine o'clock, they came across a clearing and gorged on a veritable feast of blackberries. Continuing on, they arrived at Fort Dayton at three in the afternoon. They had traversed a remarkable fifty miles. Colonel Wesson gave them a "hearty welcome" and the welcome news that Learned's brigade was marching to relieve the siege. After some refreshment, the exhausted pair fell into bed.[611]

At Albany, General Schuyler was mounting to ride to the army at Stillwater when a dispatch arrived from Congress. His political masters wanted news of what had been done to relieve Stanwix. His advice about sending Learned's brigade was preceded with a preamble:

> In vain have I exerted every nerve to procure a body of
> men to march to its relief. The militia of this county
> [Albany], in every part of it, are borne down by the
> tories. A great majority of the inhabitants of Schohary
> district have laid down their arms. Accounts are this
> moment arrived that four hundred tories are lying on
> the road between this and Schenectady, and have inter-
> cepted provisions going to the westward.[612]

Congress's question prompted Schuyler to write to Colonel Gansevoort advising that "a Body of Troops" had passed through Albany the previous day "and others are following to raise the Siege of Fort

A Cohorn being discharged — the Indians thought that the mortar's shells were
no more effective than "Apples that Children were throwing over a Garden Fence"

Pencil and ink drawing by John W. Moore, 2000, incorporating uniform details after
F. von Germann, 1778.

Schuyler. Every body here believes you will Defend it to the last and I must
strictly enjoin you so to do."[613]

The Schoharie Valley was indeed a scene of unrest. A Tory uprising
was underway and the insurrectionists were expecting assistance from
the four hundred men on the Albany road and St. Leger's army, which
they believed was marching through the Mohawk Valley.

For all of the hubbub elsewhere, on Sunday, August 10, in and about
Stanwix it was remarkably quiet. St. Leger marked the Lord's Day with
a cessation of arms, and religious services were held in the camps. With
the advantage of the universal Latin liturgy, Father MacKenna spent the
day saying Mass for his multi-ethnic charges.[614]

During the day, a party of Tory soldiers ran "across a Field near the Garrison and set . . . Fire to some Cocks of Hay." The fort's officers debated the meaning of this strange exercise. Some thought the besiegers were about to leave, as they would hardly "Destroy the Hay, it being out of our Reach and much wanted by them for their Troops to lay on[,] as tis certain they have Nothing to Shelter themselves from the Weather except their Blanketts, which they make Tents of."[615] This note is the only hint of the hardships endured by the Royal Yorkers during those nippy August nights.

On one quiet day during the siege, the young Mohawk Valley Tory, Ensign Philip Frey of the 8th, was on picket observing the fort. He was pacing back and forth on a fallen tree trunk when he saw a redcoat venture out of the shadows into a field of peas, his regimental blazing in the bright sun. Frey shouted a warning, but the Irishman had that humorous twist of indifference to danger common to his breed. Frey kept a sharp eye on the embrasures and saw the flash of a gun. A roundshot screamed over, just missing the Irishman and sending him scrambling back to camp. Frey had dropped behind the tree trunk and felt something strangely cold under him. Glancing down, he discovered "he was lying upon a large snake with a brood of little ones." It was his turn to scramble.[616]

Some Indians had been using a burnt-out barn as cover while foraging for chickens. When a Continental marksman sniped at them, they would dart behind the burnt timbers and the framework stopped the ball. On one occasion, an Indian had shot a fowl and was greeted with the usual response. He leapt behind a post, but his back was exposed and the ball grazed his spine and paralyzed him. He shouted for help and his mates dragged him to camp with a tumpline.[617]

Gansevoort was disconcerted by St. Leger's languor and fretted that he was disguising preparations for a night storming of the fort. He "Order[ed] the Guard & Piquet doubled and the Troops to lay on their Arms." Shortly after midnight, the British opened a bombardment that persisted until daylight during which a youngster had his thigh bone broken. The lad was indentured to a local farmer and had been betrothed to the late Lenea Stephane, one of the berry pickers whose scalps lay in the fort as a gruesome reminder of the peril outside the walls.[618]

In the early morning of August 11, St. Leger wrote a dispatch to General Burgoyne advising of his arrival at Stanwix: "[a]fter combating the natural difficulties of the St. Lawrence and the artificial ones the enemy threw in my way at Wood Creek." He gloated over the Oriskany ambush, "[t]he completest victory was obtained, above four hundred lay dead on the field . . . [a] number of whom were almost all the principal movers of rebellion in that country." He predicted that "[t]he militia will never rally," and only apprehended "a reinforcement of what they call their regular troops, by the way of Half Moon." He requested "a diversion" to "greatly expedite my junction with either of the grand armies."[619] Obviously, he continued to believe that an army was coming north to Albany from New York City, which begs the question of whether Howe's plans had been revealed to him by Burgoyne or Carleton. Claus selected one of his most reliable native horsemen to ride express with this message through the woods.

Gansevoort ordered a rotating detail of twelve men to be constantly employed "to keep the Fort sweet and clean as our present Situation will admit of." The quartermaster was ordered to keep as many barrels as possible constantly filled with water.[620] That very day, the besiegers diverted the creek, which provided most of the garrison's water, but the measure had been anticipated and two new wells had been opened within the fort. With these new sources and the old well, there was sufficient water for drinking and cooking, and rainwater was most likely collected for fire control, laundry, and ablutions.

At Fort Dayton early that morning, Willett penned a long report and then set off to find Learned, which he accomplished that "very same night."[621]

At Albany, affairs had reached a nadir and the committee was in turmoil. Chairman Barclay wrote to the State Council at Kingston saying that the city had requested assistance from the New England States only to be told that their militia had been ordered southwards. An appeal to the lower New York counties yielded nothing, as "all their Force are ordered to repel an intended Invasion [from New York City], when a real one is entirely neglected." He commented on Deygart's letter of the ninth and a visit by Herkimer's scout, Adam Helmer:

> [Y]ou'l be informed that the Troops [Stanwix garrison] have done their Duty, and the [Tryon] Militia have behaved very brave; Genl. Herkeimer merits the greatest Praise . . . We can assure you at the same time, that our warmest Advocates and bravest friends of Tryon County fell in that Skirmish. They are dispirited and call for help. None can be sent from this Quarter. The People from Schoharie have informed us, they will be obliged to lay down their Arms . . . We are informed that our Army intends to retreat to Half Moon [between Stillwater & Albany on the west side of the Hudson]. Should they be obliged to take this Step, the western Communication will be opened to the Enemy. The Appearance of a few of the Enemy's Troops on the Mohawk River would immediately make the Inhabitants lay down their arms.
>
> Our feelings for the brave men in that Quarter is very great. The Oneida Indians are much distressed for us. They furnish us with several useful Pieces of Intelligence . . . and beg us to stand with firmness . . . If two hundred [savages] can drive in all the Inhabitants of a well settled Country for upwards of fifty Miles . . . how must the Country suffer when perhaps a Thousand or more are necessitated to join ag't us . . . Gentlemen [, you] may probably think we are panic struck, that the fear of losing our property is the Cause of our drawing so melancholy a Picture. We have we suppose the feelings of other men on like Occasions, but the Distress which must ensue engrosses a great part of our Attention. . . .we are Apprehensive that this City will in a short time be in the Possession of the Enemy.[622]

This letter suggests that their western flank was of more concern to the Albany committee than Burgoyne's large army, which lay at Forts Edward and Miller less than thirty miles away.

At Fort Stanwix that noon, Gansevoort ordered a fatigue party with a subaltern's guard to bring in some barrels of lime, boards, and timber that lay at the foot of the glacis. They sallied under the cover of a shower of rain and, although the enemy was observed mustering "in the Road below the Landing," completed the duty without any interference. At sundown, the British fired some solid shot and shells, and at midnight they sent over another four shells, but a thundershower stopped further bombardment. The night was "very dark and excessive Rainy" and Gansevoort ordered the troops to stand to their alarm posts "lest the Enemy should attempt a Surprize."[623] The siege was working on the commandant's nerves.

Before Schuyler left Albany that day, he wrote to Colonel Van Schaick to order the militia of Dutchess and Ulster Counties to march to German Flats "as they arrive, by detachments, without waiting for the whole to come in" and "put themselves under the command of General Herkimer or Colonel Wesson."[624] He was clearly unaware of the extent of Herkimer's debilitation.

When Schuyler arrived at Stillwater, he wrote again to Wesson repeating the earlier instruction to take the whole of his regiment and "such other Continental Troops as may be at the German Flatts and what Militia you can collect to march to — the Relief of Fort Schuyler, advising Colonel Gansevoort of your approach that he may be prepared to support you in Case of an attack." Schuyler provided Wesson with an understated assessment of the enemy's strength, which he had received from the Oneidas,[625] and appealed for frequent reports, pleading, "Pray let me frequently hear from you."[626] He required prompt and accurate intelligence to make astute decisions and, from his frequent suggestions to reassemble the Tryon Militia, was unaware of how thoroughly they had been mauled. Wesson's few companies and Brooks's one hundred men and boys could not raise the siege without major militia support and that was simply unavailable. In his stress and frustration, Schuyler clutched at straws.

The German Flats committee made the fear-driven decision to release Sarah Kast McGinnis and her two married daughters, Elizabeth and Dorothy Thompson, and Dorothy's teenaged daughter, Margaretha, from confinement at Fort Dayton where they had been held as hostages. The Thompson men were Indian traders and outspoken supporters of the Crown and had been driven off. The family's chattels had been sold at public auction before the women's eyes, and after the sale they were imprisoned at Dayton in miserable conditions. When St. Leger arrived at Buck Island, the rebels' bitterness became even more pronounced, but, after the Oriskany defeat, the committee feared reprisals by the victorious Indians and Tories and allowed the women to return to their empty farmhouse. It would be a very brief respite.[627]

Willett spent the night with Learned and then rode to Albany on the morning of August 12 to bring reports to headquarters.[628]

Schuyler wrote to Herkimer and the Tryon committee to say that a Continental brigade was "on its march to relieve Fort Schuyler." He told them to "exert yourselves to the utmost . . . collect the militia of your county, & join General Learned... I confidently hope that you will act with spirit, and manfully join in repulsing the enemy."[629] His urgings fell on wounded, dispirited and exhausted ears.

As Schuyler had already sent Learned's brigade into the Mohawk, it was ironical that St. Leger's report to Burgoyne, which arrived at the general's camp on the twelfth, said that his only concern was a rebel reinforcement of Continentals.[630] Burgoyne was nonplussed to find his subordinate requesting a thrust towards Half Moon; he thought his Grand Army was already doing all the thrusting it was capable of.

At Stanwix, the besiegers "kept out of sight all day" and did "no firing till Noon when they gave us some Shott and Shells, without doing any damage." The Continentals concluded that the enemy "drew their Forces in the Day Time between us and Orisko, as we have not seen them so plenty these two or three Days as we are used to do. Neither do they trouble us all night, which gave our Troops an Opportunity of Resting." St. Leger's

inaction was perplexing. He may have put all of his hopes into the siege trench and set his troops to dig in relays, out of sight of the garrison. In any event, Capitaine de Rouville sarcastically wrote that, "after five days of bombardment, only three pickets had been cut down."[631] Scant progress indeed!

Major-General Benedict Arnold — a primary figure in the invasion of Canada, the relief of Fort Stanwix (Schuyler), and the defeat of Burgoyne

Engraving after an unknown German artist, ca. 1778. Likely published in Geschichte de Kriege, Nurnberg. Courtesy of the National Archives of Canada, C-021121.

On Wednesday, August 13, Schuyler gave orders to the bold Major-General Benedict Arnold, the great hero of the gruelling trek up the Kennebec to Quebec City in 1775 and the commander of the spirited naval defence on Lake Champlain in 1776. Arnold was about to make his mark in Tryon:

> It gives me great satisfaction that you have offered ... [to] conduct the military operations in Tryon county. You will ... repair thither with all convenient speed, and take ... command of all the continental troops, and such of the militia as you can prevail upon to join your troops...
>
> Henry Glen, Esq; is Assistant Deputy Quarter Master General at Schenectady, to whom you will apply for assistance in waggons and batteaus. If you could procure such a number of waggons as to convey the men's packs, it would greatly expedite your march. Orders are

given to send on a supply of provisions. You will, however-er, not be retarded on that account, as the country is capable of affording a sufficiency for your troops.

Colonel Van Dyck will inform you of the names of the Colonels of militia in Tryon county, and although I have already written to General Herkimer and the General Committee... it will be proper for you . . . to expedite expresses, entreating that the militia may be collected at the German Flats by the time you may arrive there.

A small regiment commanded by Colonel [James] Livingston,[632] is at Johns-Town. The inhabitants of Caghnawaga have offered to hold that post, if Colonel Livingston should be ordered up...

Although the Mohawk Indians are far from being friendly to us, yet it would greatly prejudice our cause if they were insulted. You will therefore take every precaution to prevent it. The Oneidas have friendly sentiments towards us, and must be cherished. They may perhaps be induced to take an active part in our favour. Inclose[d] you a warrant for one thousand dollars in specie . . . to make use of in order to conciliate the Oneidas, and to induce them to assist you. Be pleased to assure . . . that I have provided a genteel present for them.

The inhabitants of Tryon county are chiefly Germans, especially those at the German Flats. I think it would serve a good purpose to extol the action under General Herkimer, to praise their bravery, and give assurances that you may wish to be joined by men, who have so bravely defended themselves. Compliment General Herkimer, and please make mine to him.

It is not only impossible, but needless, to be more particular. I shall therefore only add, that if Fort Schuyler should . . . have fallen into the enemy's hands . . . you will . . . so dispose of the troops as best to cover the country.[633]

Schuyler instructed Arnold to take any ammunition he found at Albany. He expressed doubt that any more lead could be spared, as the supplies from Peekskill had not appeared, but he could take more powder if his allotment was sparse. Schuyler's instructions about the natives reflected his keen understanding of their temperament and his advice to offer praise and encouragement to the Tryon militia was well founded. Their bravery at Oriskany was becoming apparent, no matter how foolhardy their advance had been.

Willett had arrived at Albany and reported to Arnold with valuable intelligence about what lay ahead. He joined Arnold's suite when it rode westwards, but not before he found a reliable conduit through which his report could be made known to the broader world.[634]

At Kingston, the secretary of the State Council sent oddly spurious news to the governor, reporting that a second engagement had occurred at Stanwix: "American Troops there had been successful . . . killed a great Number of Indians and Tories, and some regular or British troops, and beat them with a greater Slaughter of the Enemy than any in this State during the Contest."[635]

Such wishful thinking!

CHAPTER TEN

~

THE PUNY SIEGE
Two or Three Small Popguns

A reckless scheme was launched in the British camp on August 13. Sir John Johnson, Daniel Claus, and Major John Butler were flushed with the success at Oriskany and convinced that a bold display would tumble the rebellion in the Mohawk Valley. Having been constrained by St. Leger's concern about limited manpower and his fear of unleashing the Indians, they persuaded him to dispatch a small, representative party under a flag of truce to intimidate the inhabitants. This detachment's major weapon would be the psychological power of three documents: St. Leger's proclamation, the depressing Bellinger/Frey letter, and an ostensibly forgiving, coercive message signed by themselves as the Crown's representatives for the region.

Walter Butler was chosen to command, and for the role he wore his ensign's regimentals of the 8th Regiment, perhaps to fuel his well-known conceit,[636] but more likely for sensible propaganda reasons. His scarlet coat and a section of five "Lobsters" from the 8th and five from the 34th gave the appearance of solid British support. Indian Department officers Captain Peter Ten Broeck of German Flats and Lieutenant William Ryer Bowen of Tribes Hill went as representatives of influential northern New York families.

Private Hanjost Schuyler of Gray's Company, who was from a Little Falls family, was included in the party. He knew the pathways in the German Flats area intimately and had been a serjeant of Tryon County rangers.[637] His mother and sister-in-law were Herkimers and he was a distant relation of Major General Schuyler. As he was married to an Oneida and frequently lived with his in-laws, Hanjost was as much native as white.[638] For reasons unrecorded, he had fled the county with Ten Broeck the previous October.

Private Christopher Fornyea of Daly's company was also selected. He was a Mohawk Valley farmer and may have been on a special assignment for Sir John.[639] Three Six Nations warriors — a Mohawk, an

Onondaga, and a Seneca — represented the British native alliance, bringing the party's total to eighteen.[640] With a very determined Walter Butler at their head, they set off for German Flats.[641]

During the daylight hours, military routine continued in the fort and Commissary John Hansen mustered the troops, but towards nightfall, the British batteries "Cannonaded and Bombarded for two Hours" and broke the leg of one of Mellon's soldiers.[642]

The British were again quiet throughout the day of August 14, but in the evening they opened a bombardment with shot and shell. Again, a Massachusetts soldier from one of Mellon's companies was wounded, this time in the head, but no other damage was done. At some time between ten o'clock and midnight Private Platt Sammons of Gregg's 3NY Company deserted his post outside the fort's pickets and ran off to the enemy.[643]

There is no specific record of when the British Indians took revenge on their Oneida brothers. For several days, they had been occupied with scouring the deserted battlefield, but the stench of rotting flesh put an end to that activity. They were disgruntled by St. Leger's refusal to allow a drive into the Valley and bored with his siege. His promise of the fort's public stores held them nearby for some time, but when boredom and anger overcame their patience, a party struck Oriska, destroying the crops and houses and running off the cattle.[644] The Oneidas would not be long in retaliating.

General Arnold had sent an express to Colonel Visscher with orders to muster Tryon's 3rd Regiment at Caughnawaga, but when he arrived there on August 14, he found only one hundred men with Captain David McMaster as the highest ranking officer. McMaster's 6th Company had been in the rearguard that had "pulled foot" at Oriskany.[645] Arnold had also sent expresses to the Oneidas, and their representatives were conspicuously absent. Perhaps they were preoccupied over the destruction of Oriska. Arnold hoped for a better response when he reached the German Flats.

At Peekskill, south of Albany, General Israel Putman acted upon orders from General Washington and Governor Clinton and instructed Philip Van Cortlandt's 2NY and Henry Beekman Livingston's 4NY to march immediately to join Arnold's relief force.[646]

As recruits had been disappointingly few, August 15 was a day of joy in the siege camps when more than one hundred loyalists arrived.[647] Eighty-five of the arrivals were from the New Dorlach militia company, led by Jacob Miller, who had been dismissed as their captain in January 1776 for refusing to march against Sir John. Somehow, the company had missed the muster at Fort Dayton. Johnson received the men with considerable satisfaction, but his welcome did not extend to offering their officers and NCOs equal ranks in the Royal Yorkers. Miller and ex-lieutenant Peter Sommers were inducted as serjeants, Ensign John Caldwell as a private, and Francis Clerk, one of the company's serjeants, was accepted as a corporal.[648] Perhaps Miller, Sommers, and Caldwell lacked social status or influence, or their loyalty was somewhat in question.

Whether it was the stingy treatment received by their officers and NCOs or the general despondency in the camps, thirty-six of the eighty-five men returned home. Of the forty-nine who remained, ten joined the Indian Department and thirty-nine the Royal Yorkers.

Seven men named Empey from Stone Arabia and Riemensnyder's Bush joined the Royal Yorkers. Theirs was a harrowing story that spoke volumes about the cost of loyalty so often exacted by rebel neighbours.

In the spring after suffering "ma[n]y Insults and Abuses," Philip Empey, Sr. of Stone Arabia "[was] confined in jail... till he would swear Allegiance to the Congress, but on Refusal, was put in the Dungeon, where he was continued till he expected nothing but Death ... Wherefore, to save his Life, he submitted to swear whatever they desired him."

Empey's next test came shortly after his release, when he, three of his sons, and many other Tories refused to make the muster at Fort Dayton and were made prisoners. The Empeys escaped and took to the woods, but his wife Maria and their younger children were imprisoned in the Johnstown jail. When the "Rebels Reinforcement [was] beat and dispersed" at Oriskany, Maria and the children "were set at Liberty"; however "She returned to her own House, expecting to live in it again; but they beat and abused her in such a manner, that she was carried out by four Men, and left on the high Road for dead."[649]

Philip ordered his sons and their two cousins to join Sir John, while he remained behind to attempt to save his wife. Highly motivated recruits like the Empeys were excellent material, and their service to the King would be long and persevering.

Five Scotsmen joined that same day, four of them "Mc's." An interesting additional recruit was Plat Sammons, the Continental deserter from the night before. It was a rich haul, and many days would pass before another such catch occurred.

In sober contrast, August 15 also marked a small, but significant, tragedy for loyalist aspirations in the Mohawk region when Walter Butler's bold venture came to an abrupt end.[650] His party had arrived at Rudolph Shoemaker's tavern in the German Flats early that day,[651] as the owner had been a King's Justice of the Peace during the old regime and his establishment was a natural venue. Word immediately flashed about the Flats that Walter had important messages from the camps at Stanwix, and people were told to gather that night at Shoemaker's to hear Butler's words.

Inexplicably, Walter ignored the Continental garrison at Fort Dayton, which was only two miles to the east across the river. One after another, Continental officers visited the tavern to investigate. Then Lieutenant-Colonel Brooks arrived with his detachment, perhaps in expectation of escorting the flag to Colonel Wesson at Dayton. He spoke to Butler, received his explanation, and returned to the fort. When he described Butler's version of a truce flag to Wesson, he was ordered to return to Shoemaker's with his men and arrest the party.[652]

In the meantime, several locals, including a few committeemen, arrived at the tavern and received copies of St. Leger's proclamation, the Bellinger/Frey letter, and the darkly worded missive from Johnson, Claus, and John Butler, which read as follows:

> To the Inhabitants of Tryon County
> Notwithstanding the many and great injuries we

Rebellion in the Mohawk Valley

Shoemaker's tavern where Captain Walter Butler's "Flag" party was apprehended

Ink drawing by John W. Moore, 2000,
after a twentieth-century photograph of the original building.

have received in person and property at your hands, and being at the head of victorious troops, we most ardently wish to have peace restored to this once happy country; to obtain which we are willing and desirous, upon a proper submission on your parts, to bury in oblivion all that is past, and hope that you are or will be convinced in the end, that we were your friends and good advisors, and not such wicked designing men as those who led you into error, and almost total ruin. You have, no doubt, great reason to dread the resentment of the Indians, on account of the obstinacy of your troops in this garrison but in themselves, for which reason the Indians declare, that if they do not surrender the garrison without further opposition, they will put every soul to death, not only the garrison, but the whole country, without any regard to age, sex, or friends — for which reason, it is become your indespensible duty, as you must answer the consequences, to send a deputation of your principal people, to oblige them immediately, to what in a very little time they must be forced, the surrender of the garrison — in which case we will engage on the faith of Christians to protect you from the violence of Indians.

Surrounded as you are by victorious armies, one half (if not the greater part) of the inhabitants friends of the government, without any resource, surely you cannot hesitate a moment to accept the terms proposed to you, by friends and well-wishers to the country.[653]

Walter was in full harangue when one of his guards warned that troops were outside the building. Rushing his handful of men outside, Butler deployed as if to offer resistance and, in a strange, contradictory display, flew his flag of truce. Brooks ordered the petulant Butler to surrender, but he refused, so the Colonel advanced his hundred-man detachment with bayonets fixed, and Butler capitulated.[654]

The grand design was over like a flash in the pan. Those who had shown either the temerity or timidity to come and hear Butler were astonished. Undoubtedly, the three Iroquois delegates were nonplussed and wondered what sort of incompetence had led them into this state of affairs.

General Schuyler was five miles south of Stillwater on August 15 when he wrote to Continental Congress president, John Hancock, to report about Arnold's relief mission to Stanwix and offer assurances that the brigade would be "competent to the Bussiness." He warned that once the siege of Stanwix was raised, "the Six Nations will immediately repair to Albany… [and] the bussiness to be transacted with them will be of first Importance." Although he was about to face a Congressional inquiry into his conduct, his strong sense of duty moved him to comment, "[I]t is therefore necessary that commissioners be immediately appointed, permit me to add, that no Time ought to be lost on this Occasion."[655]

Lieutenant Colbrath wrote that the British batteries had "thrown" a total of 137 shells into Stanwix during the siege. He added that they were "very troublesome with their Small Arms this Afternoon," wounding two soldiers, one a Yorker, the other a Yankee. More mortar shells struck in the evening, slightly wounding a woman and an artilleryman.

St. Leger's report explained the silence of his 6-pounders:

> It was found that our cannon had not the least effect upon the sod-work of the fort, and that our royals had only the power of teazing, as a six-inch plank was a sufficient security for the powder-magazine, as we learnt from deserters. At this time, Lieutenant Glennie of the artillery, whom I had appointed to act as assistant-engineer, proposed a conversion of the royals (if I may use that expression) into howitzers. The ingenuity and feasibility of this measure striking me very strongly, the business was set about immediately.[656]

Gansevoort continued to dread "the disgrace of a Supprise" and ordered "all Troops . . . to turn out to their Alarm Posts at 2 oClock every morning And remain at their different posts till Revalee beating. [N]o Officer[,] Non Commissioned Officer or private belonging to the Piquet shall be absent from his Guard from Sun Rise till Sun Sett."[657]

In view of his limited manpower, it is doubtful that St. Leger at any time entertained a night attack on the fortress. Certainly, his natives would not have joined such a venture. Nonetheless, the vigilant Peter Gansevoort was not going to be found wanting.

On August 16, Colbrath noted in his journal: "This Morning the Enemy threw some Shells Horrisontally at our Works but fell Short. One of those Shells falling on the parade killed a Man of Colonel Melon's Detatchment. They continued to throw them all Day and some part of the Night but did no farther damage... At Midnight they threw four Shells at us but did no damage."[658]

Needless to say, St. Leger was disappointed that Glennie's innovation did not yield better results. He reported: "[I]t was found that nothing prevented their operating with the desired effect, but the distance, their Chambers being too small to hold a sufficiency of powder[659] — there was nothing now to be done, but to approach the place by sap, to a proper distance, that the Rampart might be brought with their portes; at the same time all materials were preparing to run a mine under their most formidable Bastion."[660]

Capitaine De Rouville was not as sanguine about the efficacy of the trench. He derisively recalled that "our trenching is pushed with vigour — one hundred feet long and all of three feet deep." He also noted that Rudyerd, the engineer, made an error in surveying the trench lines, which resulted in three men losing their lives to enfilading fire from the fort. A halt of six hours occurred so the correction could be made in the dark.[661]

At German Flats, Willett visited General Herkimer's home in the company of a surgeon of Arnold's suite named Robert Johnston.[662] The doctor examined the hero's wound and determined that he had no chance of recovery unless his leg was removed, and, accordingly, the limb was amputated. As the general had no sons of his own, his house was often overrun with boys and, on this occasion, two lads were staying at the house. John Roff, a sixteen-year-old who had been sent down from Fort Stanwix, and a local ten-year-old named Adam Garlock[663] were instructed to take the severed limb outside and bury it.[664] Surgeon Johnston spent the day attending his patient.

Tryon committee chairman Deygart ordered the arrest of Colonel Hendrick Frey, the outspoken and unrepentant Tory. The committee viewed him as too dangerous to remain at large, as he had promised to "cut the Tongues of the Whigs out of their Jaws, roast and give them to a repast."[665]

At Albany, Jonathon Trumbull, Jr., wrote a letter to his father, the Connecticut governor, containing the speculation that would launch the legend of the militia's stand at Oriskany. Marinus Willett had met with Jonathon before he rode west with Arnold and gave him the glorious, but spurious, information that the Crown forces had lost "at least three hundred dead" on August 6. Either Willett stated, or Trumbell inferred, that if "the whole of the militia [had] stood firm, in all probability General Herekerman would have given the enemy a total overthrow."[666]

Rebellion in the Mohawk Valley

A Royal Artilleryman of the 1777 campaign stands beside a howitzer

Watercolour by G.A. Embleton. Courtesy of Parks Canada.

At the U.S. Northern Army's headquarters at Stillwater on the Hudson, Schuyler wrote a long letter to General Washington, much of it dealing with Walter Butler's capture. He spent no words explaining who young Butler was; he assumed the commander-in-chief would know, and undoubtedly the Virginian did.

Schuyler had received a letter from Dr. William Petrie, chairman of the German Flats and Kingsland committee of safety, advising that Walter claimed "his business lay with individuals and that he did not inquire for any officer either civil or military." Schuyler was unwilling to accept this charade and forwarded orders to "General Arnold to send him and the party with him prisoners to Albany."[667]

Late in the afternoon, Dr. Johnston found that Herkimer had taken a bad turn and was complaining of pain. He administered "thirty drops of laudanum" and then went to visit Dr. Petrie, who had also been dangerously wounded at Oriskany. Johnston's assistant, Mr. Hastings, was left in care of Herkimer, but when the surgeon returned, he found the general "taking his last gasp, free from spasm and sensible." Herkimer told the two lads to dig up his leg, as he would soon join it. Johnston reported, "[n]othing more surprised me, but we cannot always parry death."[668]

At Stanwix, some additional excitement occurred that evening when a small party was sent out to gather some firewood and was "discovered by some sculking Indians near the Garrison." These "gave the Alarm to the rest" and more natives came up from the camps:

> [They] advanced near where our Men were at work but luckily our Men had been called in before they came nigh Enough to do any Mischief. They finding our Men had got in began a most Hideous Shout. A Cannon being fired at them[,] they Departed. The Regulars' Drums were heard beating to Arms . . . We suppose they Expectd us to Sally out again upon them with a Field piece.[669]

St. Leger's forces were extremely quiet on Sunday, August 17, which led to more questions in the garrison — was the Sabbath being held sacred and gunfire withheld, or was everyone digging the siege trench and building new batteries? In bewilderment, Savage's artillerymen directed a number of solid shot towards the British batteries.[670]

Arnold arrived at Fort Dayton that evening and was immediately regaled with accounts of Butler's strange mission. Arnold was a decisive, quick-thinking individual and, in concern that this "Flag to the inhabitants" had gained some currency, he moved to stiffen local resolve and quash all thoughts of loyalism by calling for a court martial of some members of Walter Butler's party.[671] Arnold named Colonel John Bailey as president of the court, assisted by Lieutenant-Colonel John Brooks and Major William Hull, all Massachusetts officers. Marinus Willett was appointed Judge Advocate. As a professional lawyer, Butler chose to defend himself. The charges read:

> Walter Butler, an Ensign in the King's or 8th Regiment, in the service of the King of England with whom these States are at war was brought Prisoner before the court and charged with being a trayter and Spy, in that under the pretense of being a Flagg from the enemy he was found endeavoring to sudduse [seduce] a number of the inhabitants of this state from their alegiance to the United States of America.[672]

In the "Camp before Fort Stanwix," John Butler wrote a detailed dispatch to Governor Carleton about the Oriskany battle and the conduct of the siege. He concluded his letter by bemoaning that "the pleasing prospect . . . of having the direction" of the Indians had been given to Claus by the King. If Butler hoped to keep Carleton's sympathy and obligation alive with this mild complaint, he was successful. He added a postscript: "This moment we have accounts that my son sent by General St. Leger with proposals to the inhabitants of the Mohawk River, is taken prisoner by the Rebels but I give no credit to it."[673]

The balance of the Hanau Jäger battalion was on the St. Lawrence River en route to join St. Leger. In one of his regular reports to his Crown Prince, Lieutenant-Colonel Carl von Kreutzbourg wrote from Oswegatchie about how very different duty in Canada was from Europe, describing the loads of flour, hard tack, and salt meat carried in the bateaux.

> At times these heavy boats must be pulled by 40 or 50 men or even lifted over stretches of from six to 700 paces where the rocks among the whirlpools reach up to various heights . . . our men . . . stand in the rapids up to their armpits for three hours and longer. This may occur as often as four or five times a day . . . our men have lost more than 60 pairs of boots which were tore off their feet by the force of the current . . . Today

we encamped near a fort which is said to be thirty hours distant from Montreal, but it took us 12 days to reach here without a day of rest . . . many cases of sunstroke have occurred . . . One can ride downstream from here to Montreal in 24 hours.[674]

In the morning of August 18 at Stanwix, a soldier was wounded in the cheek by a sniper's ball, and, not long after, a puzzling device was observed in the British "Bombattery." The rest of the day was unremarkable, but August 19 brought far more activity, as the besiegers were "Busy in their Trench all day" and a flurry of shells was thrown at the fort around noon.[675]

Four women emerged out of the woods with a drove of cattle and entered the siege camps. Their arrival led to reunions in the Indian Department — Sarah McGinnis with her son, Lieutenant George, and her daughter Elizabeth Thompson with her sons, Lieutenant Andrew and Senior Ranger Samuel. The women had been warned that rebels were coming from Fort Dayton to seize them and took to the bush, taking just what could be carried on their backs and some of Dorothy Thompson's cattle. Sarah, who was known far and wide for her influence with the Iroquois Confederacy, had been fearful that the rebels would force her to work for the U.S. Indian Commission, as she had refused their previous offer of "12 shillings York Currency per Day, and a guard of 15 men to protect her against any harm from [the] Government side." Her decision to run was wrenching, as she was forced to abandon her deranged son William, "still bound in Chains," to the doubtful mercy of her enemies. The rigour of their march through hostile country defies imagination, as driving cattle was far from a secretive business, and they were in constant fear of stumbling upon a hostile patrol.[676]

This was a sensible concern, as Colonel Gansevoort had been keeping his Oneida scouts in motion around the siege lines. One of the boldest was Chief Paul Powless Tahaswaugatotees, known as The Saw Mill. One day, he was on a solo scout and was discovered by a party led by Brant. Instead of running him down, Joseph chose to parley and, hailing the Oneida, promised on his honour that "he shd

neither be hurt nor detained." Powless told Brant to advance separately and, raising his rifle with his finger on the trigger, "[He] bade
Brant deliver whatever message he had to offer. Brant insultingly
offered him a large reward, & a plenty as long as he should live, if he
would only join the King's side, and induce other Oneida to so do, &
help the British take Fort Stanwix."

Powless firmly declined and, true to his word, Brant let him go. The
chief set off for the fort and was joined by other Oneidas who had been
on similar patrols, but when they neared the works, they discovered that
Brant's men had "run with signal speed" and cut them off, forcing them
"to fight their way in."[677]

At midnight on August 19, Gansevoort sent Eli Pixly of his own regiment and Ely Stiles of Badlam's detachment express to Colonel Wesson
or the nearest committee with news that the "Garrison [was] Still in
high Spirits and determined to defend it to the last" and urging a relief.
He mentioned the location of the siege trench so "that [Wesson] might
Govern the Attack accordingly." The two privates were sworn to return
to Stanwix with all the intelligence they could discover.[678]

As darkness fell, the trench diggers angled towards the northwest
bastion, which brought a response from the garrison. "We fired some
Grape Shot at them now and then all night. At every Shott Fired[,] they
threw Shells at us but did no Damage." By dawn, the trench was within
150 yards of the fort's ditch.

In their cramped and fetid quarters, the garrison was growing
restive. The threat of the advancing trench was palpable, and everyone
remembered the Indians' warnings of brutal retribution, but, worst of
all, they had no word of Willett and Stockwell, or indeed, from anyone,
so tight was St. Leger's native cordon around the works. In this atmosphere of uncertainty, a few officers were said to have approached
Colonel Gansevoort with suggestions of capitulation, but he remained
resolute and refused to hear all such talk.[679]

The court martial convened at Fort Dayton on August 20 and opened with
the case against Walter Butler, who pled "not guilty" to the charges. Dr.
William Petrie testified that, when he heard that Butler was at

Shoemaker's, he inquired of the agitated local folk whether the Tory "had sent to any of the Committee." They thought not, so he went to the tavern where he found Peter Deygart, the county chairman, with copies of the papers brought by Butler. They examined these together and then warned Butler about the law. Butler replied to this testimony with the claim that he was ignorant of any such laws. In fact, his entire defence was based upon his ignorance of Colonel Wesson, Fort Dayton, or any magistrate or other person in authority at German Flats, other than Rudolph Shoemaker. Colonel Brooks testified that during his first visit, Butler had argued that he had "seen the committee who had promised to answer him," implying that he had no need to see Colonel Wesson or any other rebel authority.

Major William Hull of Jackson's Massachusetts Regiment — he and Brooks apprehended Walter Butler at Shoemaker's tavern and sat on his court martial

Engraving after a portrait by Gilbert C. Stuart. Courtesy of the Fort Ticonderoga Museum.

According to Major Hull, Walter Butler "conducted himself with great fearlessness," stating that "he was a British officer and acted under the authority of the King." He was "in the King's dominions and was amenable to no other power than what was derived from his sovereign." In other words, none of the rebels' political or military apparatus had any status in his loyal eyes. It was a bold and clever gambit, but hardly one to gain any sympathy or point of law in a court staffed by hardened enemies of the British government.[680]

Willett recorded the court's decision regarding two of the prisoners:

> The Court upon due consideration of the whole matter before them, is of opinion that Walter Butler the said prisoner is Guilty of being a spy and adjudge him to suffer the pain and penalty of Death —
>
> Joseph [Hanjost] Schuyler charged with deserting

from the armey of the American states and going over to the Enemy, was brought Prisoner before the Court, who upon being Challenged pleads. Guilty —

The Court adjudge that the said Joseph Schuyler receive 100 Lashes upon his bare back.[681]

Christopher Fornyea was also sentenced to death, but the court's deliberations have not been found. In contrast, the British Regulars were simply treated as prisoners of war, as were the three Iroquois.[682]

As to the tavern owner, Rudolph Shoemaker, he was well connected to the local Whig hierarchy and his sister Gertrude was the wife of Brigade Major John Frey.[683] As well, Butler's defence strategy implied that he was an unwitting pawn in the scheme, so he walked free.

Peter Ten Broeck, who was every bit as culpable as Walter Butler, escaped the death sentence by co-operating with the court, claiming that, although he had twice taken "the Neutral oath," he had forgotten his duty to his country when he ran off to the enemy. He discredited Butler's defence by admitting he had been taken during "the pretended play" at Shoemaker's. Ten Broeck's waffling saved his neck and, of course, damaged his reputation amongst his loyalist peers.[684] Nothing has been discovered about William Ryer Bowen's case.

Arnold saw that further action was needed to stiffen Tryon County's backbone, and, in the grand manner of the times, he issued a bombastic proclamation:

> By the Hon. Benedict Arnold, Esq., Major-General and Commander-in-chief of the army of the United States of America on the Mohawk River.
>
> · WHEREAS a certain Barry St. Leger, a Brigadier-general in the service of George of Great Britain, at the head of a banditti of robbers, murderers, and traitors, composed of savages of America, and more savage Britons, (among whom is the noted Sir John Johnson, John Butler, and Daniel Claus,) have lately appeared in the frontiers of this State, and have threatened ruin and destruction to all the inhabitants of the United States. They have also, by artifice and misrepresentation, induced many of the ignorant and unwary subjects of

these States to forfeit their allegiance to the same, and join with them in their atrocious crimes, and parties of treachery and parricide.

Humanity to those poor deluded wretches, who are hastening blindfold to destruction, induces me to offer them, and all others concerned, (whether Savages, Germans, Americans, or Britons,) PARDON, provided they do, within ten days from the date hereof, come in and lay down their arms, sue for protection, and swear allegiance to the United States of America.

But if, still blind to their own interest and safety, they obstinately persist in their wicked courses, determined to draw on themselves the just vengeance of heaven and of this exasperated country, they must expect no mercy from either.[685]

Arnold had fought fire with fire, and if words could inspire devotion to the cause, or cause submission in fear of it, he had delivered the correct balance. While the militia did not flock to join him, neither did recruits stream to join St. Leger.

At Stanwix on August 20, a sniper wounded yet another of Mellon's men. With the trench so near to the fort, the besiegers performed little work during daylight, as "small Arms as well as Cannon Shott was too hott for them. In the Evening they began their trench again, and worked all Night at it under fire of our Cannon and small Arms but did not approach any nearer."[686] The diggers may have been working underground on the mineshaft, which would have been disguised from the fort's walls.

In his camp near Saratoga, Burgoyne wrote to Lord George Germain that "in spite of St. Leger's victory [Oriskany], Fort Stanwix holds out obstinately." Unaware of St. Leger's orders against a thrust into the Valley, he commented, "I am afraid the expectations of Sir J. Johnson greatly fail in the raising of the country."[687]

~

CHAPTER ELEVEN

THE IGNOMINIOUS END OF THE SEIGE
Cowardice in Some, Treason in Others

A firewood detail sallied out of Stanwix at two in the morning on August 21 and secured a great quantity of wood without being discovered. All the while, the enemy's batteries cannonaded and shelled, which caused a distraught soldier of the 3NY to break and desert.

At daybreak, the garrison observed that the trench was much closer and enemy soldiers were seen constructing a new bomb battery. During the day, three wounded men died — an artilleryman with a putrefied knee, one of Mellon's men, and the indentured lad who had lost his fiancée.[688]

At Fort Dayton, General Arnold received a letter dated August 19 from Major-General Horatio Gates advising that he had taken command of the Northern Army. He urged Arnold to complete his assignment expeditiously, as Learned's brigade was urgently required for redeployment against Burgoyne. Arnold instantly wrote a detailed reply:

> I leave this place this morning with Twelve hundred Continental Troops . . . & a handful of Militia for Fort Schuyler, which is still beseiged by a Number equal to ours. [N]othing shall be omitted that can be done to raise the Seige, you will hear of my being Victorious or no more, & as soon as the Safety of this part of the Country will Permit[,] I will fly to your Assistance... I am credibly informed that Genl St. Leger has sent to Genl Burgoyne for a reinforcement.[689]

Arnold's plan was disrupted by the appearance of an Oneida and Tuscarora deputation who brought advice that their chiefs would arrive in two days.[690] The Indians provided a great deal of information about

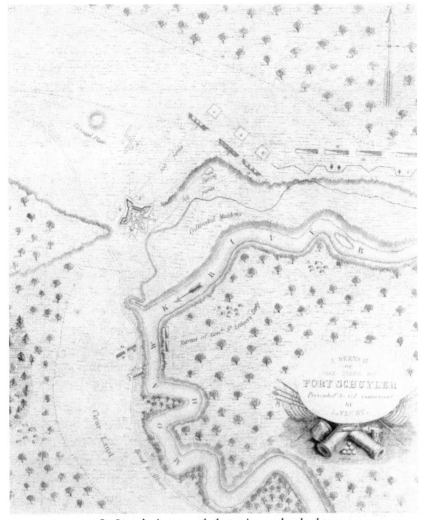

St. Leger's siege trench, batteries, and redoubts

1. Battery position for 6PR 2. Battery Position for Cohorn Mortars 3. Battery position for 6 PR 4. Redoubts manned by 34th regt. 5. Seige trench (lines of approaches) 6. St. Leger's headquarters and camp for artillery, 34th and Quebec militia A. Fort Stanwix (Shuyler) I. Main Gate K. Covert Way L. Glacis M. Sally Port Spring — Water supply stopped up by British Note: De Fluery showed three guns in each 6pr battery position; however, St. Leger employed only two 6prs during the siege. The 3prs were in a large redoubt at the Lower Landing manned by the 8th Regt to the south-east of the fort.

Detail from a formal engraving of a sketch by Capt. François Louis Teisseidre de Fleury, 1777. Courtesy of the Emmet Collection, New York Public Library.

St. Leger's expedition, information that caused Arnold to delay marching and call for a council of war with his senior officers.

Several luminaries of the Continental Army attended — Brigadier Ebenezer Learned and his colonels, John Bailey, James Wesson, and John Brooks, and the New York colonels, Cornelius Van Dyck and Marinus Willett.[691]

Arnold explained that the native messengers had said that their foes included every nation of the Iroquois Confederacy, excepting themselves, plus "foreign [Mississauga, Canada, and Lakes] Indians," which together numbered one thousand, and the white troops were "near 700, besides some Tories who have joined." Willett agreed with these numbers, and further questioning of the Flag prisoners provided further confirmation. Arnold advised the council that the morning's return of the relief totalled "933, and 13 artillerymen, exclusive of a few militia, the whole not exceeding 100 on whom little dependence can be placed," and asked whether it was wise to march with the present force. They resolved:

> [O]ur force is not equal to that of the enemy, and it would be imprudent and putting too much to the hazard to attempt the march to the relief of Fort Schuyler, until the army is reinforced: the council are of the opinion that an express ought immediately to be sent to General Gates, requesting he will immediately send such reinforcements . . . that in the meantime the army remain at the German Flatts, at least until an answer can be had from General Gates, and that all possible method be taken to persuade the militia and Indians to join us.[692]

These concerns were uncharacteristic of Arnold, who had a well-earned reputation for being bold, if not rash. Conservative voices such as Learned's may have contributed,[693] yet there are indications that Arnold was genuinely concerned. Traditional tactical doctrine held that an attacker should outnumber the defence by at least three to one, yet he had not been overly concerned about such stodgy details in the past. Besides, St. Leger would have to guard against a sortie by the garrison in his rear and would be unable to deploy all of his troops against the relief. Clearly, the most significant factor forming these resolutions was the fear of the British Indians, that and the fact that Willett was "fully of [the] Opinion there is no Danger of the Fort's Surrendering for some Time." Yet Marinus had been absent from Stanwix for several days and, in offering this assurance, assumed that nothing material had occurred. His statement produced a sense of calm that was not entirely warranted.

At the council's close, Arnold again wrote to Gates, advising of the decision not to march and requesting a reinforcement of "One thousand light Troops," which were to march with only "one Shift of Clothes" and be sent off "by Companies or small Detachments." In another uncharacteristic display, he asked, "If it is not in your Power to spare us a Reinforcement, you will please to give your Positive Orders which Shall be obey'd at all Event." He repeated his earlier comment, "No Dependance can be placed on the Militia of this County, Notwithstanding my most earnest Intreaties, I have not been able to Collect one hundred." His words were such a contrast to the inspiring phrases that had been lavished on them about their great courage and resounding victory. Had the glowing words been mere fluff, a sham to bolster confidence and encourage a fresh response? Flattery was a sensible ploy, but it would take more than sugared words to rally the brigade. The truth was that despite their collective courage, the brigade had been shattered at Oriskany, and mauled, battle-shocked men did not leap from their hearths to a muster, no matter how much cajoling took place. After the savage horror of Oriskany, the men were unwilling to again abandon their families. Yet with the success that was soon to follow, the truth of the brigade's state would become buried in legend.

Arnold informed Gates that he would write to the "Colonels of the Different Districts to turn out, at least half their Men." He had native and white scouts gathering intelligence and promised that "if any thing can be done, I will attempt it."[694] The ubiquitous Marinus Willett was entrusted to carry these latest dispatches to headquarters.

Arnold then wrote to Schuyler, advising that he had not had an opportunity to send Butler's party downriver and enclosing details of the court martial with the note that the sentences had not been fulfilled.[695] Again, he bemoaned the failings of the militia, saying that not one of the brigade's senior officers had turned out. Perhaps the surviving colonels and majors were preparing their precincts against the hovering savage horde. Arnold chose exaggeration to explain his caution: "I have been obliged from Intelligence I have received of the Enemies Strength to ask for Reinforcements. Our Force does not exceed one thousand Men, the Enemy, by the last accounts, have near two."

Earlier in the day, the mother and brother of the Tory prisoner Hanjost Schuyler had been pestering General Arnold.[696] Although the court martial had awarded the said Schuyler one hundred lashes, a rumour had been circulated that all of Butler's Tories would be executed as a method of dissuading loyalism. Not knowing better, his kin came to entreat for his life, not the forgiveness of a flogging.[697]

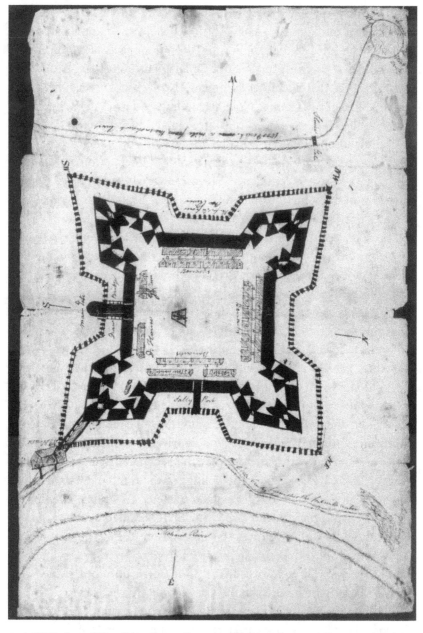

A 1777 plan of Fort Stanwix — Captain Abraham Swartwout commanded a company of the Third New York during the siege

Pen and ink drawing by an unidentified artist, ca. 1780, in the Barnardus Swartout Papers. Collection of the New-York Historical Society, Negative no.55024.

Hanjost's brother Nicholas later recalled that his brother was to be shot, whereas George M. Weaver, a young fifer of Tryon's 4th Regiment, believed he was to be hanged. Faced with the imminent demise of her youngest son, Elizabeth Schuyler begged Arnold for clemency.[698]

What transpired is difficult to unravel. It seems that Arnold at first ignored their pleading, as he had more important issues on his mind. Some of his officers must have been discussing Hanjost's reputation with the natives when an idea popped into the head of Lieutenant-Colonel Brooks.[699] He went to Arnold with a proposal to expand the execution subterfuge and Arnold accepted. The game was on.

It was announced that Hanjost would hang that day. He was brought from his cell and led to the gallows while fifer Weaver played an appropriate air. A rough coffin was laid out for all to see. His mother must have wept for mercy while Nicholas wrung his hands. As Hanjost prepared himself for the noose, an officer stepped forward to offer a conditional pardon.

Whether Hanjost immediately accepted the bargain is unknown. Nor do we know if his mother and brother were taken in by the charade or were part of it, but we do know that Nicholas agreed to be held hostage for his brother's compliance in the very same cell Hanjost had just vacated.[700]

Hanjost was to have his coat shot through with holes as proof of his narrow escape. Then he was to ride express to the siege camps, seek an interview with St. Leger, tell him the story of the Flag's capture and his fortuitous flight, and lard it on about the number of Arnold's Continentals. A series of co-opted Oneidas would arrive one after the other to confirm and embellish his story.

Lieutenant-Colonel John Brooks of Jackson's Regiment, Massachusetts Continental Line — the mastermind of the ruse that raised the siege

Engraved by A.B. Durand after a portrait by Gilbert C. Stuart.

As Hanjost was known to the Indians and spoke Oneida, he was to visit the British native alliance camps after leaving St. Leger and feed them the story of Arnold's great army. If the rebel Oneidas were correct about their brothers' boredom and declining morale, the lie would sew the seeds of "alarum, dissension and despondency."

Meanwhile in the siege camps, St. Leger received grave news:

> [I]ntelligence was brought in, by our scouts, of a second corps of 1000 men being on their march. The same zeal no longer animated the Indians; they complained of our thinness of troops, and their former losses. I immediately called a council of the chiefs, encouraged them as much as I could; promised to lead them on myself, and bring into the field 300 of the best troops. They listened to this, and promised to follow me, and agreed that I should reconnoitre the ground, properest for the field of battle, the next morning; accompanied by some of their chief warriors, to settle the plan of operations.[701]

Daniel Claus detected the natives' waning enthusiasm and later wrote that they "began to be dispirited, and fell off by degrees."[702] Certainly, they were uninspired by St. Leger expecting them to face this new threat with the support of only three hundred troops, a prospect reminiscent of Oriskany where they had borne the brunt of the fighting. And who were these "best troops" — the "lobsters" who had made such a farce of opposing Willett? They had much to contemplate.

The digging of the siege trench continued under constant fire from the fort:

> [I]n the evening 12 of the best Marksman were pick't out to harrass [the diggers] when at work in the Night, which galled them so much that their Indians were sent for to draw off our Attention, who Advanced near the Fort, which caused a General Alarm by which a heavy and continual firing was kept up for near two Hours

during which their Cannon & Mortars were playing on us very briskly, in which interim we had a man of the Artillery wounded & a Woman big with Child wounded in the Thigh.[703]

The cacophony of gunfire and musketry provided a diversion that allowed a corporal and three men of the 3NY to desert. The very next morning, they mustered in the Royal Yorkers.[704] The timing of their decision to bolt proved most ironic.

Gansevoort began to feel uneasy on several counts: the oncoming sap; the seeming decline in his troops' confidence; his shrinking provisions; and, worst of all, the complete lack of any news or sign of a relief. He decided that if help did not arrive soon, he would distribute the remaining rations to the men and lead a night breakout through the siege lines or perish in the attempt. Death would be preferred to the dishonour of surrender.[705]

Dawn of August 22 was greeted by a very smart bombardment by the British artillery that wounded the serjeant-major and two men of the 3NY.[706]

Early that morn, St. Leger and the war captains went forward to select suitable ground for opposing Arnold's column. They had made their choice and were at the point of discussing dispositions when Hanjost Schuyler appeared. He had ridden post-haste down the road from Fort Dayton and fallen in with a scout of British Indians who led him to St. Leger and the reconnaissance party.[707] As instructed, he described his capture and mock escape and gave exaggerated intelligence about Arnold's relief. There was no reason to doubt him. He had been selected for the Flag and reports that the party had been seized preceded his arrival.

True to plan, first one and then another Oneida arrived after Schuyler, each with more and more alarming information. As many Oneidas were serving with Brant and their Cayuga and Seneca clan relations, there was no reason for instant distrust; differentiating between loyal and rebel natives was never straightforward. St. Leger reported: "[S]scouts came in, with the account of the first number [i.e., 1000,] swelled to 2000, immediately after a third [saying] that General

Burgoyne's army was cut to pieces, and that Arnold was advancing, by rapid and forced marches with 3000 men."[708]

Although St. Leger "suspect[ed] cowardice in some and treason in others," he immediately returned to camp and, with the "Assistance of my gallant Coadjutor Sir John Johnson and the influence of the superintending Colonels Claus & Butler," called a new council to induce the Indians "to meet the Enemy."

Meanwhile, at Fort Dayton, Gansevoort's couriers, Pixly and Stiles, arrived with up-to-date intelligence. Arnold was alarmed to hear of the siege trench's progress, the garrison's desertions, and other evidence of their peril and declining morale. In an action more typical of his energy and spirit, he decided to force march all of the men at hand, rather than wait for the reinforcement. First, he cleverly crafted a dispatch to Gansevoort:

> Dear Colonel — I wrote you on the 19th, that I should be with you in a few days; since which your express is arrived, and informs me you are in high spirits, and no apprehensions at present. I have been retarded by the badness of the roads, waiting for some baggage and ammunition wagons, and for the militia, who did not at first turn out with that spirit I expected; they are now joining me in great numbers; a few days will relieve you; be under no kind of apprehension; I know the strength of the enemy, and how to deal with them.[709]

The letter continued with an account of the defeat of part of Burgoyne's army at Bennington, then offered contrived news that Howe's "shattered remnant" was on shipboard and becalmed and that Burgoyne was in full retreat to Ticonderoga pursued by "near fifteen thousand." It was masterful propaganda, sure to put fight into the garrison, if they received it, or utter despair into the enemy, if it fell into their hands. In either case, the cause of the rebellion stood to gain. As Pixley and Stiles had proven their woodsmen's skills, they were probably employed as the couriers.[710]

At St. Leger's Indian council, he asked to hear his allies' resolutions. The chiefs and war captains made clear recommendations — "retreat to Oswego and get better artillery from Niagara, and more men, and so return and renew the siege."[711] As St. Leger digested these rather familiar and disquieting suggestions, word arrived that two hundred Indians had already decamped. These departures may have been only the sick, elderly, women, and children, but even so, they were unnerving. The council closed. An hour later, St. Leger received advice from the chiefs that he had better retreat or face the possibility of total abandonment.[712]

Recognizing how ineffective his troops would be without native support, St. Leger hastily assembled a council of war of his senior military commanders. Opinions on what should be done were varied. Some wanted more information, others to decamp immediately. A decision was made to send all non-combatants, the sick, wounded, prisoners, and the artillery "down the Wood Creek."[713] The native headmen were advised of this decision and the order issued.

During St. Leger's two councils, Hanjost and the Oneida agents spread the story of the imminent arrival of a large column of Continentals and artillery. The information percolated through the camps and resulted in much unease, so that when the "tail of the army" was seen moving to the Wood Creek landing, the feet of the nervous began to twitch.

Bogus messengers continued to arrive at St. Leger's marquee with ever more alarming news. The last one to come in claimed that Arnold was only two miles from Lernoult's post at the

Ann (Nancy) Claus, elder daughter of Sir William Johnson and wife of Daniel — she and her children were part of the tail of the army

Unknown artist, brown wash on ivory, ca. 1770. Courtesy of the National Archives of Canada, C-083498.

Lower Landing. St. Leger's suspicions were now fully aroused, and he told his native allies that he would hold to his plan to retire that night. But, according to him, "they grew furious and abandoned, seized upon the officers liquor and cloaths, in spite of the efforts of their servants; and became more formidable than the Enemy we had to suspect." St. Leger suspected even his most confidential native allies of perpetrating a great treachery,[714] and when the warriors fell upon the goods in the camps, he thought they were making up for losing the enemy's public stores.

It is difficult to say which came first — panic amongst the troops, or the natives' sacking. An anonymous letter written at Montreal two weeks later maintained that the Indians plundered the camps only after they were abandoned.[715] In any event, as the rumours flew about Arnold's proximity, the officers began to lose control of their men, and perhaps, in some cases, of themselves.

Meanwhile, at Gates's headquarters at Half Moon on the Hudson, Governor Clinton reacted to the news that the Tryon militia was failing to respond to Arnold's appeals. Like all the politicians and soldiers who had not been at Oriskany, Clinton had little appreciation of the slaughter vested upon the brigade. There seemed to be no concern that the Valley's ripened crops stood in the fields and the harvest had to be completed before all was lost.[716] His letter to the regimental commanders began with the customary flattery: "While I have the highest Sense of the Loyalty Valor & Bravery of the Militia of Tryon County manifested in the Victory gained by them under the Command of their late worthy Genl. Hakimer." But he continued in a forceful manner: "It gives me the greatest Pain to be informed that any Difficulty should arise in their joining the Army under Genl. Arnold." Then came positive orders to muster one half of each regiment "compleatly armed equipt & accoutred & march under [Arnold's] Command to the Relief of Fort Schuyler." The colonels were to report the names of all who failed to answer their summons "that they may be dealt with . . . the utmost rigour of the law."[717] Fortunately for everyone in the militia, from colonels to the lowliest private, events eclipsed this stringent set of instructions.

St. Leger reported that when the Indians began to boldly pillage the camps, he ordered Lernoult and the troops from the Lower Landing to assemble at the ruins of Fort William, where they could confront a sally.[718] His memory must have been faulty, as this location stood less than 450 yards from Stanwix, well within range of 6- and 9-pounder guns firing canister or round shot. Undoubtedly, he meant to write Fort Newport on Wood Creek, as its ruins were out of effective range and the bateaux could be loaded without risk. As well, Newport was ideally placed to prevent a sortie from disrupting the withdrawal.[719]

The troops from the main camp were ordered to march to the bateaux depot at old Fort Bull's ruins on Canada Creek. Leaving his subordinates to decamp, St. Leger mounted his horse and departed, probably to Newport, where he could oversee affairs.[720]

Once the retreat was ordered, Claus met with the Mohawks to discuss their options. They decided against retiring to Oswego: "Brant proposed . . . to pass the Mohawk Villages[,] secure their Women and Children and collect what Indns he could in his way to join Gen. Burgoyne by way of Saraghtoga wch Col. Claus agreed to."[721]

Claus provided Brant with some funds, presumably to be shared with his fellow Mohawk leaders. Some 150 of Joseph's men left for their settlements, including the Delawares and Brant's white volunteers, who went with the Oquagas.[722]

After taking leave of the superintendent, a few Mohawks decided to search for treasures in the siege camps. If necessary, they could melt into the woods at the blink of an eye, so there was no need to be hasty.

Mississauga Indians' bark shelter, ca. 1790

Painting by Elizabeth Posthuma Simcoe.

The rangers had very little to pack. Each man was issued with sufficient rations for the trip to Oswego, then they abandoned their bark shelters, shouldered their firelocks and packs, and set off for the assembly. Similarly, the Royal Yorkers had little to be concerned about, having lost their camp gear to Willett's adventure of the sixth. As for personal goods, all the men had to do was fold their blankets into their knapsacks, stuff in a few trifling possessions, tie up the packs, and be off.

Lieutenant Joseph Anderson, who had been transferred to the Colonel's Company from Major Gray's to replace the late Donald John McDonell, had a chest of possessions that had been missed by Willett's lads. He dragooned a couple of recruits to bring it off and they struggled for a while to keep up, but soon grew tired and disgruntled and hit upon a plan of their own.[723]

The British, Canadiens, and Germans were faced with shifting a staggering amount of material — tents; barrels of clothing, shoes, flour, and musket cartridges; kegs and bottles of liquor and nails; entrenching tools; ropes . . . in short, all of the appurtenances of a military siege camp. To their great relief, an order came through to abandon the lot, excepting a food supply for the return trip to Oswego.

Hoyes was instructed to have one of the 6-pounders removed from the gun battery and taken to Canada Creek to safeguard the bateaux. Gunners, mattrosses, and artificers dismounted the second 6-pounder tube and loaded it into a wagon. Others cut up its carriage wheels and those of some wagons that were no longer needed.

In their panic-tinged haste to get away, the 34th's officers forgot the 150 men in the trench constructing the new bomb battery. One of the labourers chanced to look back towards the camp and saw troops marching off. When he told his mates, they all cheered, as they were heartily fed up with the work. Snatching up muskets, coats, and packs, they hurried to catch up.[724]

The artillerymen of this forgotten detachment were faced with the problem of four heavy Cohorn mortars, whose tubes alone weighed seventy-five pounds each.[725] Their officer decided they must be carried off, and his twelve men struggled with the awkward burdens as they followed the retreating backs of the labourers.

At the Lower Landing, the 8th's soldiers and artillerists abandoned their camp kit and prepared to move one of the 3-pounders to the

Wood Creek assembly point. The other gun's carriage was cut up and discarded, its tube hastily buried in a nearby ditch.[726]

At noon, one of the Royal Yorkers who had been wrestling with Lieutenant Anderson's chest deserted to the Stanwix garrison. He brought the story that "Burgoyne's Army was Entirely Routed and that three Thousand men was Coming up to reinforce us," proving that Hanjost and his Oneida accomplices had performed well. Further, he advised that St. Leger's expedition "was retreating with great precipitation." Gansevoort "Ordered all the Cannon bearing on their Works to Fire several rounds each to see whether they woud return it." There was no reply, yet remarkably, no further action was taken. Gansevoort's indecision and lethargy were of the same order as St. Leger's during Willett's sortie.

"Some time after 4 [deserters] came in and reported the same and that they had left part of their Baggage, upon which the Colo ordered 30 Men and two Waggons under the Command of Capt. Jansen to go to their Camps."[727] He also dispatched a rider to alert the lower Valley about what seemed to be happening.[728]

Some British-alliance natives found rich pickings in the camps, especially liquor, while others, who were more mischievous, followed the retreat, thinking that more amusement and loot might be found amongst the troops.

When Captain Jansen's party arrived at the British headquarters' camp, the eerie scene of silent, empty streets of tents generated much caution. Jansen ordered a search of the camp, redoubts, and trench. The soldier sent to St. Leger's marquee came to the entrance and was startled to find two Indians enjoying a meal from the brigadier's table. Snapping up his musket, he fired a charge of buck and ball. The buckshot caught John Deserontyon full in the meat of his left arm and breast and he crashed to the floor while his comrade bolted through the tent's sidewall and made off.[729] The nervous soldier did not linger to examine his victim.

When the 8th, Royal Yorkers, and rangers were assembled at Wood Creek, the next stage of the withdrawal began. The two outsized artillery bateaux, which had required an epic effort to bring up the creek, were sunk in deep water near the landing.[730] Several small bateaux were loaded with provisions and salvaged chests and sent down Wood Creek towards Lake Oneida, probably in the care of Hon Jost Herkimer's men. As there was no sign of pursuit, the 3-pounder tube was loaded into a small bateau after its carriage was cast aside with its wheels cut to pieces. Then the troops marched for Canada Creek along the rebuilt road that had given many of them so much sweat and pain scant weeks before.

When the artillerymen lugging the Cohorns arrived at Newport, they found the place deserted. An array of empty bateaux lay on the shore, but their officer had no desire to struggle with the unwieldy craft and, in disgust and anger, ordered the mortars cast aside and their fuses destroyed.[731] That done, his men followed the retreat down the road.

There was probably little dialogue between the Crown's soldiers and officers. A pall of disappointment and urgency hung over everyone. That haste was necessary went without saying, as at any moment the garrison could sortie or the relief force make its appearance.

The Jägers were assigned as the rearguard on the Canada Creek road. Johnson and Butler had doubted their determination and separately warned them not to fall behind and be taken, as the rebels hanged all prisoners. The Hessians were about ten miles from the fort when the parties of trench diggers, artillerymen, and other stragglers passed through their screen. Suddenly, erstwhile friendly Indians fell upon "the Scattering Tories, took their Arms from & Stabb'd them with their own Bayonets."[732] During this fracas, nine Jägers broke discipline and ran into the woods in fear of the Indians. Other Jägers had their rifles ripped from their hands, the thieves bounding away into the trees. When some of his men reported that "old Freyburger" had been scalped,[733] Lieutenant Hildebrand ordered his men to resist and he believed that five Indians had probably been killed.

According to the prisoner Moses Younglove, some Crown officers "engaged the Indians to take their baggage, but they secreted & kept the most of it." During the uproar, Father Mackenna lost all of "his vestments, missal, alter silver and much personal property" and surgeon Charles Blake of the 34th, his instruments and some cash. The natives were drunkenly amused by their allies' attempts to maintain order and discipline and took great delight in taunting them with warnings that the rebels were close behind, then watching their pace increase in panic.[734]

In the grey of twilight, two Oneida sachems reported seeing Sir John arguing with St. Leger. Supposedly, St. Leger reproached Sir John over the natives' defection, and the baronet charged his commander with "an indifferent prosecution of the siege." Both were said to have skeddadled when some Indians shouted, "they are coming! — they are coming."[735] As this was the perfect story to warm Whig ears, it must be wondered whether it contained even a grain of truth.

As darkness fell, most of the expedition had reached Fort Bull and an orders group was held to plan the next phase. Someone, a Provincial officer or one of the many faithful Indians who accompanied the withdrawal, voiced the possibility that "the enemy might have possessed themselves of [Wood Creek's mouth] by a rapid march by the Oneyda-Castle." This prospect worried St. Leger and he decided on a quick movement to the lakeshore. The tubes of both 6-pounders were dumped into the creek basin and the wheels of the intact carriage were butchered. Then the troops boarded the bateaux and rowed down the creek towards Lake Oneida.[736]

Captain Jansen's men left St. Leger's siege camp at nightfall and returned to the fort with their wagons loaded with booty. Gansevoort decided not to go for another haul in the dark because of the wandering Indians.

When Jansen's wagons disappeared, Deserontyon's companion crept into the marquee and found the war captain "weltering in his Blood: — his Shoulder was broken, but the Vital Parts were untouched, — he carried him off."[737]

St. Leger reported that "the whole of the little army arrived [at the lake] by twelve o'clock at night, and took post in such a manner as to have no fears of any thing the enemy could do." De Rouville recalled that the men "stretch[ed] out in the grass" each "cursing in his heart both savages and enemies." The men now had time to reflect on what had occurred and there were many sober second thoughts about the useful items that had been so cavalierly abandoned. Even in this hoped-for sanctuary, "our devilish savages" reappeared, each as "dignified as a . . . mandarin," and began to loot.[738] The officers and men were loath to challenge them, as they were painfully aware of likely reprisals — natives had long memories of perceived affronts.

Two more Tory deserters appeared at the fort. One was the second man involved in carrying Anderson's chest and the other, Hanjost Schuyler. Colonel Gansevoort convened a council of field officers to hear Schuyler's remarkable tale. He recounted his adventures with Walter Butler's Flag, his capture and trial, the conditions of Arnold's pardon, and claimed that his actions had caused St. Leger to decamp. He said that St. Leger "Ordered his Troops to strike their Tents and pack up . . . [and] after he had done his Errand he hid himself in the Woods till Night," where he came across the two men carrying the officer's chest and the three came in together. There was no explanation of why they arrived at the fort hours apart, but no matter. In their joy, the officers wondered if they were dreaming.

Hanjost reported that fifty-seven drunken Indians were at Fort Newport, and Major Cochran was ordered out with a party "to go and take them." Cochran returned in an hour to report that he had found no Indians, but there were eight new bateaux abandoned at Wood Creek, and, most important, St. Leger's troops were gone, completely gone! The fantastic night was capped by the woman who had been wounded on the twenty-first giving birth to a daughter. As might be imagined, the garrison luxuriated in the "Liberty to walk about and take the free Air." Gansevoort dispatched another three men "to inform General Arnold of the precipitate retreat of the Enemy." Adding to the reverie, another deserter came in with news that the mortars were abandoned below the Wood Creek Bridge.[739]

St. Leger's troops lay on the shore of Lake Oneida till three o'clock in the morning of August 23, "when the boats which could come up the creek arrived." Before voice contact was made with these new arrivals, hasty, ill-advised orders were given to embark and set off across Lake Oneida. The men rowed and sailed the twenty-two miles to the ruins of old Fort Brewerton at the lake's far western end. When the craft were beached, a bateauman of the Wood Creek party gave the startling information that some boats had "still [been] labouring down the creek, after being lightened of the best part of their freight by the Messasagoes . . . Captain Lernoult proposed, with a boat full of armed men, to repass the lake that night, to relieve them from their labour, and supply them with provision."[740]

As it transpired, Arnold's column had been unable to leave Fort Dayton on the twenty-second. The brigade marched the next morning and by five in the afternoon had arrived about ten miles above German Flats when Gansevoort's messenger rode up with the momentous news that "at 11 o'clock yesterday morning a heavy cannonade had been fired at the enemy's works." It had been immediately returned with a flurry of shells and round shot, but at three o'clock "several Deserters came in who informed that Genl St. Leger with his army was retreating with the utmost precipitation."[741]

Arnold immediately dictated a letter to Gates explaining why he had marched without waiting for the requested reinforcement — "I was determined at all events to hazard a battle rather than suffer the garrison to fall a sacrifice." He continued:

> [T]he excessive bad roads and necessary precautions in Marching thro' a thick wood retarded us so much that we have but his moment reached this place, where I have met an Express with the Inclosed Letter from Colo. Gansevoort [742]. . . the Enemy had yesterday retired from Fort Schuyler with great precipitation; I am at a loss to Judge of their real intentions; whether they have returned home or retired with a view of engaging us on the road; I am inclined to the former from the acco't of the Deserters, and from their leaving their Tents and considerable Baggage.[743]

He advised that he would "immediately Detail Abt. Nine hundred Men and make a forced March to the fort in hopes of coming up with their rear, & securing their Cannon and heavy Baggage." To facilitate his march, he left behind his artillery, tents, and baggage to join his bateaux brigade of provisions that was on the river.

Then he remembered himself and sent a second dispatch to intercept and turn about the reinforcement of light troops in the event that Gates had already responded to his request. As to the publicly flattered, but secretly maligned, Tryon militia, he simply dismissed them home.[744]

So, it was done. Burgoyne's version of Carleton's right hook through the Mohawk Valley had fizzled. Next morning, Gansevoort sent parties to all the British camps, where they took four prisoners. One was a frightened Jäger who told of the looting and stabbing by the Indians.[745] Another was an Indian, so drunk that a stick was run through his hair at the nape of the neck and he was dragged face down into the fort.[746] The garrison now held sixteen deserters and prisoners: one Hessian rifleman; one soldier of the 8th; five of the 34th; two Royal Artillerymen; one bateauman; and six Royal Yorkers, including Hanjost Schuyler. Other than Singleton, the highest-ranking prisoner was Serjeant John Lawrence of Duncan's company.[747] By comparison, the garrison had suffered seven dead, eighteen wounded, and nine desertions amongst the troops and local inhabitants since August 3.[748]

There was a great haul of useful loot, including St. Leger's escritoire,[749] which contained many letters and journals. Every Crown tent stood where it had been pitched, so if Hanjost's story was correct, St. Leger's order had not been obeyed. It was clear that a siege had been anticipated, no matter how much St. Leger had hoped it would be avoided. A list of the booty reveals what a monumental effort had to have been made by St. Leger's troops to forward the expedition's supplies and stores.

Tools & Supplies: 1 coil and 300 fathoms of rope; 1 set of men's dragging harness; 1 set of horse's harness; 106 spades; 100 picks; 80 felling axes; 1 set of blacksmith's tools; 2 casks of nails; 2 whip saws; 3 crosscut saws; 2 handsaws; 27 oil and 2 hair cloths; 30 copper hoops; 2 barrels of tar; 1 barrel of pitch; 2 tanned hides; 5 deer skins; 128 hundred weight of steel and 250 of iron.[750]

Ordnance and Ammunition: 4 Cohorn mortars; 2 travelling and limber carriages; 1 set of 3-pounder implements; 155 3- and 6-pounder round shot; 87 ditto, fixed with flannel cartridges; 128 Cohorn shells and 27 boxes of mortar cartridges; 2,160 musket cartridges; and 8 boxes of loose ball.

Transport: 23 bateaux; 19 wagons with cut wheels; and a number of horses.

Camp Equipage: 100 tent poles; 54 wedge tents;[751] 5 bell tents; 1 brass and 24 camp kettles; 12 pewter plates; 4 frying pans; 5 camp stools; 6 mattresses; 1 pair of curtains; 6 pairs of sheets; 18 bed cases; and a case of soap.

<u>Provisions</u>: a number of milch cows and 30-40 staved-in, but unspoiled, casks of flour.

<u>Clothing, etc.</u>: 40 coats; 36 capotes; 36 pair of breeches; 20 white and 49 speckled shirts; 10 knapsacks; 54 pair stockings; 20 handkerchiefs; 40 canteens; 56 blankets; and numerous smaller articles.[752]

The precipitate retreat of St. Leger and his troops has been the subject of much scorn. No attention has been given to the threat of a sortie by the garrison; instead, all concentration has been on the bogus threat of Arnold's column, which was miles away. Much has been made of the abandonment of so much equipment, yet in the face of the combined threat of the relief force and the garrison, it would have been foolhardy to attempt its removal. No one has commented about the somnolent garrison, which, throughout the withdrawal, remained safe behind the fort's walls, seemingly unaware that anything of note was happening outside. Surely, this hive of activity was visible from the sentry boxes, but not a word is said in contemporary Whig reports or later historical analyses about this inattention. To the victors the spoils, the kudos, and forgiveness.

During his forced march to Stanwix on August 24, General Arnold proceeded cautiously, advancing through thick woods rather than risking the roadway. For sure, the Albany road was in an atrocious state; however, more to the point, the lesson of the Oriskany ambush was not lost on Arnold, cocky and rash though he may have been.

In his reports, Arnold failed to mention an event that many of his men remembered for the rest of their lives. Reasoning that a second ambush would not be set amongst the militia's corpses, the column marched on the road through Oriskany. How the men coped with the stink of decomposition and the scenes of horror is unknown. Possibly they covered their noses and mouths with dampened handkerchiefs in an attempt to filter the choking smell. Lieutenant William Scudder of the 1NY recalled "we had to march over the ground where Herkimer's battle was fought, and as the dead had not been buried, and the weather warm, they were much swoln and of a purple color . . . we must have marched over and very near, about four hundred dead bodies."[753]

A few hours later, a sobered column entered the fortress to a very warm welcome: "They were Saluted with a Discharge of powder from our Mortars, formerly the Enemy's, and all the Cannon from the Bastions amounting in the whole to 13, Attended with three Cheers from the Troops on the Bastions."[754]

Arnold noted in his report to Gates written at ten o'clock the night of the twenty-fourth — "At 5 o'clock this evening . . . I reached this place . . . in expectation of harassing the enemy on their retreat," but Colonel Gansevoort had "anticipated my design" and sent out a party that brought in prisoners. That evening, Arnold dispatched a fresh scout of "faithful" Oneidas to scour the woods and pathways and issued orders to alert five hundred troops to advance to Lake Oneida the next morning.

In Garrison Orders, Arnold formerly offered his thanks to Gansevoort, the officers, and enlisted men "for their Gallant Defence of Fort Schuyler[,] they may be assured of his Warmest Recommendations to Congress." He advised that the plunder from St. Leger's camps, except the public stores, would "be sold by public Auctions without the Gate as soon as the Weather will permit it, and the proceeds to be divided amongst the Garrison in proportion to the pay of Officers and Men."[755]

Captain Lernoult's crew had retraced the lake on their rescue mission in a heavy, persistent downpour that added to the gloom of recent events and met the straggling bateaux at the outlet of Wood Creek. The weary, sodden boatmen told frightening tales of the "rascally" Indians who had leapt aboard their craft and sacked the cargo. After pushing clear, they discovered that all the other boats had disappeared. In fear of abandonment, they jettisoned the 3-pounder tube near the junction of Canada Creek,[756] and, their load lightened, made better time, but no one was in sight when they got to the mouth of Wood Creek. They were contemplating captivity when Lernoult's boats came in sight. After a quick meal, the two parties set off across the lake.

Arnold's five-hundred-man detachment marched out of Stanwix early the next morning, but the majority soon turned back due to the heavy rain. A small force pushed on to Lake Oneida and arrived at the shore to watch the British boats disappear into the teaming downpour.[757] If this small force was indeed part of the relief column, their brief glimpse was the closest that any of Arnold's men came to contact with St. Leger's forlorn expedition.

~

CHAPTER TWELVE

Retracing Its Steps
An Astonishing Detour

Arnold reported to Gates that the garrison "deserved great applause for their spirited conduct and vigorous defence, their duty having been very severe."[758] He found that Gansevoort had "suffered much by the severity of the siege" and granted him leave to go to Albany, leaving Willett in charge. Although Arnold believed the fort was "out of danger this year," the works were still not complete. As the Massachusetts troops were being withdrawn, he detached six companies of the 1NY.

He also complimented the Oneidas and Tuscaroras, but noted that "the other tribes of the Six Nations are villains and I hope will be treated as such."

One such villain, Towasguate, an Onondaga chief, came to Arnold to plea for recognition of his nation's neutrality. This was a critical matter, as Fort Stanwix was just fifty miles from their towns.[759] A skeptical Arnold saw a perfect opportunity to obtain the release of St. Leger's militia prisoners and told Towasguate that his success with this task would prove his nation's good faith. The anxious chief set off in pursuit of the retreating expedition.[760]

Prior to leaving Lake Oneida, John Butler obtained St. Leger's permission for Senior Ranger James Secord and fifty rangers to return to the settlements to collect and drive cattle to Fort Niagara.[761] The rest of the troops and their faithful native allies left Brewerton the morning of August 24 and were at the Onondaga Falls portage the next day when they were overtaken by a native express from Burgoyne. The Indian had overheard information about Arnold's attempts to call out the Tryon militia and reported that the relief column was made up of simply "the same kind of rabble as before." While this misleading information was deflating enough, to St. Leger's utter chagrin, he was told there was not "an enemy within forty miles of Fort-Stanwix."[762] Of course, Arnold had a solid force of Continentals and Fort Dayton was really within thirty miles of Stanwix, but the kernel of the issue was clear; St. Leger had been gulled. His despair reached new depths, and if his resort to the bottle had been frequent before, perhaps now it was constant.

Arnold's express to Gates arrived at the Albany headquarters on the morning of August 25. After digesting the joyous news, Gates wrote a letter claiming that "300 Indians were killed in Genl Herkermers engagement."[763] The raising of the siege had spawned even more exaggeration.

Colonel James Livingston's First Canadian Regiment (1CDN) guarded Arnold's provisions brigade as it toiled up the Mohawk. It was a small battalion of three hundred rebel Canadiens and recently absorbed New Yorkers who had been garrisoning the Johnstown area, when the local citizenry offered to assume their posts and free them to march with Arnold's relief.

As the 1CDN marched out of the shattered town of Oriska, their vanguard was assailed by the cloying stench of putrefaction. A firelock was found leaning against a tree with a pair of boots, and a search found the owner decaying in the creek. Another man was discovered a little way from the creek, "genteely dressed" without a coat or hat. A serjeant attempted to remove a silk handkerchief from the corpse's head, but the hair came away and he cast it aside. Undeterred, he scavenged the dead man's silver shoe buckles, observing that his deerskin breeches were rent from top to bottom by swollen, decomposing flesh. Then the van came across nine bodies laid side by side across the road. At the request of the committee, Arnold had ordered the burying of the dead, but the stink was so gagging, nothing could persuade the soldiers to dig graves. Further on, they found an Indian trussed up in a horse harness hanging from a tree limb. Some thought the militia had swung him up,[764] but more likely, he was being degraded as a traitor by one native faction or the other.

No one recorded what happened when the guard came opposite the battlefield, but if the odour of death was strong from eleven bodies, it was utterly intolerable from hundreds.[765] Again, the instructions to inter the dead were ignored and the guard passed along the river's shore. A few hours later, they entered Stanwix. Their arrival was most welcome, as the garrison had been supplementing their salt provisions by killing the inhabitants' "Milch Cows, Hoggs, pigs."[766]

On August 25, the Tryon committee of safety proved conclusively that it was again in the ascendancy at a meeting in the Palatine district. They resolved that Colonel Hendrick Frey would be sent to Governor Clinton at Kingston with details of his "inhuman Threatenings and horrid Assertions." That afternoon, they prepared a report for Governor Clinton. Although St. Leger had been thwarted and an uprising in nearby Schoharie quelled, they knew the fight was far from over. They wrote that "The late Triall of this County drove Numbers of hidden Enemies into the Woods, severall have joined the Enemy, a considerable Number is absconding yet in the Woods, supplied by their Families . . . Women of those Enemies is still living among us, some behave very rudely . . . and have proved very active to support and spirit up the opposite Cause." They advised that the wives of John Butler, Peter Ten Broeck, William Bowen, Gilbert Tice, John McDonell Scotus, and several others would be rounded up with their children and confined in Tice's tavern at Johnstown.

The need to seek retribution for the Oriskany disaster was very strong. Clinton was advised of charges levelled against a fellow committeeman, "Michael Ittig [who] did forget his Duty as Captain . . . so far as to consent to the Enemy's Protection." Further, Captain Jelles Fonda was "very little trusted; an Oneida Indian declared . . . that [he] . . . had sent up three letters to the Indians, showing and by trading with them . . . that he was not such a fool as the other Tories, Ten Broeck and others; he had more wit than them, if they had stood at home they would be in possession of their goods if the country would loose or gain the point . . . Doctor Younglove, who is now a prisoner with the enemy, declared openly that he heard Jellis Fonda say it was best to lay down arms . . . and all sensible men of America was of the same opinion."

A list was enclosed of committeemen and militia officers killed at Oriskany and those unable to serve due to wounds. The committee asked the governor to "give such Directions . . . to restore this County to proper Vigour in civil and military Affairs, and to issue such further orders, as will most effectually destroy Disaffection, and restore harmony."[767] Clinton's attentions were focused on Burgoyne's advance and the threat of the British at York City; consequently, it was several months before he took action to stabilize Tryon County.

At Stanwix, the weather cleared in the evening of the twenty-sixth, and the 1CDN and Jackson's regiment boarded the bateaux and set off downriver. The next day, Bailey's and Wesson's regiments followed with Arnold's suite.[768]

St. Leger arrived at Oswego on August 26 and immediately held a council of his senior commanders and staff. The meeting was underway when Lieutenant-Colonel Carl von Kreutzbourg came ashore with the balance of the Hesse Hanau Jägers to be greeted by his "Vacant" company as it straggled out of the woods.

Von Kreutzbourg had originally been told that St. Leger's expedition was composed of "1000 light English Infantry . . . and 3000 Aborigines," and this misinformation may have explained his reactions when he discovered the facts. Certainly, nothing had prepared him for the bedraggled, dispirited little army that met his sight. In agitation von Kreutzbourg attended the council and found St. Leger "in such as state of consternation, that he did not know what to say." Von Kreutzbourg recorded that the following issues were discussed:

1. Whether we were to advance or retire.
2. In case the former were preferred, where were they to get their lost guns, provisions and ammunition from, and how were the men to be provided with large and small articles of equipment again?
3. In case the latter were chosen, which was the safest way to take?

Sir John "voted for advancing" and von Kreutzbourg agreed, provided his men were given shoes and time to repair their rifles. He complained that he wanted to avoid the "ruinous journey" on the St. Lawrence again. What effect this newcomer's words had is unknown.

Likely, St. Leger found him rather insolent, as no one went any distance in North America without using the waterways, a fact the Hessian had obviously yet to absorb. His report continued:

> The most votes were for advancing, St. Leger, the officer of artillery and the Commissary-general voted for the contrary, as there was neither a supply of ammunition nor of provisions, and they did not know either where such were to be procured. To cut the matter short we shall return tomorrow or the day after to [La] Prairie opposite Montreal by batteaux, where the Corps will be supplied with what is necessary, and when that has been done we shall cross Lac Champlain to join General Burgoyne's Army.[769]

Later that day, St. Leger wrote to Burgoyne advising that "the overplus provisions" would be sent to Fort Niagara, except for sufficient stores "to carry my detachment down" to Montreal. The sloop at Oswego had already been sent off "with her full lading" and the snow[770] had been ordered for the same purpose. "Officers from each corps are sent to Montreal to procure necessaries for the men, who are in a most

Representative Hessian Jägers, ca. 1784

Hand-coloured, engraved plate by J.C. Muller after J.H. Carl, Hochfurst, Hesse-Cassel. Courtesy of the Anne S.K. Brown Military Collection, Brown University Library.

deplorable situation from the plunder of the savages." Of course, this blame conveniently ignored the stores so cavalierly abandoned. He closed with a promise to move his troops "with every expedition in my power" and "that no time may be lost to join the army."[771]

The next day, St. Leger completed his detailed report and sent it off in the care of Lieutenant James Lundy, Royal Highland Emigrants (RHE), the quartermaster-general.[772] Perhaps his intimate knowledge of the expedition's lost equipment was expected to elicit some sympathy. St. Leger included a return of his "Secret Expedition," showing that he had lost 37 men since August 1 — 17 Regulars, 14 Royal Yorkers, and 6 Jägers. No Canadiens, rangers, or natives were reported as casualties. Forty-two men were sick, 15 were "On Command," and 585 were "fit for Duty." This enumeration did not include the 345 Jägers of the three newly arrived companies.[773]

Indian matters required a great deal of attention. John Butler was sent to Montreal to obtain presents for the disappointed natives. This assignment would prove personally advantageous to Butler, as he had clandestine plans to discuss with Carleton before his mentor was recalled to Britain.

Claus recognized that when the expedition retired to Montreal, the Six Nations' territory, except for the far western border at Niagara, would be abandoned and the Mohawk castles left open to retaliation. He was able to "as much as possible, reconcil [them] to this resolution [for St. Leger to join Burgoyne]" and promised that a council would be "conven'd as soon as Col. Butler cou'd return from Montreal with some necessarys for them." He clothed the Indians who had lost their packs to Willett's sortie and reported that they "return[ed] home contented."[774] This last comment was a considerable overstatement; he knew very well that the natives were dangerously discontented. Perhaps his personal concerns warped his thinking, for he was in a stew about his future employment and irritated by Butler's rising importance while his brother-in-law Guy squandered his advantage in York City.[775] Claus recognized that once Carleton left for home, he might fill the vacuum between Guy Johnson and Butler.

Relations between the Hessian colonel and the Anglo-Irish brigadier were strained from the outset.[776] Von Kreutzbourg sarcastically described St. Leger as the leader "under whom . . . we were to gain all the laurels we possibly could." With evident relish, he reported to his Crown Prince that

St. Leger had "fled from Fort Stanwix after losing his tents and the rest of his baggage." Of course, the German had the cheap advantage of hindsight and he damned St. Leger thoroughly: "St. Leger is a man who is quite unfit for the work the King has given him to do . . . [he] does not display the least solicitude for his troops, has little initiative, almost always acts upon others' (sometimes bad) advice, so that I have resolved to beg General Bourgoyne when I join the army to withdraw me and the Corps from this man's orders, as I foresee a second disgrace in consequence of his irresolution." To a distraught St. Leger, whose world had come tumbling down about his ears, this imperious German must have been the last straw.

Von Kreutzbourg found the "Vacant" company in deplorable condition. During the retreat, the lieutenants and the sergeant-major lost much of their personal kit, and eight rifles and twenty-two knapsacks had been mislaid or stolen. Although the loyalist officers were moved by training and inclination to respect native customs, von Kreutzbourg was entirely unburdened by a sympathetic outlook towards "these horrible tribes." Like many men fresh from overseas, he failed to recognize that their value in forest warfare often outweighed the annoyance caused by their unfamiliar customs and expectations. When he discovered one of his missing Jäger rifles in the hands of a warrior, he went after it, sword drawn. In this manner, he recovered four of the missing rifles. Soon after, he found the natives "so afraid of our hunting swords" that he simply put his hand on the hilt and they jumped away "fifty paces in two bounds." The affronted Indians levelled their firelocks, "but so far none of them have shot." He ordered "all these scoundrels flogged out of camp."

The chiefs complained to St. Leger, who counselled von Kreutzbourg about the traditional native right to retain booty. The Hessian was incredulous that goods looted from allies during a retreat were viewed as legitimate gains and, in wry amusement, replied that it was the German custom to forcibly regain stolen goods and flog all thieves. Flummoxed, St. Leger had no reply.

When the Mohawks had left the siege camps, they had travelled stealthily eastwards through the Valley. John Deserontyon's wounds hardly slowed the Fort Hunter party. When he reached home, the war captain shrugged off his affliction and with characteristic energy set about preparing the village for a mass departure.

Jospeh Brant took the Canajoharies directly to Burgoyne's army and arrived on August 28. While infiltrating the rebels' outposts, they handily brushed aside all opposition. As they passed through the outlying native camp, Brant spoke to some Seven Nations headmen and received an earful. When he gained an audience with Burgoyne, Brant gave him his first news of St. Leger's retreat. After the Bennington debacle, this intelligence must have jolted even the callously optimistic Burgoyne.

Word of Burgoyne's restrictions on native warfare had led Brant to conclude that "affairs with that Army [were] being mismanaged." Brant had a marked preference for native methods and independent operations, and he may also have sensed another defeat in the offing.

Having decided he could be of no service, the crafty Mohawk took the measure of Burgoyne's vanity and told him that the rebels had spread word "all over the Continent" that his army was defeated and retiring to Canada. He said he had come in person to see whether these rumours were true so "that he might take back certain News to the Indians with Col. St. Leger." Burgoyne accepted this explanation as both sensible and credible and Brant was able to slip away without recriminations.[777]

At Stanwix, Willett struggled to return the ebullient troops to a sense of duty. On August 28, he forbade the soldiers to fire their muskets without leave. A few days later, he instructed the quartermaster to remove "every kind of Nusance from around the Camp and Garrison." Some men had a habit of remaining outside the fort all night, so he ordered the "Gates be shut at Dusk on beating the Long Roll." A few days later, he noted:

> [I am] very sorry to hear the Idle as well as Sinfull Custom of profane Cursing and Swearing practiced in this Garrison. A practice that while it can afford no kind of pleasure or profit to the person who uses it, is a Transgression of the laws of our Country as well as off our God, and can be productive of no other Consequences than those of procuring the Displeasure of Heaven, and offending the Thoughtfull Virtuous Ear.

Shortly after, he ordered the severe punishment of "any Person . . . easing themselves, in any other places about the Camp, or Garrison, except the Necessaries provided for that purpose."[778] Clearly, fort life had returned to the mundane.

Some of the men who were ranging about outside the fort made a grim discovery when they came upon the body of a militiaman impaled a few feet off the ground by a bayonet driven into a tree. This macabre display drew regular voyeurs, and after a few weeks it was found that the rotted corpse had fallen to the ground, but the blade refused to be dislodged from the trunk.[779]

With fresh memories of the vengeance wreaked upon Oriska, Brant force-marched his party to the upper castle. His intuition was timely, for the process of revenge was already underway. Chairman Deygart was aware that many Mohawks were in considerably better circumstances than their white neighbours and was eager to get his covetous hands on some plunder. He reasoned the pickings would be easy, as most of the men were away on campaign. To gain the Oneidas' complicity and assistance, Deygart encouraged the Oriskas to make up for their losses by raiding Canajoharie and to take two horses, two sheep, and two oxen where they had lost one.

The attacks began with rather mild harassment. In the dead of night, a small group that claimed to be searching for Joseph Brant entered Mary Brant's house and threatened to move her family to Albany. Young Margaret Brant recalled, "I was in one of the beds of which they drew back the Curtains, & seeing only Children in it, they declined ferther Search." After a similar experience a few nights later, "my Mother . . . determined to leave the Country as she found her residence... no longer Safe. She left her House with reluctance & with a Sore heart taking her Children[,] Seven in number[,] two black men Servants & two female Servants."[780]

Brant arrived in time for his family's departure. He warned his neutralist neighbours what to expect if Burgoyne was defeated. A great many heeded his advice and left for Indian Territory. Brant led his family through rebel-patrolled country to the Cayuga towns, where they were cared for by relatives.[781]

The Oriska war captain Honyery Tewahangaraghkan, Peter Deygart, Hanjost Schuyler, and other opportunists entered the almost deserted castle and looted the homes, paying particular heed to Mary Brant's. Deygart and Tewahangaraghkan shared a great haul, as Mary's belongings included "Sixty half Johannesses, two Quarts full of silver, several Gold Rings, Eight pair silver Buckels; a large Quantity of Silver Broaches. Together with silk Gowns." Deygart took wagonloads of loot and, to add insult to injury, his daughter traipsed about in Molly's silks. Encouraged by Deygart, Honyery and his Oriska brothers plundered Han Jost Herkimer's nearby house. Some days later, Tewahangaraghkan's dispossessed family moved into the widow Molly's home.[782]

Amherst's bateaux brigade shoots the rapids of the St. Lawrence en route to Montreal in 1760. Without adequate pilots, his army lost eighty-four men and sixty-four bateaux before arriving at the Lachine rapids.

Drawing in pencil, pen, and ink by Thomas Davies, 1760. Courtesy of the
National Archives of Canada, C-000577.

At Albany on September 2, the city's committee requested that General Gates allow several Tory families to "be sent to the Enemy," including Major Gray's and those of several others who were serving under Burgoyne.[783]

St. Leger's quartermaster, Lieutenant Lundy, made excellent time from Oswego and arrived at Burgoyne's headquarters at Fort Edward on September 2,[784] bringing formal confirmation of Brant's news — the siege of Stanwix was abandoned.

Claus anticipated a surge of rebel diplomatic effort, yet surprisingly, one of the first overtures came from the natives. The sachems of Oquaga and nearby Coolateen in Indian Territory, two towns that had supplied Brant with many of his volunteers, requested that New York State recognize their settlements as neutral and asked forgiveness for their young men who had joined Butler. They said their people would not take offence if any of their young men had been killed at Stanwix and asked that the Whigs do the same. This typical native message — utterly pragmatic, yet to white eyes so artful and dissembling — was forwarded to Governor Clinton for his instructions.[785] When he presented the requests to the State Council, the members were insulted and resolved that the two towns should be considered enemies, unless their warriors were immediately recalled. In contrast, they found the Oneidas were allies of the State and "any attack upon them [would be] an attack upon our own People." Clinton was "empowered to take into Pay such of the Indian Warriors as may choose to enter into the Service of this State."

On September 3, Clinton sent instructions to the Oquaga and Coolateen sachems:

> [I]f their young Men are fond of Fighting and choose to be in War that they can come & join us who are their Brethern born, in the same Country against our common Enemies and we will pay them as we do our own young Men who go out & fight for us.
>
> The Indian may see what Reliance is to be put on the Promises of Butler and his Friends by the shameful Manner they have fled from Fort Stanwix leaving their Cannon Tents ammunition & even their Provisions behind them, tho' they boasted they would take that Fort & proceed to Albany in a Short Time & that our People dare not fight them.[786]

Although St. Leger knew the importance of joining the Grand Army, he was unable to leave Oswego, as so many vessels were on other urgent business.[787] As the days dragged by, he occupied his men with firing practice. On September 4, von Kreutzbourg was in command when he discovered the expedition's left wing would be firing ball into the camp hospital and he blamed St. Leger for not examining the firing range before sending the troops out. Obviously, some subordinate officer had made a silly mistake, and, in any event, St. Leger expected his detachment commanders to make any necessary adjustments, but the German saw the error as another nail in the coffin of his leader's competence. That von Kreutzbourg also had "to beg for every portion of bread . . . whilst the English always get what is due to them" did not help St. Leger's cause and drew "down upon him the hatred of all the Jägers without gaining him the goodwill of the English."[788]

At Burgoyne's camp at Fort Edward on September 4, Captains John Deserontyon, Aaron Kanonraron, and Isaac Hill Onoghsokte and Chief Canadagaia arrived with the Fort Hunter families and several prominent white loyalists.[789] The villagers had abandoned their homes after hearing of the sack of the upper castle.

Many Fort Hunters abandoned considerable fortunes, so rich spoils again fell to the Whigs and their Oneida friends.[790] Captain John's handsome house and barn was on eighty-two acres "of rich flat Land." Grains had been left in the barn and barracks with a wagon, plough, harrow, and ten beaver traps. In the house were several broadcloth suits, four scarlet blankets mounting silverwork and ribbons, six blue stroud blankets, six kettles, pewter basins and plates, his bed, bedstead, and curtains, and "5,000 Wampum in Bolts, &c."[791] Kanonraron had abandoned a similar list of possessions plus "2 cows and 16 sheep, 6 horses, 1 wagon, 2 common slays with harness, 1 plough and harrow . . . 2 guns and 4 large kettles . . . 2 suits cloaths, 2 suits womens cloaths . . . all worth £544."

A few neutralists like sachem Little Abraham Tyorsansere and his associate Johannes Schrine Unaquandahoojie, who were dedicated to peace, clung to the settlement, but they were faced with distrust and resentment instead of receiving understanding or appreciation from their Whig neighbors.[792]

Once the warriors were gone, the rebels jailed the Reverend John Stuart, the Fort Hunter Anglican chaplain, and pillaged the parsonage. Queen Anne's Chapel was looted and desecrated, first used as a tavern and later as a stable. Fortunately, the Mohawks had the foresight to bury the cherished Communion plate given to them by Queen Anne in 1712.[793]

The Mohawks had sent a messenger ahead requesting assistance in breaking through the rebel outposts. Captain-Lieutenant Thomas Scott and a party of Kanehsatakes were sent out, but failed to make contact. Instead, a forty-man scout of the 3rd New Hampshire blocked the refugees' progress. Ever alert, the warriors took cover in the woods and laid an ambush. A sharp firefight ensued in which one of the Hill brothers was killed and Captain John was freshly wounded. Punching through, the Mohawks killed seven, wounded two or three others and brought in four scalps.[794]

The Fort Hunters numbered about 150 souls and brought with them "cattle, horses, and sheep." Burgoyne planned to have the elderly, women, and children travel to Canada;[795] however, the Mohawks refused to be separated. The addition of 40 warriors was most welcome, as his contingent had shrunk from a peak of 900 to only 150 Canada Indians.[796]

On the same day that the lower castle Mohawks joined Burgoyne, General Gates received a letter from proud young Walter Butler. Walter had arrived from Fort Dayton a few days before. He had avoided the humiliation of asking for a public favour, but now he sought a private audience and was confident of a positive response, as his grandfather had served with Gates. Likely, Gates was insulted by the presumption. His reply, if any, has not been found.[797]

Claus knew that the Iroquois Confederacy's affairs would require firm action over the fall and winter to offset the inevitable storm of United States diplomacy. He called the headmen together and urged them to "be revenged upon the rebels for the loss of their chiefs at Fort Stanwix and for some of their peoples being put in irons and confined at Albany." Their response was clear:

> [O]ur Hatchet is dull, on account of being restrained
> these 2 years from acting agst the rebells, and our expe-
> dition to Fort Stanwix not sufficiently equipt, that they
> intend taking up the Hatchet their forefathers gave

them, wch was burried in a deep pit, but very sharp, and would force its way wherever pointed, without controul; at the same time they declare that they only mean to restore peace to the country, and make the King's children to repent and return to their duty.[798]

The chiefs sent belts to the Western Indians advising them of their plans and recommending that they "follow their example." Claus included messages, confirming them "by large strings of Wampum." Before Claus left Oswego, the couriers returned with the western nations' answer that "all [were] in the King's interest . . . [and] will act with more vigor and spirit."

Claus ordered ranger Captain John Johnston and his nephew, Lieutenant William Johnston, to return to their previous station at the Seneca settlement of Canadasaga. Lieutenant George McGinnis and the Docksteder brothers, Lieutenants John and Frederick, were sent to the Cayuga castle. The men were supplied with wampum, trade goods, and liquor and given orders to obstruct all rebel intercourse with the Senecas and Cayugas and keep those nations firmly joined to the British alliance.[799]

Claus asked the sexagenarian Sarah Kast McGinnis to join her son George at Cayuga. She "was much beloved by the 6 Nations," and in her youth, her parents had allowed her to "live among them, and [they] adopted her as one of themselves[;] she acquired the language perfectly." The great affection and respect held for Sarah by the matrons, sachems, and war captains of the Iroquois Confederacy proved of great value over the winter in holding the western nations to their treaty with the Crown.[800]

Moses Younglove, who rivalled Benjamin Franklin for imaginative accounts of native atrocities, recalled a quite different aspect of native affairs. He claimed that the Indians were allowed to remove a prisoner from the Oswego guardhouse at will and, with a keg of rum, go to an island for a feast. Once there, they bent a small tree, split it open, and thrust their victim's arm through the slit. When the tree was released, the captive flew up and was suspended above a fire pit and roasted. Younglove claimed to have lain in his cell listening to the victims' shrieks.

Claus had reported that Major Isaac Paris, a virulent Tryon Whig, had been killed at Stanwix to prevent his recapture by Willett's sortie.

Younglove claimed that Paris was taken from the guardhouse and tortured to death within sight of the prisoners and a party of British officers. When Younglove protested to St. Leger, the brigadier exclaimed, "Damn the rebels; they deserve no better treatment."

When Younglove's turn came, he "sprang to a bar of iron which was in the room and got between the Indian and the door and made at him . . ., but he escaped through the window and no Indian after that came into the guardhouse."[801] Why an iron bar would be left in the guardhouse is a mystery, and why an Indian could dive through a window, but the prisoners could not, is another. A third puzzle is how such tales received so much credulous currency throughout the United States during and after the war.

For the second time in as many months, John McDonell Scotus arrived at Oswego, this time with forty-four recruits fresh from an abortive uprising against the rebel regime in the Schoharie. The unexpected intervention of a troop of continental cavalry thwarted the attempt, and they fled the Valley to join Sir John.

Johnson gave McDonell the heart-rending news of the death of his son, Captain-Lieutenant Donald John, which was a particularly bitter blow coming on top of his decision to abandon his wife and children. The majority of the men were enrolled in a new company under Scotus and the others were distributed across the regiment.[802]

On September 8, after a two-week delay to collect transport, the expedition was about to board the boats for the trip down the turbulent St. Lawrence to join Burgoyne's Grand Army, when an express dispatch came for Captain Lernoult. Governor Carleton ordered the 8th's companies not to accompany St. Leger, but to sail to Buck Island and forward from there all provisions and merchandise to the upper posts. When that task was complete, the Lights were to return to Oswegatchie and the hatmen to Niagara.[803]

When Younglove was afloat on Lake Ontario with his fellow prisoners, he was pleased to see "several boats loaded with Indians with Hessian uniforms." He mused that the natives had killed the Jägers and "sold their scalps to the British and dressed in their clothing." It is difficult to believe that the volatile von Kreutzbourg would have ignored, or failed

*Fort Oswegatchie — the only British post on the St. Lawrence River between
Lachine and Lake Ontario*

*Detail from a watercolour by an unknown artist after Henry Rudyerd, ca. 1780. Courtesy of the
National Archives of Canada, C-040330.*

to record, such a challenge. Yet surely the doctor could tell the difference
between natives and Europeans. Or was he again fantasizing?[804]

St. Leger had gone on ahead, leaving von Kreutzbourg to command the
expedition. The boats were not long on the lake when "steady rains and
stormy weather" forced them to take shelter "at the influx of . . . la
Rivière au Sable," where one of the Jägers, who was suffering from "a
kind of dementia," wandered into the woods. A daylight search was
unsuccessful, and during the night, the Hessian horners attempted to
guide him back by blowing their instruments. A rearguard detachment
of Jägers was left behind the next day to continue the search.

The expedition was further delayed by the sandbars at Ile aux
Gallots. The Royal Yorkers and 34th companies passed through, but the
Jägers' thirty boats lagged behind for some nine miles. Once they caught
up, a Hessian party hunted pigeons and grouse to make a broth for the
regiment's seventy sick men. They had been without bread for four to
five days and were subsisting on tough flour dumplings boiled in water.
Von Kreutzbourg fumed that St. Leger refused to supply the rations
stipulated in the contract between the Hessians' Crown Prince and the
British monarch, supposedly because the document had been printed in
Germany.[805] This charade more likely reflected the dearth of provisions
of any type, but the relationship between the two men was now beyond
rational discussion.

Shooting the river's cataracts was an extremely hazardous undertaking, and a Buck Island merchant lost four new bateaux valued at
eighty pounds while transporting the inexperienced Hanau battalion.[806]

At Albany, U.S. native diplomacy was enjoying great success. Three hundred Oneida and Tuscarora men, women, and children, an Onondaga chief with a few followers, and several Mohawk neutralists arrived on September 14 for General Schuyler's council. The next day, there was a mutual exchange of congratulations over St. Leger's retreat, followed by the Oneida chiefs metaphorically drawing the Six Nations' axe out of the Whigs' heads with the promise that "it should be struck no more." The commissioners probed whether the natives would support General Gates's army and, to their pleasure, found the Oneidas and Tuscaroras very keen. Schuyler repeated the mantra that Butler had almost brought ruin upon the confederacy and encouraged them "[t]o avenge yourselves of those people who have deceived you, and to turn the vengeance upon their heads which they so well deserve." He then said, "I now put into your hands this Axe" and tendered a large black and white belt bearing a hatchet decorated with the initials "U.S."[807] The Onondagas and Mohawks declined the war belt, but the Oneidas and Tuscaroras eagerly took hold and sang their war songs.

After a grand war feast the next day, the chiefs of the two rebel nations solemnly and formally accepted the war hatchet, and, in doing so, reconfirmed the splitting of the Iroquois Confederacy. Circumspectly, the delegates proclaimed they would use the axe only against the King's men and not their native brothers.

A steady dribble of loyalists was arriving at Burgoyne's camp, but never enough to satisfy the general's thirst for men. On September 15, a party of six appeared with John Munro. They had trekked for nineteen days through enemy-infested territory after escaping from the prison hulks at Esopus. Munro had been through two miserable bouts of imprisonment because of his recruiting activities for the Royal Highland Emigrants and was under a sentence of death when he and his five cellmates bribed two guards to gain their freedom.[808]

The U.S. Indian Commissioners spent two days equipping their native allies. On the evening of September 19, Honyery Tewahangaraghkan,

Peter Bread, and the exiled Kahnawake, Louis Atayataghronghta, were dining with the commissioners when word arrived about a major battle at Freeman's Farm. The Indians were spurred into action and most of the warriors departed that night, followed by the remainder early the next morning.[809]

A total of 112 Oneidas and Tuscaroras joined Gates's army. Added to the Stockbridge Indians, this brought the total of natives under U.S. arms to double Burgoyne's shrunken contingent.[810] One of their stated objectives was to collect prisoners to use as bargaining chips for the freedom of the three Iroquois held in Albany who had been captured with Walter Butler at German Flats.[811] Perhaps this measure was intended to restore relations with their brethren, but just as likely, it stemmed from their pride as Iroquois.

Over the next few days, Oneida and Tuscarora scouting and raiding parties caused havoc amongst Burgoyne's troops. Gates had made great play in the press about Burgoyne's use of savages against his army, but when the tables were reversed, he exhibited few scruples. On September 21, the natives returned from their first foray with two terrified Tory sentries, whom they had painted black. The hapless men were presented to Gates, and he coolly returned them to their captors for their amusement. The warriors "drove them shouting & whooping thro the Street," then took one and "Buried him up to his Neck & had their Pow-wow around him, after that, they had him up and Laid him a side of a great fire & turn'd his head & feet a while to the fire, hooting & hallowing round him."[812]

On September 23, Gates's Indians circled around to the north of the Grand Army's perimeter and snapped up a party of Tories carrying dispatches to Ticonderoga and Montreal. Such successes became regular occurrences and forced Burgoyne to operate in isolation.

On September 22, St. Leger's expedition beached at La Prairie on the south shore of the St. Lawrence opposite Montreal. Alarming news awaited them — the rebels had besieged and perhaps retaken Ticonderoga. The pressure was extreme to push the regiments forward so they could resecure the Ticonderoga posts and join Burgoyne on the Hudson River.

As the expedition was now in Brigadier Allan Maclean's district, von

Kreutzbourg was under the impression that the Scotsman would take command, but he was to be disappointed.

The next day, von Kreutzbourg dispatched twenty-three Jägers to hospital in Montreal. As well, the very worst of the British and loyalist sick and wounded were similarly transferred. Judging by von Kreutzbourg's action, the Royal Artillery, the 34th, and the Royal Yorkers were brought up to strength by drawing men from those elements that had been originally left in lower Quebec.

Von Kreutzbourg examined the demented Jäger whom the rearguard had found wandering in the woods and concluded that the man was mentally unbalanced. Lacking any alternative, he gave him an honourable discharge and left him to his own devices.

A few hours later, St. Leger's regiments set off overland to Fort St. John's, where they would be resupplied with necessaries, ammunition, and provisions for a waterborne assault to recapture Ticonderoga.[813]

For all the time that the expedition had been away from lower Quebec, Governor Carleton continued his battle of words with his superior, Lord George Germain.[814] His stream of invective over his displacement resulted in a tartly worded rejoinder reminding him that the King had directed the awarding of command in North America, and, in Germain's opinion, "there was not a part of it which I did not think most wisely calculated for the public service." As to Carleton's abbreviated campaign in 1776, the secretary scalded his junior's wounded ego with the advice that intelligence revealed that "the Rebels intended to have abandoned their Post at Ticonderoga, had you marched your army towards it."[815]

Carleton found Germain's opinions about the earlier campaign particularly galling, and his resentment boiled while he impatiently awaited the King's permission to return to Britain. His inner turmoil did not greatly affect his management of political and military affairs across Quebec and at Niagara; however, on the few occasions where he might have been expected to offer aid to Burgoyne, he hid behind the strictest interpretation of the King's instructions.[816]

On the other hand, he hastily forwarded a corvée of several hundred Canadien workers and one hundred Brunswick recruits, who were immediately employed at the Ticonderoga posts by the commandant.[817]

Fort St. John's on the Richelieu River with a British soldier, woman, child, and four ships of the Lake Champlain fleet

Detail from a watercolour over pencil, pen, and ink by James Hunter, ca. 1779. Courtesy of the National Archives of Canada, C-1507.

Carleton continued to hold strict views about native utilization. His belief that an Indian war had been foisted on his province was confirmed by the tales of Indian "excesses" that filtered back to his office. He complained to Germain on August 11: "[Y]ou have also taken the conduct of the war entirely out of my hands even within the strict limits of my commission; and (where your Lordship does not direct), you have entrusted it to Lieut. Gen. Burgoyne, to Lieut. Col. St. Leger . . . till General Howe shall give them further Instructions."[818]

In consequence, he avoided many matters relating to the natives' military employment, except for the forwarding of native contingents previously assigned to Burgoyne and St. Leger. Yet, for all his studied disinterest, Carleton did not lack warnings about native discontent. Lieutenant-Colonel Mason Bolton, the new commanding officer of the 8th Regiment at Niagara, sent news on September 9 that Schuyler was "very industrious in spreading reports to our disadvantage amongst the Indians" and had invited the Six Nations to a council at German Flats "to settle what had passed and renew their former chain of friendship." More alarming, Schuyler said that "as soon as Colonel St. Leger was gone he would take post at Ontario [Oswego] with a considerable force."[819]

Butler and three principal Iroquois chiefs arrived at Governor Carleton's Quebec City headquarters around September 14. The chiefs advised the governor of the Iroquois Confederacy's deep concern that their country lay entirely open to rebel incursions since the retreat of the troops and recommended that the British take permanent post at Oswego to demonstrate their commitment to protect their friends. Without that safeguard, they said their "Warriors could not go from Home while the Enemy were so near them, without exposing their villages, their Women and Children to Danger."[820]

Carleton had already heard of Schuyler's threatening promise to occupy Oswego, an action entirely inimical to British interests. The Crown had persuaded the nations to take an active role in the conflict and exposed them to the rebels' wrath. The governor recognized that their request to rebuild and garrison Oswego was reasonable, as it would forestall the rebels as well as guard Iroquoia and provide additional protection for the upper posts' communications.

Although Oswego was within Carleton's military jurisdiction, the diplomatic relationship with the Iroquois Confederacy rested with Guy Johnson and ultimately Sir William Howe. In addition to that conundrum, he was without the resources to act, as his army was small, overcommitted, and widely dispersed. As well, he was on the verge of being recalled and could sensibly leave the decision to his replacement. Finding himself between an anvil and hammer, he promised the army would occupy Oswego the next spring. It may have been better if he had continued to avoid such issues, as this hollow commitment later haunted the Quebec administration.

Privately, Major John Butler adroitly presented his earlier idea, but not before priming Carleton by repeating Claus's snide comments about Carleton's conduct of affairs in 1775 and the gossip this had engendered in England.[821] Carleton's mind seethed in resentment, and his obligation to Butler was sharpened by this confidence. Butler requested a beating order to raise a corps of rangers, claiming he already had the makings of two companies and that many recruits simply awaited his call.

Carleton was empathetic. The ranger's deserving aspirations had been crushed by the home government, just as his own had been, and the request meshed perfectly with the native alliance's desire to have white troops "to go out to the War" with their parties. He gave Butler the following Beating Order:

> To John Butler Esqr appointed Major Commandant of a Corps of Rangers to serve with the Indians.
>
> By virtue of the power and authority in me vested by the King, I do hereby authorize and empower you, or such officers as you shall direct, by the beat of the Drum, or otherwise, forthwith to raise, on the Frontiers of this Province, as many able bodied men, of His Majesty's loyal subjects, as will form one Company of Rangers, to serve with the Indians, as occasion shall require: which Company shall consist of a Captain, a first Lieutenant, Second Lieutenant, three Serjeants, three Corporals and fifty private men; and when you shall have compleated one Company as aforesaid, you are further empowered to raise and form another in like manner, and of like numbers as the first, and so on, untill you shall have compleated a number of companies of rangers as aforesaid, not exceeding in the whole eight companies; observing that the first be compleated, armed and fit for service, and have passed muster, before such person as shall be appointed for that purpose, by some one of the Commanding Officers of His Majesty's Troops, nearest to where the said companies so raised, shall be at the time, before another be begun to be raised. And of which eight Companies, or such part thereof as you shall be able to raise, you shall be Major Commandant, two of the Companies aforesaid (to be composed of people speaking the Indian language and acquainted with their Customs and Manner of making War) for their encouragement shall be paid at the rate of four shillings New York Currency by the day, non Commissioned Officers in proportion from the day of their inlisting, and the other said companies (to be composed of people well acquainted with the Woods) in consideration of the fateague they are liable to undergo, shall be paid at the rate of two shillings New York

Currency by the day; Non Commissioned Officers in proportion, the whole to cloath and arm themselves at their own expense. You and the Officers so raised, to be paid as is customary to the Officers of like rank, in his Majesty's service, and you are carefully to obey and follow such orders and directions; as you shall from time to time receive from me, or the Commander in Chief for the time being, or any other of your superior Officers, according to the rules and discipline of War, in pursuance of the trust hereby reposed in you.

Given under my hand and Seal at Quebec this 15th day of September one thousand seven hundred and seventy seven and in the Seventeenth year of the Reign, Guy Carleton[822]

Carleton advised Burgoyne of this decision and enclosed copies of the warrant and the instructions he had issued to Butler.[823] His instructions read:

[Y]ou shall, as soon as possible, march, with such part of the said Rangers, as are already raised, or you shall immediately raise, and as large a body of the Six nations, or other Indians, as you can collect without too much exposing their country to the incursions of the Rebels, to join and put yourself under the command, of Lieutenant General Burgoyne, giving him notice, as expeditiously as possible, of your approach toward him, and of the force you bring along with you; and all orders which you shall receive from the said Lieutenant General Burgoyne you are to observe and Obey.[824]

While the significance would not have dawned on Burgoyne, Carleton had blatantly ignored Claus and, in the process, trod firmly on Germain's toes and into Guy Johnson's bailiwick.

Butler also presented Carleton with an account of his expenses incurred at Niagara and on campaign. Although the governor felt the total excessive, his review was so cursory that he approved payment in Halifax currency, rather than York, at "better than 1/3 more" value.[825]

Carleton advised Bolton at Niagara about the warrant and Butler's instructions and forwarded a proportion of the Indian presents recently received from England.[826]

Carleton was deeply concerned by the rebel attack on Ticonderoga and travelled from Quebec City to Fort St. John's to spur on the expedition.[827] The regiments were quickly on their way up the lake, heading for the threatened fortress complex of Ticonderoga.

Before returning to headquarters, Carleton had a further opportunity to exercise his wrath against Germain, in this instance on a most convenient surrogate — the superintendent of the Western Expedition, Daniel Claus.

Claus had set out from Oswego in company with St. Leger and arrived in lower Quebec some two weeks after Butler.[828] During a visit with Brigadier Maclean, the Montreal district commander, he was told that a Kahnawake party had already been dispatched to Burgoyne. Undeterred, he sent his officers to recruit Kahnawakes and Kanehsatakes who had not left on their seasonal hunt.[829]

Claus had received no government funds to meet his expenses and was embarrassed by the badgering of the Montreal traders who had advanced him credit for Indian goods two months before. Adding to his discomfort, he met with John Butler and heard of Carleton's Beating Order for the ranger battalion and the instructions that his rival, not he, was to raise a new force from the native alliance to assist Burgoyne.

Although Claus was greatly agitated, he calmly set about organizing the department with Butler. Captain Tice, seven lieutenants, and some fifteen rangers chose to serve with Claus, while five veteran lieutenants would serve with Butler in Iroquoia. Pay lists were prepared, and once the details were complete, Butler headed west for Oswego and Claus set off to join St. Leger with a party of Kanehsatakes, who had refused to go forward without him because of Burgoyne's earlier abuses of their customs of war.[830]

At Fort St. John's, Claus met with Carleton to request a cash warrant to pay his creditors, but his reception was as chilly as Butler's had been warm. Carleton brusquely stated "that there was no farther Service for him in Indn Affairs, that he gave Mr Butler the direction of Indn Affairs in Col Johnson['s] absence and [Claus] might return to Montreal." The governor informed Claus that he had examined Butler's accounts, and Claus unwisely answered that these were of no concern to him, as his appointment was "to be paid from a different channel." This oblique reference to his preferment through the home government was ill received, and none of Claus's remonstrations persuaded Carleton. Deflated and embarrassed, he returned to Montreal to give some manner of satisfaction to his creditors who "want[ed] to send remittances by the London vessells which were ready to sail."[831]

By mid-September, Burgoyne made the momentous decision to cut off his route of retreat to Canada by destroying a bridge of boats that the Grand Army had used to cross to the west shore of the Hudson River.[832] This act was neither a show of bravado nor a means of forcing his army's advance; such artifices would come later. While his decision seems foolhardy, he could not afford to detach a sufficiently large force to guard a bridge, unless he faced up to the possibility of retreat, a thought that had scarcely touched his consciousness.

CHAPTER THIRTEEN

THE CURTAIN FALLS
This Damned Place — Reduced to Ashes

S t. Leger's vanguard of ten companies of the 34th and the Royal
Yorkers beached at Ticonderoga in the evening of September 27.
To their relief, their landings were unopposed. Their arrival had
been greatly anticipated, as the garrison was in turmoil over the rebels'
recent bold attacks, which resulted in the remarkable capture of 325
men,[833] including 13 officers and 143 privates of the 53rd, 10 naval rat-
ings, and 119 Canadien artificers. As well, the damage was extensive to
both the adjacent Lake George landing and the dominating gun position atop Mount Defiance.[834]

On the second day of the attacks, the fort's commandant, Brigadier Henry
Watson Powell,[835] had angrily refused a summons by the rebel commander, a Massachusetts militia colonel named John Brown. Powell had twenty-six years' experience as an officer. He had become the 53rd Regiment's
lieutenant-colonel in 1771 and, in the spring of 1776, led the regiment to
Canada, where he was appointed a brigadier by Carleton. In August of the
next year, Burgoyne had chosen him to command the Grand Army's dis-
tended lines of communication, and now, to his mortification, his own
regiment had been caught napping by mere militiamen.

The rebels had settled down to besiege both Ticonderoga and
Mount Independence across the lake, which was garrisoned by five
companies of the Prinz Friedrich Regiment (PFR) and five weak companies of the 53rd,[836] but it was soon clear that a stalemate had been
reached. Brown had received intelligence about a considerable reinforcement of Canadians and Indians that were "hourly expected at the
lake under command of Sir John Johnson." Consequently, he was content when orders arrived to join General Gates's army at Saratoga, having no desire to face a fresh force in his rear. Brown sent off his prisoners under guard and set his troops to destroy wagons, stores, and all

"View of the Old French Fort, Redoubts and Batteries at Ticonderoga on Lake Champlain Taken from Mount Independence, New York," 1777

Detail from an unknown artist after St. Leger's engineer, Lieutenant Henry Rudyerd. Courtesy of the National Archives of Canada, C-040336.

unneeded boats. On September 22, his force sailed from the Lake George landing; two days later it attacked Burgoyne's forwarding depot at Diamond Island and was handily repulsed.[837]

Powell's troops were faced with an immense amount of brute work to restore the Lake George landing so that supplies and troops could be forwarded. The commanding height of Mount Defiance could not be ignored and flaws revealed in the defences of Ticonderoga and Mount Independence begged attention. Powell imposed a severe duty regimen; the troops would be worked to their limit while they simultaneously guarded against repeat surprises.

It was into this gloomy atmosphere that Barry St. Leger stepped ashore on September 27. He immediately sought refuge in his usual remedy, causing Ensign Julius von Hille, PFR, to write in his journal that "L.Col. St. Leger is a very thirsty soul."[838]

The affairs of his expedition were now thoroughly enmeshed with Burgoyne's fortunes. On September 19, the Grand Army had fought a bloody, major action known to the British and loyalists as Freeman's Farm. When darkness fell, the Crown forces retained the battlefield and

Burgoyne claimed a victory, but his contention was as hollow as the Whigs' posturing after Oriskany, for like the Tryon Militia, his army had suffered disproportionate casualties.[839]

Prior to the nineteenth, the British had held a poor opinion of their opponents' fighting capability. They were suspicious that the incredible losses of the Germans and loyalists at Bennington had been due to inefficiency or worse, but now they were shocked by the ferocity of the fighting. A Continental officer recalled that Burgoyne's troops were "bold, intrepid, and fought like heroes [and] our men were equally bold and courageous & fought like men, fighting for their all." Another ruminated that the Whigs' fervour was due to having "Something more at Stake than fighting for six Pence Pr day."[840]

Burgoyne's army had bled profusely at Hubbardton and Bennington and now at Freeman's Farm. Its battle losses, plus the detachments made to man the lengthy supply route, had shrunk its combat strength alarmingly.

Many of the Continental troops who had driven St. Leger from Stanwix were present at this first battle of Saratoga. Learned's Massachusetts brigade, which now included Livingston's 1CDN,[841] was at the right-centre of the line and formed part of Arnold's wing of Gates's army. The brigade's first commitment was a three-hundred-man detachment of Jackson's led by William Hull, the major who had helped to secure Walter Butler at Shoemaker's tavern. A New Hampshire veteran described the action as "the hottest Fire of Canon and Musquetry that ever I heard in my life." Hull's men proved very cool indeed. They were posted on a rise at the south end of the main battlefield, when Hull observed a line of "lobsterbacks" five hundred feet away and advancing towards their position. Hull instructed his men to wait for his command and aim for the knees. At 150 feet, he ordered a volley and large gaps appeared in the British line, but the redcoats came on bravely. Hull ordered his men to fix bayonets, and the detachment repelled the British with steel, shattering the 62nd Regiment, which suffered 217 dead and wounded that day. This feat was followed by another crisis, which Hull met by taking a position in the woods, where his detachment fought till dusk. When they retired that evening, half were casualties.[842]

The balance of Learned's brigade was committed later in the action against the British far right and fended off dangerous enveloping attacks by British and German flank battalions. Lieutenant-Colonel Brooks's

battalion (Jackson's regiment) was the last to leave the field, abandoning their wounded to the mercies of Burgoyne's natives.[843]

Little has been discovered about the New York State militia in this battle. Several Tryon County companies served under Brigadier Ten Broeck in a combined Albany/Tryon brigade assigned to Arnold's left wing, but no mention is made of Tryon men in various accounts of the fight, nor are there records of Ten Broeck's brigade being committed as a unified force on September 19.[844]

Burgoyne had been eagerly expecting news of an expedition from York City that would open the communications to Albany by driving up the Hudson. He

An Ensign of the Prinz Friedrich Regiment of the Duke of Brunswick's troops

A watercolour by Herbert Knötel, ca. 1948. Courtesy of the Anne S.K. Brown Military Collection. Brown University Library.

reasoned that the diversion caused by an attack in Gates's rear might yet save the day. At last, on September 21, a coded dispatch dated the twelfth arrived from the senior officer in York City, Sir Henry Clinton, with word that he would "make a push at Montgomery [a fort on the lower Hudson] in about ten days." Burgoyne ignored Clinton's comment that he was expecting "reenforcements every day," although he should have recognized that there would be no "push" until after the fleet from Britain arrived with fresh troops. Instead, he focused on Clinton's promise to start in ten days' time, which by his calculation was the next day — the twenty-second.[845]

Burgoyne turned the courier about that same night with the message that "An attack . . . upon Montgomery . . . will draw away part of

The Curtain Falls

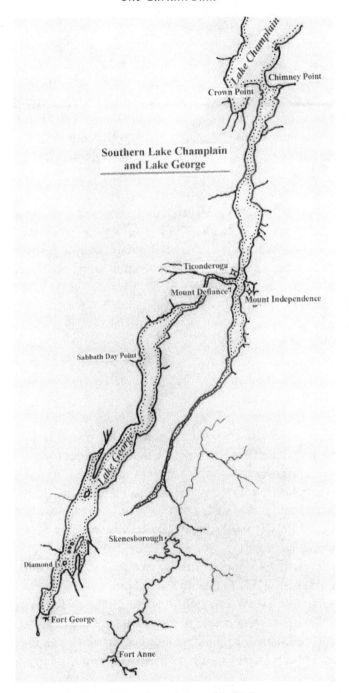

Southern Lake Champlain and Lake George

Gavin K. Watt, 2000.

[Gates's] Force, and I will follow them close. Do it, my dear Friend, directly." He described his supply shortages and, as Clinton represented a surrogate for Howe, requested instructions for his future operations.

Burgoyne then made a fatal mistake; he encamped to await Clinton. Every day, he expected a new dispatch with the happy tidings that his saviour drew near. In the words of a Brunswick officer, "At no time did the Jews await the coming of their Messiah with greater expectancy than we awaited the coming of Clinton."[846] Six long, anxious days passed, but no word came.

On September 27, Burgoyne asked Captain-Lieutenant Thomas Scott of the Quebec Indian Department to carry a dispatch to Sir Henry. Scott undertook this "difficult and dangerous piece of Service"[847] on the promise of a full captaincy. In case of capture, Burgoyne gave him verbal, rather than written, messages: the expedition could not reach Albany unless the communication to New York City was opened; with Clinton's aid, he could hold out at Bemis Heights until October 16, and if not, he would have to retreat to Canada; he needed "the plainest and most positive" reply "whether he should proceed to Albany or to make good his retreat to Canada." Lastly, his Grand Army was reduced to five thousandtroops with many sick and wounded.[848] His enemy had twelve thousand in his front and rear.

On the morning that Scott left, a Brunswick officer who had been captured at Bennington arrived under a flag of truce and delivered the shocking news that the rebels had attacked Ticonderoga.[849] So completely had Burgoyne severed his rear communications and so effectively had the rebels stymied his courier system that this startling news came as a double blow to the general. Not only had Ticonderoga been attacked, but now it was brutally clear how thoroughly he was cut off from all intelligence.

He immediately summoned a second Indian officer, Captain Colin Campbell, RHE, the brother of Major John, who commanded the department. Like Scott, Colin had a reputation for daring deeds and, as if to prove it, he chose to pass through the enemy lines wearing a rebel uniform. Campbell memorized the same messages and an additional observation that the army would be out of provisions by October 20.

With no news of Clinton, St. Leger's arrival grew in importance. Burgoyne may not have known the exact strength and composition of

St. Leger's forces, but he had every reason to anticipate more than eight hundred men-at-arms, which would increase his Grand Army by sixteen percent. As well, he expected a large number of Indians, whose services he had belatedly come to appreciate. Because the bridge of boats had been destroyed, he organized "secret means" to enable St. Leger to join him.[850]

On September 21, rather spurious details of St. Leger's failure at Stanwix and his anticipated arrival became widely known throughout the army. The commander of the Hesse Hanau artillery recorded:

> [R]eports were confirmed how Colonel St. Leger with his light expeditionary corps withdrew to Oswego, from the Mohawk River and its rough terrain, because of the enemy's superior strength and a shortage of provisions. [H]e will have to repass Lake Ontario and the St. Lawrence River in the region of Montreal. Now we eagerly anticipate the arrival of his relief via the [Richelieu] River . . . across Lakes Champlain and George, and then overland. This is an astonishing detour. It is also assumed that this unfortunate, failed expedition by St. Leger's corps must have been known here for some time because a trusted, secret, and small detachment from our army has quietly been sent back in order to hide a small number of batteaux in the earth for his use.[851]

Burgoyne's secret instructions to his German brigade commander, Major General von Riedesel, were as follows:

> I have, my dear general, to intrust a little matter to your care during your stay at Fort Edward. I desire to have two batteaux, with their oars, buried as quietly as possible. It would also, be well to shovel earth upon them, and to give them more the appearance of graves. [A] cross might be placed upon each hillock. All this must be done in the night, by trustworthy soldiers . . . The use for which these batteaux are intended is to help Lieut. Col. St. Leger in crossing the river, in case of circumstances forcing him to march without his ships . . . I have sent him orders as to

the necessary measures of precaution he is to take upon arriving on [Diamond] island at the lower end of Lake George. If he finds that the enemy are not in the vicinity of the road leading to the army ... he is to cross the river near Fort Edward, at the same time notifying me in advance of his movement, that I may be able to facilitate it from my side. I have told him where he will find the batteaux, viz. inside of Fort Edward. I had given orders to Brigadier General Powell to have your reserve cross at the same time with Colonel St. Leger, and to leave those only behind that belong to the regiment of Prince Frederick.[852]

Governor Carleton was now fully awakened to Burgoyne's distress. He ordered Brigadier Maclean with four fieldpieces, an assistant engineer, his Highland Emigrants, and the 31st Regiment to follow St. Leger's troops to Ticonderoga.[853] He was to assist in driving off the rebel attackers and help Watson Powell forward St. Leger's troops to Burgoyne. Once those tasks were accomplished, he would take post at Chimney Point to prevent the rebels from interdicting the lifeline further to the north.

On September 27, Powell wrote to Carleton reporting that St. Leger had arrived at Ticonderoga. "[I]t will not be possible for Lieutenant-Colonel St. Leger's Detachment to join General Burgoyne, as he has not be[en] supplied with boats and Horses to transport his Provisions and Baggage, when he had crossed Lake George." [854] He finished with the ominous advice that Burgoyne's most recent express boat had been taken.[855]

Spanish John McDonell and his new company of Royal Yorkers had been bundled aboard the bateaux at Oswego, rushed through the short layover at St. John's, and arrived at Ticonderoga with the personal firearms they had brought from the Schoharie. McDonell received permission to "receive the Kings Arms" and the men were given the option of retaining their guns or delivering them into the safekeeping of regimental stores. Thirty-six men assigned their property to acting quartermaster Gummersall,[856] and he issued the King's musket to all of the company.

Watson Powell was still isolated from his commander and in need of advice and two days later he wrote again to Carleton to say he had Burgoyne's permission to retain St. Leger's Regulars if the situation at Ticonderoga so warranted. This order had been issued before Brown had

captured the three companies of the 53rd, and, as the 8th had not arrived, he ruminated that retaining the one hundred Brunswickers and the two companies of the 34th would put his posts on nearly "the same footing" as previously. He tacitly sought Carleton's blessing and, as an alternative to retaining Burgoyne's troops, suggested the possible assignment of the 31st Regiment from the Canadian army to his garrison.[857]

Major-General Horatio Gates, commander of the U.S. armies that defeated Burgoyne

Engraving after an unknown artist.

Brigadier Maclean and his mini-brigade arrived at Ticonderoga soon after St. Leger. In a detailed report to Carleton on September 30, he mentioned that a verbal message had arrived from Burgoyne about the battle at Freeman's Farm. He noted that Burgoyne urged that "St. Leger [be] pressed forward, but the destruction of carriages on the Portage, and the very shocking situation of the Quarter Master Generals department at this place will make it impossible to pass St. Leger for a few days." Further, "Brigadier Powel has resolved not to let [St. Leger] go untill he hears again from General Burgoyne." He closed his letter with the information that Ticonderoga was in "the greatest distress" for carts, harness, bateaux, pitch, oakum, and an assistant quartermaster-general. Maclean decided he could be more useful fortifying Chimney Point and used the excuse of the governor's orders to extricate himself.[858]

To judge from Maclean's report, he and Powell had spent some time in heart-to-heart discussion and he had made it clear that Carleton would not release the 31st Regiment. In any event, when Powell wrote to the governor that same day, he noted that Maclean was leaving Ticonderoga on the morrow with the artillery detachment and the 31st. As the Highland Emigrants were not mentioned, they probably stayed on for a few more days. Powell had rethought his position of the day before and advised Carleton that St. Leger's force would be advanced to join Burgoyne as soon as possible, although he could not resist pointing out that his posts were much exposed "if not assisted from Canada."[859] Security was tightened yet again due to concerns about repeat raids. On October 1, it was ordered that every man who left the lines would require a pass and none were to leave unarmed. On the second, 130 Jägers occupied an advance camp outlying Mount Independence. Two days later, all troops were ordered to sleep in their clothing and to fall in fully armed when the reveille gun fired or if they heard a bugle alarm. An investigation revealed that the companies of the 53rd had been over-run due to sloppy challenging, so all troops were reminded about the correct procedures for countersigns and paroles.[860]

Burgoyne's army was still encamped at Freeman's Farm on October 2 when Richard Duncan, one of Sir John's chosen officers, slipped through the rebel cordon. He had managed to flee Albany, where he had been under intense suspicion for over a year. He brought with him a handful of recruits for the Royal Yorkers.[861]

Burgoyne's General Order of the day advised the Grand Army of the enemy's attempts against Ticonderoga. Of course, the very best face was put on these events and their grave implications tacitly ignored.[862]

The next day, Burgoyne confidently issued another encouraging General Order: "[T]here is reason to be assured, that other powerful Armies of the King are actually in Cooperation with these Troops." After claiming that "the present supply of provisions is ample," he cut the troops' rations. In the face of mounting evidence of the expedition's peril, the majority of the troops continued to hold the general in high regard. His heartfelt, flowery phrases about their stalwart nature and courage appealed to them, such as, "The Lieut. Genl. is confident he shall meet with universal, and cheerful obedience to this order, and as a Testimony of his Attention to the Spirits, and good will of the Troops on all occasions" he suspended all stoppages from their pay and gave the officers 165 days' forage money "during the Diminution of the Ration."[863]

About this time, he decided to make another attempt to get a dispatch through to Clinton. This time, the volunteer was an ardent loyalist named William Schermerhorn from the Helleburg in Renssalaerwyck, who was a recruiter for Sir John Johnson. As he knew the ground to be traversed intimately, he had an excellent chance of success.[864]

On October 6, six hundred rebels ferociously struck the Grand Army's outposts across the entire perimeter. Immediately, the natives and Provincials were sent out and a two-hour skirmish ensued during which they drove the rebels in upon their own pickets, burned some sheds, and sniped at a clutch of rebel generals at a nearby house.[865]

Brigadier Powell wrote to Carleton on October 10 advising that Sir John Johnson had sent Captain John Jones to Burgoyne with a proposal "to join the army through the woods, which was accepted, and Mr. Jones returned here on that account, but Sir John Johnson wishes to delay his march till Colonel Clause arrives with some Indians which are daily expected, so that it is very uncertain when he will set out."[866] Johnson was unaware of Claus's agonizing experiences with Carleton and his wait was in vain. Mysteriously, it was Sir John, not St. Leger, his commanding officer, who had made the offer to march overland.

Powell reported to Carleton the next day that Jones had again made the round trip to Burgoyne's camp and brought news that the army was in retreat. As he had crossed the enemy's lines repeatedly, his prediction that the withdrawal would "be attended with great difficulty" had considerable weight. He provided details of a battle fought by the Grand Army on October 7 in which "eight Pieces of Canon" had been lost and an alarming number of senior officers killed and taken prisoner. Although Carleton had warned Powell to ignore rumours, he nervously observed, "I am informed this Garrison is to be attacked by nine thousand Rebels & should General Burgoyne not be able to effect a Retreat the consequences may be fatal to it."[867]

Burgoyne had waited in his camp in vain for St. Leger to join him and for Clinton to bring relief, but neither had appeared. In a rare display of uncertainty, he assembled his senior officers to a council of war and, after reviewing the army's options, proposed a deep thrusting, enveloping attack against Gates's flank. The concept did not receive universal approval, and the next morning, the generals conducted a reconnaissance. Von Riedesel observed that unless the attack could gain the enemy's rear in a single day's march, the army would be separated for too long. He recommended a withdrawal to Canada, but the contemplation of the shame and ridicule that would reward such a retreat was too much for Burgoyne. Secretly, he contrived a desperate venture and disguised his true intentions by describing the movement as a reconnaissance in force. To mollify the doubters, he advised his generals that, should the rebels' flank prove too strong for a full attack, he would authorize a retreat to Batten Kill, but his true intention was to commit his troops to a piecemeal attack that would draw the whole army forward. Deserters had informed Burgoyne that Gates's army had increased dramatically, but he was unaware that fully thirteen thousand Continentals and militia opposed him.[868]

To improve his chances, Burgoyne assigned Captain Alexander Fraser's Company of Marksmen with some Provincials and all the natives to work their way round the rebels' rear and divert their attention.[869]

When Burgoyne ventured out of his positions on the clear, crisp October morning of October 7, he took fifteen hundred British and German Regulars and two 12-pounders, six 6-pounders, and two six-inch howitzers. As Gates had predicted to his officers, "the old gamester" was about to "risque all upon one throw."[870]

A complete account of Bemis Heights, or Second Saratoga, is not germane; however, the deeds of the troops who had confronted St. Leger in the Mohawk Valley should be noted.

On the morning of October 7, a long-standing feud between Arnold and Gates culminated in the former being dismissed from an officers' council that had met to discuss Burgoyne's advancing "reconnaissance."[871] With the waspish Arnold out of the way, Gates planned to make a moderate deployment of riflemen and light infantry to oppose Burgoyne. Concerned about such a weak response, his generals persuaded him to send three additional battalions, including two from Learned's brigade. After some ineffectual skirmishing, Learned's was reunited and committed as a whole to the centre of the developing action. Learned was ordered to hold in place while light troops enveloped one flank and a mixed New Hampshire/New York brigade, the other. When Learned saw that the two flanking operations were underway, he launched his attack.

Arnold was unable to stay away from the fighting. After downing a dipper of rum, he rode forward to the centre where Learned's brigade was heavily engaged and, seizing command,[872] led the troops in a charge against a German brigade. The Germans were forced to withdraw, as their wings were dangerously threatened by the flanking operations. Soon all of the Crown forces were falling back to secondary positions. Arnold then took control of the whole attack. He was in his element, acting "more like a madman than a cool and discreet officer." This was the frenzied commander all had come to expect who displayed an impetuosity directly opposite to his cautious, measured march to relieve Stanwix.

He ordered Lieutenant-Colonel John Brooks with Jackson's and Livingston's 1CDN to attack the German-held Breymann Redoubt. Brooks exhibited cool courage as he led his men against a two-hundred-yard-long breastwork that fronted the redoubt. The Germans held their fire until the rebels were 135 feet from the position, but Brooks and his men absorbed their fusillade and pressed forward.

Arnold and a body of riflemen and lights circled behind the redoubt and, while Brooks's men were pressuring the front, the general jumped his horse through a rear sally port and demanded a surrender. The Germans replied with musketry, dropping Arnold's horse and then hitting the general's same leg that had been injured two years before at Quebec City. The riflemen and lights following him carried the redoubt. When Brooks and his men climbed the parapet, they discovered that the Germans had been defeated. Learned reassumed command, and after combining with another brigade, precipitated the rout of the enemy.

To cap this thrust, Ten Broeck's 1,850-man New York militia brigade was brought forward, but they were scarcely required. The deed was done. Burgoyne's last "throw" had been forcefully and bloodily repulsed.[873]

For some reason, Fraser's troops and natives had failed

A chastened John Burgoyne
after the defeat

Engraving after an unknown artist.

to create a diversion and, upon returning to camp, they discovered that Burgoyne's "reconnaissance" had been a disaster. The natives prudently decided to melt away.[874] That night, the army abandoned six fieldpieces and, leaving their campfires burning as a ruse, began to retreat.[875]

By mid-October, John Butler was at Buck Island on his return trip to Niagara where he conferred with Captain Potts, who was still occupied with transporting stores. Potts told him that the Indian goods sent by Carleton had already been forwarded to Colonel Bolton at Niagara and spoke of a visit by some Senecas who claimed that the Tuscaroras, Oneidas, and most of the Onondagas had accepted Schuyler's hatchet. Butler was in no way surprised about the former two, but a commitment by the Onondagas was alarming, if it was true. He had planned to call the alliance to a council at Oswego to raise his new contingent, but the old fort was at the back door of Onondaga territory. In any event, his idea was nullified by the lack of presents, so he went to Niagara to assemble his force under the impressive shadow of that symbol of the Crown's power.[876]

Powell again wrote to Carleton on October 16 expressing the fear that "all [Burgoyne's] expresses have been taken." A Royal Yorker captain, Samuel Anderson, who had left the Grand Army at Saratoga on Friday the tenth, arrived with some recruits and news the night before. Anderson had earlier been prevented from joining the Yorkers in Canada and, after months of rebel confinement, escaped to serve as a supernumerary officer on Burgoyne's staff. As the campaign unfolded, he was assigned to the Loyal Volunteers to serve with Captain Robert Leake, who was married to Lady Polly Johnson's sister.[877] The same day, an Indian, "in whom Sir John Johnson & Major Gray place great confidence," arrived with important news. When he left Saratoga on the thirteenth, "Burgoyne was then surrounded on all sides by the Rebels and as the firing had ceased he took it for granted the General was then capitulating." Powell believed this report was true and, speculating that Carleton would not want to keep Ticonderoga, sought orders to abandon it. He worried about all the provisions, stores, and guns on Diamond Island, remarking that "it will probably be attended with great difficulty to bring off that Post." Entrusting these gloomy reports to the intrepid Captain John Jones, he sent him express to Quebec.

Major Gray wrote these same details to his fellow Scotsman, Brigadier Allan Maclean, at Chimney Point, adding that the Indian was only able to get away "with great difficulty" and that the rebels had captured "50 boats loaded with provisions." He thought that the cessation of firing signalled "that it is all over with them" and noted in frustration that

> General Powell does every thing in his power to secure this damned place which ought to have been burned when you was here . . . I think this place should be abandoned and soon, as in the best of times its not worth the keeping and should a Garrison be attempted to be kept here its only laying a baite for those Rascalls to be more troublesome during the winter.[878]

That night, a number of Jägers deserted and a party of Indians and Royal Yorkers tracked them down and brought them back to Ticonderoga. The battalion orderly book noted that these men had been extremely fortunate to keep their scalps and a new order made it clear that if any others deserted, "a party of savages will immediately be sent out with full permission to scalp immediately."[879]

Powell wrote Maclean from Mount Independence noting that unless Carleton gave orders to "destroy and abandon" his posts, he would have to "submit to cannon and numbers." He asked Maclean to send all the bateaux that he could spare so that "we may be prepared for the worst event." If he was required to defend Ticonderoga, he postulated that "very strong reinforcements will be necessary as well as provisions."[880]

On Friday, October 17, Ensign von Hille, the Brunswicker journal-keeper, noted, "It was peculiar that the large Engl[ish] flag on the barracks of Mt. Indep. fell down from the tall pole twice today. Many saw this as a bad omen."[881] And it was, for even as the flag surrendered to gravity, so did Burgoyne's army surrender to Gates's.

That same day, loyalist Captain Samuel MacKay arrived at Ticonderoga with a mixed party of Loyal Volunteers and Canadiens. He had been sent out with Fraser's Marksmen, the 47th Regiment, and some artificers "to Reconoitre and Repair the Roads and Bridges to facilitate the

Brigadier-General Allan Maclean, Royal Highland Emigrants — Maclean had been Carleton's second-in-command during the defence of Quebec City in 1775 and '76

A miniature by an unknown artist.

Retreat of the army from Saratoga to Fort Edward." When the other units were ordered to turn back, the Loyal Volunteers were instructed to act as "a covering Party for the Artificers," but a body of five hundred rebels cut off their retreat. They set off through the woods to Fort George to join with St. Leger, only to find that his presence there was nothing but rumour. On hearing that Burgoyne was treating with the rebels, they "Repaired to Ticonderoga."[882] Over the next two days, small parties of loyalists drifted in to Ticonderoga. On October 19, Powell wrote to Carleton with details of Burgoyne's capitulation provided by "Hugh Daveny [Devinnay] a Deserter from the Rebels" who was vouched for by McKay, both as a pre-war acquaintance and for his recent behaviour under arms for the King. Devinnay claimed that Burgoyne had said "that his Army was to surrender, and lay down their Arms between the Hours of eight and ten that Morning . . . the British Troops were to go to Boston, and embark from thence for England, the Germans were to go home to their own Country, and the Volunteers [loyalists] and Canadians to Canada."[883] Mindful of Carleton's warnings about verbal accounts, Powell sent Devinnay express to Canada carrying his dispatches.

Two days after the Grand Army's thrashing at Bemis Heights, a number of family bands of Fort Hunter Mohawks left the camp. Baroness von Riedesel watched them go and caustically wrote, "The slightest setback makes cowards of them." How very, very little she knew or understood.[884]

Unlike their white allies, they refused to abandon their sick and wounded, so each band was burdened with litters. During their hazardous exfiltration through the rebel cordon, some of the fugitives were forced to subsist on a thin gruel made from small birds. Although the groups were well dispersed, at least one fell prey to the thousands of militiamen scouring the countryside. North of Fort Edward on October 14, a force of New England militiamen confronted one of the larger bands, killed a warrior, and captured fifty-three men, women, and children. A heavy guard was required to protect the Indians from the crowds who wanted to revenge the murder of Jane McCrae, the young woman who had been scalped by British Indians. It meant nothing that the Fort Hunters had no hand in McCrae's killing — after all, Indians were Indians.

The more elusive and fortunate bands straggled into Ticonderoga to be met by the Canada Indians, who were there with Captain Tice and Sir John. Powell sent them to Fort St. John's by ship.[885]

On Monday the twentieth, the flood tide of rumours was confirmed when Captain Alexander Fraser arrived with a copy of the thirteen articles of surrender agreed to by Burgoyne and Gates. After a brief stopover, Fraser pushed on to Quebec City with his distressing news.[886]

Like the fall of a final curtain, nature provided a signal that the campaign season was drawing to a close, when heavy snow and frost blanketed the Ticonderoga posts that night.[887]

The next day, Powell received a petulant reply from Carleton responding to his frequent appeals for direction. The governor said he could not give him orders, "not alone because the Post you are in has been taken out of my command," but also because he was so distant from the scene. Carleton's advice to Powell was

"act by your own judgement . . . by your own prudence and resolution . . . either you resolve with vigour to put the place in such a situation as to be able to make the longest and most resolute defence, or that you prepare in time to abandon with all the Stores, whilst yet your retreat may be certain. Your own sense will tell you that this latter would be [a] most pernicious measure if there be still hopes of General Burgoyne's coming to your Post."[888]

Rebellion in the Mohawk Valley

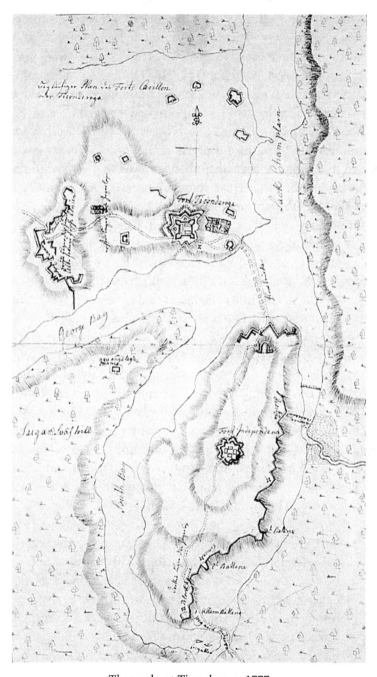

The works at Ticonderoga, 1777

Pen and ink drawing by Lieutenant-Colonel Carl von Kreutzbourg, Hesse Hanau Jäger Regiment, 1777. Courtesy of Staatsarchiv Marburg, Bestand, WeI/20, Germany.

Lieutenant-Colonel John Peters arrived on October 21 with the remnants of his Queen's Loyal Rangers. In the dying hours of the Grand Army, he had been "in great anxiety and distress of mind," as so many of his men who had been taken at Bennington had been viciously abused. Convinced that his people were in particular peril, he obtained written permission from Burgoyne to withdraw to Canada and, after many adventures, reached Ticonderoga.[889]

The Prinz Friedrich Regiment spent much of October 22 building "huts of boards to protect themselves from the cold weather." Von Hille wrote that the work over the past few weeks had been "so demanding that even on Sundays not a single man was in the camp during the day." All the regiment's spare baggage was sent off to Quebec in three boats.[890]

The Jägers' orderly book noted on October 24 that "shameless[,] malicious rumours, contrary to the ... honour of army service" were being spread amongst the men and "augmented" by the officers. The battalion was "sharply admonished not to give ear to such absurd lies ... and even less believe and repeat them." Von Kreutzbourg provided his version of events. "The army was struggling against a force ten times its own strength and was forced to capitulate after an obstinate encounter during which it was cut off from retreat." Ten times! Maybe three; however, the troops' morale had to be bolstered, even with fairy tales.

In the freezing isolation of the Ticonderoga posts, the good will between the allies was becoming frayed. Von Kreutzbourg's explanation of the army's defeat was followed by an earnest entreaty to "conduct yourselves peaceably and in friendly fashion, and strive for unity" in the face of the "many occasions, misunderstandings and strife" that had arisen between the nationalities.[891]

The Jessup brothers led another sizeable party of loyalists to Ticonderoga. They had remained with Burgoyne till the bitter end, and after giving the rebels their parole not to take up arms again during the conflict, had been released. John Munro had somehow avoided giving a parole, and when he arrived at Ticonderoga, Sir John persuaded him to enter the Royal Yorkers as a captain.[892]

On October 27, Major James Gray was reunited with his wife, Elizabeth, and children when a captain and serjeant of the rebel Green Mountain Rangers brought the family to Ticonderoga under a Flag from Skenesborough. Gray now had one pleasant memory of a disastrous

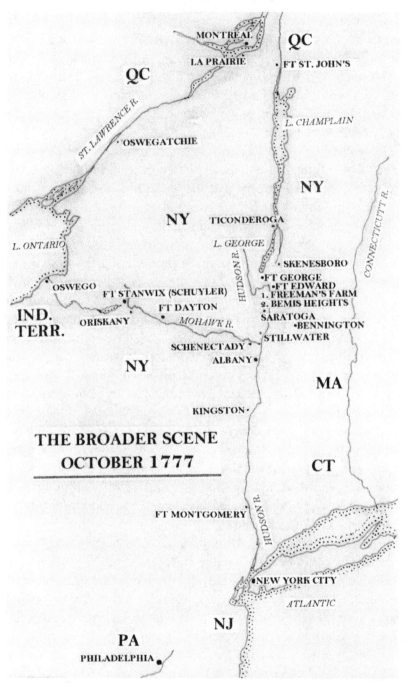

The broader scene, October 1777

Gavin K. Watt, 2001.

campaign. Several years would pass before most of his fellow Yorker officers would see their wives and children again. More snow came through the night and continued to fall all the next day until midnight.[893]

On November 1, Brigadier Maclean wrote to the governor from Chimney Point tacitly descrying Powell's nervousness by giving his opinion that the rebels probably had no more than two hundred men anywhere near Ticonderoga. Maclean reported that Sir Henry Clinton had been forty miles from Albany in the last week of October, "destroying the Country as he went, and not leaving a standing house behind him," which implied that the rebels had enough to worry about without concerning themselves with Ticonderoga.

He reported that Powell had held a council of war that "resolved to abandon Mount Independence and Ticonderoga" and withdraw "the Garrison and Stores on Diamond Island." He had complained to Maclean that the Germans, who made up two-thirds of his garrisons, "would not work" and requested his assistance. He dispatched "150 men with proper officers to assist in Embarking his Provisions, Cannon & Stores," while retaining sufficient men to defend Chimney Point. Maclean reported that "[T]he weather has been so severe since we left St. Johns that we have now got 30 Sick in the two Regiments and likely to have many more, we have now 2 feet of Snow on the Ground and freezing hard, firewood scarce and far from us, which with Entrenching our Camp keeps us at hard Labour."[894]

Powell's return of November 1 of "all ranks" at Ticonderoga and Mount Independence listed a total of 1,642 rankers, of whom a startling 378, or 23 percent, were sick in quarters or the hospital. Several parties were "on command," the largest being sixty-five Royal Yorkers who were probably patrolling the environs. The 53rd had only ninety-three men in garrison and thirteen on command. Powell had not exaggerated; of the 1,077 fit men in the two posts, over 67 percent were German — 327 PFR, 301 Jägers, and 100 Brunswick recruits.[895] German troops were generally of the opinion that they had been sent to soldier, not to navvy, although in the British service, a soldier did what was required.[896]

Meanwhile, Butler had arrived at Niagara, only to discover that there was insufficient clothing and provisions to raise a fresh corps of alliance warriors. Nonetheless, he called the chiefs to a council, but before they

*The evacuation of Ticonderoga — after torching several outlying buildings, the
garrison and St. Leger's expedition put off in bateaux on November 7, 1777*

Pencil sketch by Peter Rindlisbacher, 2000, after Henry Rudyerd, 1777.

arrived, word came of Burgoyne's surrender. It was just as well; the
rangers he had sent to collect cattle had not returned and he had only
one and a half companies for his new battalion.[897]

Preparations for the withdrawal from Ticonderoga were well underway
by November 3. At dawn, a mixed detachment of four officers and one
hundred men was sent to "the large forest at Lake George" to protect the
baggage being transferred from Diamond Island. Three PFR officers
examined their regiment's baggage to decide what to return to Quebec
and what to burn and a party of drovers was sent off through the woods
to Quebec with the remaining fifty horses and thirty oxen.

The withdrawal was characterized by many instances of faltering
morale, judgement, and energy. The weather underscored the decline
and added to the tedium and tension. On November 5, Ensign von Hille
wrote, "All of a sudden, it has become extremely warm. The most terrible thunderstorms have centred about our camp from all sides."[898]

Deteriorating weather and distressing news proved too much for
the ten Royal Yorkers who were serving as artillery boatmen. Although
the oversized bateaux had been sunk in Wood Creek at Stanwix, the
men had been retained to move stores from Oswego to Ticonderoga,

and when faced with more of the same back-breaking work for the return voyage to Quebec, they deserted en masse on November 5.[899]

An apology from a Royal Yorker officer appeared in the Jäger battalion's regimental orders. He had struck one of their guards during the night watch and "swore on his honor . . . that he did not know that the boy belonged to the watch."[900] A serious affront had been deftly defused.

That same day another council of war concluded that "all of the baggage [would be] taken on the boats." On October 7, the Jägers struck their tents and went to Chimney Point to relieve Maclean's detachment. Their orders were to leave for Fort St. John's the next day. As the next phase, Brunswicker detachments left Ticonderoga in the afternoon with their baggage.

Ensign von Hille noted that the excess guns were "blown up, spiked or deprived of their trunnions," and the remaining troops struck their tents, loaded them into the boats, and returned to bivouac in the barracks overnight.

On Saturday, November 8, the report of the morning gun was still reverberating when "all the newly built blockhouses, huts, barracks, magazines, etc. were set afire" along with "the large communications bridge between Mt. Indep. and Ticonderoga as well as the small one toward the portage to Lake George." Fifty barrels of powder, which had been placed underneath the walls of Fort Ticonderoga, were detonated and the works "blew up high into the air." The Brunswick ensign philosophically recorded:

> [T]he many expenses incurred by the [rebels] and by the Crown of England (from which the commissaries and engineer officers had probably been taking considerable sums for themselves) became a victim of the fire and changed to ashes in little time . . . No theater director could present the Moors of Jarbar so alert at lighting the spreading fires as quickly as the Eng[lish] artillerymen were in setting everything afire. Rebuilt Carthage had probably not been reduced to ashes as quickly as this circuit of a few leagues.

With dirty smoke drifting overhead and buildings blazing on every quarter, the PFR detachment took to their boats. Everyone was gone from the ruins before noon and the vessels proceeded north through a heavy, sombre snowfall under a leaden sky.[901]

All had come to a close. Burgoyne and his troops were prisoners of the detested rebels. The Grand Army's small remnant and St. Leger's light expeditionary corps withdrew into the frozen sanctuary of Quebec. The great fortress complex of Ticonderoga, whose capture had been such a glorious achievement for Burgoyne and a stimulant for St. Leger, lay in tumbled, smoking ruins to mark the dénoument of the two tragic expeditions.

Incredibly, rebellion had prevailed! — the troops row north to winter quarters in a heavy, sombre snowfall under a leaden sky

Pencil sketch by Peter Rindlisbacher, 2000.

Epilogue

Of Grand Strategy

Now that the story of St. Leger's expedition is complete, it is interesting to consider an observation made by Alexander Hamilton, a brilliant twenty-one-year-old captain who was one of General Washington's aides. In April 1777, he commented on the "secret" British grand strategy:

> And as to the notion of forming a junction with the northern army, and cutting off the communication between the Northern and Southern States, I apprehend it will do better in speculation than in practice.
>
> Unless the Geography of the Country is far different from any thing I can conceive, to effect this would require a chain of posts and such a number of men at each as woud never be practicable or maintainable but to an immense army. In their progress, by hanging upon their rear and seizing every opportunity of skirmishing, their Situation might be rendered insupportably uneasy.[902]

With the benefit of hindsight, Piers Mackesy, a modern British historian, saw the issue somewhat differently:

> The irony of the campaign is that the keys rested for a moment in British hands. To check Howe in the south and Burgoyne in the north, the Americans had fatally weakened the nexus between the two fronts. By one of those bold tactical strokes, which contrasted so oddly with his strategic timidity, Clinton had seized the forts

of the Highlands which six days earlier or six hours later would have resisted the whole army of Howe. In spite of Burgoyne's disaster and the coming intervention of France, it is conceivable that the future pattern of the war would have been altered if the gateway could have been kept.[903]

Perhaps, as Mackesy suggests, the 1777 grand strategy of splitting the rebellion would have had some real merit if it had been properly supported and executed.

Of Peter Gansevoort

On October 4, 1777, an act of the Continental Congress resolved "[T]hat the thanks of Congress be given to Col. Gansevoort and the officers and troops under his command for the bravery and perseverance which they have so conspicuously manifested in the defence of Fort Schuyler and that he be appointed Colonel-Commandant of the fort, so gallantly defended."[904] News of Gansevoort's promotion was received at Stanwix eight days later and the officers delivered a warm address to their colonel. In part it stated:

> Hon'd Sir: From a just sense of that Conduct which has hitherto so conspicuously been shown, to advance the Third New York Regiment to Honor and Public notice,
> We congratulate you that those characteristics which so eminently point out the Gentlemen and Soldier have by your Personall bravery been deservedly noticed, by our Bleeding Country.
> Altho' we rejoice at your Promotion yet we cannot but regret the loss of so worthy a patron.[905]

It would seem that the exact nature of the honour had not been revealed in the message that reached the frontier, as the officers and Gansevoort appear to have assumed that he had been promoted to brigadier-general. As this rank would result in his removal from command of the 3NY, he responded as follows:

Your polite address on my Promotion merits my Sincere thanks. Justice & Gratitude I hope Shall Never be wanting in me to the Third N.Y. Regiment who have by their firmness & Discipline been the Chief Author of my Promotion. Therefore, Gentlemen, please accept my Warmest wishes for the prosperity of the Corps, that all their Virtuous endeavours in the defence of their Bleeding Country may be Crowned with Honor & Success.[906]

Gansevoort's actual promotion was a recognition similar to the awarding of a medal for noteworthy service and possibly carried some remuneration; however, the reality was likely quite disappointing to everyone. His promotion to state brigadier did not occur until March 26, 1781.

Of Marinus Willett

On the same day that Gansevoort was honoured, Congress resolved "in the highest terms of approbation, on your bravery and conduct" to present Willett with "an elegant sword."[907] By mid-1780, Marinus was lieutenant-colonel commandant of the 5NY. The next year, he returned to the Mohawk region as lieutenant-colonel commandant of a regiment of New York Levies and, simultaneously, as acting brigadier of the restored Tryon brigade. In his usual spirited manner, he solidified the region's defences and enjoyed considerable success against Tory and Indian incursions. In 1782, he became a full colonel in command of a regiment of New York Levies in Tryon County.[908]

Of Fort Stanwix (Schuyler)

The 3NY continued a dangerous and dreary existence at Stanwix until late November 1778. Desertions and ugly incidents were frequent. Native and Tory scouts hovered about the works and frequently killed or carried off unsuspecting and careless men, but tension and excitement aside, time wore heavily on the officers and troops without the distractions of a town. Gansevoort's November 1778 letters to his new wife Caty reflected the garrison's unrest over their awaited relief, "We are all most out of patience to [hear] of Colo. Van Schaick and his Regiment being on their march," and only a few days later he bemoaned Van Schaick's delays.[909]

The 1NY was soon as disgruntled with Stanwix as their sister regiment had been. Most wearying was the futility of garrisoning a dangerous post that had become ineffective. Native and Tory raiders simply skirted the Oneida Carry to deliver continuous attacks throughout the Mohawk region.

There was a constant flow of complaints lodged with higher authorities, which prompted Governor Clinton to write that "the troops of this State conceive it a hardship to . . . perpetually . . . garrison that Post, it is become extremely disagreeable to them."[910] In September 1779, thirty mutinous soldiers were thwarted in a plot to spike the guns and blow up the powder magazine. In the following February, Van Schaick wrote to General Washington requesting a relief, and the commander-in-chief answered that "as soon as the Season and circumstances will admit" it would be effected, but the months dragged on. In May, thirty-one men deserted and a party of Oneidas was sent to secure them. Only a few were retrieved after a very bloody action.[911]

Fires plagued Stanwix. A month before the desertions, the guard-house burst into flames and an adjacent barrack had to be razed to prevent it from spreading. Thirteen months later, a larger fire destroyed all the barracks, followed soon after by torrential rains, which extensively damaged the sod walls. The new commandant, Colonel Robert Cochran, who had been major of the 3NY during the siege, wrote, "the works are all tumbling into the ditch."[912]

A decision was made to abandon the post and move the garrison to German Flats, where it could be of more use in the defence of the region. It was an ignominious end to the gallant Stanwix, whose defence had been such a beacon of pride and hope for American arms in the stressful days of August 1777.

Of the British Failure

For a decade and a half, the French had smarted over their extensive losses in the Seven Years War, and when rebellion shook America, every embarrassment and reverse suffered by Britain was relished in Versailles.

Epilogue

The Continental Congress soon found that France was approachable and envoys were sent to procure ships, small arms, cannon, powder, and uniforms. In addition, large numbers of adventurous French officers volunteered to serve in the Continental Army, but the key outcome pursued by Congress was France's direct entry into the war. This commitment would spell disaster for the British, who had far more interests to protect from her arch-enemy than thirteen rebelling colonies. As late as mid-June 1777, the French denied having an interest in the war, which led a British parliamentarian to write, "France to us sends most fair words, to America, stores and officers."

Burgoyne's defeat proved that the rebels had an excellent chance of taming the British lion, and France decided she could profit from the disruption. In January 1778, two treaties were signed with the United States, a Treaty of Commerce and the more important Treaty of Alliance.

The French presence altered the character of the war. Britain's armies in America went on the defensive to protect her footholds on the Atlantic coast at York City and Rhode Island and to safeguard the colonies of Quebec, Nova Scotia, Newfoundland, and the Floridas. With her worldwide concerns, Britain never fully regained the momentum of offensive on the American continent, and France's navy and armies ensured the rebellion's ultimate success.[913]

Of the Oriskany Myth

The continued assertion of Herkimer's success became an important element in the development of the overall "legend of the Revolution." In 1945, the national myth of a great victory was cemented when the U.S. Navy named an Essex Class aircraft carrier the USS *Oriskany*.[914]

Two elements of the myth of the militia's victory are analysed below. First, a comparison of militia casualties to those of their opponents, and second, a scrutiny of the success of the brigade's mission.

The Casualties

Soon after Oriskany, it became common to offer proof of a victory in Whig accounts by minimizing the brigade's casualties while exaggerating those of the enemy.

The legend got off to an early start when Gansevoort provided a report for public consumption stating that the brigade marched into the ravine with only three or four hundred men against the enemy's twelve hundred. This set the odds against the militia at three or four to one. Yet Gansevoort had been told in Herkimer's message that one thousand militiamen had marched from Fort Dayton and he knew from captured documents that St. Leger's force was no larger than twelve hundred. And he was equally aware that not all of St. Leger's troops were sent to the ambush, as he had seen the 8th and 34th companies deploy against Willett's sortie. His version of the battle's conclusion was also misleading.

> [The Indians and Tories], it seems, were ordered back to the fort, in consequence of the sally made or intended to be made under Lieut.Col. Willet. This occasioned their sudden retreat, leaving our people in possession of the ground, and providentially saved them from being cut off [contemporary euphemism for killed.][915]

Readers of his account could be excused for concluding that the militia had faced an overwhelming foe, suffered few casualties, and emerged the victor. As the report was so at variance with what actually happened, Gansevoort must have been either protecting the readers' sensibilities or altering the facts for political purposes. His description set the tone for the next 175 years.

Well, what were the losses of the Tryon County Militia Brigade? The analysis begins with Herkimer's report to Gansevoort that he had one thousand men. In ignoring the several detachments he had made at Fort Dayton, he either "rounded-up" to bolster the garrison's morale or had a memory lapse. Whatever the case, I will deduct two hundred men for those detachments. About half of the 3rd Regiment fled at the commencement of the ambush. Assuming that the four battalions marched into the ambush with about even strengths, half of the 3rd would be one hundred men.[916] For want of better information, I will accept Father Mackenna's report that 30 militiamen were captured[917] and the Whig reports that 150 Tryon men marched out carrying 50 wounded when the battle ended.[918] Definitive information about the number of men who escaped through the woods during the six hours of the battle has not been found, so a rough guess would be that one hundred men managed to work free. A summary of these factors looks like this:

Assembled at Dayton	1000
Subtract detachments	-200
Marched in the column	800
Less rearguard that fled	-100
Trapped in the ambush	700
Less escaped through woods	-100
Remained in the ambush site	600
Less Survivors	-200
Total dead or captured	400
Less those taken prisoner	-30
Number Killed	370

Note well: This calculation excludes the sixty to one hundred Oneidas who joined at Oriska village and also ignores the number of the rearguard who were pursued and killed by Brant's volunteers and the Mohawks — let's say fifteen. Here is a summation of casualties, ie. dead, wounded, and captured.

Killed at ambush site	370
Add pursued, run down and killed	+15
Total dead	385
Add wounded	+50
Add captured	+30
Casuals from all sources	465

Although the number of militiamen who were killed is a warmly debated topic, there are several contemporary sources that shed light. On August 23, 1777, William Scudder, the 1NY lieutenant, "marched over and very near, about four hundred dead bodies."[919] Of course, this was an estimate made by a man marching along the road, not a precise enumeration. As to the corpses' identities, they were not native, as those had been removed by their brothers in the days following the battle. The bodies Scudder saw must have been militiamen, Royal Yorkers, Hessians, and rangers. Enumeration of Crown casualties will be addressed later.

Benjamin Dickson's highly detailed pension application stated that the militia "lost 346 men killed and prisoners;" [920] however, he offered no specific reason for such an oddly precise number.

Forty years after the battle, at a time when a pension applicant stood to gain no censure or reward by exaggerating the carnage, George Stine recalled that four hundred men had been killed. He added that "the slaughter would have been much greater but for the gallant conduct of Colonels Gansevoort and Willett."[921]

Hugh McMaster stated in his application that "the destruction of the whole militia was prevented" due to the timely assistance of Willett's sortie.[922] Jacob A. Young recalled that "the whole army was routed and driven back."[923] John Frank wrote that the brigade "proceeded as far as Oriskany where the Indians and tories fell upon them, and they were[,] after a great many men killed[,] obliged to fall back and retreat in great disorder."[924] Peter P. Bellinger used the phrase, "the defeat of the Continental [sic] forces at Oriskany."[925]

Other Whig accounts, most often by non-participants, placed the number of militiamen killed at just over two hundred. I suspect that concerns for public morale originally dictated a reduction of the truth; however, Jim Morrison, the Mohawk Valley historian who has studied this issue for three decades, believes that 225–235 perished. The truth is evasive.

British contemporary accounts consistently claimed that five hundred militiamen were killed,[926] but these reports must have been "singing from the same song-sheet," as the number is too rounded, too pat.

As a participant, one might think to trust John Butler more than most, as he had heard from the Indians after they re-examined the carnage afresh. Nine days after the battle, he wrote that the rebels suffered "the loss of 500 Killed, Wounded, and taken."[927] It may be assumed that his "wounded and taken" were all prisoners, as he had no way of knowing the number that had been taken home.

As noted, the only contemporary record that reported the number of militia prisoners was Father MacKenna's; he claimed thirty. If this number is subtracted from Butler's total of casualties, the dead would have numbered 470. On the other hand, MacKenna claimed that only two hundred "Bostannais" had been killed, roughly substantiating some rebel reports![928] So the mystery continues.

The Crown's casualties are impossible to assess from contemporary Whig sources, which were universally imprecise and vague. On August

8, Adam Fonda named only two Crown deaths, both inaccurate, and then added "a great many others."[929]

When Chairman Deygart wrote on August 9, he reported a very precise figure for the number of men in Willett's sortie, i.e. 206, and a quite precise number of "whole" men who came out of the ravine, i.e. 150, but of the Crown's casualties, he could only state "all accounts agree that a great Number of the Enemy is killed."[930]

Nineteenth-century writers, even those who interviewed participants, were unable to shed any brighter light. One of the first accounts was written in 1831 by William Campbell, the son of a participant. He interviewed many Oriskany veterans and wrote, "The loss of the regulars and Tories is not known, but in the contest with Herkimer and Willet must have been nearly or quite a hundred."[931] Stone, who wrote in 1838, stated that "The loss of the enemy in this engagement was equally, if not more severe, than that of the Americans."[932] Thirteen years later Pomroy Jones wrote, "The loyalists and Indians each lost . . . killed about 100, besides many wounded."[933] In keeping with contemporary practice, no sources were provided for any of these claims.

The mysterious letter of August 18, 1777, written at Albany by someone who had seen "Col. Wallers," said that "Sir John Johnson fell in the engagement" and "[t]he killed and wounded of the enemy in both engagements [battle and sortie,] from all that can be collected, exceeds three hundred."[934] It is not difficult to see how the Whigs convinced themselves that the Indians had lost two hundred or more men.

British reports and returns have rarely been consulted, and some who have examined them have concluded that British officers employed a formula to reduce their casualty rate, either for their own delusion or perhaps to protect their careers.

Regarding the Indians, Butler advised Carleton that they "suffered much having 33 Killed and 29 wounded, the Senecas alone lost 17 Men, among whom were several of their Chief Warriors, & had 16 wounded."[935] Butler would gain no personal advantage if native casualties were more or less, so there seems no reason to doubt his accounting.

Daniel Claus's numbers were of the same order when he reported that thirty-two Indians were killed, "among which were several Seneka chiefs," and that thirty-three were wounded.[936] A year later, Claus wrote a biography of Brant in which he reported the number of Seneca dead

Rebellion in the Mohawk Valley

at Oriskany as seventeen "among whom were several Chiefs and Leaders w[hi]ch enraged them greatly."[937]

Richard McGinnis, who joined Butler's Rangers in 1778, kept a journal in which he claimed that the Indians "of Different Nations" had lost thirty-two men killed in the ambush.[938]

A later report of Indian losses by John Norton, the war captain of the Canadian Grand River natives during the War of 1812, repeated oral tradition when he recalled that the Iroquois had "lost about Fifty men, a great part of whom belonged to the Ondowaga [Senecas.]"[939]

On a different scale altogether, word was received at Burgoyne's camp on August 12 that "The Indians lost about 200 killed, and about as many wounded — A great loss for them . . . [They] . . . suffered much by the Loss of some of their favourite Chiefs, and Warriors."[940] This statistic suggests that almost half of the Indians engaged at Oriskany were casualties. St. Leger's detailed report to Burgoyne on August 27 paints a different picture, "it was not so with the Indians[,] their loss was great/ I must be understood, [by] indian computation, being only about thirty killed and wounded, and in that number some of their favourite chiefs, and confidential warriors were slain./"

The total of St. Leger's casualties from all causes was remarkably light compared to the catastrophic losses suffered by the militia. The following table is compiled from St. Leger's August 27 return prepared at Oswego and from Butler's reports.

Regiments	Killed/Capt'd/Missing		Wounded/Sick	
	Officers	Rankers	Officers	Rankers
Royal Artillery		3		2
King's or Eighth	1	5		7
34th		10		5
KRR NY	2	16	1	24
Jägers		6		7
Indian Dept	2	1		1
Subtotal	5	41	1	46
Natives	32		34	
Total (Stanwix phase)	78		81	

Of the British Regulars, two artillery rankers were prisoners at Stanwix. The King's Regiment casualties included Ensign Walter Butler and the five rankers captured at Shoemaker's tavern. The 34th casualties included five men taken with Butler and five that were held prisoner at Stanwix. The three Royal Yorker officer casualties were those named in the text, and of the sixteen ranker casualties, two had been taken with Butler at Shoemaker's and five others were prisoners at Stanwix.

A comparative examination of Royal Yorker returns for 1776 and 1777 reveals that by December 24, 1777,[941] the regiment had sustained twelve deaths (killed or died of wounds), six desertions, twenty-three missing (dead or deserted), seven prisoners with the enemy, and ten discharged from wounds or illnesses. Together, these categories total fifty-eight. That's a wastage of 19.3 percent.

Regarding the six Hessian riflemen, two went missing at Oriskany, and one was killed and two went missing during the retreat, one of whom was made a prisoner at Stanwix.

Considering that de Rouville's company had been plagued with desertions, it is interesting that St. Leger reported no Canadien casualties during the Stanwix phase. Nor did he report Indian Department casualties, although it is known that two ranger officers were killed at Oriskany, one ranker was killed, and another wounded.[942] The native casualties in the table are Butler's numbers with the addition of Deserontyon, who was wounded during the retreat. The additional casualties suffered by the Fort Hunters when they joined Burgoyne have not been included.

The Mission

The goal of the Tryon County Militia Brigade was to relieve Fort Stanwix. Presumably, this was to be accomplished by precipitating a pitched battle in which St. Leger's forces would be defeated or driven off by the combined efforts of the garrison and the brigade.

Another possibility may have been for the militia to force a path through St. Leger's lines and gain entry to the fort, thereby doubling the garrison and rendering the storming of the fort impossible; however, that would have resulted in overcrowding and almost guaranteed heavy casualties from British shelling. Provisions would have been reduced at a remarkable rate, even with the addition of the brigade's wagonloads, but, on the other hand, St. Leger may not have continued his siege faced with such overwhelming numbers.

In the event, the militia failed to accomplish a relief in any form; instead, they marched into an ambush and received a staggering drubbing. Whether they suffered 30 percent or 46 percent casualties, the Tryon militia was shattered and never fully recovered. In the aftermath, accusations of misbehaviour and cowardice caused a great deal of acrimony. On April 20, 1778, a number of depositions were heard by Justice of the Peace Jelles Fonda regarding the looting of the Mohawks' Canajoharie castle and Han Jost Herkimer's house by committee Chairman Peter Deygart and his cronies.[943] These events were viewed as dangerous personal excesses, as opposed to the State's systematic sequestration of Tory properties, which was conducted under due process of law and financial necessity, no matter how the victims viewed the process.

Deygart and his fellow-travellers initiated a counterattack. On May 28, 1778, the New York State Council of Appointment reviewed charges against several Tryon County militia officers and officials. Jelles Fonda was charged with disaffection and Colonels Visscher and Veeder and Adjutant Van Veghten were charged with cowardice during the battle. George Herkimer, brother of General Herkimer, was charged with cosseting Tories, and William Deygart, a county Justice of the Peace, was accused of assisting Butler and Ten Broeck at Shoemaker's tavern. The State Council received "sundry Affidavits and other Papers" and heard testimony from the accused and witnesses for and against. Sensibly, they "[R]ecommend[ed] it to the Complainants as they have done to the Parties complained of, that as they esteem the good of their Country, they forbear from any further Disputes that may tend to disunite the Inhabitants of Tryon County and heartily to assist each other in the most vigorous Exertions to repel the common Enemy."[944]

Governor Clinton intervened and amalgamated the remnants of the Tryon brigade with Albany County's, an arrangement that continued until 1781, when Willett was brought in to command the defence of Tryon County.

Arnold's displeasure over the failure of the Tryon militia to rally reflected his inability to recognize the depth of the tragedy that had struck the county. Even so, the Tryon men were resilient and, after a brief respite, they rose again to confront Burgoyne. Over the next five brutal years of fire and terror, they rallied again and again and again.

Of Willett's Sortie

The other half of the August 6 equation was the sortie from the fort. While it may be tempting to be derisive about the lack of risk that attended this venture and scoff at Willett's outrageous claims of enemy casualties, the sortie's lasting effects were of far greater implication than a few dead and captured soldiers and natives. As well, several Oriskany participants recorded that the sortie ensured the survival of the two hundred or so entrapped survivors, as it prompted the enemy's withdrawal.

The looting of the Royal Yorkers' camp certainly added to the Tories' discomfort and anger, but of much greater consequence was the pillaging of the Indians' camps — their blankets, their valuable finery, and, most significant, their religious articles. Enraged by their battle casualties, they were further agitated by these material and spiritual losses.

St. Leger added to their anger when he refused to release them into the Valley, and when the siege collapsed, they were disgusted and dismayed. Willett's sortie had laid the seeds of this displeasure. As a Mohawk explained a few years after the events of 1777: "[I]t was degrading of Indians to receive orders from white men, as if [the natives] had not people of sense among themselves."[945]

Final Words

We have viewed the British campaign of 1777 in America through the microcosm of the St. Leger Expedition — a small, but not insignificant, element of the whole. It should have been apparent that the entire premise and conduct of the campaign was incredibly dependent upon communications — late, inadequate, misleading, conflicting, impossible, garbled, bogus, missing, disputed, and ignored orders, reports, and requests. Germain to Howe; Carleton to Burgoyne; Guy Johnson to Butler; Carleton to Claus; Claus to St. Leger; Herkimer to his colonels; Herkimer to Gansevoort; Deygart to Schuyler; Clinton to Herkimer; Arnold to the Tryon colonels; Henry Clinton to Burgoyne; and on and on.

Most significantly, St. Leger's affairs were particularly affected by another class of communication — propaganda. Words of deliberate exaggeration and misinformation such as Butler's to the natives; the reports of Jane McCrae's death; Gansevoort's report to the Tryon committee; St. Leger's proclamation; Johnson's, Claus's, and Butler's threatening letter; Arnold's sham executions; Arnold's proclamation to Tryon County; Arnold's clever report to Gansevoort; Han Jost Schuyler's lies to St. Leger; Willett's report to the broader world . . . the old maxim was proven again: the first casualty of war is truth.

Of Oriskany And Stanwix
Contemporary Comments
The Tryon County Militia

"It is with concern we are to acquaint you that this was the fatal day in which the succors, which were intended for your relief, have been attacked and defeated with great loss of numbers killed, wounded, and taken prisoners . . . We are sorry to inform you that most of the principal officers are killed."

> Peter Bellinger and John Frey, Tryon County Militia, August 6, 1777

"[T]hey plunged blindly into the trap that was laid for their destruction . . . the militia shewed no want of courage in their deplorable situation in the midst of such extreme danger and so bloody an execution."

> London Edition, Annual Register, 1777

"I went over the ground where General Herkimer fought Sir John Johnson . . . one of the most desperate engagements that has ever been fought by the militia. I saw a vast number of human skulls and bones scattered through the woods."

> Alexander Thompson, April 20, 1783

"While the fort was thus invested, General Herkimer made an ineffectual attempt to relieve it . . . The relief of the fort being still an object of the utmost importance, and no doubt remaining on the minds of many, but that General Herkimer had been defeated."

> Marinus Willett's Manuscript, William M. Willett 1831

Historians' Comments

"Tryon County long had reason to mourn that day."
> William L. Stone, 1838

"There was scarcely a family in the Mohawk Valley but what had lost some relative, a father, brother or cousin."
> Pomroy Jones, 1851

"The battle was a severe one. The severest, perhaps, for the number engaged, that took place during the whole revolutionary war."
Nathaniel S. Benton, 1856

"Herkimer's glory is that out of such a slaughter he snatched the substance."
J. Watts De Peyster, 1882

"This was one of the most severely contested battles, and one of the most important in its results of any fought during the whole war."
Jeptha R. Simms, 1883

"In the Valley homes was great mourning. For such a small population, the losses were almost overwhelming. In some families the male members were wiped out. It was many a long, weary year before the sorrow and suffering caused by the sacrifices at Oriskany had been forgotten in the Valley of the Mohawk."
Nelson Greene, Oriskany Battlefield Plaque, 1975

Contemporary Comments
British Indians and Tories

"I thought at that time the Blood Shed a Stream Running down on the Decending ground during the afternoon, and yet some living crying for help. But [we] have no mercy . . . .. for them."
Blacksnake Tekayetu, Seneca warrior

"At length the Indians with a detachment of the Yorkers and rangers, pursuing that blow, utterly defeated them with the loss of 500 killed, wounded [and] taken."
John Butler, August, 1777

"The compleat victory was obtained; above 400 lay dead upon the field, amongst the number of whom were almost all the principal movers of rebellion in that country . . . In relation to the victory, it was equally complete, as if the whole had fallen; nay, more so, as the two hundred who escaped only served to spread the panic wider."
Barry St. Leger, August, 1777

"[A] success so signal as would in other cases and a more fortunate season have been decisive as to the fate of a stronger and much more important fortress."
London Edition, Annual Register, 1777

"All the good done by the exped'n was that the Ringleaders and principal men of the rebels of Tryon County were put out of the way."
Daniel Claus, October 1777

"The Six Nations say . . . our expedition to Fort Stanwix [was] not sufficiently equipt."
Daniel Claus, November 1777

"[T]o St. Leger was assigned the most important part in the programme with the most inadequate means of carrying it out."
Sir Henry Clinton, 1777

"They hope he will not send a handful of men with two or three small popguns, as was the case when we went to Fort Stanwix in Seventy Seven . . . And a General that loved milk better than they did themselves for they saw he drank it all, and would not give them any."
Onondaga Chiefs Teaqwanda and Teyanarunte, 1780

Historians' Comments

"The rebels behaved with resolution, but were totally defeated. In the action General Hercheimer and almost every leading man in the rebel interest in the county of Tryon were killed. Not a man got into the fort, and the wagons, provisions, and stores were all taken or destroyed."
Thomas Jones, 1879

"Then a butchery ensued such as had never occurred on this continent, and if the entrapped Americans engaged had not shown the courage of desperation they would all have been sacrificed . . . it was morally decisive in results . . . Tryon County suffered such a terrific calamity, that, . . . if it smiled again during the war, it smiled through tears."
John Watts De Peyster, 1882

BIBLIOGRAPHY

Primary Sources — Archival

American Antiquarian Society
Orville W. Carroll Collection.

Archives of Ontario
Ms521(1), Edward Jessup Papers.
Ms622, a miscellaneous selection of Haldimand Papers
H.H. Robertson Papers.

Archives of Quebec
LG V-666.

British Library
Haldimand Papers.
AddMss21678, Gen'l Orders and Letters Relating to Garrison at Niagara, 1759–78.
AddMss21699, Register of Letters from Carleton to Various Persons, 1776–77.
AddMss21700, ditto.
AddMss21734, V.3, Letters from various persons to Haldimand, 1781–82.
AddMss21743, General Orders issued by Carleton and Haldimand, 1776–83.
AddMss21756, Corresp., Officers Commanding at Mackinac & Niagara, 1777–82.
AddMss21765, Correspondence with Officers at Niagara, 1777–84.
AddMss21779, Reports on Indian Meetings, Treaties, etc., n.d. and 1778–84.
AddMss21822, V.2, as above, 1783-85.
AddMss21826, Returns of Loyalists in Canada, n.d. and 1778–87.
AddMss21827, Muster Rolls, Accounts etc., Corps of Loyal Americans, 1776–83.
AddMss21873, Memorials from Officers and Soldiers of the Army n.d. and 1778-84.
AddMss21874, V.1, Memorials from Prov Corps and Loyalists n.d. and 1777–82.
AddMss21875, V.2, as above, n.d., 1783–84.

Constitution of the Iroquois Confederacy, Grand River, Brantford, Ontario

McCord Museum, McGill University
John Munro & Jessup Family Papers.

National Archives of Canada
Claus Family fonds, MG19, F1, Vols. 25&26
Haldimand Papers (all B series are transcripts of MG21).

Bibliography

B23, Pt2, General Orders & Instructions.
B39, Register of Letters from Sir Guy Carleton to
Various Persons.
B71, as above.
B158, as above.
B162, V.2, as above.
B214, Memorials from the Provincial Corps & Loyalists
(v.1) n.d. and 1777–82.
MG 23, K4, John Fife Mss.

Colonial Office Records
  CO42 (Canada, Original Correspondence).
  42/35 (Q12), 1776, Carleton & Germain.
  42/36 (Q13), 1777, Carleton, Burgoyne & Germain.
  42/37 (Q14), 1777, Burgoyne's expedition & surrender.

War Office Records
  WO1/11, Carleton-War Office, In-Letters, North
  America, 1755-85.
  17/1571(1), as above, 1777.
  17/1571(2), as above.
  28/5, 28/9, 28/10(1), Headquarters records & returns, America, 1775–1795.
  34/14, Amherst Papers.

Massachusetts Historical Society, Collections of
  Seventh Series, Vol. II.

New York Historical Association, Library of
  Wyman Collection.

New York Historical Society, collections of.
  Gates Papers, Mf Reel 3 and Box 7.
  Schuyler Papers.
  Tryon County Mss.
  Vol. II "Minutes of the Council of Appointment."

New York Public Library
  Schuyler Papers, Indian Papers.
  Box 14.
  Emmet Collection.

New York State Library
  125th Annual Report.
  John Peters Papers.
  Manuscript No. 2428. Military Artificers, KRR NY.

Public Record Office
  CO5/140.
  WO28/2, 34th Regiment, Field Officers' Letters, 1777–1789.

Rebellion in the Mohawk Valley

U.S. National Archives and Records Center
    Records of the U.S. House of Representatives, Twenty-first Congress's committee on
    Military Pensions, RG233, File No. HR21A-D16.1. E.R. Hessler, tr., 2/87.

New York Pension Applications
    Bellinger, Peter P., R731&732.
    Cristman, Frederick, R1941.
    Duesler, John, widow of, W16244.
    Failing, Jacob J, widow of, W21092.
    Failing, John D., widow of, W19242.
    Flanders, Henry, S13037.
    Frank, John, S23644.
    Gamps, [Krembs], Henry, W16273.
    Garlock, Adam, R3917.
    Helmer, Adam F., widow of, W17067.
    Kilts, Conrad, S13658.
    Leathers, John, widow of, W20452.
    Lonis, George M., widow of W20522.
    McMaster, Hugh, widow of, W16645.
    Miller, Adam, S11073.
    Petrie, Richard Marcus & Catharine, R729.
    Quackenboss, Abraham J., R8537.
    Quackenboss, Peter J., R8537.
    Runnolds, Silas, R9078.
    Sammons, Frederick, S11350.
    Scholl, Johan Jost, widow of, W16396.
    Snell, Peter (Susannah), R9897.
    Snook, Henry, S11435.
    Spankable, widow of, W11519.
    Stewart, Finley, widow of, W16421.
    Stine, George, S11471.
    Thompson, William, R14662.
    Van Eps, Evert, widow of, W15969.
    Van Slyke, William, widow of, W2461.
    Van Vechten, Derick, S23047.
    Walrath, Henery J., S28937.
    Wolleber, Abraham & Dorothy, R17772.
    Young, Jacob A., R11960.
    Zimmerman, Jacob, widow of, W20002.

Pennsylvania Pension Applications,
    Dickson, Benjamin, S22210.
    Dickson, James, S22208.

U.S. Department of the Interior.
    Geological Survey 1955, AMS5870 II NE — Series V821.

U.S. Papers of the Continental Congress,
    Mf Group M247, 77: 83-86.

Bibliography

Wisconsin, State Historical Society
  Lyman C. Draper Manuscripts.
  Series F, Vol.10. (Joseph Brant Papers)
  Series U, Vol.11. (Frontier War Papers)

Primary Sources — Published

Newspapers and Periodicals
Daily Herald (Utica, NY) July 30, 1883.
Toronto Globe, July 16, 1877.

Published Documents, Maps, and Contemporary Works

Act for Regulating the Militia of the State of New York passed at Poughkeepske, April 3, 1778, in the Second Session of Assembly, An. Poughkeepsie: n.p., 1778.

Adler, Winston, ed., and Asa Fitch, comp. *Their Own Voices: Oral Accounts of Early Settlers in Washington County, New York.* Interlaken, NY: Heart of Lakes Publishing, 1983.

Antliff, W. Bruce, tr. *Loyalist Settlements 1783–1789.* Toronto: Ministry of Citizenship and Culture, 1985.

Bradstreet, Lieut.Col. John. *An Impartial Account of Lieut.-Col. Bradstreet's Expedition to Fort Frontenac.* Toronto: Rous & Mann Limited, 1940.

Calendar of Historical Manuscripts Relating to the War of the Revolution, in the office of the Secretary of State, Albany, N.Y. 3 vols., Albany: Weed, Parsons and Company, Printers, 1868.

Clinton, George. *Public Papers of George Clinton, First Governor of New York, 1777–1795. 1801–1804.* 6 vols.. New York and Albany: State of New York, 1902.

Colonial Laws of New York from the Year 1664 to the Revolution, The. 5 vols., Albany: 1894.

Council of Appointment, Minutes of, April 4, 1778–May 3, 1779. NYHS, V. II (1925).

Davies, K.G., ed. "The Campaigns of 1777." *Documents of the American Revolution 1770–1783,* Colonial Office Series, vol. XIV, Transcripts 1777. Shannon: Irish University Press, 1972.

De Lancey, Edward F., ed. *Muster Rolls of the New York Provincial Regiment — 1755–1764.* NYHS Collections, 1891. Reprint, Bowie, MD: Heritage Books Inc., 1990.

Fernow, Berthold, ed. *Documents relating to the Colonial History of the State of New York.* Albany: Weed, Parsons and Company, Printers, 1887. XV, State Archives, V. 1.

Force, Peter, ed. *American Archives, 4th Series, Containing a Documentary History of the English Colonies in North America from the King's Message to Parliament of March 7, 1774, to the Declaration of Independence by the United States.* 6 vols., Washington, DC: M. St. Clair Clarke & Peter Force, 1837–1846.

Fraser, Alexander, ed. *Second Report of the Bureau of Archives for the Province of Ontario.* 2 vols., Toronto: Legislative Assembly of Ontario, 1904. Reprint, Baltimore: Genealogical Publishing Co., Inc., 1994.

General Staff, Historical Section of, ed., II. "The War of the American Revolution, The Province of Quebec under the Administration of Governor Sir Guy Carleton, 1775–1778." *A History of the Organization, Development and Services of the Military*

Rebellion in the Mohawk Valley

and Naval Forces of Canada From the Peace of Paris in 1763 to the Present Time With Illustrative Documents [HSGS]. 2 vols., Canada, King's Printer, n.d.

Hamilton, Milton W., ed., and Albert B. Corey, director and state historian. The Papers of William Johnson. 13 vols., Albany: University of the State of New York, 1962.

Jefferys, Thomas. The American Atlas. London, 1776. Repring, Amsterdam: Theatrum Orbis Terrarum, 1974.

Johnson, Colonel Guy, Adjutant General for the Northern District of New York Province. Manual Exercise, Evolutions, Manoeuvres, &c. To be Observed and Followed by the Militia of the Province of New-York: with some Rules ... Albany: Alexander and James Robertson, 1772. Facsimile edition, Johnstown, NY: Lewis G. Decker, 1982.

Johnston, Charles M., ed. The Valley of the Six Nations — A Collection of Documents on the Indian Lands of the Grand River. Toronto: Champlain Society, 1964.

Knox, Captain John. The Siege of Quebec, and the Campaigns in North America 1757–1760. 1769. Reprint, London: Folio Society, 1976.

McHenry, Chris, comp. Rebel Prisoners at Quebec 1778–1783. Author, 1981.

O'Callaghan, E.B., ed. Documents Relative to the Colonial History of the State of New York. Albany: Weed, Parson, 1854. London Documents, XLVI.

Pargellis, Stanley, ed. Military Affairs in North America 1748–1765, Selected Documents from the Cumberland Papers in Windsor Castle. Archon Books, 1969.

Penrose, Maryly B., ed. Indian Affairs Papers, American Revolution. Franklin Park, NJ: Liberty Bell Associates, 1981.

——. Mohawk Valley in the Revolution, committee of Safety Papers & Genealogical Compendium. Franklin Park, NJ: Liberty Bell Associates, 1978.

——. Mohawk Valley Revolutionary War Pension Abstracts. Bowie, MD: Heritage Books, Inc., 1989.

Preston, Richard A., ed. Kingston Before the War of 1812, A Collection of Documents, Ontario Series III. Champlain Society, 1959.

Proceedings of a General Court Martial, held at Major General Lincoln's Quarters, near Quaker-Hill, in the State of New York by order of his Excellency General Washington, Commander in Chief of the Army of the United States of America for the Trial of Major General Schuyler. Philadelphia: 1778

Remembrancer or, Impartial Repository of Public Events for the Year 1777, The. London: J. Almon, 1778.

Roberts, James A., comptroller. New York in the Revolution as Colony and State. Albany: State of New York, 1897. Reprint in 2 vols., 1904.

Secretary of the Commonwealth. Massachusetts Soldiers and Sailors in the War of the Revolution. 17 vols. Boston: Wright and Potter Printing Co., 1896.

Simes, Thomas. The Regulator or Instructions to Form the Officer and Complete the Soldier. London, 1780.

Smith, Clifford Neal. Mercenaries from Hessen-Hanau Who Remained in Canada and the United States after the American Revolution. German-American Genealogical Research Monograph Number 5. McNeal, AZ: Westland Publications, 1976. Transcripts of Mss held in the Staatsarchiv, Marburg, Bestand, Germany.

Smith, Captain George. An Universal Military Dictionary, A Copious Explanation of the Technical Terms &c. — Used in the Equipment, Machinery, Movements, and Military Operations of an Army. London: J. Millan, 1779. Reprint, Ottawa: Museum Restoration Service, 1969.

Sullivan, James, and Alexander C. Flick, eds. Minutes of the Albany committee of Correspondence, 1775–1778. 2 vols, Albany: State University of New York, 1923 & 1925.

Primary Sources, Unpublished Transcripts, Letters, Documents and Journals

Bailey, DeWitt. tr. Butler's Rangers Pay Lists for 24 Dec. 1777 – 24 Oct. 1778. HP, AddMss21765.

Fort Stanwix document collection.

MacKenna, Father John. Letter to Monseignor Montgolfier from Wood Creek, 10Aug77, Archives of Quebec, MG-V666.

Gansevoort, General Peter. Military Papers of. tr. by the State Historian. Submitted 1906, NY State Archives.

Pay Lists of Butler's Rangers, 24 Dec. 1777 – 24 Oct. 1778. HP, AddMss21765.

Rimaldy, Virginia, tr. Orders of the Field Jaeger Corps from May 7, 1777, to April 30, 1783.

Smy, LtCol William A., tr.&ed. "The Butler Papers: Documents and Papers Relating to Colonel John Butler and his Corps of Rangers 1711–1977." u.p., 1994.

Willett, Marinus. LtCol Marinus Willett's Orderly Book, 1777. NYHS, NYSL, Department of Archives & Manuscripts.

———. Col Marinus Willett's Letter & Orderly Book, Ft Rensselaer 1781. Document No.15705, NYSL, Archives & Mss.

Published Memoirs, Depositions, Diaries, Journals, Poems and Correspondence

American

(see also State pension depositions noted above)

Arnold, MajGen Benedict. Proclamation to the inhabitants of Tryon County, 20Aug77. Stone, *Brant*, I, No. VIII.

Baldwin, Col Jeduthan, Thomas William Baldwin, ed. *The Revolutionary Journal of Colonel Jeduthan Baldwin*. Bangor, 1906.

Bloomfield, Joseph. *Citizen Soldier, The Revolutionary War Journal of Joseph Bloomfield*. Mark E. Lender and James Kent Martin, eds. Newark: New Jersey Historical Society, 1982.

Colbrath, Lieutenant William. *Days of Siege, A Journal of the Siege of Fort Stanwix in 1777*. Larry Lowenthal, ed. Eastern Acorn Press, 1983.

Elmer, Lieutenant Ebenezer. "Journal Kept During an Expedition to Canada in 1776." L.Q.C. Elmer, ed. Proceedings, New Jersey Historical Society, Vol. II, No. 3 (1847); Vol. II, No.4 (1847); Vol. III, No.1 (1848); Vol.X, New Series No.4, (1925).

Helmer, Adam. Statement of to the State Congress, Kingston, 12Aug77. tr. Clinton Papers, II, 212.

Minutes of the [NY] Council of Appointment, April 4, 1778–May 3, 1779. NYHS, V. II (1925).

Scudder, Lieut William. *The Journal of William Scudder, an Officer in the Late New-York Line*. Author, 1794. Reprint, Garland Publishing, Inc., 1977, as vol. 22 of *Narrative of North American Indian Captives*.

Willett, LtCol Marinus. Poem entitled "Juvinus," "General Harkemer's Battle, A New Song to the Tune of the British Boys," written at Albany, 7Dec77. NYHS, Marinus Willett Mss Collection. Folder 1775–77.

———. *A Narrative of part of the Transactions at and near Fort Stanwix since the investiture of that place by the Enemy, given in Manuscript by Lieutenant-Colonel Marinus*

Willett of that Garrison, 11Aug77. Appendix III of Willett, *A Narrative of the Military Actions of Colonel Marinus Willett.*

Younglove, Surgeon Moses. Affidavit of. Stone, *Brant,* I, App.IV.

Younglove, Samuel. A different version of Moses Younglove's experiences. NYSL, Albany, Folder #42, item 11965.

British, German and Canadian

Ainslie, Thomas. *Canada Preserved — The Journal of Captain Thomas Ainslie.* Sheldon Cohen, ed. Toronto Copp Clark Publishing Company, 1968.

Anburey, Thomas. *With Burgoyne from Quebec.* Sydney Jackman, ed. Toronto: Macmillan of Canada, 1963.

Burgoyne, Lieutenant General John. *A State of the Expedition From Canada as Laid Before the House of Commons By Lieutenant-General Burgoyne and Verified by Evidence; with a Collection of Authentic Documents and an Addition of Many Circumstances which were Prevented from Appearing Before the House by the Prorogation of Parliament, etc.* London: J. Almon, 1780.

——. "General Burgoyne's Proclamation". Hadden, *Journal,* 59-62.

——. E.B. O'Callaghan, ed. *Orderly Book of Lieut. Gen. John Burgoyne.* Albany: J. Munsell, 1860.

——. "Thoughts for Conducting the War from the Side of Canada." Burgyone, *State of the Expedition.*

Butler, Major John. Letter to Governor Carleton, Camp before Ft Stanwix, 15Aug77. HP, CO42/37.

Claus, LtCol Daniel. "Anecdotes of Captain Brant." NAC, MG2, 46 found in William Clement Bryant, "Captain Brant and the Old King." Publications of the Buffalo Historical Society, Vol. IV (1896).

——. Letter to Secretary Alexander Knox, 16Oct77, found in *CHSNY,* VIII.

——. Letter to Secretary Knox, 6Nov77, found in *CHSNY,* VIII.

De Lorimier, Claude-Nicolas-Guillaume. *At War with the Americans, The Journal of Claude-Nicolas-Guillaume de Lorimier.* Peter Aichinger, tr. and ed. Victoria: Press Porcepic, n.d.

Empey, Philip, Jr. Claim of, 16Feb88. Loyalist Petitions, II, 1123.

Empy, Philip, Sr. "The humble Petition of." *Loyalist Narratives From Upper Canada.* James J. Talman, ed. Toronto: Champlain Society, 1946.

Enys, John. *The American Journals of Lt John Enys.* Elizabeth Cometti, ed. Syracuse: Adirondack Museum and Syracuse Univ. Press, 1976.

Fornyea, Christopher. Petition of. "Petitions for grants of land in Upper Canada, second series, 1796–99." *OHSPR,* vol. 26 (1930).

Gummersall, Thomas. Declaration of, 6Aug76. *CHSNY,* VIII, *London Documents: XLVI,* 682–83.

Hadden, Lieut. James M. *A Journal Kept in Canada and Upon Burgoyne's Campaign in 1776 and 1777.* Horatio Rogers, ed. Albany: Joel Munsell's Sons, 1884.

Hertel de Rouville, Capitaine Jean-Baptiste-Melchior. Poem, "L'Entreprise Manquée," in "L'Expedition du Fort Stanwix." *Le Canada Français.* (Société du Parlés Français au Canada, Québec) vol. XXXIII (November 1945).

Hesse Hanau Jäger Battalion. "Diary of the Hanau Jaeger Corps," from the Hessian Papers at Morristown National Historic Park. *Fort Stanwix Garrison Newsletter (1981).*

Hesse Hanau Jäger Battalion. Orders of the Field Jaeger Corps from May 7, 1777, to April 30, 1783. Virginia Rimaldy, tr. (u.p.).

Bibliography

Hughes, Thomas. *A Journal by Thos: Hughes For his Amusement, Designed only for his Perusal by the time he attains the Age of 50 if he lives so long. (1778–1789).* Cambridge: Cambridge University Press, 1947.

Johnson, Sir John. *Orderly Book of Sir John Johnson During his Campaign Against Fort Stanwix from Nov. 4th, 1776 to July 30th, 1777.* William L. Stone, tr. and ed. New York: A.S. Barnes & Company, 1881.

——. Daniel Claus and John Butler. Proclamation. "To the Inhabitants of Tryon County, August 13, 1777. Stone, *Brant, I,* No.VII.

Lynn, Mary C., ed.,and Helga Doblin, tr. *The American Revolution, Garrison Life in French Canada and New York, Journal of an Officer in the Prinz Friedrich Regiment, 1776–1783.* Westport, CT, and London: Greenwood Press, 1993.

McDonell, John Scotus. *Spanish John, Being a narrative in the Early Life of Colonel John M'Donell of Scottos.* Knoydart, Scotland: Craigmyle, 1993.

McGinnis, Richard. "Journal of Occurrences Respecting Our Suffering in the Late Rebellion." , Carol Lind., ed. *NY Genealogical & Biographical Record.* Vol.105, No.4 (Oct 1974).

Norton, John. *The Journal of Major John Norton 1816.* Carl F. Klinck & James J. Talman, eds. Toronto: Champlain Society, 1970.

Pausch, Georg. *Georg Pausch's Journal and Reports of the Campaign in America.* Bruce E. Burgoyne, tr. and ed. Bowie, MD: Heritage Books, Inc., 1996.

Peters, LtCol John. "A Narrative of John Peters, Lieutenant-Colonel in the Queen's Loyal Rangers in Canada Drawn by Himself in a Letter to a Friend in London." *Toronto Globe,* July 16, 1877.

St. Leger, LtCol Barry. "Colonel St. Leger's Account of Occurrences at Fort Stanwix," 27Aug77. *Burgoyne, State of the Expedition.*

——. Expense Accounts of the St. Leger Expedition. "L'Expedition du Fort Stanwix." *Le Canada Français.* (Société du Parlés Français au Canada, Québec) vol. XXXIII (November 1945).

——. Letter to Carleton, Oswego, 27Aug77. *NAC, WO42/37.*

——. "Present State of the Detachment Sent on the Secret Expedition," 27Aug77. WO17/1571(2).

——. A general proclamation to the inhabitants. Stone, *Brant, I,* No.III.

Stanley, George F.G., ed. *For Want of a Horse, being A Journal of the Campaigns against the Americans in 1776 and 1777 from Canada by an officer who served with Lt.Gen. Burgoyne.* Sackville, NB: Tribune Press Limited, 1961.

Talman, James J., ed. *Loyalist Narratives From Upper Canada.* Toronto: Champlain Society, 1946.

Von Hille, Ensign Ludwig Julius Friedrich. *Journal of an Officer in the Prinz Friedrich Regiment, 1776–1783.* Mary C. Lynn, ed. and Helga Doblin, tr. Westport, CT, and London: Greenwood Press, 1993.

Von Riedesel, Baroness Frederika Charlotte Louis von Massow. *Letters and Journals Relating to the War of American Independence and the capture of the German Troops at Saratoga.* Claus Reuter, tr. and ed. Toronto: German-Canadian Museum of Applied History, 2001.

Von Specht, Johann Friedrich. *The Specht Journal.* Helga Doblin, tr. Westport, CT, and London: Greenwood Press, 1995.

Stone, William L., tr. *Letters of Brunswick and Hessian Officers During the American Revolution.* Albany, 1891. Facsimile, New York: De Capo Press, 1970.

Townshend, George, First Marquis, Master-General of Ordnance. "Rules and Orders for the Discipline of the Light Infantry companies in His Majesty's Army in Ireland

Rebellion in the Mohawk Valley

1772." Captain R.H. Smythies. *Historical Records of the 40th (2nd Somersetshire Regiment)*. Devonport: 1894.

Secondary Sources — Books

Abler, Thomas S., ed. *Chainbreaker, The Revolutionary War: Memoirs of Governor Blacksnake As told to Benjamin Williams*. Lincoln and London: University of Nebraska Press, 1989.

Anderson, Fred. *Crucible of War, The Seven Years' War and the Fate of Empire in British North America, 1754–1766*. New York: Alfred A. Knopf, 2000.

Atkinson, C.T. *The South-Wales Borderers — 24th Foot — 1689–1937*. Cambridge: Regimental History Committee, 1937.

Bailey, DeWitt. *British Military Longarms 1715–1865*. New York, London and Sydney: Arms and Armour Press, 1986.

Bellico, Russell P. *Sails and Steam in the Mountains, A Maritime and Military History of Lake George and Lake Champlain*. Fleischmanns, NY: Purple Mountain Press, 1992.

Bonsal, Stephen. *When the French Were Here, A Narrative of the Sojourn of the French Forces in America, and Their Contribution to the Yorktown Campaign Drawn from Unpublished Reports and Letters of Participants in the National Archives of France and the MS. Division of the Library of Congress*. Garden City, NY: Doubleday, Doran, and Company, Inc., 1945.

Bruce, R.M. *The Loyalist Trial*. n.p., n.d.

Campbell, Maria. *Revolutionary Services and Civil Life of General William Hull Prepared from His Manuscripts by His Daughter Mrs. Maria Campbell Together with the History of the Campaign of 1812 and Surrender of the post of Detroit by his Grandson, James Freeman Clarke*. New York: D. Appleton and Co., 1848.

Campbell, William W., Jr. *Annals of Tryon County; or the Border Warfare of New York*. Cherry Valley: The Cherry Valley Gazette Print, 1880.

Chartrand, René. *Canadian Military Heritage, I, 1000–1754 & II, 1755–1871*. 2 vols., Montreal: Art Global Inc., 1995.

Chidsey, Donald Barr. *The War in the North, An Informal History of the American Revolution in and near Canada*. New York: Crown Publishers, Inc., 1967.

Cruikshank, Ernest A. *The Story of Butler's Rangers and the Settlement of Niagara*. Welland: Lundy's Lane Historical Society, 1893. Reprint, Owen Sound, ON: Richardson, Bond and Wright Ltd., 1975.

——. and Gavin K. Watt, ed. *The King's Royal Regiment of New York with the additions of an Index, Appendices and a Master Muster Roll*. Toronto: Gavin K. Watt, 1984. Regimental history originally published. OHSPR, 27 (1931).

Cuneo, John R. *The Battles of Saratoga, The Turning of the Tide*. New York: Macmillan Company, 1967.

Dawson, Henry B. *Battles of the United States, By Sea and Land: embracing those of the Revolutionary and Indian Wars*. 2 vols. New York: Johnson, Fry, and Company, 1858.

DePeyster, John Watts. *The Life, Misfortunes & the Military Career of Brig. General Sir John Johnson Bart*. New York: Chas. H. Ludwig, 1882.

——. *Miscellanies of an Officer*. New York: C.H. Ludwig, 1838.

Dictionary of Canadian Biography. Toronto: University of Toronto Press, 1966.

Egly, T.W., Jr. *Goose Van Schaick of Albany 1736–789*. Author, 1992.

——. *History of the First New York Regiment*. Hampton, NH: Peter E. Randall, 1981.

Bibliography

Everard, Major H. *History of Thos. Farrington's Regiment subsequently Designated The 29th (Worcestershire) Foot 1694 to 1891.* Worcester: Littleby & Company, Worcester Press, 1891.

Flexner, James Thomas. *Lord of the Mohawks, A Biography of Sir William Johnson.* Boston and Toronto: Little, Brown, and Company, 1979.

Foote, Allan D., with James Morrision, Joseph Robertaccio & Alan Sterling. *Liberty March — The Battle of Oriskany.* Utica: North Country Books, 1998.

Fryer, Mary Beacock. *King's Men, the Soldier Founders of Ontario.* Toronto and Charlottetown: Dundurn Press Limited, 1980.

Fuller, J.F.C. *British Light Infantry in the Eighteenth Century.* London: Hutchinson & Co., 1925. Facsimile edition, Doncaster, UK: Terence Wise, 1991.

Graymont, Barbara. *The Iroquois in the American Revolution.* Syracuse: Syracuse University Press, 1972.

Greene, Nelson, ed. *History of the Mohawk Valley — Gateway to the West 1614–1925.* 4 vols., Chicago: S.J. Clarke, 1925.

——. *The Old Mohawk Turnpike Book.* Fort Plain: author, 1924.

Hagerty, Gilbert. *Massacre at Fort Bull.* Providence: Mowbray Company, 1971.

Higginbotham, Don. *The War of American Independence, Military Attitudes, Policies, and Practice, 1763–1789 — Wars of the United States Series.* Don Mills, ON: Fitzhenry & Whiteside Limited, 1971.

Hinman, Marjory Barnum. *Onaquaga: Hub of the Border Wars of the American Revolution in New York State.* N.p., 1975.

Hudleston, F.J., *Gentleman Johnny Burgoyne, Misadventures of an English General in the Revolution.* Indianapolis: Bobbs-Merrill Company, 1927.

Huey, Lois M., and Bonnie Pulis. *Molly Brant, A Legacy of Her Own.* Youngstown, NY: Old Fort Niagara Association, 1997.

Hughes, MGen E.B. *Firepower, Weapons effectiveness on the battlefield, 1630–1850.* London: Arms and Armour Press, 1974.

Jepson, George H. *Herrick's Rangers.* Bennington, VT: Hadwen, Inc., 1977.

Johnson, Ken D. *The Bloodied Mohawk, The American Revolution in the Words of Fort Plank's Defenders and Other Mohawk Valley Partisans.* Rockport, MA: Picton Press, 2000.

Jones, Pomroy. *Annals and Recollections of Oneida County.* Rome, NY: author, 1851.

Jones, Thomas. *History of New York during The Revolutionary War and of the Leading Events in the Other Colonies at that Period.* Edward Floyd DeLancey, ed. 2 vols., New York: New York Historical Society, 1879.

Katcher, Philip R.N. *Encyclopedia of British, Provincial and German Army Units 1775–1783.* Harrisburg: Stackpole Books, 1973.

Keesler, M. Paul. *One Quarter Mile to Go, the Bicentennial Re-creation of the March of the Tryon County Militia and the Battle of Oriskany August 4, 5 & 6, 1977.* Holland Patent: NY Sportsman Magazine & NYS Muzzleloaders Assoc. Inc., 1977.

Kelsay, Isabel Thompson. *Joseph Brant 1743–1807, Man of Two Worlds.* Syracuse: Syracuse University Press, 1984.

Kemp, Alan. *American Soldiers of the Revolution.* London: Almark Publishing Co. Ltd., 1972.

Ketchum, Richard M. *Decisive Day, The Battle for Bunker Hill.* Doubleday & Company, Inc., 1962.

——. *Saratoga, Turning Point of America's Revolutionary War.* New York: Henry Holt and Company, 1997.

Leach, Douglas E. *Roots of Conflict, British Armed Forces and Colonial Americans,*

Rebellion in the Mohawk Valley

1677–1763. Chapel Hill and London: University of North Carolina Press, 1986.

Lossing, Benson J. *The Pictorial Field-Book of the Revolution or, Illustrations, by Pen and Pencil, of the History, Biography, Scenery, Relics, and Traditions of the War for Independence.* 2 vols., New York: Harper & Brothers, 1851.

Luzader, John F. "Construction and Military History." *Fort Stanwix: History, Historic Furnishing, and Historic Structure Reports.* Washington: Office of Park Historic Preservation, National Park Service, U.S. Department of the Interior, 1976, 2-71.

Mackesy, Piers. *The War for America 1775-1783.* Lincoln and London: University of Nebraska Press, 1992. Previously published in Britain, 1964.

Mathews, Hazel C. *Frontier Spies.* Fort Myers: Hazel C. Mathews, 1971.

———. *The Mark of Honour.* Toronto: University of Toronto Press, 1965.

McIlwraith, Jean N. "Sir Frederick Haldimand." *The Makers of Canada.* 11 vols. Toronto: Morang & Co., Limited, 1911. Vol. 3.

MacWethy, Lou D. *The Book of Names Especially Relating to the Early Palatines and the First Settlers of the Mohawk Valley.* Baltimore: Genealogical Publishing Co., Inc., 1981.

Mintz, Max M. *The Generals of Saratoga, John Burgoyne & Horatio Gates.* New Haven and London: Yale University Press, 1990.

Mollo, John, and Malcolm MacGregor. *Uniforms of the American Revolution, Macmillan Color Series.* New York: Macmillan Publishing Co., Inc., 1975.

Monroe, John D. *Chapters in the History of Delaware County New York.* Delaware County Historical Association, 1949.

Morrison, James F. *Colonel Jacob Klock's Regiment, Tryon County Militia.* Author, 1992.

———. *A History of Fulton County in the Revolution.* Gloversville: James F. Morrison, 1977.

Parkman, Francis. *The Conspiracy of Pontiac and the Indian War after the Conquest of Canada.* 2 vols. Boston: Little, Brown, and Company, 1895.

Potter-MacKinnon, Janice. *While the Women Only Wept — Loyalist Refugee Women in Eastern Ontario.* Montreal and Kingston: McGill-Queen's University Press, 1993.

Rahmer, Frederick A. *Fort Stanwix, A Brief History.* Rome, NY: author, 1940.

Reid, W. Max. *The Mohawk Valley, Its Legends and Its History.* New York and London: The Knickerbocker Press, 1901.

———. *The Story of Old Fort Johnson.* New York and London: G.P. Putnam's Sons, 1906.

Robinson, Helen Caister, Phyllis R. Blakeley, and John N. Grant, eds. "Molly Brant, Mohawk Heroine." *Eleven Exiles, Accounts of Loyalists of the American Revolution.* Toronto: Dundurn Press, 1982.

Rossie, Jonathon Gregory. *The Politics of Command in the American Revolution.* Syracuse: Syracuse University Press, 1975.

Rural Repository, vol. XX, No. 18 (1844).

Schuyler, George W. *Colonial New York, Philip Schuyler and His Family.* 2 vols. New York: Charles Scribner's Sons, 1885.

Scott, John Albert. *Fort Stanwix (Fort Schuyler) and Oriskany — The Romantic Story of the Repulse of St. Leger's British Invasion of 1777 Told For the First Time in Chronological Order and in Detail — Mainly From Contemporary Reports, Letter and Diaries, With All Sources Indicated.* Rome: Rome Sentinel Company, 1927.

Shy, John. *A People Numerous Armed, Reflections on the Military Struggle for American Independence.* New York: Oxford University Press, 1976.

Simms, Jeptha R. *Frontiersmen of New York Showing Customs of the Indians, Vicissitudes of the Pioneer White Settlers and Border Strife in Two Wars with a Great Variety of Romantic and Thrilling Stories Never Before Published.* 2 vols, Albany: Geo. C. Riggs, 1883.

Bibliography

——. *History of Schoharie County, and Border Wars of New York; Containing also a Sketch of the Causes Which Led to the American Revolution; etc.* Albany: Munsell & Tanner, 1845.

——. *Trappers of New York: or, A Biography of Nicholas Stoner and Nathaniel Foster; together with Anecdotes of other Celebrated Hunters and some account of Sir William Johnson and his style of living.* Albany: J. Munsell, 1871. Reprinted, Harrison, NY: Harbor Hill Books, 1980.

Smith, Arthur Britton. *Legend of the Lake, the 22-Gun Brig-Sloop Ontario 1780.* Kingston, ON: Quarry Press, 1997.

Stanley, George F.G. *Canada Invaded 1775–1776.* Toronto and Sarasota: Samuel Stevens Hakkert & Company, 1977.

Stevens, Paul L. *A King's Colonel at Niagara 1774–1776.* Youngstown, NY: Old Fort Niagara Association, 1987.

Stone, William L. *The Campaign of Lieut.Gen. John Burgoyne and The Expedition of Lieut.Col. Barry St. Leger.* Albany: Joel Munsell, 1877.

——. *Life of Joseph Brant — Thayendanegea including the Indian Wars of the American Revolution.* 2 vols. New York: Alexander V. Blake, 1838. Reprint, St. Clair Shores, MI: Scholarly Press, 1970.

Swiggett, Walter. *War Out of Niagara, Walter Butler and the Tory Rangers.* Port Washington, NY: Ira J. Friedman, Inc., 1963.

Thomas, Earle. *Sir John Johnson, Loyalist Baronet.* Toronto and Reading: Dundurn Press, 1986.

Thomas, Howard. *Marinus Willett, Soldier-Patriot 1740–1830.* Prospect, NY: Prospect Books, 1954.

Torres, Louis. "Historic Furnishing Study." *Fort Stanwix: History, Historic Furnishing, and Historic Structure Reports.* Washington, DC: Office of Park Historic Preservation, National Park Service, U.S. Department of the Interior, 1976.

Tuckerman, Bayard. *Life of General Philip Schuyler, 1733–1804.* New York: Dodd, Mead and Company, 1903.

Watt, Gavin K. and James F. Morrison. *The British Campaign of 1777 — the St. Leger Expedition — The Forces of the Crown and Congress.* King City, ON: Gavin K. Watt, 2001.

Weise, Arthur James. *The Swartwout Chronicles 1338–1899.* NY: Trow Directory, Printing and Bookbinding, 1899.

Wesleger, C.A. *The Delaware Indians — A History.* New Brunswick, NJ: Rutgers University Press, 1972.

Wilhelmy, Jean-Pierre. *German Mercenaries in Canada.* Beloeil, PQ: Maison des Mots, 1985.

Willett, William M. *A Narrative of the Military Actions of Colonel Marinus Willett, Taken Chiefly from his Own Manuscript.* New York: G.C.H. Carvill, 1831.

Williams, John, ed. *The American War of Independence 1775–1783, 200th Anniversary.* London: Invasion Publishing, 1974.

Wright, Col John Womack. *Some Notes on the Continental Army.* Vails Gate, NY: National Temple Hill Association, 1963.

Wright, Robert K., Jr. *The Continental Army.* Washington, DC: Army Lineage Series, Center of Military History, United States Army, 1989.

Rebellion in the Mohawk Valley

Secondary Sources — Articles, Monographs, Booklets, Newsletters, Catalogues and Theses

Ball, Edward C. *First Stars and Stripes to Defy Foe Flown at Fort Stanwix.* n.p., 1972.

Bond, C.C.J. "The British Base at Carleton Island." *OHSPR*, Vol. 52 (1960).

Bryant, William Clement. "Captain Brant and the Old King." *Publications of the Buffalo Historical Society*, Vol. IV (1896)

Burleigh, H.C. "Loyalist Refuge, Sir John Johnson's Flight in May, 1776." *Forgotten Leaves of Local History*. Kingston: Brown & Martin Ltd., 1973.

——. *Captain MacKay and the Loyal Volunteers.* Bloomfield, ON: Bayside Publishing Company, 1977.

——. *Deforests of Avesnes and Kast, McGinness.* Burleigh, n.d.

Caruana, Adrain B. *Grasshoppers and Butterflies: The Light 3 Pounders of Pattison and Townshend.* Bloomfield, ON: Museum Restoration Service, 1979.

Cooper, LtCol Frank. "The Empeys of Stormont." u.p.

Cruikshank, Ernest A. "The Coming of the Loyalist Mohawks to the Bay of Quinte." *OHSPR*, 26 (1930).

——. "Petitions for grants of land in Upper Canada, second series, 1796–99." *OHSPR*, 26 (1930).

"L'Expedition du Fort Stanwix." *Le Canada Français*. (Société du Parlés Français au Canada, Québec) Vol. XXXIII (November 1945).

Faux, David. "The Pro-Patriot Faction Among the Mohawk Indians and the Sale of the New York Lands." *Loyalist Gazette*. (Autumn 1980)

"Fidelity." Newsletter of Toronto Branch, UEL Assoc. of Canada.

Forbes, William M. "Fort Schuyler, 1760-1766." *Annals and Recollections*, Rome Historical Society (October 1983).

Morrison, James F., ed. "Fort Klock Historic Restoration Newsletter," Vol. III, No. 6, March 1991.

"Fort Stanwix Garrison Newsletter", (1981).

Green, Ernest "Frey." *OHSPR*, Vol.33 (1939).

Herrington, M. Eleanor. "Captain John Deserontyou and the Mohawk Settlement at Deseronto." *Bulletin of the Departments of History and Political and Economic Science in Queen's University*, Kingston, Ontario, Canada, No. 41 (Nov. 1921).

Holst, Donald W. "Notes on British Artillery Flags in the American Revolution." *Journal of the Company of Military Historians*, XXXIX, 3.

"John Brown and the Dash for Ticonderoga." *Bulletin of the Fort Ticonderoga Museum*, V. II, No. 1 (Jan. 1930).

Lyttle, Eugene W. "Nicholas Herkimer." *Proceedings of the NYHA*, (1904).

MacMaster, Richard K. "Parish in Arms: A Study of Father John MacKenna and the Mohawk Valley Loyalists, 1773–1778." *United States Catholic Historical Society, Historical Records and Studies*, XLV (1957).

McCulloch, Ian. "'Within Ourselves . . .': The Development of British Light Infantry in North America During the Seven Years' War." *Canadian Military History*, volume 7, No. 2 (Spring 1998).

Morrison, James F., *Colonel James Livingston, The Forgotten Livingston Patriot of the War of Independence*. Johnstown: Col. James Livingston Historic Research Committee, 1988.

Nellis, Milo, "Col. Ebenezer Cox." *The Palatiner*, Aug 1952.

"Stone Arabia Battle Chapter Newsletter", Sons of the American Revolution, 1995.

New Jersey Historical Society Proceedings, Vol. II, No. 3 (1847); Vol. IX (1864); Vol. X,

Bibliography

New Series No. 4, (1925)

New York Genealogical and Biographical Record, Vol. LXVIII, (July 1936).

Northern Frontier Project Team, State University of New York. "The Northern Frontier Special Resource Study." Boston: NPS, Boston Support Office, 1999.

Ontario Historical Society, Papers & Records [*OHSPR*] (*Ontario History*). Toronto.

Ontario History (formerly *Ontario Historical Society, Papers & Records*). Toronto.

"Petitions for grants of land in Upper Canada, second series, 1796–99." *OHSPR*, Vol. 26 (1930).

Rees, John U. "'We are now . . . properly . . . enwigwamed.' British Soldiers and Brush Shelters, 1777–1781." *The Brigade Dispatch*, Vol. XXIX, No. 2 (Summer 1999).

Risteen, Frank B., Sr. "Children of Sir John Johnson and Lady Mary (Polly) Johnson, Married at New York June 30, 1773." *OHSPR*, Vol. LXIII (1971).

Robertson, H.H. "Burgoyne's Loyal Americans, Some notes on Burgoyne's Campaign 1777." Unpublished manuscript. AO, H.H. Robertson Papers.

Smy, William A. "The Butlers Before the Revolution." *The Butler Bicentenary, Commemorating the 200th Anniversary of the Death of Colonel John Butler.* Colonel John Butler Branch, UEL Assoc. of Canada, 1997.

—— "Standards, Guidons and Colours of the British Army and Provincial Corps During the American Revolution." *Loyalist Gazette*, Vol. XXXI, No. 1 (Spring 1993).

Stacey, Kim. "No One Harms Me with Impunity — The History, Organization, and Biographies of the 84th Regiment of Foot (Royal Highland Emigrants) and Young Royal Highlanders, During the Revolutionary War 1775–1784." Manuscript in progress, 1994.

Stevens, Paul L., "His Majesty's 'Savage' Allies: British Policy and the Northern Indians During the Revolutionary War — The Carleton Years, 1774–1778." Doctoral dissertation for the Department of History, State University of New York at Buffalo.

"Thirteenth Regt, (Stillwater-Saratoga) Albany County Militia '77." "Stone Arabia Battle Chapter Newsletter." Sons of the American Revolution, Dec. 1993.

"Tryon County Militia Newsletter". Vol. I, No. 3 (1983); Vol. I, No. 8 (1983); Vol. II, No. 1 (1983); Vol. II, No. 8 (1984); Vol. III, No. 5 (1985); Vol. IV, No. 2 (1985); Vol.V I, No. 3 (1987); Vol. VI, No. 9 (1987); Vol. XI, No. 5 (1991); Vol. XIV, No. 10 (1994); Vol. XV, No. 1 (1994); Vol. XVII, No. 6 (1998); Vol. XVIII, No. 3 (1998)

USS *Oriskany*, CVA34. *www.geocities.com/Pentagon/Bunker/2272/index. html*

Wilson, Bruce. "John Butler and Early Office Holding at Niagara." *The Butler Bicentenary, Commemorating the 200th Anniversary of the Death of Colonel John Butler.* Colonel John Butler (Niagara) Branch, UEL Assoc of Canada, 1997.

Williams, Reverend Eleazer. "The Life of Colonel Louis Cook." Papers of Franklin B. Hough. New York State Archives. U.p., ca. 1851.

ENDNOTES

Abreviations

1Bn	first battalion
2Bn	second battalion
AA	American Archives
AddMss	Additional Manuscript
AO	Archives of Ontario, Toronto, Ontario
BL	British Library
CHSNY	Colonial History, State of New York
CO	British Colonial Office Records (microfilm, held by many institutions)
DCB	Dictionary of Canadian Biography
HP	Haldimand papers (originals held at the PRO. Microfilm and transcripts held by many institutions)
HSGS	Historical Section of the General Staff, Ottawa, Canada
JAHR	The Journal of the Society of Army Historical Research
KRR NY	King's Royal Regiment New York
Ms(s)	Manuscript(s)
NAC	National Archives of Canada
NJHS	New jersey Historical Society
n.d.	no date
n.p.	no publisher
NYHS	New York Historical Society
NYSL	New York State Library, Albany, New York
NYPA	New York Pension Application
PRO	Public Records Office, Kew Gardens, England
RHE	Royal Highland emigrants (later 84th Regt of Foot)
SJJ	Sir John Johnson, 2nd Baronet of New York
TCM	Tryon County Militia Brigade
TCMN	Tryon County Militia Newletter
UELA	United Empire Loyalists Association of Canada
WO	British War Office Records (microfilm, held by many institutions)

1   Piers Mackesy, *The War for America 1775–1783* (Lincoln and London: University of Nebraska Press, 1992; previously published in Britain, 1964) 56,108-09; F.J. Hudleston, *Gentleman Johnny Burgoyne, Misadventures of an English General in the Revolution* (Indianapolis: The Bobbs-Merrill Company, 1927) 50-54,56,69-70,74-76,105-06,110-13.

2   Hudleston, 105.

Endnotes

3   Mackesy, 30,76; Max M. Mintz, *The Generals of Saratoga, John Burgoyne & Horatio Gates* (New Haven & London: Yale University Press, 1990) 72.

4   Paul L. Stevens, "His Majesty's 'Savage' Allies: British Policy and the Northern Indians During the Revolutionary War — The Carleton Years, 1774–1778," *[Allies]* a doctoral dissertation for the Department of History, State University of New York at Buffalo, 702.

5   Guy Johnson's Journal, May–Nov75, transcribed in E.B. O'Callaghan, ed. *Documents Relative to the Colonial History of the State of New York [CHSNY]* (Albany: Weed, Parson, 1854). London Documents, XLVI, 658; the Mohawks to the Oneidas, May75, Jeptha R. Simms, *Frontiersman of New York Showing Customs of the Indians, Vicissitudes of the Pioneer White Settlers and Border Strife in Two Wars with a Great Variety of Romantic and Thrilling Stories Never Before Published [Frontiersman]* (2 vols, Albany: Geo. C. Riggs, 1883) I, 498fn. Two of the Mohawks quoted were Aaron Hill Kanonraron of Ft Hunter and Joseph Brant Thayendanegea of Canajoharie. They stated, "Guy Johnson is in great fear of being taken prisoner by the Bostoners."

6   Guy Johnson's Journal in *CHSNY*, XLVI, 658. "Such of the Mohocks as were at home, and a body of armed white men, making together about 250"; Earle Thomas, *Sir John Johnson, Loyalist Baronet* (Toronto and Reading: Dundurn Press, 1986) 14-15,41; Ernest A. Cruikshank, *The Story of Butler's Rangers and the Settlement of Niagara [Butler's Rangers]* (Welland: Lundy's Lane Historical Society, 1893 — reprinted by Richardson, Bond & Wright Ltd., Owen Sound, Ontario 1975), 24-25.

7   Guy Johnson's Journal in *CHSNY*, XLVI, 658-62; Claus as first choice: Milton W. Hamilton, ed., Albert B. Corey, director & State historian, *The Papers of William Johnson* (13 vols., Albany: The University of the State of New York, 1962) XIII, 725-731.

8   Guy Johnson's Journal in CHSNY, XLVI, 662.

9   George F.G. Stanley, *Canada Invaded 1775–1776* (Toronto & Sarasota: Samuel Stevens Hakkert & Company, 1977) 125-32; George F.G. Stanley, ed., *For Want of a Horse, being A Journal of the Campaigns against the Americans in 1776 and 1777 from Canada by an officer who served with Lt.Gen. Burgoyne [Horse]* (Sackville, NB: The Tribune Press Limited, 1961) 70-76.

10 Ernest A. Cruikshank and Gavin K. Watt, eds. *The King's Royal Regiment of New York with the additions of an Index, Appendices and a Master Muster Roll [KRR NY]* (Toronto: Gavin K. Watt, 1984. Regimental history originally published *OHSPR*, 27, 1931) 1; *Quebec Gazette*, 15Dec74 , cited in Earle Thomas, 66.

11 "An Abstract of the State of the Militia In the Province of New York," 2Jun75 transcribed in CHSNY, VIII, 877.

12 Cruikshank, *Butler's Rangers*, 12.

13 Visit with Gov Tryon: Cruikshank & Watt, *KRR NY*, 8; Raising a brigade: *Calendar of Historical Manuscripts Relating to the War of the Revolution, in the office of the Secretary of State, Albany, N.Y.* (3 vols, Albany: Weed, Parsons and Company, Printers, 1868) I, 208 and ibid, II, 587-88.

14 Eliphalet Dyer to Jos Trumbull, 20Jun75, cited in Mintz, 81.

15 Tryon to Dartmouth, 7Feb76, transcribed in *CHSNY*, VIII, 663. Tryon stated, near 4,000; *Rural Repository*, Vol.XX, No.18 (1844). "Schuyler set out on this mission with 700 militia, but before he reached Caughnawaga his force had increased to three thousand"; Thomas Jones, *History of New York during The Revolutionary War and of the Leading Events in the Other Colonies at that Period*, Edward Floyd

DeLancey, ed. (2 vols., New York: The New York Historical Society, 1879) 99-100. Jones stated 3,000.

16   James Sullivan & Alexander C. Flick, eds., *Minutes of the Albany committee of Correspondence, 1775–1778* (2 vols, Albany: State University of New York, 1923 & 1925) I, 386.

17   SJJ to Claus, 20Jan77, transcribed in John Watts DePeyster, *Miscellanies of an Officer* (New York: C.H. Ludwig, 1838) L. The number 170 was given by Sir John. Carleton reported "about two hundred followers", but this included men who had joined from Canada. A detailed study of the KRR NY muster rolls found in WO28/5, 186-190 yields only 150 names of men who joined on 19Jun76 with about 20 others who either joined from Canada or had their enlistment date back-dated for reasons of seniority. It may be that another 20 of the trekkers took employment in the Indian, Engineering or Commissary Departments. See also, Cruikshank & Watt, *KRR NY*, 166-275; Declaration of Thomas Gummersall, 6Aug76, transcribed in *CHSNY*, VIII, 682-83. Gummersall, who was an eye witness, wrote "130 Highlanders & near 120 other inhabitants of the country attached to government."

18   The guides were Captains John Deserontyon and the Hill brothers, Aaron Kanonraron and Isaac Onoghsokte. See, William A. Smy, tr.&ed., "The Butler Papers: Documents and Papers Relating to Colonel John Butler and his Corps of Rangers 1711-1977" *[Smy Transcripts]* (u.p., 1994) Civil Secretary's Correspondence, Upper Canada Sundries, 1791-1800, RG5, A1, Vol.1A, 57-58; Gummersall Declaration; Cruikshank, "Coming of the Mohawks to Quinte," *OHSPR*, 26 (1930), 391; *Dictionary of Canadian Biography*, V, 255. Another spelling of Isaac Hill's Mohawk name was *Anoghsoktea*.

19   *Smy Transcripts*. Butler to Mathews, 15Aug80, found in HP, AddMss21765. Thos Butler remained a prisoner in New England for most of '77. On giving his parole, he was allowed to return to Tryon County and was held under surveillance with his mother and family. He was exchanged in '80.

20   H.C. Burleigh, "Loyalist Refuge, Sir John Johnson's Flight in May, 1776," *Forgotten Leaves of Local History* (Kingston: Brown & Martin Ltd., 1973) 48-49.

21   Major H. Everard, *History of Thos. Farrington's Regiment subsequently Designated The 29th (Worcestershire) Foot, 1694 to 1891* (Worcester: Littleby & Company, The Worcester Press, 1891) 79. This description was of Sir John when he entered Montreal a day or so before meeting with Burgoyne.

22   Carleton to Germain, 8Jul76, in NAC, 42/35 (Q12), 102. A report of Sir John's arrival, reasons for issuing the beating order and details of the order; Carleton to Barrington, 8Jul76, ibid. Reports the incident in slightly different terms; SJJ to Claus, 20Jan77, transcribed in DePeyster, Miscellanies, L. Sir John reported that a second battalion was noted in the warrant.

23   Carleton to Forster, 20Jun76 cited in Stevens, *Allies*, 702-03.

24   Mintz, 97.

25   Sullivan to Dayton, 17May76, cited in Thomas Jones, I, 586-87.

26   A metaphorical term employed by the whites for a semi-permanent, palisaded native townsite. Originally, it referred to Iroquoian towns only, but the term's use grew to include any native village, fortified or not.

27   Joseph Bloomfield, *Citizen Soldier, The Revolutionary War Journal of Joseph Bloomfield*, Mark E. Lender and James Kent Martin, eds. (Newark: New Jersey Historical Society, 1982) 65.

28   ibid, 70; Lieutenant Ebenezer Elmer, L.Q.C. Elmer, ed. "Journal Kept During an

Endnotes

Expedition to Canada in 1776," *Proceedings*, New Jersey Historical Society, Vol.II, No.3 (1847), 142.

29 Burgoyne to Henry Clinton, 7Nov76, cited in Stevens, *Allies*, 702.

30 Butler's wife was named Catherine, née Catalyntje Bradt. Also left behind were Thomas and three younger children. See, *NY Genealogical and Biographical Record*, Vol.LXVIII, (July 1936); William A. Smy, "The Butlers Before the Revolution," *The Butler Bicentenary, Commemorating the 200th Anniversary of the Death of Colonel John Butler* (Colonel John Butler Branch, UEL Assoc. of Canada, 1997) 34-52. Contains an excellent review of this important family.

31 A report of Governor Tryon to the Earl of Dartmouth, 11Jun74, gave the Civil Establishment paid by the Crown and noted Sir William as Superintendent and Sole Agent of the Indian Department with Guy Johnson and Daniel Claus as Deputies. Found in *CHSNY*, VIII, 455. The terms "Deputy Superintendent" and "Deputy Agent" were synonymous.

32 Carleton to Caldwell, 19Jul76, cited in Stevens, *Allies*, 702-03,2109.

33 Barbara Graymont, *The Iroquois in the American Revolution* (Syracuse: Syracuse University Press, 1972) 239. The author advised that Mary Brant took great satisfaction in luring away Mary Hill to stay with her at Niagara in 1780.

34 Paul L. Stevens, *A King's Colonel at Niagara 1774–1776* (Youngstown: Old Fort Niagara Association, 1987) 57.

35 Graymont, 108. From Seaver, *A Narrative of the Life of Mrs. Mary Jemison*, (Norman OK: 1992) 98.

36 Dayton to Schuyler, 1Aug76, cited in John F. Luzader, "Construction and Military History." *Fort Stanwix: History, Historic Furnishing, and Historic Structure Reports* (Washington: Office of Park Historic Preservation, National Park Service, U.S. Department of the Interior, 1976) 23; The name "Fort Schuyler" failed to replace "Fort Stanwix." Writers with royalist leanings rarely referred to the works as Ft Schuyler, preferring the more familiar and untainted, older name. Many "patriot" writers followed the same course, including prominent authors of the 19th century, e.g., Willett, 1831; Pomroy Jones, 1851; Simms 1883. Perhaps the final word should be heard from the U.S. Govt, which chose to name the reconstructed works (built on the original site in the 1970s at Rome, NY) "Fort Stanwix"; In this book, I have used the name Stanwix, except when quoting contemporary material.

37 Schuyler to Washington, 1Aug76, cited in Luzader, 23.

38 Bloomfield, 95.

39 ibid, 106-07.

40 Lieutenant Ebenezer Elmer, L.Q.C. Elmer, ed., "Journal Kept During an Expedition to Canada in 1776." *Proceedings*, New Jersey Historical Society, Vol.III, No.1 (1848), 28-29.

41 Bloomfield, 107.

42 committee meeting, 18Oct76, transcribed in Maryly B. Penrose, *Mohawk Valley in the Revolution, committee of Safety Papers & Genealogical Compendium* (Franklin Park, NJ: Liberty Bell Associates, 1978) 90.

43 committee meeting, 20Oct76, transcribed in ibid, 91-92.

44 Also known as William Brant Johnson or Brant Kaghneghtago. He left the Valley in '76 with Guy Johnson and returned after Johnson's party left for England. See Isabel Thompson Kelsay, *Joseph Brant 1743-1807, Man of Two Worlds* (Syracuse: Syracuse University Press, 1984) 177&766.

45 Second Major Augustus (Enos) Clapsaddle of the Fourth Regt, TCM was killed at Oriskany. See, Watt & Morrison, *The British Campaign of 1777 — The St. Leger*

Rebellion in the Mohawk Valley

Campaign — The Forces of the Crown and Congress (King City, ON: Gavin K. Watt, 2001) 164; Roster of the Fourth Regt found in *Tryon County Militia Newsletter [TCMN]*, Vol.III, No.5.

46   Penrose, *Mohawk Valley*, 92-94&99.

47   Carleton to Caldwell from Point au Fer, 6Oct76, cited in Stevens, *King's Colonel*, 68.

48   General Order, Chambly, 8Sep76 signed by E. Foy, Deputy Adjutant General found in Stanley, *Horse*, 88.

49   Stanley, *Canada Invaded*, 144.

50   Sir John Johnson, *Orderly Book of Sir John Johnson During his Campaign Against Fort Stanwix from Nov. 4th, 1776 to July 30th, 1777 [SJJ OB]* William L. Stone, tr. & ed. (New York: A.S. Barnes & Company, 1881) 3; Quotation: Cruikshank & Watt, *KRR NY*, 11.

51   Claus to Reverend Vardill, 15Oct78, found in AO, *Claus Papers*, MG19, F1, Vol.26.

52   Eben Jessup to SJJ, 15Nov76, found in the Jessup Papers, McCord Museum, McGill University; The beating order for the 2Bn, KRR NY was issued four years later by Gen Haldimand on 13Jul80.

53   SJJ to Claus, 20Jan77, transcribed in DePeyster, Miscellanies, L.

54   Lieut. James M. Hadden, *A Journal Kept in Canada and Upon Burgoyne's Campaign in 1776 and 1777 [Hadden's Journal]*, Horatio Rogers, ed. (Albany: Joel Munsell's Sons, 1884) 35.

55   NAC, CO42/36 (Q13), 3.

56   Germain to Carleton, Whitehall, 26Mar77, found in Historical Section of the General Staff, eds., II, "The War of the American Revolution, The Province of Quebec under the Administration of Governor Sir Guy Carleton, 1775-1778," *A History of the Organization, Development and Services of the Military and Naval Forces of Canada From the Peace of Paris in 1763 to the Present Time With Illustrative Documents* [HSGS] (2 vols, Canada, King's Printer, n.d.) II, 202. Germain's displeasure was particularly severe regarding Carleton's withdrawal to winter quarters. The Secretary believed that Washington's successful attacks at Trenton and Princeton in NJ were made possible by Carleton's withdrawal freeing U.S. forces for deployment south.

57   Germain to Carleton, 22Aug76, and Germain to Burgoyne, 23Aug76, cited in Stevens, *Allies*, 797; The letter of 22Aug76 also appeared in Lieutenant General John Burgoyne, *A State of the Expedition From Canada as Laid Before the House of Commons By Lieutenant-General Burgoyne and Verified by Evidence; with a Collection of Authentic Documents and an Addition of Many Circumstances which were Prevented from Appearing Before the House by the Prorogation of Parliament, etc... [State]* (London: J. Almon, 1780) Appendix, No.II; Mackesy, 106-07. Mackesy provides a detailed insight into Germain's attempted dismissal of Carleton in '76.

58   HSGS, II, 36. Unknown to the British, the rebel officers and men released by Carleton prior to his withdrawal into Canada alarmed General Gates at Ticonderoga with their sentiments of approval for the governor. Gates quickly removed them, lest their talk undermine the resolve of his garrison.

59   C.T. Atkinson, *The South-Wales Borderers — 24th Foot — 1689–1937* (Cambridge: Regimental History Committee, 1937) 158. From the Stopford-Sackville Mss.

60   Stanley, *Canada Invaded*, 105,125-32.

61   Thomas Anburey, *With Burgoyne from Quebec [Anburey Journal]*, Sydney Jackman, ed. (Toronto: Macmillan of Canada, 1963) 3. I am quoting Jackman, the editor. Many authorities treat Anburey with caution due to a number of inexplicable errors that appear throughout his text. I have cited his journal with caution;

Endnotes

Richard M. Ketchum, *Saratoga, Turning Point of America's Revolutionary War* *[Saratoga]* (New York: Henry Holt and Company, 1997) 72-73. Ketchum provides an excellent account of Burgoyne's machinations.

62   Stanley, *Horse*, 17.

63   Earle Thomas, 71.

64   John Hill Oteronyente may have remained with Guy Johnson and served as one of the guides.

65   Kelsay, 140. Some authors claim that Joseph was Guy Johnson's secretary at this time. Kelsay dismisses this thought by noting that Brant could not write or spell well enough for that role. Joseph Chew was the department secretary who travelled with Johnson to England.

66   Tice was repeatedly listed as the senior captain on department returns. For example, "List of Officers belonging to the Indian Department at Niagara, Montreal 4thDec1783" found in AO, Ms622, Reel 113; "List of Officers and other Employed during the Rebellion in the Department of the Indian Six Nations at Niagara..." ca. 1783 found in ibid.

67   Kelsay, 181-84.

68   Brant's speech to the Six Nations cited in ibid, 184. From NAC, Q56, PT.2: 521-22.

69   Kelsay, 184. From Norton Teyoninhokarawen, *Journal of a Voyage*, II, 701.

70   LtCol Daniel Claus, "Anecdotes of Captain Brant," found in William Clement Bryant, "Captain Brant and the Old King." *Publications of the Buffalo Historical Society*, Vol.IV (1896). "The packet [boat] fell in... with a rebel privateer of superior force... Joseph and... John [Hill Oteronyente]... having brass rifle guns... were so... good marksmen as to pick off those... whom by the dress they took to be officers."

71   Kelsay, 99-100,129&273.

72   ibid, 185. From Force, 5, III, 1500.

73   Carleton to Germain, Quebec ,16Oct77, found in NAC, CO42/37 (Q14), 270-76. "I gave a Memorandum to Lieutenant General Burgoyne . . . to apply for a Reinforcement of four thousand men, in order to enable me to give him a suitable command on the Mohawk River."

74   Burgoyne, *State*, Appendix, No.III; Donald Barr Chidsey, *The War in the North, An Informal History of the American Revolution in and near Canada* (New York: Crown Publishers, Inc., 1967) 191-92.

75   Germain to Carleton, 26Mar77, NAC, CO42/36, (Q13), 73-9. This source gives the strength of the KRR at 133.

76   NAC, CO42/36 (Q13), 16. Burgoyne mused that 500 would patrol behind the lines to intercept spies and deserters and procure intelligence. Another 2,000, raised from the "disobedient & refractory" would work at the fortifications of Sorel, Fort St. John's, Chambly and Ile aux Noix. Another 2,000 would move provisions, artillery, stores and baggage as required. Another 1,500-2,000 would be "attached to the [his] army to follow the Enemy."

77   *Hadden's Journal*, 45-46.

78   Although the Mohawk region's defence force was in flux over this time period, the assignment of two sizeable regts, the 3NY and the majority of Wesson's MA plus the smaller 1CDN and Badlam's 150 Massachusetts men, all of which were in place in Jul77, represented some 1,500 men. This accounting ignores 1,000+ Tryon County Militia.

79   Graymont, 110-111; Kelsay, 186-87.

80   ibid, from NAC, HP, B39, 360-61. A document dated 28Dec76; NAC, HP, AddMss21699. Brant's letter to Kanehsatake (Lake of the Two Mountains) is

repeated in Carleton's instructions to Lernoult of 9Feb77.

81   Stevens, *Allies*, 924. Lieut Thos Scott was at Akwesasne and Ens Wm Johnson at Kanehsatake. Both uncovered Brant's letter. Capt Alex Fraser, 34th, who was Carleton's appointee as D/Supt for the Que Ind Dept, forwarded the letter to Carleton.

82   *Smy transcripts.* Carleton to Butler and Carleton to Lernoult, 9Feb77, from NAC, HP, AddMss21699.

83   Kelsay, 187-88; Graymont, 110-11,114.

84   Kirkland to Schuyler, 25Jan77, transcribed in Maryly B. Penrose, ed., *Indian Affairs Papers, American Revolution* (Franklin Park, NJ: Liberty Bell Associates, 1981) 71.

85   Some allied nations were referred to as nephews, others as cousins. I have not been able to determine why or which. Perhaps nephews referred to those elements of a nation that had settled by invitation on Confederacy lands and cousins to those elements that lay outside.

86   Kelsay, 188.

87   Kirkland to Schuyler, 3Jan77, transcribed in Penrose, *Indian Affairs*, 63.

88   Claus, *Anecdotes of Brant.*

89   Quotations: Kirkland to Schuyler, 14Jan77, transcribed in Penrose, *Indian Affairs*, 67-68.

90   Gray to Carleton, dated 24Mar77 found in NAC, HP, MG21, B158, 16.

91   Cruikshank & Watt, *KRR NY*, 14.

92   *SJJ OB*, 24-25.

93   Cruikshank & Watt, *KRR NY*, 15.

94   Jno Harper to the *Schoharie* Committee, 12Jun77, transcribed in the *Proceedings of a General Court Martial, held at Major General Lincoln's Quarters, near Quaker-Hill, in the State of New York by order of his Excellency General Washington, Commander in Chief of the Army of the United States of America for the Trial of Major General Schuyler. [Schuyler Court Martial]* (Philadelphia: 1778) 103. "Brant came to Onioquago, hoisted the British flag"; Kelsay, 190.

95   Samuel Clyde to Herkimer, n.d., cited in William L. Stone, *Life of Joseph Brant – Thayendanegea including the Indian Wars of the American Revolution* (2 vols., New York: Alexander V. Blake, 1838 – republished, St. Clair Shores, MI: Scholarly Press, 1970) I, 182.

96   Kelsay, 190-92. Provided a list of 25 whites who served with Brant during the war. Only a handful joined him in 1777. As his volunteers were irregulars, almost no records were kept of their service.

97   *Smy transcripts.* Butler to Carleton, 31Mar77 from NAC, CO42/36 (Q13); Stevens, *Allies*, 958-59; Cruikshank, *Butler's Rangers*, 34

98   John D. Monroe, *Chapters in the History of Delaware County New York* (Delaware County Historical Assoc., 1949) 64; "Highlanders": See NYPA R14662 of Wm Thompson, a Pte in Whitaker's Cherry Valley Coy, First Regt transcribed in part in Ken D. Johnson, the Fort Plank historian, *The Bloodied Mohawk, The American Revolution in the Words of Fort Plank's Defenders and Other Mohawk Valley Partisans* (Rockport, MA: Picton Press, 2000) 590.

99   Monroe, 64.

100   Deposition of Peter MacAlpine transcribed in W. Bruce Antliff, tr., *Loyalist Settlements 1783–1789* (Ontario: Ministry of Citizenship and Culture, 1985) 345. MacAlpine said that he "joined them — but being an old man was allow'd to go Home & gave his Arms to another man." Peter was to pay dearly for his loyalty

101   G[eneral] O[rders] of Guy Carleton found in HP, AddMss21743; *SJJ OB*, 37;

Endnotes

Cruikshank & Watt, *KRR NY*, 193. Ex-corporal Edward Egnue deserted on 24Apr79.

102 *SJJ OB*, 29-30.

103 Various quotations: *Smy Transcripts*. Lernoult to Carleton from NAC, CO42/36 (Q13); Little information about the Mississaugas has been uncovered. Only one chief/war captain has been identified who was known to have participated during the war. Their activity from the very beginning of the war has been proven. They were a loyal, active ally of the Crown throughout and, by willingly granting land to their Six Nations cousins after the war, proved faithful to their alliances.

104 Lieutenant William Colbrath, *Days of Siege, A Journal of the Siege of Fort Stanwix in 1777 [Colbrath Journal]* Larry Lowenthal, ed., (Eastern Acorn Press, 1983) 11.

105 William M. Willett, *A Narrative of the Military Actions of Colonel Marinus Willett, Taken Chiefly from his Own Manuscript [Wm Willett]* (New-York: G.C.H. Carvill, 1831) 44; Marinus Willett, *Lieutenant Colonel Marinus Willett's Orderly Book (1777) [Willett OB]*, NYHS, NYSL, Dept. of Archives & Manuscripts. La Marquisie's rank was given as major at Fort Schuyler on 24Jun77. This was perhaps a local rank, so that the Frenchman would not be outranked by Maj Hubbell, as Schuyler referred to him as capt when he ordered him sent down; Gansevoort to E.B. De La Marquisie, 26May77, as noted in Stefan Bielinski, *A Guide to the Revolutionary War Manuscripts in the NYS Library* (Albany: NYS American Revolution Bicentennial Commission, 1976) 54. Doc.#1308. This source provides initials and an alternate spelling for the surname of this much-maligned officer; Carpenters' dismissal: Report of La Marquisie, n.d., in the Gates Papers transcribed in Luzader, 25.

106 Various quotations: *Smy Transcripts*. Lernoult to Carleton, 28Apr77 from NAC, CO42/36 (Q13).

107 This portrait by Gilbert Stuart is held by the Munson-Williams-Proctor Institute Museum of Art, Utica, New York; Family recollections by Catherine Gansevoort Lansing cited in John Albert Scott, *Fort Stanwix (Fort Schuyler) and Oriskany — The Romantic Story of the Repulse of St. Leger's British Invasion of 1777 Told For the First Time in Chronological Order and in Detail — Mainly From Contemporary Reports, Letter and Diaries, With All Sources Indicated* (Rome: Rome Sentinel Company, 1927) 87-88.

108 Acute sense of honour: see Gansevoort to Gates, 12Aug76, Gansevoort Papers, 67. A browse through these papers reveals his systematic approach, which was confirmed by his granddaughter's recollections.

109 Granddaughter's recollections, Scott, *Fort Stanwix*, 89-90.

110 A group letter addressed to Gansevoort, 12Oct77, *Military Papers of General Peter Gansevoort* (transcribed by the State Historian, submitted, but unpublished, 1906) 178-79.

111 Frederick A. Rahmer, *Fort Stanwix, A Brief History* (Rome: author, 1940) 6. To quote this author: "he won the distinction of successfully resisting a three-week siege in a period when every other Continental post in New York was either evacuated or surrendered." In '79 he marched with Sullivan against the Iroquois. In '81 he became a BGen and held this grade in the post-Revolutionary army. Gansevoort was born in '49 and died in 1812.

112 Leonard Gansevoort to Peter, 17May77, cited in Graymont, 115.

113 Hansen to Mathew Visscher at Albany, 13May77, transcript of document No.114 in the Wyman Collection, NYSHA Library, Cooperstown, NY. Visscher was Secretary to the Albany Committee.

114 Entries for 10&28May77, *Colbrath Journal*, 11-12.

115 Edward F. De Lancey, ed., *Muster Rolls of the New York Provincial Regiment — 1755–1764*, NYHS Collections (1891 – republished, Bowie, MD: Heritage Books Inc., 1990) 118. Marinus Willett was returned as a private in '58.

116 Lieut.Col. John Bradstreet, *An Impartial Account of Lieut.Col. Bradstreet's Expedition to Fort Frontenac* (Toronto: Rous & Mann Limited, 1940) 7-8,16. Bradstreet's force had considerably more troops than St. Leger — 155 Regulars, 60 Rangers and 1,112 NY, 680 MA, 318 RI and 412 NJ Provs and 270 bateauxmen. His artillery was of at least 4 guns and 3 howitzers, including 2 X 12pr.

117 See *Wm Willett*; Howard Thomas, *Marinus Willett, Soldier-Patriot 1740–1830* (Prospect, NY: Prospect Books, 1954)

118 Egly, 1NY, 20.

119 *Wm Willett*, 44-45.

120 Letter of William Johnson Jr., 16Jul77, cited in Jeptha R. Simms, *History of Schoharie County, and Border Wars of New York; Containing also a Sketch of the Causes Which Led to the American Revolution; etc...* (Albany: Munsell & Tanner, 1845) 220; *Schuyler Court-Martial*, 103. Harper claimed that Brant had more than 100 men.

121 Brant's speech to Haldimand, Quebec, 21May83, found in Charles M. Johnston, ed., *The Valley of the Six Nations — A Collection of Documents on the Indian Lands of the Grand River* (Toronto: Champlain Society, 1964) 38. He said, "The Indians distinguish by Bostonians, the Americans in Rebellion."

122 Marjory Barnum Hinman, *Onaquaga: Hub of the Border Wars of the American Revolution in New York State* (n.p., 1975) 29-29fn.

123 Payment for supplies: In fact, Butler later paid the loyalist suppliers of provisions; Hinman, *Onauqa* ga29-29 fn.; John Harper to *Schoharie* Committee, 10&12Jun77, cited in Graymont, 116; Stone, *Brant*, I, 180. Brant's quoted comments are Stone's words from extensive interviews with participants.

124 NAC, CO42/36(Q13), 111,156-59,188-90,297-300; NAC, CO42/37(Q14), 270-76.

125 Burgoyne to Simon Fraser cited in Mintz, 131. Apparently quoted by Fraser to John Robinson, 13Jul77.

126 Cruikshank & Watt, *KRR NY*, 14.

127 The hair was pulled back into a queue and secured by a ribbon. Regular troops had their hair treated with pomade and sprinkled with flour to give a uniform white appearance. It is possible that Provincial troops followed this practice, at least in garrison.

128 The repeated use of John Butler's militia rank of colonel is quite confusing. His rank at this time was major in the Six Nations' Indian Dept.

129 *Smy Transcripts*. Carleton to Bolton, 16May77, transcribed from NAC, HP AddMss21699.

130 Stone, *Brant*, I, 181.

131 Kelsay, 191.

132 Guy Johnson to Germain, 7Jul77, cited in Kelsay, 196; Guy Johnson to Germain, 11Nov77, found in *CHSNY*, 726; Communications: water routes such as the Hudson, Oswego or Richelieu Rivers.

133 Langan to Carleton, 20May77, transcribed in NAC, CO42/36 (Q13), 125-26; Langan was a Lieut in the Six Nations' Ind Dept. See, a return by Capt Tice, NAC, WO28/10, 406.

134 HSGS, II, 220.

135 *SJJ OB*, 41.

136 A locket-sized miniature of Colonel Daniel Claus, C-083514, held by the NAC.

Endnotes

137 This title was found on a certificate signed by Claus on a document at Buck Island, 9Jul77, and taken from an Indian killed at Oriskany, transcribed in *TCMN*, Vol. I, No.3 (March 1983).

138 Memorandum by Daniel Claus, 10Sep80, transcribed in Hamilton, *Johnson Papers*, XIII, 728.

139 ibid, 730.

140 Howe to Carleton, 5Apr77, cited in Stevens, *Allies*, 1009. From NAC, CO42/36, ff.235-36.

141 Mintz, 94&131. Burgoyne's famous brigadier, Simon Fraser, characterized Carleton as "a proud, austere, narrow-minded man, disappointed in all his views of ambition, environed by flatterers, Dependants and Sycophants."

142 Cruikshank & Watt, *KRR NY*, 209. Nicholas Hillyer, a Johnstown tailor, was at that time, a Sjt in the Col's Coy.

143 *SJJ OB*, 42-43.

144 NAC, WO17/1571(1).

145 The fife airs of the 34th have been passed down for posterity in the highly detailed, quaintly illustrated collection of John Buttrey. He served at Montreal as a 34th Drummer in '77 and as the Regt's Drum Major in 1802&03. See NAC, MG 23, K4, John Fife Mss.

146 John Williams, *The American War of Independence 1775–1783, 200th Anniversary* (London: Invasion Publishing, 1974) 29; *Hadden's Journal*, 42fn; *CHSNY*, VIII, 714fn; AO, Ms521(1), Edward Jessup Papers. Jessup's Loyal Rangers Orderly Book, 1780-1783. On 21Oct82, St. Leger was appointed "a Brigadier General in the Army in Canada." As such, he commanded the southern section of the military district of Montreal with his HQ at Fort St. John's; Hazel C. Mathews, *Frontier Spies* (Fort Myers: Hazel C. Mathews, 1971) 100,110&126. St. Leger commanded Ft St. John's in '81 before his promotion to district commander and managed the Secret Service during the attempts to kidnap several significant and notorious northern Whigs, amongst them Gen Philip Schuyler. A major Secret Service activity during his tenure was the negotiations with the independent Republic of Vermont; Jean N. McIlwraith, "Sir Frederick Haldimand," *The Makers of Canada* (11 Vols., Toronto: Morang & Co., Limited, 1911) 3, 314. McIlwraith notes that BGen St. Leger commanded all the troops in Canada when Haldimand departed for England.

147 Two youthful images of St. Leger are: a) an engraving published in 1795 by I. Roberts from a miniature painted by R. Cosway, RA as found in William L. Stone, *The Campaign of Lieut. John Burgoyne and The Expedition of Lieut.Col. Barry St. Leger [Burgoyne & St. Leger]* (Albany: Joel Munsell, 1877) 138; b) unattributed engraving found in *The Story of Old Fort Johnson* (New York & London: G.P. Putnam's Sons, 1906) opposite 88. Perhaps b) is an interpretation of the engraving by Roberts; An unattributed, undated portrait, probably painted when he returned to Britain after the war. It shows a dissipated face edged by hanks of hair with a soft mouth and rather saddened, dark eyes. This painting of St. Leger as an older man is found in Williams, 29.

148 NAC, WO28/2. Letters 34th Regt. Six years of letters reveal St. Leger as a senior officer with genuine concern and affection for both his junior officers and men. Whatever his failings, he was not one of those officers who ignored the welfare of his Regt. There were also a few instances of his sharp reaction to perceived insolence.

149 *SJJ OB*, 45-46,48.

150 Cruikshank, *Butler's Rangers*, 34.

151 *Smy Transcripts.* Carleton to Butler, 18May77, from NAC, HP, AddMss21699.

152 Claus to Knox, 16Oct77 *[Claus to Knox, 16Oct77]* transcribed in *CHSNY*, VIII, 718-19; Knox: Stevens, *Allies*, 833. The author advises that Wm Knox was on Germain's staff as an Undersecretary. He had been a Georgia resident, was well informed about American affairs and had participated in negotiations with the Creek Indians in '60-61. He was well aware of the importance of gifts in Indian diplomacy and in Jun76 inherited responsibility for their procurement. He became expert in selecting suitable presents produced by British industry and retained this responsibility throughout the war.

153 Grand Army structure: British — flank brigade, Grenadiers and Lights totalling 1,568. Two line infantry brigades, 2,388; German — flank brigade of Grenadiers and Lights and two line brigades totalling 3,217. See, Burgoyne, *State*, xv and *Hadden's Journal*, passim, and Jean-Pierre Wilhelmy, *German Mercenaries in Canada* (Beloeil: Maison des Mots, 1985)140-41. Grand total, British and German infantry, 7,173; British artillery, 257 men of the Royal and Irish Establishments, with 2 X light 24 prs, 4 X medium 12 prs, 18 X light 6 prs, 6 X light 3 prs, 2 X 8" howitzers, 4 or 6 X 5 1/2" howitzers and 4 Royals or Cohorns. See, Burgoyne, *State*, 9, App.34 and *Hadden's Journal*, 44. Hesse Hanau Artillery Company, 155 men with British guns, 2 X light 3's and 8 X light 6's. See, Georg Pausch, Bruce E. Burgoyne, tr. and ed., *Georg Pausch's Journal and Reports of the Campaign in America* (Bowie, MD: Heritage Books, Inc., 1996) Introduction and *Hadden's Journal*. Army strength including artillerists, 7,600; Provincials: fought as light and line infantry, rangers and crews & guards for the bateaux. An accurate count is difficult, as men transferred between regts for various reasons. Sample returns: Van Pfister's Loyal Volunteers, 1Aug–8Sep77 — 335 all ranks found in HP, AddMss21874, 3. Queen's Loyal Rangers, 7Aug77 — 262 men. See NYSL, Peters' Papers, #3589. Jessup's King's Loyal Americans, 25Jun–24Oct77 — 182 men less Capt Hugh Munro's Coy (other returns give numbers as high as 280) found in HP, AddMss21827, 43-44. McAlpin's American Volunteers (includes Capt Hugh Munro's KLA Coy), 24Jan78 – 67men found in ibid, 138-39. Samuel Adams' Rangers, 23Jan78 — 31 men found in ibid, 136-37. Peter Van Alstine's Bateaux Coy, 10Dec77 — 30 men found in NAC, WO28/10, Pt 1, 101; Natives: managed by the Quebec Ind Dept officers, including several noted Canadien partizans from the previous war. Canada Indians, 500. See, Stevens, *Allies*, 1022. Lakes and Western Indians, 400. See, ibid, 1025; Navy: Lake Champlain fleet, 1,000 seamen. When operating beside the waterways, he had the ships' guns, 14 X heavy 24prs, 47 X 12prs and 57 X 6-pounders. See, NAC, CO42/36, Q13, 173-74.

154 Those who enjoy calculations will have noted that Burgoyne's peak manpower was about 9,300 men. However, in giving the number of muskets deployed at peak strength, I have taken into consideration that not all Provincials were armed and that native numbers ebbed and flowed; Mintz, 225. From C.W. Snell, "A Report of the Strength of the British Army under Lieutenant General John Burgoyne" (Saratoga National Historical Park, 1951.) Snell gives the total from Canada as 9,078. He must have included loyalists and Indians who joined in NY State.

155 Stevens, *Allies*, 1009. Burgoyne received Howe's advice that he would not cooperate with the thrust from Canada at the same time as he received Germain's orders dated 26Mar77. The latter were sent for his "guidance and instruction." Stevens notes that these were the only written orders Burgoyne received; Mintz, 135-37. Mintz claims that Carleton had Howe's letter two weeks before giving it to Burgoyne. He suggests Burgoyne may have cancelled his expedition, if he had received Howe's letter earlier. As the ship *Tartar* anchored at Quebec on 26May, his contention that the dis-

Endnotes

patches were in Canada for two weeks is correct. Stevens suggests that the courier carrying the dispatches was unable to catch up with Carleton until about 6Jun and Carleton delayed to the tenth before passing them on to Burgoyne. Whatever the case, Mintz's thought is an interesting hypothesis, but in my opinion, whether there was a fourteen-day or a four-day delay, cancellation was not likely in view of Burgoyne's odd interpretation of his orders and his overweening ambition.

156 *SJJ OB*, 54.

157 NAC, B39, 522.

158 Detachments: These infantrymen were most likely expected to conduct the artillery, not man the guns; Number and weight of guns: see, Claus to Knox, 16Oct77; Cohorns: St. Leger later referred apologetically to employing Royals. One can see why by examining Captain George Smith, Inspector of the Royal Military Academy at Woolwich. *An Universal Military Dictionary, A Copious Explanation of the Technical Terms &c. — Used in the Equipment, Machinery, Movements, and Military Operations of an Army [Dictionary]* (London: J. Millan, 1779 – limited, Ottawa: Museum Restoration Service, 1969) 187. A Cohorn had a bore of 4.5", a Royal 5.8." A substantial difference.

159 All British and Provincial infantry companies had a minimum of three commis-sioned officers. The LtCol and the Maj were paid as Capts in their coys. However, as the Col was most often absent, his Coy was commanded by a Capt-Lieut, ie. an officer ranked as the junior Capt, but paid as a Lieut. The flank companies had 1st and 2nd Lieuts, the hat coys a 1st Lieut and an Ens.

160 Angus McDonell was unable to join until Jul79. Duncan joined at the end of the '77 campaign.

161 NAC, CO42/36, Q13, 329-31.

162 Corvée: A system of compulsory labour impressed upon the Quebec habitants during the French regime and continued under British government.

163 Burgoyne to Germain regarding the Canadien fighting coys and the corvées, in ibid, 245&284.

164 *SJJ OB*, 58-59.

165 Staff appointments: see, St. Leger to Burgoyne, 25May77, transcribed in NAC, CO42/36 (Q13), 418-19 and *SJJ OB*, 60-61; Ancrum: see Thomas Hughes, *A Journal by Thos: Hughes For his Amusement, Designed only for his Perusal by the time he attains the Age of 50 if he lives so long (1778-1789)* (Cambridge: Cambridge University Press, 1947) 159. Hughes described Ancrum in '87 as having the odd mixture of a violent temper and great generosity. He was not generally well liked. See also Stevens, *Allies*, 2297. Ancrum had been a capt of the 34th since '72; Lundy: see Kim Stacy, "No One Harms Me with Impunity — The History, Organization, and Biographies of the 84th Regiment of Foot (Royal Highland Emigrants) and Young Royal Highlanders, During the Revolutionary War 1775–1784," (manuscript in process, 1994). Stacy noted that Lieut James Lindin (Lundin) served in the 7th Coy, 1st Bn in '77 and transferred to the 2nd in '78, serving in the 3rd Coy. He was promoted to Capt-Lieut on 11Dec79 and transferred to the 1st Coy, serving therein in that capacity until dis-bandment in '83; and NAC, WO34/14, Lundy's appointment to the Regt as Lieut was 14Jun75, the day of the founding of the RHE. Previously, he had been a Lieut in the 35th. On a 1Bn officers' roll dated Boston, 3Sep75, Lundy was listed as a Lieut; Kusick/Kuysak, James: Kusick served as Bradstreet's bateaux master in 1758 and with Guy Johnson in 1775; Farquharson/ Ferguson: John Ferguson was the barrack-master at Montreal from 1774-78. In '78, he transferred to Carleton Is. as barrack-master and commissary. He also held these positions at Oswegatchie. In '83, he was at

Cataraqui in the same employment. In '91, Ferguson married Magdalene Johnson, daughter of Sir William Johnson and Mary Brant. See, Richard A. Preston, ed., *Kingston Before the War of 1812, A Collection of Documents, Ontario Series III* (Champlain Society, 1959) 106&241fn and Molly Brant, 86&104; Piety, Austin: Resigned his post in Boston on 7Mar77. See, *SJJ OB*, 60 and NAC, WO28/9, 59; Clergis/Clerges, George: Clerges entered the army as a Vol in the 34th. On 10Jul76, he became an Ens in the 53rd, but on 1Jan77 exchanged back to the 34th. On 5Nov82, he was promoted to Lieut. See Letters of the 34th, 1783, 46. St. Leger to Lernoult, 18Mar83. Ens Clergis was murdered by the QM (Bullies, Butters?) of the 34th while at Carleton Island. See, *Hadden's Journal*, 215fn.

166 *SJJ OB*, 61.

167 Correspondence and discussion with Peter C. Ferri, Frankford, ON. Ferri has studied, built, and crewed a variety of these craft. Bateaux were in regular use in trade on the rivers and lakes of New York and Quebec. As these waterways were the highways of America, the military relied on these craft as carriages for troops, stores and provisions. Bateaux were shallow-draft, flat-bottomed craft, propelled by rowing or sailing and occasionally poling. The vessels were steered by a 15-18 foot stern sweep and the oars were 12 feet long. The mast mounted a square-rigged mainsail and a topsail. The setting pole was 8 feet long and shod with an iron tip. The Admiralty design was the most common and carried 1,500 pounds of cargo. This vessel weighed about 1,800 lbs (816Kg) and was 30 feet (9.14m) long with a centre beam of 6 feet. Its sides were 4 feet high with a rounded bow and sides. As this design was "clinker" built (each plank overlapped), field repairs were difficult, requiring skilled artificers. This design was most useful for lake travel. Larger craft up to 60 feet long were also used for heavy loadings. This was likely the type assigned to St. Leger's artillery. Designs of this length often had a horizontal board around the gunwale on which the crew could walk when poling. A slanted bow was at times more useful, as it cut the water cleanly and would ride over obstacles. Mohawk- and Cataraqui-style bateaux were of this type with slant-sided, butt-fit "carvel" planking, allowing simple "field" repairs. The slanted sides turned away waves in rough water. These craft were somewhat smaller — 20-25 feet with a corresponding lighter payload. The military usually manned the smaller bateaux with seven men — six on the oars and one at the steering sweep. The cargo of barrels, crates and bales would lie on the boat's bottom, firmly wedged into place to prevent shifting, leaving room for the men's legs as they sat at the oars; Artillery bateaux: Letter of Jas Gray, 22May82, found in NAC, WO28/5, 98. This letter indicated that the extra-large bateaux of the artillery required extra hands.

168 *SJJ OB*, 62-63.

169 Stevens, *Allies*, 1085; The expense accounts of the St. Leger Expedition transcribed and explained in "L'Expedition du Fort Stanwix "*[St. Leger Expenses], Le Canada Français*, (Société du Parlés Français au Canada, Québec) Vol. XXXIII (November 1945) 219. Jean-Baptiste-Melchior Hertel de Rouville was from a famous military family. One of J-B-M's forefathers was infamous in MA history for leading a particularly destructive raid against the frontier village of Deerfield in 1704. His father, René-Ovide, was an active Canadien loyalist imprisoned by the Whigs during the occupation of Montreal; Claude-Nicolas-Guillaume De Lorimier, *At War with the Americans, The Journal of Claude-Nicolas-Guillaume de Lorimier*, Peter Aichinger, tr & ed., (Victoria: Press Porcepic, n.d.)30&55; DCB, V, 421: Hertel de Rouville was an Ens in the Régiment de Languedoc and saw extensive service in Corsica against the partisan Pascal Paoli. He was exchanged for rebel officers taken at The Cedars.

Endnotes

170 HSGS, II, 42. Carleton's Military Secretary, Capt Foy, wrote in '77, "The Canadians tho' not rich, yet being generally in a state of easy Circumstances, have a strong repugnance to the life of a common soldier, and a very few, if any, will embrace it from choice... To humour this prejudice against being considered as professional soldiers," the companies raised for the '77 campaign were designated as militia. The troops were to be told that their raising was merely an improvement upon the old militia law, designed for the better defence of Quebec, but they were not exempt from the obligation to serve elsewhere if required by emergency.

171 Antecedents: René Chartrand, *Canadian Military Heritage, I, 1000-1754 & II, 1755-1871* (2 vols., Montreal: Art Global Inc., 1995) I, 73-76,91,83-100,144,154-56,192,202.

172 NAC, HP, B39, 544.

173 Mens' uniforms: Johann Friedrich von Specht,*The Specht Journal* , Helga Doblin, tr., (Westport, CT & London: Greenwood Press, 1995) 46. In addition to commanding the German 1st Bde, Col von Specht commanded his own Musketeer Regiment; Officers' uniforms: A portrait of Lieutenant Ignace-Michel-Louis-Antoine de Salaberry, the coy's 1st Lieut from the René Chartrand Collection.

174 Schuyler to Van Schaick, 14Jun77 and to Gansevoort, 10Jul77, found in *Schuyler Court Martial*, 155. These letters offered proof that this was a Massachusetts' detachment commanded by Maj Ezra Badlam; Schuyler to Hancock, 14Jun77, cited in Graymont, 116; T.W. Egly, Jr., *Goose Van Schaick of Albany 1736–1789* (Author, 1992) 42. Egly states that a "contingent" of the 1NY formed part of this force; T.W. Egly, Jr., *History of the First New York Regiment [1NY]* (Hampton, NH: Peter E. Randall, 1981) 59-61.

175 Egly, *Van Schaick*, 42-43.

176 Stone, *Brant*, I, 182fn.

177 Hinman, 30.

178 *SJJ OB*, 63.

179 ibid, 64.

180 Cruikshank & Watt, *KRR NY,* 15-16. Details of the size of this corvée have not been located.

181 Claus to Knox, 16Oct77. Claus spelled Deserontyon "Odiserundy" and Oswegatchie as "Swegachy"; Scout participants: James Thomas Flexner, *Lord of the Mohawks, A Biography of Sir William Johnson* (Boston & Toronto: Little, Brown and Company, 1979) 101. The French settled a number of Onondagas and Cayugas at Oswegatchie in 1750 as a Christian satellite town. The scout likely included men of the old settlement and Inroquois Confederacy warriors, Akwesasnes and Mississaugas. *TCMN*, Vol. I, No.3 (March 1983). A certificate taken from the body of an Indian killed at Oriskany. "The Bearer, Schoughyowote, a young Cayuga Chief has been upon a scouting Party to Fort Stanwick's in the Beginning of July 1777"; Size of party: Gansevoort to Schuyler, 4Jul77, quoted in Stone, *Burgoyne* , 161. "Yesterday a party of at least forty, supposed to be Butler's emissaries"; *St. Leger Expenses,* 220. Expense Documents, Item 8 — an invoice signed by Capt John Hare for presents given to an Indian chief on 9Jul77 at Buck Island must relate to the scout to Stanwix.

182 Claus to Knox, 16Oct77.

183 P. Gansevoort to C. Van Schaick, 23Jun77, transcribed in John Albert Scott, *Fort Stanwix* , 130-31.

184 *Colbrath Journal*, 16.

185 Smy transcripts. U.S. Papers Continental Congress, Mf Group M247, 77: 83-86.

186 Governor George Clinton, *Public Papers of George Clinton, First Governor of New York,*

Rebellion in the Mohawk Valley

1777-1795. 1801-1804 (6 Vols., New York & Albany: State of New York, 1902) II, 62.

187 Capt Bull: C.A. Wesleger, *The Delaware Indians — A History* (New Brunswick, NJ: Rutgers University Press) 246. Capt Bull was from the lower Susquehanna. Possibly, he was recruited by Brant when Joseph stopped at the Delaware towns on his way to Niagara. In the later war, Bull was very active in his home territory; Francis Parkman, *The Conspiracy of Pontiac and the Indian War after the Conquest of Canada* (2 vols., Boston: Little, Brown, and Company, 1895) II, 113. Capt Bull was a "formidable chief" against the Pennsylvania frontiers during the Pontiac Uprising; Kelsay, 101. Brant was with the Oneida/Mohawk party that seized Capt Bull at Oquaga during the Pontiac Uprising and sent him prisoner to Sir William. How ironical that Bull 'ran' with Brant in the early days of the revolution; Pool: Bailey, DeWitt, tr. Butler's Rangers Pay Lists for 24 Dec. 1777 – 24 Oct. 1778 found in HP, AddMss21765. A Henry Pool was a Pte in Capt "Tin Broock's" Coy. He did not appear in the '83 Butler's roll. This was likely the same man that was with Brant at Unadilla; Stone, *Brant*, I, 183; Simms, *Schoharie*, 221. From the Joseph Wagner/Waggoner deposition.

188 Kelsay, 195. Declaration of John Dusler, 12Feb1833; NYPA W16244 of Dusler's widow.

189 Claus to Knox, 16Oct77. Claus reported less than 200 men and gave the volume of powder; Simms, *Schoharie*, 223. John Harper reported that Brant had 137 men; Herkimer to Schuyler, 2Jul77, transcribed in Penrose, *Indian Affairs*, 81-82. Herkimer reported 200 men; William W. Campbell, Jr., *Annals of Tryon County; or the Border Warfare of New York* (Cherry Valley: The Cherry Valley Gazette Print,1880) 68. States 130 men.

190 Flexner, 227-28,248. The author details George Ury Klock's lack of principles regarding his dealings with the Mohawks.

191 Kelsay, 195. Dusler declaration; Herkimer to Schuyler, 2Jul77, transcribed in Penrose, *Indian Affairs*, 81-82.

192 Some sources suggest that Waggoner and his men were instructed to kill Brant and his key men whenever an opportunity presented itself, but they were outfoxed by Brant and his party, who were too alert. See Stone, *Brant*, I, 184-85. Stone was scandalized over this plan; Simms, *Schoharie*, 222-23. Simms objects to Stone's interpretation, claiming to have interviewed Waggoner who denied that an overt killing was ordered.

193 ibid, Deposition of Joseph Waggoner; James F. Morrison, *Colonel Jacob Klock's Regiment, Tryon County Militia* (author, 1992) 3&8. Jos Waggoner is noted as a Sjt. Abraham and George Herkimer as Ptes in Klock's Second Regt.

194 Graymont, 117; Herkimer to Schuyler, 2Jul77, transcribed in Penrose, *Indian Affairs*, 81.

195 ibid. Herkimer later wrote, "We have allmost been engaged there in a battle."

196 Simms, *Schoharie*, 223.

197 William W. Campbell, 69.

198 NAC, CO42/36(Q13), 188-90; Claus to Knox, 16Oct77; Germain to Carleton, 26Mar77 quoted in John Watts DePeyster, *The Life, Misfortunes & the Military Career of Brig. General Sir John Johnson Bart. [Career]* (New York: Chas. H. Ludwig, 1882) cii. "It is the King's further pleasure that you put under... St. Leger... [the] Hanau Chasseurs, [totalling] 342; Carleton to Germain, 26Jun77 quoted in Cruikshank & Watt, *KRR NY*, 16. "about a hundred of the Hanau Chasseurs have since arrived, and they are on their way to join him"; St. Leger's return, Oswego, 27Aug77, found in NAC, WO17/1571(2), 207, shows the Jäger Coy as 89 all ranks, including casualties; Entry for 12Jul77 found in the "Diary of the Hanau Jaeger Corps *[Jaeger Corps'*

Endnotes

Diary]," held at Morristown National Historic Park and published in the *Fort Stanwix Garrison Newsletter*, 1981. LtCol von Kreutzbourg wrote that 19 men of the Vacant coy had been ordered to guard some Brunswick recruits, indicating that the coy was understrength by that number when it joined St. Leger; For a complete roll of the Vacant Coy, see Watt & Morrison, *Campaign of 1777*, 30-32.

199 *Willett OB.*.

200 *Schuyler Court Martial*, 140.

201 Earlier effectiveness of Canadiens: see Chartrand, I, 45-202.

202 Herkimer to Schuyler, 2Jul77, transcribed in Penrose, *Indian Affairs*, 81-82.

203 Gansevoort to Schuyler, 3Jul77, ibid, 82-83.

204 Spoor and sod party: Gansevoort to Schuyler, 4Jul77, cited in Stone, *Burgoyne & St. Leger*, 161. "a party... attacked Ensign Sporr with sixteen privates"; *Fort Klock Historic Restoration Newsletter*, Vol. III, No.6 (March 1991). From Mohawk Valley Pensions — John Spoor was the ensign of Dewitt's Coy, 3NY. He was taken prisoner by the enemy at Fort Stanwix in July 1777 and held for about six months"; Chris McHenry, compiler, *Rebel Prisoners at Quebec 1778–1783* (Author, 1981) 22. Ens John Spurrs taken at Ft. Stanwix on 3Jul77 was returned to the States in Oct77; Casualties: *TCMN*, Vol. I, No.3 (March 1983). Schoughyowote's certificate – "has been upon a scouting Party to Fort Stanwick's... where 5 prisoners and 4 scalps were taken.

205 Gansevoort to Schuyler, 4Jul77, Penrose, *Indian Affairs*, 84-85.

206 Court-martials had been held on 5,9,12&28Jun and would continue on 19&21Jul. None were held during the siege, but shortly after, on 26Aug, the cycle started again. The following punishments were awarded: 5Jun, one man — 150 lashes, 9Jun, one man — 100 lashes, 12Jun, two men — 150 lashes each, 28Jun, one man — 100 lashes, 19Jul, one man — 200 lashes, another man — 100 lashes. The outcome of the 21Jul courtmartial was not recorded; While the Cont Army exhibited some unique features such as limited enlistment terms, it was a typical 18C army. Harsh discipline in harsh times.

207 JA Scott, 138.

208 *Schuyler Court Martial*, 135-36.

209 ibid, 155; JA Scott, 139.

210 *Schuyler Court Martial*, 135-36.

211 ibid, 137&140.

212 JA Scott, 138.

213 Thomas Jefferys, *The American Atlas* (London: 1776 – republished, Amsterdam: Theatrum Orbis Terrarum, 1974) Map by Maj Saml Holland, Surveyor Gen, Northern District in America '76 shows three different leagues, e.g., 65 Marine leagues = 226mi. 65 Cdn leagues = 162mi; 65 Travelling leagues = 121mi. One of the latter two were meant.

214 Langan to Carleton, 20May77, found in NAC, CO42/36 (Q13), 125.

215 British attitudes and colonial perspectives: Richard M. Ketchum, *Decisive Day, The Battle for Bunker Hill* (Doubleday & Company, Inc., 1962); Douglas E. Leach, *Roots of Conflict, British Armed Forces and Colonial Americans, 1677–1763* (Chapel Hill & London: The University of North Carolina Press, 1986); Fred Anderson, *Crucible of War, The Seven Years' War and the Fate of Empire in British North America, 1754–1766* (New York: Alfred A. Knopf, 2000); How British attitudes affected loyalists: John Shy, "Armed Loyalism: The Case in the Lower Hudson Valley," *A People Numerous & Armed, Reflections on the Military Struggle for American Independence* (New York: Oxford University Press, 1976) 181-92.

216 St. Leger to Carleton, Oswego, 27Aug77 [St. Leger to Carleton, 27Aug77] found in

NAC, CO42/37(Q14), 140.

217 Like tragic comedy, St. Leger's return of 27Aug77 at Oswego was entitled a "Present State of the Detachment Sent on the Secret Expedition." NAC, WO17/1571(2), 206.

218 Edward Spencer to Gansevoort, 6Jul77, transcribed in Penrose, *Indian Affairs*, 85-86.

219 *Schuyler Court Martial*, 160; Jos Robertaccio collection – William M. Forbes, "Fort Schuyler, 1760-1766," *Annals and Recollections*, Rome Historical Society (October 1983). Fortuitously, young Capt Nicholas Herkimer commanded a party clearing this same road from Ft Herkimer to Ft Stanwix in '59. His knowledge of the roadway was intimate.

220 Number of Indians: Claus to Knox, 16Oct77; Buck Island: Was renamed Carleton Island in '78 when it was fortified as the major staging depot for the upper posts. The fort was named after Gov Haldimand. See C.C.J. Bond, "British Base at Carleton Island," *OHSPR*, V. 52, 1.

221 Stevens, *Allies*, 1089. This author provides the given name "John" and the spelling "Burnett." Burnett was commissioned a Lieut in '64 and was with the 8th throughout its service in America. He became expert in the use of watercraft. Burnett rose to MGen before his death in 1817.

222 *SJJ OB*, 65-66.

223 Volkert Douw to Schuyler, 9Jul77, transcribed in Penrose, *Indian Affairs*, 88-89.

224 Schuyler to Gansevoort, 10Jul77, cited in JA Scott, 139.

225 Orville W. Carroll Collection, American Antiquarian Society, Worcester, MA. Letter #1834.

226 JA Scott, 141-42.

227 Announcement: *SJJ OB*, 66; Rank of brigadier: *Hadden's Journal*, lxxxvii. Rogers noted, "the grade of brigadier-general was formerly a distinctive one in the army, but it was abolished as such, about the year 1748; after which time it was only conferred temporarily, and ordinarily upon regimental lieutenant-colonels. It was usually conferred for a war, or for as long as the bearer should serve in practically the same field of operations; as, for example, during the Revolutionary War."

228 *Jaeger Corps' Diary*; PRO, CO5/140, 70&71. "Corps des Chasseurs de Son Altesse Serenissime le Prince Hereditaire de Hesse – Compagnie du Capitaine Kornrumpff"; ibid, 68. "Etat... une Companie du Corps des Chasseurs de S.A.S. Mgr Le Prince Hereditaire de Hesse Cassel à Hanau le 7e Mars 1777" signed by C.A. Kornrumpff; In keeping with Hessian usage, the company was referred to as the "Vacant" company, as its captain had died in Montreal.

229 Lieut Chas Collerton saw much service later in the war at Ft Niagara and on the frontier. On 31Oct80, he perished in the tragic wreck of the brig *Ontario* when all hands and passengers were lost on L. Ontario. See, Arthur Britton Smith, *Legend of the Lake, the 22-Gun Brig-Sloop Ontario 1780* (Kingston, Ont: Quarry Press, 1997).

230 *SJJ OB*, 67.

231 Why St. Leger set off later than Burgoyne is undetermined. Obviously a timetable guided both commanders' movements. Given the belief that Stanwix was an ineffectual block to St. Leger's advance, it may have been advantageous for him to reach the upper reaches of the Mohawk Valley ahead of Burgoyne's investment of Ticonderoga. A large force, which would have otherwise been arrayed against Burgoyne, might have been sent to block St. Leger's advance and the U.S. command would have been in a deeper quandary than the actual events created. In any event, a timetable must have been carefully weighed and balanced, but its exact details have not been discovered. As the Royal Yorkers were paid to 24Aug, this may have been the estimated date of joining Burgoyne in Albany.

Endnotes

232 Henry Rudyerd was one of a handful of British artillery officers who left a portfolio of superb paintings of early North America that are so important to historians. Many of these are held by the NAC.

233 Butler to Hay, 15Jun77, transcribed by Smy from NAC, CO42/36(Q13). Butler requested "Mr. Hay at Detroit for a body of the western Indians to join their brothers of the Six Nations on this expedition, agreeable to mutual treaties subsisting between them."

234 Irondequoit Bay is the site of modern Rochester, NY.

235 Graymont, 120. Details of the Irondequoit council from Mary Jemison's account of her life amongst the Seneca. She cites accounts by the Senecas, Cornplanter and Blacksnake and the Oneida Thos Spencer to the U.S. commissioners.

236 Claus to Knox, 16Oct77. Claus stated he was put in orders upon St. Leger's arrival on 8Jul. Sir John's Orderly Book indicated the announcement occurred four days later; Stands of Arms: in military usage, a musket, cartouche and belt with bayonet and scabbard. Indians had little tactical application for a bayonet. Most often, they preferred to load from powder horn and loose ball carried in a leather bag. Claus may have meant he received muskets only, unless the arms at Oswegatchie were already destined for the Indian trade, and then, a stand could refer to a trade musket, powder horn, tomahawk and ball bag.

237 *SJJ OB*, 77-78.

238 Herkimer to Schuyler, 15Jul77, transcribed in Penrose, *Indian Affairs*, 89-91.

239 Stevens, *Allies*, 1103.

240 Various quotations and description: Graymont, 120fn,121,123.

241 Cornplanter: Cornplanter was also known as Capt Abeel (O'Bail) after the surname of his white father, see Kelsay, 367.

242 *Schuyler Court Martial*, 174.

243 Letter to Jas Deane, 10Jun77, cited in Stevens, *Allies*, 1069. This visit to the Canadian villages was at the request of Schuyler; Deane to Schuyler, 25Jun77, cited in *Schuyler Court Martial*, 118fn. Provides details of this scout.

244 Stevens, *Allies*, 2236. Spencer stated he visited "Cassasseny." Stevens interpreted this to be Akwesasne, a contention I have accepted.

245 Various quotations: Tyron County committee meeting, 17Jul77, transcribed in Penrose, *Mohawk Valley*, 121-23.

246 Carroll Collection, American Antiquarian Soc., letter #1824.

247 A transcript of Herkimer's 18Oct76 order to Col Peter Bellinger found in Eugene W. Lyttle, "Nicholas Herkimer", *Proceedings of the NYHA*, 1904. In part, this order read – "Ser you will order your bodellgen [battalion] do mercks [march] immiedettleh [immediately] do ford edouard [Fort Edward] wid for das profiesen and amonieschen [provision and ammunition] fied [fit]for an betell [battle] etc..." If this transcript is credible, Herkimer's English was too poor for him to have composed the proclamation and it would also indicate how St. Leger spoke English.

248 Transcribed in William W. Campbell, 76-77.

249 *SJJ OB*, 84-85.

250 Claus to Knox, 16Oct77.

251 Entry 18Jul77 in *SJJ OB*, 87-88.

252 Stone, *Burgoyne & St. Leger*, 146-47.

253 *Schuyler Court Martial*, 175.

254 Carroll Collection, American Antiquarian Soc., letter #1879.

255 Jelles Fonda letter in Herkimer's papers cited in Stone, *Brant*, I, 182.

256 *Willett OB*.

257 *Colbrath Journal*, 17.

258 Carleton to Maclean, 24Jul77, transcribed in HSGS, II, 232. Carleton's outrage over this treason was plain. Maclean was instructed to visit the parishes of each of the deserters and claim, "upon pain of military execution," two men as replacements for each. The militia capts of the parishes were ordered to find the deserters and forward them to their coys for punishment.

259 One of these men was Adam Shades, who volunteered for the Royal Yorkers just before Oriskany. The other two, James Empson and John Jones, joined Butler's Rangers on that corps' formation in Sep77.

260 Howe to Guy Johnson, 7Apr77, cited in Stevens, *Allies*, 1004. Stevens's endnotes are confusing, but it appears this commission was found in British Army Head Quarters Papers, #479.

261 Graymont, 124.

262 Wesson's Regt is often referred to as the 9MA. Michael Thompson, the MA ContLine historian, advises that in '77, any use of numbers to designate MA regts was unofficial. After the '76 campaign, the MA Line was entirely rebuilt and the State authorities were reluctant to indicate seniority by numbering the new regts. John Bailey was convinced that he was senior and made common use of the designation "1st MA," but when numbers were assigned two years latter, his Regt became the 2MA.

263 Schuyler to NYS Council, 21Jul77, *NYHS Collections*, Schuyler Papers.

264 JA Scott, 145.

265 Number of men: Claus, *Anecdotes of Brant*, 27. Claus was not specific about who these men were. An amalgam of other information led me to conclude that Mohawks from the two Valley castles were with Brant and his volunteers.

266 illiterate interpreter: A phrase describing Butler found in Claus to Vardill, 15Oct78, found in the *Claus Papers*, MG19, F1, Vol.25.

267 Various quotations: Claus to Knox, 16Oct77.

268 Stevens, *Allies*, 1114.

269 Claus, *Anecdotes of Brant*.

270 Stevens, *Allies*, 1035&1092. Egushaway led 6 Ottawas, Sastaretsi and Orindiacky led 6 Wyandots, Windeego and sachem Okia led 5 Potawatomis and civil chiefs Mettusawgay and Massigayash led 22 Chippewas. The Quebec rangers were M. Pierre Drouillard and the interpreter, William Tucker.

271 Bruce Wilson, "John Butler and Early Office Holding at Niagara," *The Butler Bicentenary, Commemorating the 200th Anniversary of the Death of Colonel John Butler* (Colonel John Butler Branch, UEL Assoc. of Canada, 1997) 12 and William A. Smy, "The Butlers Before the Revolution," ibid, 49. This cousin was Walter Butler Sheehan, the son of Capt Wm Sheehan and Anne Butler, John's half sister. Sheehan finished the war as a Lieut of the 8th.

272 Claus, *Anecdotes of Brant*.

273 John McDonell, *Spanish John, Being a narrative in the Early Life of Colonel John M'Donell of Scottos* (Knoydart, Scotland: Craigmyle, 1993) McDonell's great grandfather had been the chief of Glengarry in the late 17th century, and through him, John was a descendant of the legendary Donald, Lord of the Isles. Scotus married his cousin Catherine in 1747. She was the daughter of Donald McDonell, "reckoned the bravest man of the clan," who had fallen at Culloden moor. John McDonell had been a Lieut in the Spanish army in 1744, which earned him his nickname "Spanish John." He returned to Scotland from Spain to serve Prince Charles Stuart as a Capt in "the '45."

274 AO, HP, AddMss21822, Reel 82, 124.

Endnotes

275 Carleton to BGen Maclean, Quebec 24Jul77, transcribed in HSGS, II, 232.

276 "Colonel St. Leger's Account of Occurrences at Fort Stanwix," [St. Leger to Burgoyne, 27Aug77], Burgoyne, State, lxxvii; St. Leger to Carleton, Oswego, 27Aug77 in NAC, WO42/37 (Q14), and transcribed in MG11, 135-43.

277 Stone, Brant, I, 218-20. The written plan and drawing of this arrangement were abandoned with St. Leger's papers during the hasty retreat; The Military Papers of General Peter Gansevoort [Gansevoort Papers], transcribed by the State Historian (NY State Archives: u.p., 1906) 172-73. This source transcribes St. Leger's material and is more reliable than Stone's interpretation.

278 "Indian files" was a tactical evolution for moving troops through constrictions or over difficult topography. As a formation, it could not produce any volume of fire to the front. The file was long and often winding, so thoughtful officers prepared for attack from any quarter.

279 The historian Stone credits the "refugee Provincials" for these dispositions. His supposition failed to acknowledge the many painful lessons absorbed by the British during their operations against woods-wise Canadiens and crafty native allies, lessons that had become an informal syllabus of instruction for Regulars on the frontiers. That such knowledge may have come from the native war captains, whose men formed a key element of the formation, was entirely ignored. Stone's comment that the dispositions were "extraordinary precautions" was odd, particularly after what was to occur at Oriskany.

280 St. Leger to Burgoyne, 27Aug77.

281 ibid; Stevens, Allies, 1114. Stevens says that Clerges joined Bird with some 34th men. This was not mentioned by St. Leger.

282 Willett OB..

283 Gansevoort to Schuyler, 26Jul77, transcribed in Penrose, Indian Affairs, 91-92.

284 Gansevoort to Caty Van Schaick, 26Jul77, transcribed in JA Scott, 146.

285 Stevens, Allies, 1114. Stevens theorized that these Indians were members of the scout sent by St. Leger from the Salmon River on July 23.

286 Fort Stanwix Document Collection, #14250.

287 Quotation and facts: Colbrath Journal Journal, 19,20.

288 A dozen contemporary maps do not reveal the location of Nine Mile Point on L. Oneida. I suspect it was on the north side, as the Advance and Main parties followed that shore because the south shore was controlled by the Tuscaroras' castle of Ganasaraga and the Oneidas' castle of Kanawolohale/Old Oneida.

289 Spencer to Gansevoort, 29Jul77, in the Gansevoort Papers, 151-52; Transcribed in Stone, Burgoyne & St. Leger, 149-51.

290 Herkimer to Gansevoort, 29Jul77, Gansevoort Papers, 153.

291 Garrison Order, 13Aug77, found in Willett OB.. The order named John Hansen; Richard Varick to Gansevoort, 1Aug77, transcribed in Gansevoort Papers, 158. Noted that Hanson was appointed to muster the troops of the garrison.

292 John Bradstreet, An Impartial Account of Lieut.Col. Bradstreet's Expedition to Fort Frontenac (Toronto: Rous & Mann Limited, 1940) 13. The Oneida River "is the same stream that is called the Onondaga river, at its discharge into Lake Ontario. But as the Senecas River runs into it, at about twenty miles distant from the Oneida Lake; the intermediate part between this river and the lake, is call'd the Oneida river; and that part when the Seneca River runs into it, is call'd the Three Rivers, tho' in fact, there are but two"; Jefferys, Holland's map shows Three Rivers at the junction of the "Seneka" River with the east and west branches of the Onondaga River.

293 Colbrath Journal, 20-21.

294 Thomas Spencer to Gansevoort, 29Jul77, *Gansevoort Papers*, 151-52.

295 Mintz, passim. The author provides superb detail of Gates, his service and ambitions. Use the index to follow his ascendancy; For another viewpoint, see Jonathon Gregory Rossie, *The Politics of Command in the American Revolution* (Syracuse: Syracuse University Press, 1975). Rossie details the struggles in the U.S. Army upper command throughout the war; Bayard Tuckerman, *Life of General Philip Schuyler, 1733-1804* (New York: Dodd, Mead and Company, 1903) 137-237. An account strongly biased against Gates, shedding much light on Schuyler's struggles; Horatio Gates ended the war as the second senior general officer in the U.S. Army and enjoyed George Washington's confidence and friendship.

296 *SJJ OB*, 94. This was the final entry in the book.

297 ibid, 93&94fn. Information provided by the editor.

298 Jefferys, Holland's map placed the Royal Blockhouse at the east end of Lake Oneida where "Oneyda" Creek flowed into the lake.

299 *Colbrath Journal*, 34.

300 JA Scott, 170. Named this man "Watson," but no one of that name was in the Ind Dept; Bird to St. Leger, 2Aug77 in the *Gansevoort Papers*, 171. Gave the name "Wilson." This makes sense, as Capt Jas Wilson was with Bird.

301 Stone, *Brant*, I, 220-22. Transcripts of Bird's reports and St. Leger's replies.

302 Stevens, *Allies*, 1119.

303 Kelsay, 198-99. From the "Life of Governor Blacksnake."

304 Graymont, 127-28. Her account drew from Draper's, "Conversations with Governor Blacksnake" Mss4848, 65-66, "Life of Blacksnake" and Seaver's, "Mary Jemison"; Thomas S. Abler, ed., *Chainbreaker, The Revolutionary War Memoirs of Governor Blacksnake As told to Benjamin Williams [Chainbreaker]* (Lincoln & London: University of Nebraska Press, 1989) 58-80. Includes a discussion of Blacksnake's confused memory.

305 St. Leger to Butler, 4Aug77, the *Claus Papers*, XIV, 252 cited in Stevens, *Allies*, 1124.

306 Rev MacKenna: Richard K. MacMaster, "Parish in Arms: A Study of Father John MacKenna and the Mohawk Valley Loyalists, 1773-1778." United States Catholic Historical Society, Historical Records and Studies, XLV (1957) 121. Detail from John G. Shea, *Life and Times of Most Rev. John Carroll*, 143n. This source noted MacKenna's proficiency in German; Hessians' sickness: *Jaeger Corps' Diary*.

307 Thos Spencer to Tryon Committee, 17Jul77, transcribed in Penrose, *Indian Affairs*, 121-23; Cruikshank & Watt, *KRR NY*, 16. Cruikshank noted the presence of Lady Johnson and family; Kelsay, 198. Kelsay included Nancy Claus and her children.

308 Frank B. Risteen, Sr. "Children of Sir John Johnson and Lady Mary (Polly) Johnson, Married at New York June 30, 1773," OHSPR, Vol.LXIII (1971), 93-95.

309 SJJ at Lake George: Earle Thomas, 29. From the *Johnson Papers*, 2, 346-48; Their relationship: Regarding their later friendship, see ibid, 132-35,138,140-44,147-69; Wm Claus: Cruikshank & Watt, *KRR NY*, 181. In '81, Wm Claus was an Ens, 2KRR. He was promoted to Lieut 24Aug83 and trans'd to the 1Bn. At disbandment, he was 8th senior Lieut. He served as Sir John's D/Supt Ind Affairs during the War of 1812 and died on 11Nov1826 at Niagara.

310 E.B. O'Callaghan, ed., *Orderly Book of Lieut. Gen. John Burgoyne [Burgoyne OB]* (Albany: J. Munsell, 1860) 192.

311 Bateaux brigade size: *Colbrath Journal*, 24 and *Wm Willett*, 49. Variously reported as 2-7 bateaux. Colbrath stated 4, Willett 5; Mellon's troops: Colbrath stated 100, Willett 200. As the Willett account was the son's rework of his father's manuscript, I accepted Colbrath's figure.

Endnotes

312 Gilbert Hagerty, *Massacre at Fort Bull* (Providence: Mowbray Company, 1971) 68&97. Ft Newport was built on The Carry in '56 at the eastern terminus of the creek system. It was destroyed later that same year when the British withdrew in fear of a French attack.

313 Details of the attack: *Colbrath Journal*, 24; Capt John Martin: Affidavit of Moses Younglove transcribed in Stone, *Brant*, I, App.IV. Younglove claimed Martin was given to the Indians at Oswego and was tortured and killed. However, Martin was paroled and returned uninjured to the States later in the war. This blatantly erroneous claim throws doubt on Younglove's entire affidavit; McHenry, 1. Martin was on a Quebec prisoner list of 27Jun78 as "John Martin, Captain 30 years of age from Schenectady, NY... taken near Ft. Stanwix on 2Aug77"; The second man: NYPA W16421 of the widow of Finley Stewart transcribed in Ken D. Johnson, 580. Stewart was pensioned for wounds he received when captured while serving in Martin's Bateaux Coy at Stanwix.

314 Definitions for various elements of fortifications: see, Smith, *Dictionary*.

315 William Willett, 50; Size of garrison: For a complete enumeration, see Watt & Morrison, *Campaign of 1777*, 102-56.

316 *Colbrath Journal*, 24; Canister: MGen E.B. Hughes, *Firepower, Weapons effectiveness on the battlefield, 1630–1850* (London: Arms and Armour Press, 1974) 34-35. Describes the utilization of case or canister shot. Canister was employed primarily as a defensive projectile. Fired from a British 6-pounder, a lightweight tinned case held 85 X 1 1/2-ounce balls. A heavyweight tinned case held 41 X 3 1/2-ounce balls. The case disintegrated on discharge, launching the balls in a controlled pattern similar to a modern shotshell. As the spread of the balls was 32 feet at 100 yards, one might imagine the area covered at maximum range for light case, which was 250 yards. Hughes noted that contemporary authors often described canister as grape shot, which was a very heavy version of case shot usually used against ships and boats at close ranges. Colbrath wrote "Grape Shott" in his journal, likely in reference to canister.

317 *Colbrath Journal*, 26. He wrote, "a Continental Flagg"; Luzader, 37-41. This flag raising has been the subject of legend since the revolution. Many claimed it was the first time the Stars and Stripes were raised in the face of the foe. Luzader researched this contention in depth and concluded that the flag was not the Stars and Stripes, but rather, the Grand Union flag of the United Colonies. British history students will be confused by the term "Grand Union" in this context. To them, the Grand Union is formed by the crosses of St. George of England and St. Andrew of Scotland superimposed. In the American sense, the Grand or Great Union Flag (also known as the Cambridge Flag) was first raised on 1Jan76 at Washington's HQ at Cambridge, MA. It had 13 horizontal stripes of red and white representing the rebelling provinces and employed a British Grand Union (referred to in American journals as the British Union flag) in the first canton. This design became widely known as the Continental or Congress Flag, but the later Stars and Stripes was also frequently referred to as the Continental or Congress flag. It is no wonder that confusion arose. For a brief account of the flags flown by the rebels and the United States, see Alan Kemp, *American Soldiers of the Revolution* (London: Almark Publishing Co. Ltd., 1972) 54-69; For further analysis regarding the flag flown at Stanwix see, Edward C. Ball, *First Stars and Stripes to Defy Foe Flown at Fort Stanwix* (n.p., 1972); JA Scott, 173-176, 345-351; Arthur James Weise, *The Swartwout Chronicles 1338–1899* (NYC: Trow Directory, Printing and Bookbinding, 1899) 205-19. Ball and Weise bring too much emotion to this issue

to "feel" trustworthy; Willett's quotation: Luzader, 39. From Marinus Willett's "Narrative" in the Tomlinson Collection, NYPL.

318 Burgoyne's proclamation: *Hadden's Journal*, 59-62. To maintain the original document's emphasis, I used spellings and capitalization from Hadden's transcript; St. Leger's proclamation: Stone, *Brant*, I, App.III, xxxi-ii. This source showed how St. Leger's wording was different. My paragraphing duplicates Stone's.

319 St. Leger copied his commander's proclamation, yet he was vilified for the thinly disguised threat of the tomahawk. Ironically, he eliminated a critical, most threatening section from Burgoyne's version.

> In consciousness of Christianity, my Royal Master[']s clemency, and the honour of Soldiership, I have dwelt upon this invitation, and wished for more persuasive terms to give it impression; and let not people be led to disregard it by considering their distance from the immediate situation of my Camp. I have but to give stretch to the Indian Forces under my direction, and they amount to Thousands, to overtake the harden'd Enemies of Great Britain and America, (I consider them the same) wherever they may lurk.

How much more ominous were the final lines of the proclamation when the above section was included, especially to troops garrisoned in the Mohawk Valley hard by the centre of the League. St. Leger had already indicated his concerns about the sanguinary customs of native warfare in his instructions to Bird. The omission of this section speaks well for him.

320 *Colbrath Journal*, 26.

321 *Wm Willett*, 50.

322 Graymont, 131.

323 St. Leger to Carleton, n.d. cited in Cruikshank & Watt, *KRR NY*, 17. "Three nines, four sixes, two threes with a considerable number of wall-pieces, were... made use of during the siege"; Louis Torres, "Historic Furnishing Study," *Fort Stanwix: History, Historic Furnishing, and Historic Structure Reports* (Washington: Office of Park Historic Preservation, National Park Service, U.S. Department of the Interior, 1976) 82-83. In Mar-Jun78, the number and weight of guns at Stanwix were essentially the same – 3 X nine-pounder, 4 X 6-pounder, 4 X three-pounder, a total of 11 guns. Also listed were 4 X 4.4" mortars which were those abandoned during St. Leger's retreat. There were "4 travelling carriages for 3-pound cannon... 9 garrison carriages for 6- and 9-pound cannon"; The weight of metal fired by Stanwix's 9's was considerably more effective than St. Leger's 6's and 3's when used against personnel or siege works. See, E.B. Hughes, 29,32-35.

324 *SJJ OB*, 112-17. An appendix — an undated article entitled "Sir Darby Monaghan" from the publication "London Clubs" about an amusing, drunken evening in Dublin involving Barry St. Leger after his return from America.

325 *Colbrath Journal*, 28; Willett to Gov Trumbull, 21Aug77, transcribed in Henry B. Dawson, *Battles of the United States, By Sea and Land: embracing those of the Revolutionary and Indian Wars* (2 vols., New York: Johnson, Fry and Company, 1858) I, 248-50. Willett reported the "German riflemen." He listed 7 Continentals wounded, 1 dead.

326 Quotations and facts: *Wm Willett*, 51.

327 *Colbrath Journal*, 28. Before the war, Roof kept a tavern at The Carry and worked with the bateaux servicing the Indian trade.

Endnotes

328 Claus to Knox, 16Oct77.

329 St. Leger to Burgoyne, 27Aug77.

330 From the Continental Congress papers, reel 183, item 166 cited in Ken D. Johnson, 431.

331 Haldimand to Clinton, 26May79 cited in Cruikshank & Watt, *KRR NY*, 28. "Sir John Johnson's Regiment tho' a usefull Corps with the Ax, are not altogether to be Depended on with the Firelock." Damned with faint praise after their strong effort at Oriskany. Of course, he qualified the comment with the words, "not altogether." Except for Butler's, the loyalists corps in the Cdn Dept spent as much time on pioneering duties as on active campaign, precisely because they were so "usefull."

332 Erie Canal Village historic site was built around old Fort Bull, which was destroyed by the French in 1756.

333 Quoted phrases and facts: Bradstreet, 9-11.

334 Pine Ridge was likely near the modern hamlet of Pine Crest located in the Rome Sand Plains on a pond-tributary to Fish Creek. Pine Crest and the Rome Sand Plains can be found in the Verona Quadrangle, Oneida County Map, NE/4 Oneida 15 Quadrangle, US Dept of the Interior, Geological Survey 1955, AMS5870 II NE – Series V821.

335 St. Leger to Burgoyne, 27Aug77.

336 Graymont, 145. St. Leger's men abandoned 19 wagons on 22Aug. Of course, some of these may have been obtained from around Ft Stanwix and at the Oriskany ambush.

337 Joseph Robertaccio, a Utica-area historian, advises that the abandoned wrecks of the artillery bateaux were discovered sunk in the creek basin at the ruins of old Fort Bull during the building of Erie Canal Village; Details of beach: See Hagerty, *Massacre at Fort Bull.*

338 *Clinton Papers*, I, 169.

339 *Colbrath Journal*, 29. Freshly-cut boards had been hauled upriver from Canajoharie to build the barracks. The Frenchman had been strangely oblivious to the structure's vulnerability.

340 *Wm Willett*, 51.

341 Quotation: Indian council of 19Feb80 cited in Kelsay, 202. From HP, AddMss21787, pt.3, 112.

342 Butler to Carleton, Camp before Ft Stanwix, 15Aug77, found in NAC, CO42/37 (Q14), 153-55. Butler said the militia was "on their march to throw themselves into this place"; Claus to Knox, 16Oct77; Claus, *Anecdotes of Brant*, 28.

343 St. Leger to Burgoyne, 27Aug77.

344 Butler to Carleton, 15Aug77.

345 St. Leger to Burgoyne, 27Aug77. "Sir John Johnson put himself at the head of this party"; Claus to Knox, 16Oct77. "Sir John Johnson asked leave to join his company of Light Infantry and head the whole, which was granted."

346 Claus, *Anecdotes of Brant*, 28; St. Leger did not report sending Brant, unless the phrase, "the whole corps of Indians," was meant to include him. Butler's report to Carleton also failed to mention Brant; No source gave the disposition of the Mississaugas, but this, and other accounts, suggested they were left to guard the siege lines at Stanwix.

347 The order of these events is in question. Butler to Carleton, 15Aug77, 153. Butler stated that he was sent first by St. Leger with Sir John following later. While the ranger did not give command control to Johnson in his report, he recognized Sir John's seniority by mentioning his name ahead of his own; St. Leger to Burgoyne,

Rebellion in the Mohawk Valley

27Aug77. His description begs the issue of who was first sent; Claus, whom it must be remembered never give any credit to Butler, wrote in his *Anecdotes of Brant* that "Sr. John Johnson offered his services to command a party of Light Infantry and what Indians were assembled and ready for service"; Claus to Knox, 16Oct77. "Col. Butler and other Indian Officers were ordered with the Indians." From these sources, we can construct a table of white participation.

Sir John Johnson	1
Light Infantry Coy, KRR NY	55
(at full strength)	
Six Nations' Indian Dept Rangers	21
(from Butler's account)	
Quebec Indian Dept Rangers	2
Total	79

348 Graymont, 131; Stevens, *Allies*, 1125. Both sources agree that only the most committed Cayugas and Onondagas were present.

349 Butler to Carleton, 15Aug77; Claus to Knox, 16Oct77; Stevens, *Allies*, 1233-34,2285; Lakes Indians' participation: Stevens cited Henry Hamilton to Germain, Detroit, 5Sep77 found in NAC, WO42/37, f.172 and Hamilton and Jehu Hay, "Return of Parties of Indians sent from Detroit against the Rebels after the 2d July 1777" found in NAC, WO28/10, f.396.

350 St. Leger to Burgoyne, 27Aug77. St. Leger gave the time of leaving.

351 Stevens, *Allies*, 1234. Quoted from *Life of Governor Blacksnake*, Draper MSS, 16F135-36.

352 Butler to Carleton, 15Aug77, 153.

353 *Wm Willett*, 51.

354 Robertaccio research. Fort Stanwix Document Collection, #14250. I believe this letter was written by Gansevoort, as so many phrases match his letter to Van Schaick on the same topic. I believe he sent it to the Tryon Committee, ca. 29Jul77 with the intention of rousing the populace.

355 Warriors' identities: Stevens, *Allies*, 1169en. Stevens cites a great many confusing sources; The women: Winston Adler, ed., Asa Fitch, compiler, *Their Own Voices: Oral Accounts of Early Settlers in Washington County, New York* (Interlaken: Heart of Lakes Publishing, 1983) 55&58. They had been sitting outside their cabin when they saw Indians pursuing some retreating rebel soldiers. In fright, they hid in the cellar, but the Indians found them; Provincial officer: Lieut David Jones of Jessup's King's Loyal Americans.

356 Kelsay, 204. From the *Gansevoort Papers*.

357 Lou D. MacWethy, *The Book of Names Especially Relating to the Early Palatines and the First Settlers of the Mohawk Valley* (Baltimore: Genealogical Publishing Co., Inc., 1981) 143; MacWethy claimed that the Canajoharie precinct was subdivided after the '77 campaign and that John Harper was given a colonelcy to command the Fifth Regiment. Morrison agrees with the boundaries, but places the split in '76.

358 The 1778 NY militia regulation mentioned Grenadier companies, but not Light Infantry. Quite confusing!

359 Company structure: The 56 men were composed of 1 Capt, 2 1stLieut, 2 2ndLieut, 1 Ens, 4 Sjts, 4 Cpls, 2 Drs (a fife and a drum) and 40 Ptes. In the '78 regulation, the officers supplied the fife and drum at their own expense; Examples of actual Coy strength: *TCMN*, Vol.IV, No.2 (Aug 1985). From NA, Rev War Rolls 1775-83, Roll 75. Capt Chris'r Fox's Coy, 2nd Regt, showed 77 all ranks including 4 officers, 3 Sjts, 3 Cpls; ibid. Capt Jellis *Fonda's Papers*. A return of 13-22May77 gave only 24 men,

all ranks, including 2 officers, 2 Sjts, 3 Cpls; ibid, Roll 74. Capt Chris'n Getman's Coy, ? Regt (surnames suggest 2nd) for '76-77 gave 69 all ranks, including 3 officers, 3 Sjts, 3 Cpls; Morrison research. Capt Michael Ittig's Coy, 4th Regt had 59 all ranks including 4 officers, 4 Sjts, 3 Cpls and 1 Dr. Morrison concluded that only 33 all ranks from Ittig's were at Oriskany and, in his opinion, that size of turnout was typical in all coys of the Bde. Of course, certain classes were likely designated for home defence, to man fortified houses and stone churches.

360 At Oriskany, deaths and disabling wounds fell unevenly upon the various coys. Many beats had to be restructured to allow coys to recruit to full strength. As the war intensified, the Tryon Bde was stressed to the limit. Individual regts were reduced to a level of ineffectiveness due to deaths, disabling wounds, flight from the area and desertion to the Crown. While the KRR NY numbered 300 at the outset of the '77 campaign, it grew to 395 by the campaign's end, even after suffering a wastage of 22%. By the end of '80, the 1KRR was at full strength of 650 and a second battn was authorized with an initial strength of approximately 400. The primary recruiting base for both battns was the Mohawk Valley region. As well, Butler's Rangers recruited over half its numbers from this same area. Its strength was about 500 in '80. Add to this the Mohawk Valley Highlanders of Maclean's 84th RHE Regt, which represented perhaps three of his ten, 65-man coys and Guy Johnson's Ind Dept with Claus's little unit in Montreal and it becomes clear that the drain on manpower from Tryon was staggering. In late '80, the defence of the Valley was put into the capable hands of Marinus Willett. Despite manpower and morale problems, he developed a very effective fighting force composed of Levies and the valiant remnants of the Tryon County Militia, who had clung strongly and bitterly to their original convictions.

361 Bloomfield, 64,102. 3NJ Continental officers amused themselves in Jun76 over a threatened duel between 4TCM officers. On 28Aug, NJ officers were again entertained at the militiamen's expense. Capt Bloomfield wrote, "[We] attended... a ludicrous Beating up for Volunteers by a High-German appointed Capt. who can neither read nor write. The oddity of the Capt., his officers & Recruits with their dress excited the Laughter of all our officers." Unsurprisingly, Bloomfield spent "the Eveng. engaged in Settling a fray between the Soldiers & Inhabitants."

362 Robert K. Wright Jr., *The Continental Army* (Washington: Army Lineage Series, Centre of Military History, United States Army, 1989); Col John Womack Wright, *Some Notes on the Continental Army* (Vails Gate, NY: National Temple Hill Association, 1963).

363 Mackesy, 31.

364 John Mollo & Malcolm MacGregor, *Uniforms of the American Revolution, Macmillan Color Series* (New York: Macmillan Publishing Co., Inc., 1975) 52. There were large bodies of militia in the various colonies; in '75, Connecticut fielded 26,000 men and Pennsylvania 31,800.

365 Bloomfield, 64. For example, on 21Jun76, Tryon militiamen of the 4TCM were drafted to reinforce the army in Canada.

366 John Shy, "A New Look at the Colonial Militia," *A People Numerous & Armed*, 30-31.

367 Colden to Halifax, 3Aug54, transcribed in Stanley Pargellis, ed., *Military Affairs in North America 1748-1765, Selected Documents from the Cumberland Papers in Windsor Castle* (Archon Books, 1969) 19.

368 Wraxall to Henry Fox, 27Sep55, transcribed in ibid, 141.

369 Loudoun to Duke of Cumberland, 17Oct57, transcribed in ibid, 400.

370 Shy, 31fn. From the *Loudoun Papers*, No.5668.

371 Companies of Associated Exempts were created in many districts. In an act dated 3Apr78, the official designation for this special class of militiaman read "All persons under the age of sixty who have held civil or military commissions and are not or shall not be reappointed to their respective proper ranks of office, and all persons between the ages of fifty and sixty." They were to be called out "in time of invasion or incursion of the enemy." James A. Roberts, *New York in the Revolution as Colony and State* (Albany: State of New York, 1897 – reprinted in 2 vols., 1904) I, 10.

372 Janice Potter-MacKinnon, *While the Women Only Wept — Loyalist Refugee Women in Eastern Ontario* (Montreal & Kingston, etc: McGill-Queen's University Press, 1993) 35. From the Journals of the Provincial Congress, Provincial Convention, committee of Safety and Council of Safety of the State of New York 1775-1776-1777, 115.

373 The system of short terms of duty was so engrained in the American psyche that it plagued the Continental Army, in which the duration of service, while longer, was also limited. On the other hand, their British, German and Provincial opposition reaped the benefits of continuity, enjoying the assurance of retaining both officers and men for the duration of the conflict. See Watt, *Burning of the Valleys*, 256-59 for some of Washington's observations on short-term enlistments.

374 Ken D. Johnson, 214. An intersection of two important roads, which was later the site of Fort Plank, was well known to Capt Samuel Pettingell's Coy and served as its rendezvous; ibid, 571. NYPA S11435 of Henry Snook.

375 *The Colonial Laws of New York from the Year 1664 to the Revolution* (5 vols, Albany: 1894) V, 736. The act of 1Apr75 called for each militiaman to provide "a good well fixed Musket or Fuzee, a good Sword, Belt and Cartridge Box, Six Cartridges of Gun Powder and Six sizeable Bullets"; Berthold Fernow, ed., *Documents relating to the Colonial History of the State of New York*, XV, State Archives (Albany: Weed, Parsons and Company, Printers, 1887) V.1, 31. By 22Aug75 the regulation was altered to, "every man between the ages of 16 and 50 do with all convenient speed furnish himself with a good Musket or firelock, Bayonet[,] Sword or Tomahawk, a Steel Ramrod, Worm, Priming Wire and Brush fitted thereto, a Cartouch Box to contain 23 rounds of cartridges, 12 flints and a knapsack agreeable to the directions of the Continental Congress"; Torres, *Fort Stanwix*, 84. A resolution passed by the NY Prov Congress in Aug76 - each man in the militia of Albany city and county and Tryon County was to provide a "good Musket or firelock and Bayonet Sword or Tomahawk, a Steel Ramrod[,] Worm, Priming Wire and Brush fitted thereto, a Cartouch Box to contain 32 rounds of cartridges, 12 flints... That every man shall at his place of abode be also provided with one pound of powder and three pounds of bullets of proper size to his musket or firelock." While the latter requirement sheds some additional light, the former listing is an exact repeat of the Aug75 requirement except for the number of cartridges, which suggests one of the transcribers made an error and transposed the numbers 2 and 3. From the other evidence, 23 is likely correct; *An Act for Regulating the Militia of the State of New York passed at Poughkeepske, April 3, 1778, in the Second Session of Assembly* (Poughkeepsie: n.p., 1778) 34. Called for only 16 rounds and a bayonet, without mention of a tomahawk as an acceptable alternative.

376 The '75 regulation required each man to supply "sizeable" balls for his firearm. This was in recognition of the notorious variety of bore sizes found within the militia. Although bore sizes of the same pattern of military muskets varied within a range

allowed by govt inspectors, the ammunition supplied was of uniform diameter which compensated for this variation. Therefore, amongst the Crown troops, who were generally issued with a reasonably consistent pattern of musket, ammunition was not a great problem. British Light Infantry was supposed to be issued with fusils of carbine bore, ie. 67 inch. See, DeWitt Bailey, *British Military Longarms 1715–1865* (New York, London & Sydney: Arms and Armour Press, 1986) 53. It is unlikely that the KRR Lights were so favoured, as fusils were scarce and preference given to Regulars. The Cont Line suffered with irregular bore diameters, as the States had no large scale manufacture of military firearms and often relied upon stores taken from the Crown, or purchased from European sources, or provided by their *Allies*, principally the French. See, letter of Leonard Gansevoort to Peter, Jun77, cited in Torres, *Fort Stanwix*, 84. "Lieut. McClallen... has drawn out of the Store sixty good new French muskets and the like number of Quality Bayonets, Cartouch Boxes and Bayonet belts". Torres stated that a dig at Stanwix confirmed the presence of French muskets at Stanwix. He noted that the majority of the arms would have been of British Land patterns. This necessitated the supply of two calibres, British at nominally 0.75 inch (19mm) and French at nominally 0.69 inch (17.53mm); While the majority of muskets were of British type or origin, fully 1/3 of those used at Stanwix during the siege were French, as the MA troops that reinforced the garrison were almost all so armed. Conversation with Anthony Tommell, who is preparing a study of the French stands of arms supplied to America in Apr/May77. He advised that 18,000 stands were imported into Portsmouth, NH and 12 of the 15 MA Regts were so equipped. This specifically included Wesson's Regt, which was extensively rearmed with French muskets and bayonets.

377 Whether the militia were able to furnish the 23 balls demanded in the Nov75 regulation or the 16 prescribed in the '78 version is an open question. In '81, the NY Levies, i.e., quasi-regulars, had difficulty with the quantity of ammunition at hand and with balls of the wrong diameter, as the men were still equipped with muskets of differing bores. Willett wanted each man to have "at least seventeen charges of Ammunition," a long way from 23 each. Of course, this was the backwater of the Northern Dept and the "real" war had shifted to the south. See, *TCMN*, Vol.II, No.8. From *Col Marinus Willett's Letter & Orderly Book, Ft Rensselaer 1781*, document No.15705, NYSL, Archives & Mss.

378 Robertaccio research. Joseph has two identical examples of a pattern of cartridge box found in the old Tryon County area. They are wooden blocks/boxes drilled for 24 cartridges and covered with a single leather flap. He believes these were issued to the Tryon Militia Bde and are evidence that the State provided a great deal of equipment. Of course, they may have instead been issued to NY or MA Levies who served in the county. As yet, there has been no information uncovered to date their time of issue.

379 Returns of the Tryon County Militia indicated that belt axes were carried in the place of bayonets. The Aug75 regulation had given alternates, ie. sword, bayonet or tomahawk. The '78 regulation prescribed, "a sufficient Bayonet with a good Belt." Of course, that requirement was easier said than done, as many firearms were of hunting designs, unable to socket a bayonet; *TCMN*, Vol.II, No.8. From NYHS Proceedings (1915), 490-91. A return of the arms of men stationed at Caughnawaga under Maj Jelles Fonda, 17Jun78. Of 14 men, four had a gun and sword, the rest a gun only, except one who had neither. One man had no accoutrements. Whether the nine with a gun only had a tomahawk was unstated; Marinus Willett, *Willett's OB, Fort Rensselaer 1781*, Document No.15705, NYSL, Archives & Mss. The availability of bayonets to fit the various firearms haunted

U.S. forces throughout the conflict. This was confirmed by Willett's Orderly Book entry for 17Jul81 noting that the NY Levies were expected to be equipped, "if possible [with] a Bayinet"; Colonel Guy Johnson, Adjutant General for the Northern District of New York Province, *Manual Exercise, Evolutions, Manoeuvres, &c. To be Observed and Followed by the Militia of the Province of New-York: with some Rules...* (Albany: Alexander and James Robertson, 1772 – facsimile edition – Johnstown, NY: Lewis G. Decker, 1982) Johnson's pre-war manual for the NY Militia contained no bayonet drill. Hunting Swords and Hangers were popular, perhaps many militiamen, especially officers and NCOs, carried them rather than a tomahawk.

380 In a letter of 7Jul1999, William H. Watkins, former site manager of the Herkimer Home State Historic Site, advised that although the fragment of a brocaded waistcoat on exhibit at the site is labelled as belonging to the General, its provenance is in doubt due to its later fashion.

381 Breadbake's Coy: *TCMN*, Vol.XV, No.1 (September 1994). NYPA R11960 of Jacob A. Young of Breadbake's; Howse's Coy: ibid, NYPA W19242, the widow of Pte John D. Failing of Howse's and *NYPA W20002*, the widow of Pte Jacob Zimmerman, of the same coy; Davis' & Visscher's Coys: *TCMN, Vol.XIV, No.10 (August 1994). NYPA S11350* of Frederick Sammons; Tories rounded up: *NYPA R8538* of Peter J. Quackenboss, partially transcribed in Ken D. Johnson, 529; Old men as guards: Peter S. Deygart to Schuyler, 6May77 and endorsed as 6Aug77, transcribed in the *Clinton Papers*, II, 192; Rev Gros: *TCMN, Vol.XI, No.5 (September 1991)*. From the Palatiner, Aug1952; Number of forts: James F. Morrison prepared a study of fortified homes and forts in the Mohawk Valley and found 24 in use in '81.

382 Morrison research. *PA Pension Application S22210* of Benjamin Dickson. Benjamin declared that Whitaker's Coy was not in the battle at Oriskany and only joined the remnants as they withdrew; *PA Pension Application S22208* of James Dickson. Benjamin's brother James stated that Whitaker's Coy was in the battle. Another mystery.

383 *Colbrath Journal*, 29. He wrote that Herkimer's message to Gansevoort said 1,000 militia were on the march; Butler to Carleton, 27Aug77. Butler wrote there were 900; Claus to Knox, 16Oct77, stated "upwards of 800"; St. Leger to Burgoyne, 27Aug77, reported "a reinforcement of eight hundred militia"; MacKenna to Abbe Montgolfier, 10Aug77 found in the Archives of Quebec, LG V-666. MacKenna wrote – "attacked 1000 Bostonnais"; Wm Willett, 51. Wm wrote 1,000. His father's narrative in Appendix III did not give a number; Juvinus (believed to have been Marinus Willett), "General Harkemer's Battle, A New Song to the Tune of the British Boys" *[Willett, Juvinus]* written at Albany, 7Dec77, NYHS, Willett Mss Collection, Folder 1775-77. This heroic poem advised 760 men; Letter of James F. Morrison to Watt, 3Nov93. Morrison believes the Bde raised 800-900 out of a potential 1,200+; CHSNY, VIII, 303. In '72, Gov Tryon visited the county and Sir Wm Johnson mustered three regts of the Bde for his inspection. Tryon reported they numbered "upwards of 1,400 effective men." Therefore, the four regts might easily have been 1,800+ men in '72, before the defection of loyalists for the RHE, KRR NY and the Ind Dept.

384 *TCMN*, Vol.XIV, No.10 (Aug 1994). NYPA S11435 of Henry Snook, son of 1Lieut Wm Snook of Pettingell's Coy; *NYPA W15969* widow of Evert Van Eps. Van Eps' son recalled his father having a horse shot out from under him at Oriskany. Van Eps was a Pte in Fonda's Coy of Exempts, but he may have been allowed a mount due to age or a handicap.

385 *TCMN*, Vol.XIV, No.10 (Aug 1994). NYPA S8537 of Abraham J. Quackenboss of

Endnotes

Capt Jacob Gardinier's Coy, Third Regiment; Morrison research. NYPA W16396. The widow of Johan Jost Scholl recalled that all of Rechtor's Coy was assigned to this duty, but it is clear from other pension applications that some of his men served in the battle.

386 JA Scott, 203.

387 *TCMN*, Vol.XV, No.1 (Sep 1994). NYPA W16273 of Pte Henry Gamps [Krembs, etc...] of Capt Andrew Dillenbach's Coy; ibid, Vol.XIV, No.10 (Aug 1994). NYPA's R731&R372. Pte Peter P. Bellinger in Ittig's Company, Fourth Regt was ordered "to return to Fort Herkimer and from there to go to Little Falls about six miles east."

388 Butler to Carleton, 15Aug77.

389 Based upon occurrences in the ravine, it is Morrison's contention that the Third Regt was split around the wagon convoy. With little doubt, the following coys of the Third were engaged in the later battle: 1st — Jacob Gardinier's; 2nd — John James Davis's; 5th — Samuel Pettingal's and that of Jelles Fonda, which was perhaps numbered the 9th. This grouping of coys did not follow the order of march prescribed in Guy Johnson's regulations which would have placed the 1st and 5th coys in the leading wing, (ie., ahead of the wagons) and the 2nd and 9th in the following wing.

390 Colour of horse: Thomas Jones, I, 344; Details of halt: Willett, Juvinus.

391 Location of halt: Letter of 1977 from Roger Myers, Historic Site Assistant, Oriskany Battlefield, Central NYS Park & Recreation Commission; Paul M. Keesler, *One Quarter Mile to Go, the Bicentennial Re-creation of the March of the Tryon County Militia and the Battle of Oriskany August 4,5&6, 1977* (Holland Patent: NY Sportsman Magazine & NYS Muzzleloaders Assoc. Inc., 1977) 22 (map); Capt Henry Staring: Watt & Morrison, *Campaign of 1777*, 165; MacWethy, 165.

392 Maryly B. Penrose, *Mohawk Valley Revolutionary War Pension Abstracts* (Bowie, MD: Heritage Books, Inc., 1989) 26. From the NYPA S23644 of John Frank; Watt & Morrison, *Campaign of 1777*, 179.

393 Morrison research. The deposition of Henry Flanders in support of the NYPA W16396 of the widow of Johan Jost Scholl; Henry Flanders: Watt & Morrison, *Campaign of 1777*, 181; Frederick Helmer: ibid, 180.

394 Sponable/Spanable: ibid, 182. Capt Rechtor's 6th Coy; Ken D. Johnson, 573. NYPA W11519. Elizabeth Spanable recalled that John was in Capt Frederick Getman's Coy, but this may have been earlier or later. She says that John had been "about five miles west of Herkimer" when he was captured; MacWethy, 152; Sponable/Spanable's captivity: Simms, *Frontiersman*, II, 109; James F. Morrison, *A History of Fulton County in the Revolution [Fulton County]* (Gloversville: Author, 1977) 47. Sponable was taken to Canada and imprisoned there until released in '81, which suggests that his captors were Mississaugas; Jacob J. Klock: Watt & Morrison, *Campaign of 1777*, 162.

395 Elmer, II-4, 187.

396 The exact number of Oneida and allied warriors who joined Herkimer is unknown. The village of Oriska housed about fifty souls. (Schuyler to Laurens, 15Mar7, Penrose, *Indian Affairs*, 119). The normal ratio of 1/4–1/3 warriors suggests about 15 came from that village. They were joined by allied warriors, such as the two Kahnawakes who were in the locale and probably Tuscaroras from Ganaghsaraga and Oneidas from nearby Old and New Oneida; Cruikshank, *Butler's Rangers*, 36. Although he has proven remarkably accurate in his facts, he cited no sources for his contention of 60 participants; Stevens, *Allies*, 1230. Stevens agrees with Cruikshank's number of 60 rebel Indian participants as does Graymont, 132; Interview with Polly Doxtator, 1877 found in the Draper Mss,

Series U (Frontier War Papers), Vol.11, 196-97. From stories related by her family, she recalled that "perhaps a hundred" participated.

397 Bloomfield, 65-66. Bloomfield stated the Oneidas were the most warlike and competent of the Six Nations, but his sentiment likely mirrored the fashion of the times of praising one's friends and disdaining one's enemies.

398 Oneida participation: Stevens, *Allies*, 1230en2284. He noted that most of the evidence of Oneida participation came from later testimony and cited several 1850's pension applications; Honyery Doxtator Tewahangaraghkan: Graymont, 132&197. Doxtator was made a U.S. Capt on 1Jan79. The 1828 declaration of Peter Doxtator transcribed in Penrose, *Indian Affairs*, 350. Stated that Peter was the son of Honyery. He gave his father's name as Tewahangaraghkan and advised that the name, Doxtator, a corruption of the German name Dockstader from the Valley, was adopted after the war; Senagena, Honyery's wife and his son: Graymont, 134; JA Scott, 224. From Frank Moore, *Diary of the American Revolution*. Scott's quote from Moore indicated that Doxtator's wife was armed with pistols and that his son was with him. Moore's source for this information is unknown; Honyery's wife's name was found in an interview with Elijah Skenando, Draper Mss, U, Vol.11, 243-44; A declaration of Peter Doxtator in 1852 transcribed in Penrose, *Indian Affairs*, 351. Peter, son of Honyery gave his mother's Christian name as Dolly, née Cobus; Honyost Tewahangaraghkan: Jinney Doxtator's declaration, 22Dec1852 transcribed in Penrose, *Indian Affairs*, 354. Jinney was the wife of Honyost Doxtator, who had been a Lieut; Henry Cornelius Haunnagwasuke: Stevens, *Allies*, 1230; Blatcop: Graymont, 135; Thomas & Henry Spencer: ibid, 132,134; Stevens, *Allies*, 1230 and MacWethy, 177; James Powless Wakarantharaus: Henry Wakarantharaus Powlis's (Powless) declaration, 23Aug1853, transcribed in Penrose, *Indian Affairs*, 360. James Powless was promoted to Capt in '78 and served under Col Louis; Louis Atayataghronghta: Pension file of Nicholas Cusick in Penrose, *Indian Affairs*, 365. Cusick advised that Atayataghronghta was also known as "Colonel Luie or Lewis Cooke"; Stevens, *Allies*, 368&1230. Stevens offered many references to Louis' early orientation towards the Whigs. Due to his black blood, he was sometimes called "Black Louis"; ibid, 392. Louis was fluent in French and well versed in English. Obviously, he spoke Mohawk, the primary language at Kahnawake, and likely other dialects of the region; Reverend Eleazer Williams, "The Life of Colonel Louis Cook," Papers of Franklin B. Hough (New York State Archives, u.p., ca. 1851). May be found in the website of Darren Bonaparte — <www.wampumchronicles.com>; Graymont, 197. Schuyler promoted Louis to LtCol in the Continental army in '79. See, a "List of Indians to have Commissions", NYPL, *Schuyler Papers*, Box 14.

399 Demuth: MacWethy, 169; Watt & Morrison, *Campaign of 1777*, 144,150,166,171; Helmer: NYPA W17067 of Adam F. & Anna (née Bellinger) Helmer; A letter by McKesson, Kingston, 12Aug77, transcribed in the *Clinton Papers*, II, 212. Document #698. This details Adam Helmer's testimony of his role as a scout sent to advise Gansevoort; Graymont, 132; MacWethy, 169. Named him as John Adam F. Helmer; Folts: MacWethy, 169. He named the third man as Hon Jost Folts. This came to light in 1930 when the pension papers of John Adam Helmer were examined.

400 *Colbrath Journal*, 29.

401 NYPA W16244 of Pte John Duesler of Cox's Regt, who may have been in hearing range of the 6Aug council stated that he wanted to wait for Gen Arnold. This was likely a trick of memory, as Arnold was not in the picture until Schuyler dispatched him on 13Aug.

Endnotes

402 Stone, *Brant*, 234. In statements of Ptes George Walter, Second Regt and Henry Seeber, First Regt, Cox and Paris were named. It was mentioned that others joined in the baiting; Milo Nellis, "Col. Ebenezer Cox," The Palatiner, Aug 1952 found in the *Stone Arabia Battle Chapter Newsletter*, SAR, 1995, 15. Jacob Klock was the son of Georg (Jury) Klock and Cox's sister; NYPA S13037 of Henry Flanders. He named Helmer, a committeeman; W. Max Reid, *The Mohawk Valley, Its Legends and Its History* (New York & London: The Knickerbocker Press, 1901) 418; Penrose, *Mohawk Valley*, 226. Peter Bellinger was married to Delia Herkimer, sister of Nicholas; ibid, 253. The mother of John Frey's wife, Gertrude Schoemaker, was born a Herkimer.

403 Ernest Green, "Frey," *OHSPR*, Vol.33 (1939), 54-59. The story of Philip Rockell Frey's escape from the Valley, his service at Oriskany and later as Ens, 8th Regt; Bolton to Carleton, 21May78 found in HP, AddMss21873. Frey a Vol in the 8th Regt at Stanwix, "[A]t the utmost risk of his life, made his escape from the Rebel country where his family have since gone through great persecutions in their persons and estates for their attachment to the Crown"; Penrose, *Mohawk Valley*, 253. Born to Henrick and Anna Margreth (née Keyser) Frey, 9Oct59 — christened Philippus.

404 Watt & Morrison, *Campaign of 1777*, 77.

405 First to run: Stone, *Brant*, I, 234. From the *Travels of President Dwight*, III, 192; Flankers: Willett, Juvinus; Statements by Adam Miller and George Walter cited in Stone, *Brant*, I, 235. These confirmed that an advance guard and flankers were set; Statement by Conrad Mowers cited in Simms, *Frontiersman*, II, 70. Stated that a van was set and that three of its number were "cut off," i.e., killed; William W. Campbell, 79. Stated that Spencer insisted on a van and flankers; Cruikshank, *Butler's Rangers*, 36; Indians as flankers: Evidence on this matter is very sparse. It would have been the height of folly not to employ Indians in this role, yet it is clear that many Tryon militiamen distrusted their friendship; Stevens, *Allies*, 1236. Stevens placed some rebel Indians in the flankers and vanguard, but gave no clear source for his conclusion.

406 Willett, Juvinus. "We then proceeded in three Files"; Stone, *Brant*, I, 235. He wrote, "They marched in files of two deep." "Files two deep" was delineated in Guy Johnson's '72 manual, 21, but Juvinus was contemporary to the event and, as such, I accepted his information. Yet, it must be recognized that Guy Johnson's militia regulations formed the militia in two ranks, as was the practice of British Regulars in America. Johnson's regulations do not contain a "three file" marching manoeuvre.

407 A commonly used, contemporary diminutive for a British Light Infantryman.

408 Scouts: Cruikshank & Watt, *KRR NY*, 17; Pomroy Jones, *Annals and Recollections of Oneida County* (Rome: author, 1851) 344.

409 John Norton, Carl F. Klinck & James J. Talman, eds, *The Journal of Major John Norton 1816* (Toronto: Champlain Society, 1970) 272. "[B]y some neglect, — there was not provided a sufficient Quantity of Arms for these Warriors, so that nearly one half of them fought with no other arms than a Short Spear or Tomohawk."

410 Stevens, *Allies*, 1233. Stevens contended that the Ft Hunter men and some Onondagas joined Brant. That Deserontyon, Kanonraron and Onoghsokte, all senior war captains, would subordinate themselves to Brant seems unlikely, but to take side with him was understandable, as they shared concern for the vulnerability of the two Valley castles.

411 ibid, 1231-34. An excellent analysis of the nations involved; Ind Dept commissioners to Henry Laurens, President of Congress, 12Jan78, transcribed in Penrose,

Indian Affairs, 103. "[T]he Senecas and Cayugas in particular... the latter... continued to threaten revenge for the loss and disgrace they sustained in the engagement with the late Genl. Herkemeyer."

412 Claus, *Anecdotes of Brant*, 28. Claus wrote this account when his rancour against Butler was at its peak, so exactly what the Maj's position on a parlay with the militia is unknown; Cruikshank & Watt, *KRR NY*, 17-18; Graymont, 132; Stevens, *Allies*, 1234-36. Stevens made no mention of hesitancy on anyone's part.

413 Corduroy roads were a common feature in North America and were constructed by laying logs across the roadway in wet, boggy areas. The timbers' buoyancy and toughness created a strong surface, but the roadway could be treacherous, shifting and bucking abruptly.

414 JA Scott, 206. He offered no source for this information.

415 Jos Robertaccio, a member of the Oriskany Battlefield Committee, advised that a plan of the ambush site was developed using aerial, infra-red photography to define the old roadway; Interview and correspondence by author with John Auwaerter, Research Assistant, State University of New York, College of Environmental Science and Forestry. John participated in a 1999 study of the battlefield which cast some doubt on previous conclusions about the placement of the road. The results of this investigation have yet to be published.

416 St. Leger to Burgoyne, 27Aug77. "[T]o suffer the attack to begin with the troops in front, while [the Indians] should be on both flanks and rear"; Claus, *Anecdotes of Brant*, 28. "Brant signalized himself highly by advancing on the Rebels Rear and harassing their Retreat"; Butler to Carleton, 15Aug77. "Sir John was posted on the road to give the Enemy a Volley as they advanced... Myself, with the Indians, & 20 Rangers were posted to flank them in the woods."

417 In European warfare, it was not generally acceptable to single out officers as targets, but the practice was common in democratic America amongst Americans of both political stripes whose anger ignored old-world niceties; Thomas Ainslie,*Canada Preserved – The Journal of Captain Thomas Ainslie* , Sheldon Cohen, ed. (The Copp Clark Publishing Company, 1968) 27. In the British view it was also unacceptable to snipe at sentinels. Of the siege of Quebec in '75, Ainslie, a Scots-Canadian, wrote, "Lie in wait to shoot a sentry! a deed worthy of Yankey men of war." By '77, such compunction had disappeared. St. Leger set his Indians and Germans to that very task.

418 Historians debate about whether ambushers were deployed on both sides of the road. Immediately to the west of the eastern, or first ravine, the north side fell off abruptly to very marshy ground. Probably, no one was stationed there. Next came the deep ravine on the north side, which was skirted by the roadway. The slope of the walls of this feature would have prevented posting men along that stretch. Where the road ran westward on somewhat higher ground, there was no reason why men could not have been secreted on both sides of the road. However, it was clearly preferable to fire downwards into the militia, as "overs" from level firing might hit your own men, but there were very few positions of appropriate height; Norton, 273. "The arrangement for the Battle was made about half way between the Fort and a Stream called Orhiska or Ariska [after Oriska village.] The Line extended obliquely to the right, along the path by which the Enemy were to advance. The left Wing extended a small distance beyond the path. Immediately where it [the road] met the Line, Sir John Johnson, with a part of his Regiment, took position. The Ondowaga [Seneca] were on the right." This reference to the "left Wing" indicated that men were posted on the north side.

419 *Colbrath Journal*, 29.

420 No record has been found confirming when the Jägers were dispatched to the ambush. I see two possibilities: a) the loyalists failed to mention the Germans, as they wanted all the credit for themselves and their Indian allies, or b) the Germans were dispatched to Sir John in the early morning. St. Leger should have recorded their presence, but on that count we must consider LtCol von Kreutzbourg's comment that St. Leger was very anti-German and he may have chosen to ignore them; Robertaccio research. Kreutzbourg to Gall transcribed in "German allies" (NYHS, 1873). This source quotes Lieut Hildebrand's report stating that Oriskany was "not the great victory which it is represented as, but a close fought affair." While this note has the ring of truth, it should be recognized that it was not necessarily the comment of a participant; DePeyster, *Career*, cxxxiii. From von Eelking, *Deutchen Hülfstruppen*, I, 3-23. "On the 5th, a relieving column of nearly 1,000 men drew near. St. Leger was aware of its approach in time, and for its reception placed an amuscade in the woods. This for the greater part[?] consisted of regular[?] troops, and among these were the Hesse-Hanau Jagers"; John Merz research. Clifford Neal Smith, *Mercenaries from Hessen-Hanau Who Remained in Canada and the United States after the American Revolution*, German-American Genealogical Research Monograph Number 5 (McNeal, AZ: Westland Publications, 1976) This source included transcripts of Mss held in the Staatsarchiv, Marburg, Bestand, Germany. From regtl rolls, Smith noted that two Jägers went missing on 6Aug77. Their fate is unknown. Willett's highly detailed report of his sortie made no mention of killing, capturing or being opposed by Hanau riflemen. I conclude that it is very likely that the two men were lost at Oriskany; Who commanded the Jägers at Oriskany is unknown. Von Kreutzbourg to his Crown Prince at Oswego, 5Sep77, transcribed from the *Jaeger Corps' Diary* reported that Lieut Hildebrand led the Vacant Company at Stanwix. As 1Lieut Phillip Hildebrand was the ranking officer of the coy, I have assumed that he had the honour. Another possibility was his 2Lieut, Johan August Krafft.

421 Butler to Carleton, 15Aug77. "[T]his disposition was soon after a little altered by the Indians while the Enemy were advancing."

422 William W. Campbell, 84; Morrison research: NYPA W16244 of John Duesler's widow. This source claimed the ambush was sprung between 8 and 9 o'clock; NYPA S28937 of Henery J. Walrath. This application stated "between nine & ten o'clock."

423 Robertaccio research. In 1995, the U.S. Weather Service confirmed that violent windstorms occurred in the upper Mohawk Valley area in the late summer of '77.

424 Cruikshank, *Butler's Rangers*, 36.

425 Morrison research. The van: Moses Younglove's statement to his father Dec77, recorded by his brother Samuel Younglove, NYSL, Albany, Folder #42, item 11965; William W. Campbell, 84; Jacob Casler: Draper Mss, F10, 130-31; Watt & Morrison, *Campaign of 1777*, 179. Morrison records two Jacob Caslers as Ptes in Bellinger's Regt and notes that Jacob Sr. was in the van; MacWethy, 166. He listed three Jacob Casler's in Bellinger's and advised that Jacob H. was engaged at Oriskany; From this sparse evidence, it appears that the vanguard and perhaps the white flankers were chosen from the Fourth Regt.

426 Willett, Juvinus; Pomroy Jones, 344.

427 Samuel Younglove; An unauthorized digging on the battlefield in 1996 uncovered a period surgeon's instrument which may have belonged to Moses Younglove.

428 Cox's voice: William W. Campbell, 101; Forming in roadway: Nelson Greene, *The Old Mohawk Turnpike Book* (Fort Plain: the author, 1924) 277; Cox kills militia-

man: Moses Younglove Affidavit, in Stone, *Brant,* I, App. IV. The two Younglove documents, i.e., Moses' personal deposition, given to John Barclay of the Albany committee shortly after his return from captivity, and his notes and stories recorded by his brother Samuel, were indicative of the passion of the battle, but are so contradictory and highly coloured as to be extremely suspect.

429 James F. Morrison lists a Pte Henry Smith as an Oriskany participant in Bellinger's Regt. As a bodyguard, Smith would have been chosen for his cool head and superb marksmanship.

430 Allan D. Foote with James Morrision, Joseph Robertaccio & Alan Sterling, *Liberty March – The Battle of Oriskany* (Utica: North Country Books, 1998) 193. Foote provided Rufus Grider's superb drawing of the sniper's large powder horn. The scrimshaw work included "patterns, birds, trees, fishes, antelopes, deer, cows" and the inscription, "James Clement 1757." Smith thought his foe was native. While an Indian may have carried the horn, it is probable that James Clement was an Ind Dept ranger. Lieut Lewis was the only Clement listed as serving in the dept at the time, but he had an older brother James who would have been 58 in '77. Lewis was not the carrier of the horn, as he lived long after the battle. Of course, it is possible, that Lewis had loaned James's horn to a native or James had traded it. Clement genealogists do not know the date of James' s death. Considering all of this evidence, I believe James was the sniper.

431 Cruikshank, *Butler's Rangers,* 36. "Elated by the sight, and maddened by the smell of blood and gunpowder, many of the Indians rushed from their coverts to complete the victory with spear and hatchet"; A letter dated Fish-kill, 21Aug77, cited in *The Remembrancer or, Impartial Repository of Public Events for the Year 1777* (London: J. Almon, 1778) 394-95. This was an extract of a letter from Albany of 18Aug. The information was from a Colonel "Wallers" who was generally believed to have been Marinus Willett; Senecas' Drunk: Stevens, *Allies,* 1234. Denied by Blacksnake in Conversations with Gov Blacksnake, Draper Mss4S23-25.

432 *Chainbreaker,* 88. From the Draper Mss, 4-S-24; Graymont, 216. These youngsters were not chastised for their cowardice. In native society, individuals were allowed to make such choices; Red Jacket later became a renowned orator, political leader and warrior.

433 Morrison's transcript of the deposition of Garred Van Brocklen (Ens Garret S. Van Bracklin, 4th Coy, Third Regt,) 13Jun78, found in the NYHS, NYC, Tryon County Mss.

434 Morrison research. Draper Mss, Series F, V.10, 130-31.

435 NYPA W15969 of Evert Van Eps' widow, transcribed in *TCMN,* Vol.II, No.1 (1983).

436 Roy Najecki research. (George) Townshend, (1st Marquis, Master-General of Ordnance), "Rules and Orders for the Discipline of the Light Infantry companies in His Majesty's Army in Ireland 1772," in Captain R.H. Smythies, *Historical Records of the 40th (2nd Somersetshire Regiment)* (Devonport: 1894) App.IV, 549. "It is to be particularly observed that each file has an entire dependence upon itself and that the Firelocks of the front and rear Men, are never to he unloaded at the same time, when the front Rank Man Fires, the Rear Rank Man is to make Ready and step up briskly before his Comrade, but is by no means to discharge his Firelock untill the other has loaded, and then he is to step briskly before the Rear Rank Man, and this to be followed untill a signal shall be given for ceasing to Fire. This Mutual Defence and Confidence is one of the most Essential Principles of Light Infantry... The Men when in a wood are to be taught to Cover themselves with Trees by placing the Right Foot about six inches behind the left, and presenting to the Right of the tree, and after firing to step back two paces, and give Room to the Rear Rank man to come

up to the same Tree and to fire alternately, according to the directions before mentioned"; Claus Reuter collection. That the Jägers also employed a similar tactic is proven in Virginia Rimaldy, tr., *Orders of the Field Jaeger Corps from May 7, 1777 to April 30, 1783*. In a detailed order dated at L'Assomption 4Sep79, the following instruction was issued by von Kreutzbourg. "If the Jaegers have an encounter in the woods, they are to proceed two by two and one only will be allowed to shoot at one time, so they will be able to assist one another"; J.F.C. Fuller, *British Light Infantry in the Eighteenth Century* (London: Hutchinson & Co., 1925 – facsimile edition, 1991); Ian McCulloch, Ian, "'Within Ourselves...' The Development of British Light Infantry in North America During the Seven Years' War", *Canadian Military History*, Volume 7, No.2 (Spring 1998) 41-55. A study of the development of light infantry tactics during the 7 Yrs War in America and a commentary on the Rev War.

437 Townshend. "The Light Infantry are to be taught to fire at Marks, and each Soldier is to find out the proper Measure of Powder for his own Firelock and to make up his Cartridges accordingly."

438 Von Kreutzbourg, Oswego , 5Sep77, in the *Jaeger Corps' Diary*. "I found that the muskets (rifles?), which were distributed among this company during their hurried departure, were not worth a shot of powder."

439 Norton, 273. "A celebrated War Chief of the Ondowaga [Seneca,] – (of the Ottigaumi [Fox/ Squacki] race,) appeared to have fallen by their Fire"; Stevens, *Allies*, 1105; Blacksnake's Conversations, Draper Mss, He denied a story circulating in the 1850s which claimed that the Indians shot the loyalists "in their rear, supposing they had fired on them."

440 Simms, *Schoharie*, 307-13. Simms claimed that Han Yerry (Doxtator) Tewahangaraghkan was captured during the Sullivan Expedition and hacked to pieces by the Senecas. This tale was apocryphal. A ritual mutilation may have been done to an Oneida, but not Honyery, as his sister-in-law, Jinney Doxtator, stated that he survived the war and died at 94 on 4Jul1839 at Oneida Castle. See, her declaration transcribed in Penrose, *Indian Affairs*, 352; His wound: JA Scott, 224.

441 This story told by Dr. George Lintner, a Schoharie Dominie (pastor) was cited in Simms, *Frontiersman*, 108-09. Lintner claimed that Louis said "there is one of the black serpents!" An unlikely exclamation from a man of mixed black and red blood.

442 An 1877 interview with Elijah Skenando found in the Draper Mss, Series U, Vol.11, 243-44.

443 As Senagena rode to the settlements to seek help for the Bde's wounded after the withdrawal from the battlefield, did the rebel Indians remained to the very end and, more puzzling, did they count as part of the 150 who survived?

444 Northern Frontier Project Team, SUNY, "The Northern Frontier Special Resource Study," 4. The study provides this translation of the Oneida name for the Oriskany battlefield.

445 George Walter: Simms, *Frontiersman*, II, 92-93; Merckley and Fralick: ibid, II, 102-03.

446 Morrison research. NYPA R9897 of Susannah Snell for her husband, Peter.

447 NYPA W16244, widow of John Duesler.

448 Depositions of John Garrison & Garred Van Brocklen, Caughnawaga, 13Jun78, transcribed by James F. Morrison from the NYHS, Tryon County Mss; Simms, *Frontiersman*, II, 92.

449 Bronk-a-horse must be an English corruption of a Mohawk name; Simms, *Frontiersman*, 95-96; Stone, *Brant*, II, AppV, xxxvfn.

450 NYPA S28937 of Henery Walrath; Most warriors carried a stoutly-made, woven fibre "prisoner" cord as part of their war equipment.

451 Willett, Juvinus. This source named Van Veghten; Samuel Younglove . Reported the incident, but did not name the individual; Van Veghten was specifically named in William Wills to Gov Geo Clinton, 10Feb78, transcribed in *Clinton Papers*, III, 741.

452 Jacob Seeber: Stone, *Brant*, I, 236-37fn. Named Seeber as being responsible for introducing this tactic without giving recognition to his rank; Jacob Seeber was the son of LtCol William of the First Regt; Penrose, *Mohawk Valley*, 319. This source offers details of Jacob's earlier service in the Valley as a capt of the 4NY at German Flats in '76; Jacob Beeler/Peeler: Henry Seeber credited Pte Jacob Beeler/Peeler with implementing this simple tactic throughout the Brigade. See, *TCMN*, Vol.VI, No.9 (1987). From Greene, *Mohawk Valley — Gateway to the West*, III, 833; Watt & Morrison, *Campaign of 1777*, 175. Morrison placed Beeler in Klock's Second Regt.

453 Butler to Carleton, 15Aug77.

454 Simms, *Frontiersman*, II, 93-94.

455 *Remembrancer 1777*, 394. Quoted a letter — "[T]heir cartridges being made up of three buck shot and a bullet." The writer claimed 300 Indians were killed and wounded at Oriskany. Norton stated there were only 500 Iroquois at Stanwix and that not all of these fought at Oriskany. We can be positive there were not 60% casualties.

456 Samuel Younglove. Moses reported that the defensive circles held against all charges by the enemy, red and white. How doubtful! Indeed, reading Samuel's account, one wonders how any Royal Yorkers or Indians survived the fighting.

457 *TCMN*, Vol.XVII, No.6 (Feb 1998). A pre-1916 booklet "Colonel Samuel Clyde — A Brief Biography" found by James F. Morrison in the Cherry Valley folder, Gloversville Free Library. The booklet noted that Clyde had served as a NH Capt in '58 under Abercrombie at Ticonderoga and Bradstreet at Ft Frontenac; Clyde Papers cited in Simms, *Frontiersman*, II, 80fn.

458 ibid, II, 72-73. Herkimer's actual view of the battle would have been extremely limited, yet he made many excellent observations and dispositions.

459 NYPA W20522 of George M. Lonis's widow transcribed in *TCMN*, Vol.XVIII, No.3 (Nov 1998). Information about Henry Sits was included in an affidavit supporting the George Lonis' widow's application. Lonis was also spelled Lonas/Lohns.

460 Simms, *Frontiersman*, II, 96-97; Watt & Morrison, *Campaign of 1777*, 177. Garret Walrath was a prisoner at the battle's end. He must have been recaptured in the later fighting.

461 Samuel Younglove.

462 This Sjt was one of three men — Duncan Murchison, Alexander McPherson, or Murdock McLean. See, Watt & Morrison, *Campaign of 1777*, 45.

463 Moses Younglove Affidavit, in Stone, *Brant*, I, App. IV.

464 Jägers were armed with a short hunting sword rather than a bayonet. The sword was a weapon of last resort rather than a weapon of attack. See Mollo & MacGregor, plate#80 and a drawing in Philip R.N. Katcher, *Encyclopedia of British, Provincial and German Army Units 1775-1783* (Harrisburg: Stackpole Books, 1973) 117.

465 Henery Walrath Pension.

466 Singleton: *"Fidelity"*, Newsletter of Toronto Branch, UEL Assoc, Vol.24, No.4 (1999). Singleton settled in CT#3, Fredericksburgh, in '84, but moved in '88 to the mouth of the Moira R. near the Mohawk settlement to trade. Indian traders had command of the appropriate Indian dialect required to conduct business; Davis: Moses Younglove Affidavit in Stone, *Brant*, I, App. IV; Watt & Morrison, *Campaign of 1777*, 78,85,86. Davis had been brought up by Cherokee Indians and may very well have taken revenge in this manner.

Endnotes

467 Simms, *Frontiersman*, II, 105; MacWethy, 168.

468 Stone, *Brant*, I, 237.

469 Black powder is extremely sensitive to moisture. Water entering the muzzle or touchhole can drown the main charge and cause misfires, making it necessary to worm out the ball and main charge and swab the barrel dry before reloading. Moisture on lock parts can spoil the priming. A few drops in the pan are often enough to dissolve the priming into ineffectual black soup.

470 The KRR was equipped for a major campaign from stores in Montreal, I believe to a scale similar to that recommended by many British experts. For example, see Thomas Simes, *The Regulator or Instructions to Form the Officer and Complete the Soldier* (London: 1780) 13.

471 An address by Maj MM Jones delivered during ceremonies at Oriskany and reported in the *Daily Herald* (Utica, NY) July 30, 1883, 2.

472 Butler to Carleton, 15Aug77; Stone, *Brant*, I, 237; Graymont, 134-35. From the Draper Mss; *Chainbreaker*, 128-130.

473 Robertaccio research. Several typically German large-calibre rifle balls were dug up in the 1990s in the SW corner of the defensive perimeter near the monument. As a great deal of earth was moved about during the building of the monument and the pathway to the interpretative centre, it is difficult to say where these balls were fired from. A likely site is along the edge of the deep ravine, where a little height could be gained for observation into the blowdown.

474 Simms, *Schoharie*, 263.

475 The account: Simms, *Frontiersman*, II, 93; Peter Deygart's report, 9Aug77, in *Clinton Papers*, II, 204. He named Wm Johnson as a fatality; William of Canajoharie: Fox was mistaken, the redoubtable William was very much alive the following year. See, Hazel C. Mathews, *The Mark of Honour* (Toronto: University of Toronto Press, 1965) 57. She noted that Capt Wm Johnson was cited for his humane actions at Cherry Valley in '78; Letter from Wm Johnson Jr. to U.S. officers explaining the conduct of the Indians at Cherry Valley quoted in Graymont, 190.

476 Junior captain: It may appear strange that the Regt's junior capt led the reinforcement, but Maj Gray and Capts Daly and Alex McDonell were very likely at work along The Carry and young McDonell was the most senior officer available. As well, it makes sense that the Col's Coy had been assigned to the camp guard, when the Light Coy was sent to the ambush; Troops involved in reinforcement: See KRR NY casualty returns, Watt & Morrision, *Campaign of 1777*, 38-63; Total number sent: MacKenna to Montgolfier, 10Aug77. The priest wrote that Sir John had 80 troops, but it is unclear whether he referred to the force in the morning or the reinforcement in the afternoon.

477 Byrne & Lipscomb: Simms, *Frontiersman*, I, 306. Byrne was given his land in Sir William Johnson's will; NAC, WO28/9, 50. Byrne was a "a Volunteer from Quebec"; For both men, see Cruikshank & Watt, KRR NY, 175,219.

478 Simms, *Frontiersman*, II, 74. Simms believed this gunfire was the requested signal. This would seem unlikely as its timing was too late.

479 Stone, *Brant*, I, 238; Stone, *Burgoyne & St. Leger*, 182-83.

480 Dawson, I, 243. Some sources claim that the Royal Yorkers exchanged hats with militia casualties and prisoners rather than turning their coats. Dawson wrote that there were few distinguishing differences between the hats worn by either side; Conversation with Michael D. Thompson, recreated 2MA, Continental Line. Michael advised that on 14May77, Bailey's Regt was issued 102 hunting shirts and 47 suits of clothes. He believes these shirts were natural in colour, i.e., light brown;

Rebellion in the Mohawk Valley

At the 200th anniversary of the Oriskany battle, the recreated Royal Yorkers reversed coats to simulate Butler's ruse. The effect was dramatic. At 25 yds, their appearance was remarkably similar to three nearby men clothed in natural linen frocks, illustrating how the ruse was so effective against the distraught militia in their smoke-filled lair 200 years previous.

481 The ruse was by no means far fetched. Captain John Knox, *The Siege of Quebec, and the Campaigns in North America 1757-1760* (1759 – reprinted, London: The Folio Society, 1976) 19. Knox tells of British Regulars wearing their coats reversed aboard a ship bound for America. This was a common practice to keep the coats clean in the cramped and dirty lower decks. Observing them, a Massachusetts privateer reported they were Frenchmen.

482 Nelson Greene, ed., *History of the Mohawk Valley – Gateway to the West 1614-1925 [Gateway]* (4 vols., Chicago: S.J. Clarke, 1925) III, 832-33. Adam Miller stated, "the enemy advanced with fixed bayonets, [a] close attack... without the firing of guns from either side."

483 Col Waller's (Willett's?) account, Fishkill, 18Aug77, quoted in the *Remembrancer 1777*. "[T]he regulars marched on very boldly three deep"; Conversation with Michael D. Thompson, 2MA recreated. He advised that MA troops continued to employ three ranks in this period and, as noted in a previous chapter, the militia was said to have marched in a long column of threes.

484 Jacob Sammons: Watt & Morrison, *Campaign of 1777*, 163. Sammons was 2Lieut of John James Davis's 2nd Coy; Jacob Gardinier: Simms, *Schoharie*, 263. His blacksmith shop was on the river opposite Caughnawaga; Gardinier's struggle and wounding: Stone, *Brant*, I, 238-39; Simms, *Schoharie*, 263. Simms recorded that Gardinier received 13 wounds.

485 Watt & Morrison, *Campaign of 1777*, 178. Adam Miller, Third Regt from the town of Mohawk in the 2nd Coy's beat.

486 McDonell's death: Claus to Knox, 16Oct77. "Captn Lieut McDonald of Sir John's Regt... killed"; Butler to Carleton, 15Aug77. "Of the New Yorkers, Capt. McDonald was killed"; Miller's wound: NYPA S11073 of Adam Miller.

487 William W. Campbell, 85.

488 Waiter: A less demeaning U.S. army term for "servant"; Gardinier continued to fight: William W. Campbell, 85.

489 Walter: Watt & Morrison, *Campaign of 1777*, 177; MacWethy, 153; Dillenback: ibid, 144; Watt & Morrison, *Campaign of 1777*, 162. Andreas was Capt, 4th Coy of Klock's; Dillenback's fight: Stone, *Brant*, I, 240.

490 Casler: Neither Morrison nor MacWethy listed a George Casler in the First Regt; Watt & Morrison, *Campaign of 1777*, 173. Listed a John Casler from the town of Canajoharie; Cox: ibid, Morrison listed William Cox, First Regt as an Oriskany participant; Diefendorf's death: I combined two accounts. Simms, *Frontiersman*, II, 97-98 and Draper Mss, F, V10, 130-31.

491 Butler to Carleton, 15Aug77.

492 Greene, *Gateway*, III, 832.

493 Butler to Carleton, 15Aug77; Stone, *Burgoyne & St. Leger*, 190fn; de Peyster, *Career*, cxxiv-v.

494 Ken D. Johnson, 469. NYPA W20452 widow of John Leathers. This document contained a deposition by Joseph Waggoner, giving this account; swarming: I came to this conclusion from the number and nature of Watts' wounds.

495 Norton, 273. "[A] remnant of the Enemy retreated... to a Pine Wood Thicket, of very difficult access, encumbered with fallen Trees, — where they could not be

assailed, but at great disadvantage. The Warriors, returning from the pursuit and slaughter of the routed Enemy, had begun to surround this hold, when their Attention was called to their own encampment at the Fort, which from the firing they heard from that Quarter, — they had reason to suppose had been attacked." Norton was referring to Brant's men and the Valley Mohawks who had been pursuing the rearguard; *TCMN*, Vol.I, No.8 (1983). Victor Putman of De Graf's Coy, Third Regt stated that the enemy retreated on hearing musket and cannon fire at their encampments and Hugh McMaster of McMaster's Coy Third Regt stated, "the destruction of the whole militia was prevented" by the intervention of the sortie. NYPA W16645 widow of Hugh McMaster; Stone, *Brant*, I, 240; Graymont, 139.

496 Simms, *Frontiersman*, II, 79.

497 Only 130 left: James Dickson, S22208; 150 stood the field: Deygart to Albany committee Chairman, 9Aug77, in *Clinton Papers*, II, 203; 150 in a circle: *Willett, Juvinus*; This was likely the final circle in the "Pine Wood Thicket of difficult access" of Iroquoian memory; Morrison found that 30 of the 150 unwounded survivors were from Ittig's Coy!

498 Simms, *Frontiersman*, II, 98. Gave Putman's given name as Richard and claimed he was the Ens in Davis's Coy; Morrison has not found an Ens of that name at Oriskany. He noted the Ens of Davis' Coy was Garret S. Van Bracklin and that he was at the battle. Victor C. Putman had served as a Pte in Davis' Coy prior to Oriskany and he served as Lieut in the battle, but in which coy is not known. He served later as a Sjt and a Pte in various Third Regt Coys, 1778-80 and also in the Willett's NY Levies in '81. He never served as an Ens during the war. See, *TCMN*, Vol.I, No.8 (1983).

499 Miller's capture: *TCMN*, Vol.VI, No.9 (1987). From Greene, *History of the Mohawk Valley – Gateway to the West*, III, 832. That Miller was captured by Hare just after Davis' death was noted in this source; Wilson's death: Richard McGinnis, *Journal of Occurrences Respecting Our Suffering in the Late Rebellion*, Carol Lind, ed., NY Genealogical & Biographical Record, Vol.105, No.4 (Oct 1974) 198-99.

500 Narrative of Jacob Sammons cited in Stone, *Brant*, I, 242; Frederick Cristman's NYPA R1941 transcribed in *TCMN*, Vol.XIV, No.10 (1994). Cristman was a Pte of Capt Frank's Coy, Fourth Regt. "That the Indians belonging to the enemy endeavored to take the scalp of General Herkimer but... they did not succeed in their attempt."

501 Geo Lonis's widow's NYPA W20522. This was the only mention I have found of prisoners being taken by the militia at Oriskany. Lonis's captive was described as "a British soldier" and the horse as belonging to a "British officer." Perhaps he meant Tory in both references, yet every missing British and Loyalist officer noted in St. Leger's return has been accounted for. As well, other than St. Leger, there is no mention of "British" officers being mounted on this campaign, let alone participating in the ambush. Was Lonis mistaken, had he actually taken a militia officer's horse?

502 NYPA S23047 of Derick Van Vechten.

503 Jones's address reported in the *Daily Herald* (Utica, NY) 30Jul1883, 2.

504 Wounded carried out: William W. Campbell, 87. He noted that 40–50 wounded were carried, obviously the most seriously injured. The number makes sense. Considering their exhaustion, 130 whole men, even when assisted by Whitaker's coy, would be hard pressed to carry more than 50 wounded. Of course, this begs the question of how many grievously wounded men were abandoned to a frightening, lonely death in the woods; Morrison documented 56 men who were wounded at Oriskany and not captured. Four were officers who later died of their wounds.

In his exhaustive study, he noted 22 men whose wounds were in the upper body, which may have allowed them to walk out, assuming they had the strength. And, these men may have been considered in the "whole" category; Whitaker's Coy: Benjamin Dickson's pension, S22210. "Capt. Whitaker's Company however did not reach the ground until after the engagement when his men assisted in taking care of the wounded."

505 Watts's watch: MacWethy, 139. He recorded the name as "Fehling." Morrison believes this was Henry Nicholas Failing; Col Charles Briggs, Johnson Hall curator in the 1970s, advised me that he had seen the watch in the possession of the Failing family in his youth. Its whereabouts in 1976 was unknown. Briggs also mentioned that he had heard that a fusil, reputedly taken from a Yorker officer at Oriskany, was with some family in the Valley, but could not locate it. This is likely the fusil taken by 2Mjr Samuel Clyde and was probably Singleton's; Watts's sash: I believe Col Briggs told me that the Sanders family owned the sash.

506 NYPA W16396, widow of Johan Jost Scholl.

507 NYPA R8537 of Abraham J. Quackenboss.

508 Morrison research. John Lewis's deposition of 13Jun78 transcribed from NYHS, Tryon County Mss. Lewis was in the Third Regt.

509 Timmerman litter party: Morrison research. NYPA W21092, widow of Jacob J. Failing; Snell litter party: Morrison research. NYPA S13658 of Conrad Kilts, a Pte of Klock's from Stone Arabia.

510 Simms, *Frontiersman*, II, 79.

511 NYPA W19242, widow of John D. Failing.

512 An interview with Cornelius Doxtator in 1877 found in the Draper Mss, Series U, V11, 202-04.

513 JA Scott, 229.

514 William W. Campbell, 107.

515 These deaths lead to a question — of the fifty wounded carried from the ambush, how many others died?

516 Timmerman litter party: NYPA W21092, widow of Jacob J. Failing. This group arrived home on 9Aug; Snell litter party: NYPA S13658 of Conrad Kilts, a Pte of Klock's from Stone Arabia; MacWethy recorded five Snells who died at Oriskany. Frederick Jr., Joseph, Jacob, Johan (John) and Johan Jr.; Watt & Morrison, *Campaign of 1777*, 175,177. Morrison lists eight dead Snells, including Jacob Jr., a fifer.

517 Marinus Willett, *A Narrative of part of the Transactions at and near Fort Stanwix since the investiture of that place by the Enemy, given in Manuscript by Lieutenant-Colonel Marinus Willett of that Garrison, 11Aug77* appears as Appendix III in *Wm Willett*.

518 *Colbrath Journal*, 29.

519 ibid; His relationship to Capt Henry Diefendorf who died at Oriskany has not been established.

520 Adam Helmer to McKesson, 12Aug77, transcribed in *Clinton Papers*, II, 212. Helmer entered the fort at "one O'clock"; Willett Narrative, 11Aug77, in *Wm Willett*, App. III, 131. Willett said they arrived "about eleven o'clock"; *Colbrath Journal*, 29. His 6Aug77 entry stated they arrived between 8 and 9 o'clock in the morning; As Helmer was personally involved, perhaps he knew best. As Willett led the sortie, one might assume his memory would be most accurate. Colbrath, who wrote his journal on the day that events occurred, may have been the most accurate, yet such an early arrival would have allowed the sortie to be made long before the storm arrived. Another mystery of history.

Endnotes

521 Question of volunteers: Some historians believe that Willett called for volunteers. I believe he did not; Sortie Composition: The reported composition was strange. Willett's account indicated that most of the officers were Yorkers and that Massachusetts's men made up half the party. It makes little sense that Badlam's and Wesson's men provided a higher proportion of enlisted men, as the officers of each State were jealous of their prerogatives and unlikely to surrender control to officers from another. Perhaps Willett forgot, or ignored, the unfamiliar Massachusetts officers. It was very much in his interest to emphasize the work of the Yorkers and his propensity for self-aggrandisement must not be ignored; Artillery Coy: see Watt & Morrison, *Campaign of 1777*, 103,107-09; Savage: Adam Helmer to McKesson, 12Aug77, transcribed in *Clinton Papers*, II, 213.

522 Capt Allen: Morrison research. This was Capt Jacob Allen of Bailey's Regt. He was killed 19Sep77 at Freeman's Farm fighting Burgoyne. From, Secretary of the Commonwealth, *Massachusetts Soldiers and Sailors in the War of the Revolution* (17 Vols: Boston: Wright and Potter Printing Co., 1896) I, 154-55; Sortie composition: *Willett Narrative*, 11Aug77, in Wm Willett, App. III, 131. Marinus Willett reported the detachment numbered 250 (his son later wrote 200); Deygart to Albany Committee, 9Aug77, transcribed in *Clinton Papers*, II, 203 gave the oddly precise number of 206; Adam Helmer to McKesson, 12Aug77, transcribed in *Clinton Papers*, II, 212. Helmer noted another precise number — 207; *Colbrath Journal*, 29. He gave the number as 200. A simple calculation favours Marinus Willett's report, as the lower numbers do not leave enough men to make his eight subdivisions of sufficient strength to be useful. For example – advance guard, 30 men. rearguard, 30 men. flank guard, 30 men. gun guard, 50 men. This totals 140. With a Gun crew of 6 we would have a subtotal of 146. Then, the eight subdivisions could have been of 13 each for 104, giving a grand total of 250 men, as Marinus recorded. By deduction, if only 200 men were assigned to the sortie, then only 56 men would have been available for the eight subdivisions, ie. 7 men each. That is so small as to seem unlikely.

523 Pomroy Jones, 23; *Wm Willett*, 51.

524 Willett Narrative, 11Aug77, in *Wm Willett*, App. III, 132.

525 St. Leger to Burgoyne, 27Aug77. St. Leger referred to this Indian as "cowardly," indicating that he believed he was from an British alliance nation. The quoted word "pressed" was from his account.

526 Graymont, 146. Peter and Paul Powless and Han Jost were Oneida scouts in the fort during the siege; Draper Mss, Series U, V11, 202-04. Cornelius Doxtator stated that Chief Paul Powless, a.k.a. The Saw Mill and Ta-ha-swan-ga-to-tees, was at Stanwix and that some Oneidas were inside the fort, others were outside acting as pickets and spies.

527 Luzader, 45. He dealt succinctly with the question of Willett's motivation, that is, why he chose to plunder the camps rather than directly assisting Herkimer, and concluded that Willett made this decision after exiting the fort. I conclude that his plan was made before he set out, that the camps were thoroughly scouted and a rebel Indian sent to lure Bird away; *Wm Willett*, 51-54. Willett's son made no suggestion that his father had any goal in mind other than raiding the camps; Willett Narrative, 11Aug77, 131-32. Willett offered no indication that any other target was considered other than the two encampments; Adam Helmer to McKesson, 12Aug77, in *Clinton Papers*, II, 212. Helmer reported that Willett "attacked an Encampment of the Enemy... in Order to facilitate General Herkemer's March to the Fort."

528 Willett Narrative, 11Aug77, in *Wm Willett*, App. III, 133. The quoted words are from this account.

529 I have accepted secondary sources that place Sir John's family in the Royal Yorker camp; *Wm Willett*, 53. Stated that Sir John fled in his shirtsleeves. As a scarlet coat with gold lace was amongst the plunder taken, Willett Jr. may have concluded that Sir John abandoned it. However the Royal Yorkers were clothed in green with silver as their metal colour in '77, not red with gold. The subject coat may have belonged to one of the native war captains, or Willett's looting may have extended to the Lower Landing where Bird was encamped. The coat may have been Bird's, as the 8th Regt wore red and their metal colour was gold.

530 *Wm Willett*, 54.

531 Willett Narrative, 11Aug77, in *Wm Willett*, App. III, 133.

532 Colours: ibid, 132. Marinus reported that "five colours" were taken; Over the years, there has been much debate as to what type of colours these were. The West Point Museum holds an Artillery-style Grand Union, said to have been taken at Fort Schuyler (Stanwix) from the Royal Yorkers, but later evidence suggested that it may have been taken at the capture of Fort George in 1813; The Artillery Grand Union was "a curious hybrid of garrison flag and regimental color." Unlike the Grand Union, the Artillery Grand Union's St. Andrew's Cross lacked symmetry. See, Donald W. Holst, "Notes on British Artillery Flags in the American Revolution," *Journal of the Company of Military Historians*, XXXIX, 3, 117-21 and LtCol William A. Smy, "Standards, Guidons and Colours of the British Army and Provincial Corps During the American Revolution," *Loyalist Gazette*, Vol. XXXI, No.1 (Spring 1993) 16-25. The Artillery Colour was often used as a national camp flag; Goods destroyed and fouled: *Colbrath Journal*, 31; Adam Helmer to McKesson, 12Aug77, transcribed in *Clinton Papers*, II, 212; Flankers: ibid.

533 Stevens, *Allies*, 1256. Stevens noted Claus as the source for these quotations.

534 Two sick Indians: Gov Blacksnake's Conversations, Draper Mss; Native booty: Claus to Knox, 16Oct77; Medicine bundle: Seneca oral tradition cited in Stevens, *Allies*, 1247.

535 Prisoners: Claus to Knox, 16Oct77. "taking... Lieut Singleton and a private of Sir John's Regt who lay wounded in the Indian Camp"; Willett Narrative, 11Aug77, in *Wm Willett*, App. III, 132. "We brought in four prisoners, three of which were wounded. One of the prisoners is a Mr. George Singleton of Montreal"; Adam Helmer to McKesson, 12Aug77, in *Clinton Papers*, II, 212. Helmer reported, "one Regular Capt'n and four privates"; *Colbrath Journal*, 31. "four prisoners, three of whom were Wounded, a Mr. Singleton of Montreal who says he is a Lieutenant"; Carrying of loot: ibid, "[Willett] ordered his men to take as much baggage as they could... each one carrying with him as much as they could"; *Wm Willett*, 54. He wrote that seven wagons were brought out from the fort to gather the plunder. I have accepted Colbrath's account.

536 St. Leger to Burgoyne, 27Aug77.

537 NYPA S28937 of Henery Walrath.

538 Rev Thomas Scott: McIlwraith, 3, 256. "[Scott]... proved a constant source of annoyance to... Barry St. Leger, of whom he made so many unjust complaints to the commander-in-chief that he was told that no more such scurrilous epistles would be received, and he was forbidden to exercise the function of a clergyman in the province; Capt D. Forbes, 15Mar82, found in NAC, WO28/2(1782), 6. The subaltern officers of the 34th "gave it as their opinion that his Conduct was so highly improper & unbecoming the Sacred Character he bore, that it would be for the

Credit & Service of the Regiment, that he shou'd be dismissed." They referred to him as the "irreverend" Scott. Apparently, Scott was accused of consorting with young native women during his service at Ft Niagara; Scott's letter to St. Leger: Rev Thos C.H. Scott to St. Leger, 13Oct81 transcribed by Wm Smy from HP, AddMss21734. This is a brutally accusatory letter.

539 St. Leger to Burgoyne, 27Aug77

540 Willett gave the name as "Bedlow," which is surely Badlam. See, Willett Narrative, 11Aug77, in *Wm Willett,* App. III, 132; Adam Helmer to McKesson, 21Aug77 in Clinton, II, 213.

541 Willett Narrative, 11Aug77, in *Wm Willett,* App. III, 132.

542 Adam Helmer to McKesson, 12Aug77, in *Clinton Papers,* II, 213.

543 Quotations are from St. Leger to Burgoyne, 27Aug77.

544 No casualties: Adam Helmer to McKesson, 21Aug77, in *Clinton Papers,*II, 213; Willett Narrative, 11Aug77, in *Wm Willett,* App. III,. He wrote "not one man killed or wounded"; Three cheers: *Wm Willett,* 55; Colours hoisted: ibid; *Colbrath Journal,* 31. Colbrath claimed that only four colours were captured.

545 Clifford Neal Smith, "Mercenaries from Hessen-Hanau who remained in Canada and the United States after the American Revolution," German-American Genealogical Research Monograph No.5 (McNeal, AZ: Westland Publications, 1976) These men were Jost Stein and Johan Strott.

546 Watt & Morrison, *Campaign of 1777,* 31,32,38-63.

547 Stevens, *Allies,* 1253-54. From Seaver, *Life of Mary Jemison,* 116–17. This quote of Jemison's words referred to her village's reactions to the losses in the ambush, but there is no doubt that these same traditional, involuntary outpourings occurred in the camps at Stanwix.

548 St. Leger to Burgoyne, 27Aug77; Stevens, *Allies,* 1253-54. Besides Tocenando, the Senecas lost Axe-Carrier Asquishahang (principal warrior of Genesee castle,) Things beside the Stump Dahwahdeho, Black Feather-Tail Gahnahage, Branch of a Tree Dahgaiownd, Fish Lapper Dahohjocdoh and an unnamed captain of the affil-iated Squakis.

549 Claus to Knox, 16Oct77.

550 Stevens, *Allies,* 1259.

551 Preston, 4fn. Glennie was commissioned in '75. He served as Deputy Engineer at Carleton Is. (see en80) during the building of Ft Haldimand and transferred to the Engineers in '79. A noted mathematician, he was elected a Fellow of the Royal Society that same year. In '80, he was cashiered for insubordination to Captain Thos Aubrey, 47th, a very unpopular commander at Ft Haldimand. This finding was overturned in Britain and Glennie was restored to his rank. He later settled in New Brunswick where he entered politics.

552 St. Leger to Burgoyne, 27Aug77.

553 *Willett's OB.*

554 Willett to Trumbull, 11Aug77, transcribed in the *Remembrancer 1777,* 448-49.

555 *Colbrath Journal,* 31.

556 Catherine Van Schaick to Gansevoort, 31Jul77, transcribed in JA Scott, 198; *Colbrath Journal,* 55-56. This source has a reproduction of the original; Possibly, she referred generally to Indians, not just the Oneidas.

557 ibid, 31; What a strange fabrication! Perhaps he glimpsed Johnson or Butler in con-ference and made an honest mistake in identity.

558 William W. Campbell, 91. The exact time of writing was noted in the letter's head-ing; McHenry, 22. On a list entitled "Return of Rebel Officers sent from Quebec to

New York on their Paroles" the prisoners' given names were noted, but the wrong date of capture was recorded.

559 Butler to Carleton, 15Aug77, 154; Stevens, *Allies*, 1257. Noted that the British officers attempted to ransom every captive; Claus to Mathews, 15May80, found in the *Claus Papers*, Vol.25, 169-71. As Claus explained to Haldimand's secretary, revenge was a key element of the native character. "The only means to make them act heartily is to endeavour to draw them on to lose blood, when revenge will outdo all bribery." The Indians' great losses at Oriskany sustained their activity against the rebels throughout the war, although their opinion of their British ally's management of the conflict was never overly favourable.

560 Pomroy Jones, 339-41. Testimony of Jabez Spicer.

561 *Chainbreaker*, 89; variations of the gauntlet were used as punishment in the German forces and the Royal Navy.

562 Simms, *Frontiersman*, II, 100; whether this tale should be credited is highly questionable. I have previously noted that the bateaux-master, Capt Martin was reported by Younglove as eaten by the Indians, yet he returned to the States during the war. Simms was assured by John L. Groat that his brother Lieut Peter/Petrus Groat and Andrew Cunningham "were captured at Oriskany and murdered at Wood Creek – slices of their thighs being roasted and feasted upon by the savages." A fellow prisoner, Peter Ehle claimed to have seen these men killed and communicated their fate to the Valley; Morrison research. Petrus Groat returned to the Valley long after the war. He was mentally disturbed, but very much alive and whole. See, the notice of John Sanders, Western Repository, 30Jun1807, cited in NYSL, 125th Annual Report, 18-19. Sanders advised that on 4Jun1807 he discovered Petrus "Groot" sitting beside the Mohawk Turnpike. He offered many details of Groat's appearance and his captivity with Indians "north of Quebec;" Morrison does not list an Andrew Cunningham as a participant in the battle, but MacWethy, 133, lists Cunningham as a fatality. Yet, unlike other similar instances, he did not record that he was a prisoner before his death; Crouse: He may have died running the gauntlet and was maimed afterwards in the traditional native fashion.

563 NYPA S28937 of Henery Walrath/Wallradt indicated that it was Lakes Nations Indians from the Detroit region who captured him.

564 Artificers: Todd Braisted research. NYSL, Mss 2428. This document, dated 27Jun78, gave the names of a work party of 13 Royal Yorkers who acted as a foreman, carpenters and sawyers during the siege. In this instance ,they were "Employed in . . . laying Platforms for the Guns"; St. Leger to Burgoyne, 27Aug77.

565 Pomroy Jones, 361.

566 Norton, 273.

567 Simms, *Frontiersman*, II, 109. His captors' misinterpretation saved Sponable from running the gauntlet when they got to their settlement.

568 Claus, *Anecdotes of Brant*, 28; Claus to Knox, 16Oct77.

569 Stevens, *Allies*, 1260. In Stevens's opinion, St. Leger "was inhibited by an orthodox European tactical view, [he] did not see any military advantage for himself or Burgoyne in launching an incursion into the frontier settlements in the rear of Schuyler's army while his troops continued to coop up Gansevoort's garrison"; Claus to Knox, 16Oct77; Claus's comment about the inhabitants was overstated, but St. Leger's decision not to take advantage of the shattered morale of Tryon's populace presents one of those fascinating "what ifs" of history.

570 *Colbrath Journal*, 33. He recorded that Capt Ancrum advised that "St. Leger had held a Counsel with them for two Days."

Endnotes

571 Greene, *Gateway*, I, 822. Herkimer's first wife was Deygart's sister.

572 *Clinton Papers*, II, 191-92.

573 Deserters: One was Thomas Cavan of Aorsen's 5th Company, who by month end, had been enlisted in the Col's Coy by Sir John. See, HP, MG23, B23, Pt2; Fernow, XV, State Archives, V.1, 203. Gave the name as "Cavin"; Cruikshank & Watt, *KRR NY*, 180. Cavan served the King's cause throughout the war. He transferred to the 2Bn in '80 and was a Sjt in Capt Wm Redford Crawford's Coy in '82-84. He may have returned to the States, as he did not settle in Canada prior to '89.

574 Schuyler to Congress, 8Aug77, transcribed in the *Schuyler Court Martial*, 184-86.

575 Morrison research. NYPL, NYC, NY, Emmet Collection, Document #4611.

576 Sister's name: Penrose, *Mohawk Valley*, 129. This was perhaps Maria Yates (née Frey), sister of Henry, John and Barent and wife of Committeeman Christopher P. Yates who at the time was the Maj of the 1NY. See Egly, 1NY, 51; This event: Simms, *Frontiersman*, II, 104.

577 Peter Ehle's deposition before the Tryon Committee, 25Aug77, transcribed in Penrose, *Mohawk Valley*, 129. Peter S. Deygart gave evidence that Henry Frey said he would kill his son Philip if he took up arms in the rebel militia. Clearly, Hendrick Frey was a man of strong words and principles.

578 NYPA S28937 of Henery Walrath. When the party arrived at Ft Niagara, he was put in prison for five days, during which time the Indians were drunk and not permitted to see him. When they arrived at Detroit, Walrath was in such poor condition from mistreatment and lack of food that his captors decided he would die and they sold him to Gov Hamilton, who immediately sent him and another rebel captive to Ft Erie. The two men continued eastwards till arriving in Quebec City. After some delay, Walrath and 73 prisoners were sent aboard a vessel bound for NYC. He arrived home in Jan78. To obtain this release, Walrath had taken an oath to refrain from taking up arms against the King, but he fought again on "the first opportunity that presented."

579 St. Leger to Burgoyne, 27Aug77; Young: NYSL, Mss2428. Showed Sjt Andrew Young (whose trade was a gun carriage maker) as foreman. His party, now composed of himself and 8 carpenters were "Employed in making Cheeks for a field carriage."

580 Butler to Carleton, 17Aug77.

581 Haldimand to Germain?, 27Sep78, found in NAC, WO1/11, Pt.1, 94. "[I]t is necessary for Captain Watts lately of Sir John Johnson's Corp Serving with which he received a wound in the action last Summer, upon the Mohawk River near the German flatts, and has had his leg cut off, and now of the 8th regiment[,] having been permitted to purchase a company in it, to go to England for the benefit of the hot bath to recover the flexibility of the joint of the Knee, otherwise he will not be able to make use of an artificial Leg."

582 Willett Narrative, 11Aug77,. in *Wm Willett*, App. III.

583 John Brooks, born in Medford, MA, trained as a physician and practised at Reading before the Revolution. He commanded Reading's Minute Company and was active on the fateful day of Lexington and Concord. On the formation of the Continental Army, Brooks was made a major of Bridge's MA Regiment. In '76, Brooks was attached to the Connecticut Line and served therein during the battles of Long Island and White Plains. In '77, he was promoted to LtCol of Jackson's MA Regiment. As Col Jackson had been gravely wounded in '76, command fell on LtCol Brooks throughout the '77 campaign and he served with great distinction, as will be seen in the text. He continued to serve the cause for the balance of the war and was appointed MGen of MA militia postwar and was governor of the State in

1812, serving for six successive terms. See the National Portrait Gallery (1835).

584 *Smy Transcripts.* Col Jeduthan Baldwin, *The Revolutionary Journal of Colonel Jeduthan Baldwin*, Thomas William Baldwin, ed. (Bangor: 1906) 114; Lieut William Scudder, *The Journal of William Scudder, an Officer in the Late New-York Line* (Author, 1794 – reprinted, Garland Publishing, Inc., 1977 as Vol.22 of *Narrative of North American Indian Captives*) 16-17.

585 *Colbrath Journal*, 32,33&54. The latter page was a summation of the garrison's casualties from 25June–22Aug as recorded by Colbrath; Wm Willett, 55.

586 *Wm Willett*, 56-57. I quoted from the son's interpretation of his father's memories, as the sentiments were so in keeping with the occasion and events.

587 Willett Narrative, 11Aug77, in *Wm Willett*, App. III, 134; I chose not to quote from Wm Willett's version of his father's speech as found in *Wm Willett*, 57-58. As Colbrath's report was very detailed, there is every reason to believe that he was present and he made no mention of a speech by LtCol Willett. In addition, Willett (11Aug77) does not credit himself with delivering the answer to the proposal, yet he was certainly not shy about mentioning other events and occasions in which he took a principal role; Despite the "patriotic" outrage that has occurred over the years concerning the tone of St. Leger's summons of the fort, it is wise to recognize that he simply followed the customs of the time. His reference to being unable to control his native *allies* was a known truism of North American warfare. See, Anderson, 192. When Montcalm summonsed Fort William Henry, he stated, "nor would it be in his power to restrain the cruelties of a mob of Indians of so many different nations." Of course, Montcalm was French. The furor over St. Leger's veiled threat was due to him being a British officer, who, in theory, should not have relied upon "savages." This posturing ignored the fact that the rebels had employed natives from the earliest stages of the war.

588 *Colbrath Journal*, 34.

589 Sources disagree over who proposed this cessation of hostilities. I suspect that some "patriotic" historians did not wish to even contemplate that Gansevoort would show such weakness. Colbrath indicated that the answer was deferred till the following morning and "a Cessation of Arms [was] agreed to by both parties till then." As this truce improved Willett's chances to creep through the British lines, I take the view that Gansevoort knew exactly what he was about and accepted a truce as a clever ploy to reduce vigilance and gain time.

590 *Wm Willett*, 58.

591 *Colbrath Journal*, 34&54. Colbrath recorded there was only a single deserter, yet Fernow, XV, State Archives, I, 203 claimed that Thos Benson and J'thon Huggins deserted the night of 8Aug. Benson was serving in Butler's Rangers in '83. No record of Huggins has been found.

592 Willett and Colbrath agreed that this meeting was in the evening, after the emissaries departed; NYPA R9078 of Silas Runnolds. He deposed that Pte Asa Monroe accompanied Willett and Stockwell on their perilous trip through the siege lines. A Silas Runnolds/Reynolds or Asa Monroe were not listed by Roberts or Fernow in the 3NY, nor was there any mention of a ranker travelling with Willett, although there was an Alexander Monrow/Munro/Munroe serving in Bleecker's 8th Coy. A mystery; Miscreant band: Willett Narrative, 11Aug77 in *Wm Willett*, App. III. Ah Willett! Such phraseology, such a keen eye for personal immortality!; To urge the militia: *Wm Willett*, 59. It was felt that Marinus had a particular cachet with the county's militia. Perhaps, this was due to his reputation for bold activities in the early rebellion in New York City, or, for a closer-to-home reason, his bloodless

intercession to quell a mutiny of the 1CDN Regt at Ft Dayton on his way upriver to Stanwix. See, James F. Morrison, *Colonel James Livingston, The Forgotten Livingston Patriot of the War of Independence [Livingston]* (Johnstown: Col. James Livingston Historic Research Committee, 1988) 6.

593 *Wm Willett*, 58. Marinus's son said the time of leaving the fort was 10:00 PM. Strangely, he also stated that it was the night of the 10Aug77; *Colbrath Journal*, 34. I have favoured Colbrath's contemporary journal that stated 1:00 AM, the morning of 9Aug.

594 *Wm Willett*, 59-60.

595 Willett's address to the troops, 8Aug77, transcribed in the *Gansevoort Papers*, 159-60.

596 Morrison research. Carroll Collection, American Antiquarian Society, letter #1833.

597 Claus to Knox, 16Oct77. "The rebels knowing... the insufficiency of our field pieces to hurt them, and apprehensive of being massacred by the Indians for the losses they sustained in the action; they rejected the summons."

598 *Colbrath Journal*, 37.

599 St. Leger to Gansevoort, 9Aug77, transcribed in William W. Campbell, 92-93. The letter was signed, "Barry St. Leger, Brigadier General of his Majesty's Forces."

600 ibid; A complete transcript found in Stone, *Brant*, I, xxxvi-vii.

601 *Colbrath Journal*, 34.

602 Stone, *Brant*, I, 253-54. Contains a plate of the original letter and a transcript.

603 *Colbrath Journal*, 37.

604 J-B-M Hertel de Rouville's satirical poem, "L'Entreprise Manquée" found in *Le Canada Français* (Société du Parlés Français au Canada, Québec) Vol. XXXIII (November 1945) 225-29. I concluded that the Canadiens were assigned to this task from the details in de Rouville's poem; NYSL, Mss 2428.

605 *Colbrath Journal*, 37. All details and quotations were from this source.

606 Barclay to the "President of the Council of Safety for the State of New York," 9Aug77, transcribed in *Clinton Papers*, II, 201.

607 Simms, *Schoharie*, 234.

608 *Wm Willett*, 59-60.

609 Penrose, *Mohawk Valley*, 236. Prior to his election on 25Aug77, Deygart (Deygert, Dygert Tygert) assumed the role of chairman of the County Committee.

610 *Clinton Papers*, II, 203-04.

611 *Wm Willett*, 60-61.

612 *Schuyler Court Martial*, 185-86.

613 Carroll Collection, American Antiquarian Soc., letter #1828.

614 MacKenna to Montgolfier, 10Aug77. MacKenna advised the vicar-general that "it is very difficult for me to say mass daily because of the war"; MacMaster, 121. Sir William would not have brought MacKenna from Ireland if he could not converse with the Highlanders. From circumstantial evidence, I have concluded that he spoke English. Obviously, his vocation as a priest required that he spoke Latin and he very likely spoke French as well.

615 *Colbrath Journal*, 38; Without doubt the KRR also made use of brush huts, a common substitute for tents. See, John U. Rees, 2ndNJ, "'We are now... properly... enwigwamed.' British Soldiers and Brush Shelters, 1777-1781," *The Brigade Dispatch*, Vol.XXIX, No.2 (Summer 1999) 2-9.

616 Simms, *Frontiersman*, II, 106.

617 ibid, II, 107. Simms wrote that the Indian was taken to Canada and recovered from his paralysis. How he discovered this is a mystery.

618 *Colbrath Journal*, 38.

619 I have no evidence regarding the time of day when St. Leger wrote this report, but it supposedly arrived at Burgoyne's camp the next day; *Remembrancer 1777*, 392.

620 Entry for 11Aug77, in *Willett's OB*.

621 *Wm Willett*, 61.

622 *Clinton Papers*, II, 209-11.

623 *Colbrath Journal*, 39.

624 *Schuyler Court Martial*, 186. For some reason, this order was ignored or later changed.

625 This misinformation about troops strength suggested that the Oneidas outside of the siege lines held no intercourse with their brethren inside the cordon, otherwise they would have had detailed information from Sir John's captured papers.

626 Carroll Collection, letter #1905.

627 H.C. Burleigh, *Deforests of Avesnes and Kast, McGinness* (author, n.d.) 6,12-13; Sarah Kast McGinnis's father founded the native trading business at German Flats. Her husband, Teady McGinnis was killed at Lake George in 1755 while serving as an Indian Dept officer under Sir William. Her sons-in-law, the brothers, John and Samuel Thompson, took over the family business. Their establishment hosted Guy Johnson in 1775 when he left the Valley. John & Samuel, and the latter's sons Timothy, Samuel Jr. and Andrew were all implicated in inimical activities and taken up by the rebels, leaving behind 62-year-old Sarah with her demented son, William, who was bound in chains for his own safekeeping, and her daughters Elizabeth and Dorothy and the latter's daughter. As the Six Nations held Sarah in great esteem, the committee questioned her about Indian Affairs and only "with difficulty [did she get] clear of [their] Resentment." When the rebels sold the family's farming and trading goods at public venue, the women stood by watching their neighbours buy up their goods and chattels. Afterwards, they were "confined... ill used, and left in a very disagreeable situation" in Fort Dayton; Watt & Morrison, *Campaign of 1777*, 77,227. Andrew and Samuel Jr. served with Butler at Fort Stanwix. John got away to join the KRR at Ticonderoga on 25Oct77 and was noted as sick on an end-of-year return. Andrew served later as a capt in Butler's Rangers and drowned in the service. Timothy Thompson served as an Ens in the 2KRR.

628 *Wm Willett*, 61. He wrote that his father discovered from Learned that Arnold was to command the relief force and that he rode to Albany to meet him and offer current reports. As Schuyler's orders to Arnold were issued on 13Aug, it seems unlikely that Learned already knew of his appointment on the 11th.

629 *Schuyler Court Martial*, 186.

630 Stanley, *Horse*, 128; This feat prompts many questions about wilderness express riders. Did they operate in relays with fresh riders and mounts, or was there only one rider, who relied on stations of remounts somewhere along the way, or was there a single rider and a string of mounts, which allowed the animals to rest after a set distance? Of course, it is also entirely possible that the recorded dates of dispatch or receipt were incorrect.

631 De Rouville, 226.

632 Morrison, Livingston. The First Canadian (1CDN) Regiment.

633 *Schuyler Court Martial*, 187-88.

634 *Wm Willett*, 61; A letter from Albany was excerpted in a letter from Fishkill of 18Aug77 which was printed in the *Remembrancer 1777*, 394-95. The latter letter found its way into the "Impartial Repository of Public Events For the Year 1777." Another account of the events was found in the British Register for '77 as quoted

Endnotes

in *Wm Willett*, 61fn. I see Marinus's deft hand in all of this exposure.

635   Jno McKesson to Clinton, 13Aug77, transcribed in *Clinton Papers*, II, 220-21.

636   Haldimand to Sir John Johnson, 7Sep79, cited in Cruikshank & Watt, *KRR NY*, 31. The Governor wrote, "[John Butler's] son... conceited and petulant."

637   Morrison research. Hanjost Schuyler was a Sjt in Capt Demuth's 1776 ranging Coy, which was disbanded in Mar77.

638   Capt Lathrop Allen to Schuyler cited in George W. Schuyler, *Colonial New York, Philip Schuyler and His Family* (2 Vols., New York: Charles Scribner's Sons, 1885) 2, 463&474. The book details Hanjost's background and his service and rank in the County's rangers.

639   Petition of Christopher Fornyea [Fornyea Petition] transcribed in Ernest A. Cruikshank, "Petitions for grants of land in Upper Canada, second series, 1796-99," *OHSPR*, 26 (1930), 186.

640   A letter dated Fishkill 21Aug77, transcribed in the *Remembrancer 1777*, 394-95. The writer reported Walter Butler's party as "fourteen white men, and fourteen Indians"; Claus to Knox, 16Oct77. "Ensign Butler of the 8th Regt 10 soldiers and 3 Indians"; Stevens, *Allies*, 2299. He cited a Dec77 Indian council at Niagara which confirmed that three Iroquois went with Butler; NAC, WO17/1571, 207. St. Leger's return prepared at Oswego noted that 1 Ensign and 5 Other Ranks of the 8th were casuals and, of the 34th, 1 Sjt and 9 Other Ranks. Stevens concluded from this return and similar evidence that the Regulars were evenly drawn from both regts.

641   The date of Walter Butler's departure is unclear. Walter Swiggett, *War Out of Niagara, Walter Butler and the Tory Rangers* (Port Washington, NY: Ira J. Friedman, Inc., 1963) 90. He claimed that Walter left on the 10th or 11th, but offered no sources; Butler to Carleton, 15Aug77. Butler's postscript of 17Aug stated, "my son, sent by General St. Leger." This is our only clue.

642   Order: *Willett's OB*; Casualty: *Colbrath Journal*, 40.

643   Sammons as deserter: ibid, 41. Recorded that the man was from Gregg's; Fernow, XV, State Archives, V.1, 205. Noted only one deserter from Gregg's, but gave the date of desertion as 5Aug. Sammons' enlistment in the KRR was 15Aug77. NAC, WO28/5, 212.

644   Claus to Knox, 6Nov77 [Claus to Knox, 6Nov77] transcribed in *CHSNY*, VIII, 723-26. Claus, whose language was always quite precise, made note that the party was Six Nations, not just Mohawk; Schuyler to Henry Laurens, 15Mar78 transcribed in Penrose, *Indian Affairs*, 119-20.

645   Morrison, *Livingston*, 7. He gave Arnold's arrival at Caughnawaga as 16Aug. I believe Arnold departed Albany on the 13th with Schuyler's orders of that day in his pocket. My contention is confirmed by *TCMN*, Vol.VI, No.3 (1987) which provided an excerpt from Russell W. Knight, ed., *General John Glover's Letterbook 1776-77*, 30. A letter, written at Van Schaick's Island on Aug 19, stated "Arnold left us on the 13th." For men on horseback, the trip from Albany to Caughnawaga could not have taken longer than one day. Therefore, I place Arnold at Caughnawaga on the 14th. This theory is reinforced by Arnold visiting Herkimer on the 16th See, *TCMN*, Vol.VI, No.9 (1987) From Greene, Gateway, I, 829.

646   JA Scott, 267; Full names and regtl designations from Roberts, I, 29&47.

647   Cruikshank & Watt, *KRR NY*, Appendix III. The primary document revealing enlistment dates for these men is, HP, MG21, B158, 208-10; The petition of Jacob Miller, John Peter Sommer and John Caldwell to Haldimand [Miller Petition] found in HP, AddMss21874, 112-13. They hoped to receive "farther

Acknowledgments" for bringing in their coy to Stanwix as recruits; Butler's Rangers' pay lists found in HP, AddMss21765.

648 KRR muster rolls, 25Jun-24Dec77, prepared 22Jan78 found in NAC, WO28/5, 211-20.

649 Quotations and account: Frank Cooper research. "The humble Petition of Philip Empey, lately an Inhabitan of Stoneraby, near the Mohake River, Tryon County," Montreal, 6Dec82 transcribed in James J. Talman, ed., *Loyalist Narratives From Upper Canada* (Toronto: Champlain Society, 1946) This surname was various spelled, 'Empy, Empie, Oempy, Emichen; A committee of safety examination of William P. Empie of Riemensnyder's Bush transcribed in Penrose, *Mohawk Valley*, 111-12. Also contained details of Philip P., John P., John W. Empie and John McCaffery (the latter also joined the KRR on 15Aug77) who were persuaded to take an oath of association. This oath was given in complete detail and is of considerable interest; Three sons: Claim of Philip Empey, Jr., 16Feb88 transcribed in Cruikshank, *Loyalist Petitions*, II, 1123. Advised that Philip Jr. (christened Johan Philip) was one of three sons of Philip Sr.; LtCol Frank Cooper, "The Empey's of Stormont," u.p. Johannes F. was the oldest, followed by Philip Jr., then William P., Adam P. and Jacobus; HP, MG21, B158, 208-10. This record indicated that the five sons of Philip Sr. joined on 15Aug77; Two cousins: These were John W. and Adam Empey from Riemensnyder's Bush. Their father was known as William Sr.; Maria Empey: Philip Empey Sr.'s petition, 6Dec82. She died in 1779 as a result of her horrific experiences. In '79, after a 13-week imprisonment, Philip Sr. "went to Sir Johns Settlement [Johnstown]" and hid. In the spring of '80, when Sir John raided the area, Philip, three more of his sons — Christopher, Peter and Henrich and a son-in-law, Michael Van Koughnett, joined the KRR. Philip's petition advised that a 7th son joined the KRR prior to the St. Leger expedition, but that has not been substantiated by enlistment dates. According to several KRR muster rolls, his five sons joined on 15Aug77 and one son on 22May80. The date of Peter and Henrich joining has not been found, but Philip Sr claimed that they also served.

650 Fornyea Petition. Stated that Butler's party was captured ten days after Oriskany. From other circumstances, I have placed the event nine days after.

651 German Flats and Kingsland committee meeting, 17Jun75, Penrose, *Mohawk Valley*, 18. On 17Jun75, Rudolph Shoemaker, Joost Herkimer Jr. and John Thompson signed an association stating they would "support our American Liberties to the utmost of our power." While Han Jost Herkimer and John Thompson later ran off to Niagara to serve in the Ind Dept, Shoemaker somehow managed to avoid the acrimony of either party. Proponents of both political stripes visited his tavern throughout the war and, on several occasions, the building was spared by loyalist 'incendiaries'; John Ruch research. NAC, HP, MG21, AddMss21826, f37. A Rudolph Shomaker served in Hanjost Herkimer's Bateaux Coy at Coteau du Lac in '80. This may have been his son, Rudolphus, b. 1762. See, Penrose, *Mohawk Valley*, 322.

652 Howard Thomas, *Marinus Willett, Soldier-Patriot 1740-1830* (Prospect, NY: Prospect Books, 1954) 84-85. Brooks said that the taking of Butler was done "not without a considerable deal of difficulty."

653 A proclamation to the Inhabitants of Tryon County, 13Aug77, transcribed in the *Remembrancer 1777*, 451; Howard Thomas, 80; Luzader, 49, and in Stone, *Brant*, I, Note VII, xxxvii-viii. As this proclamation was dated 13Aug, Walter Butler must have left the camps no earlier than that day.

654 Maria Campbell, *Revolutionary Services and Civil Life of General William Hull prepared from His Manuscripts by His Daughter Mrs. Maria Campbell Together with the*

Endnotes

History of the Campaign of 1812 and Surrender of the post of Detroit by his Grandson, James Freeman Clarke (New York: D. Appleton and Co., 1848) 82-84.

655 Schuyler to Hancock, 15Aug77, Penrose, *Indian Affairs*, 95-96.

656 St. Leger to Burgoyne, 27Aug77.

657 *Willett OB.*.

658 *Colbrath Journal*, 43.

659 Glen Smith, gun commander in the recreated Royal Yorkers and a muzzle-loading artillery specialist, notes that the Cohorn tubes would have been mounted on the three-pounder carriages. He predicts that this "mortizer" combination would have produced a vicious recoil.

660 NYSL, Mss 2428. Sjt Young's artificers were "Preparing Materials for Mining"; Smith, *Dictionary*, 228. "SAP, in sieges, is a trench, or an approach made under cover of 10 or 12 feet broad"; St. Leger to Carleton, 27Aug77, 139-40.

661 De Rouville, 225. He accused the expedition's engineer, but did not specifically name Rudyerd.

662 Robert Johnston to Dr. Jonathon Potts, General Hospital Northern Department, dated "General Harcomers" 17Aug77 found in *TCMN*, Vol.VI, No.3 (1987) taken from Greene, Gateway, I, 829.

663 *Colbrath Journal*, 28. Editor Lowenthal identified the Roof who was present; Stone, *Brant*, I, 247. Offers the story from John Roof that the amputation was performed by "a young French surgeon in the army of General Arnold... contrary to the advice of... Doctor Petrie." Roof (Roff, Rouf) claimed the operation was "unskilfully performed, and it was found impossible by his attendants to stanch the blood;" Ken D. Johnson, 413-14. NYPA R3917 of Adam Garlock. Garlock claimed a Dr. Wright was the attending physician. Another mystery.

664 Simms, *Frontiersman*, II, 91.

665 *Clinton Papers*, II, 229; Tryon committee minutes for 25Aug77, transcribed in Penrose, *Mohawk Valley*, 128.

666 Jonathon Trumbull Jr. to Jonathon Trumbull dated at Albany, 16Aug77 found in the Collections Massachusetts Historical Society, Seventh Series, Vol.II, 117-20.

667 Swiggett, 91. Schuyler advised Washington that the letter came from "Mr. Petry, Chairman of a committee in Tryon County"; committee minutes, 25Aug77, transcribed in Penrose, *Mohawk Valley*, 127. Showed "Wm. Petrea" to be a member of this subcommittee.

668 Simms, *Frontiersman*, II, 91. Claimed the disinternment of the leg was two or three days later, not the same day; Johnston to Potts, 17Aug77, *TCMN*, Vol.VI, No.3 (1987).

669 *Colbrath Journal*, 43.

670 ibid,46.

671 A record of this courtmartial may be found in Howard Thomas, 81-86; Swiggett, 90-97. His pro-Tory observations and conclusions were so highly coloured, opinionated, and obviously inaccurate, I have used his material very cautiously.

672 Howard Thomas, 82.

673 A postscript dated 17Aug77 to Butler to Carleton, 15Aug77.

674 *Jaeger Corps' Diary.*

675 *Wm Willett*, 63. Claimed that St. Leger "formed two parallels, the second... brought him near the edge of the glacis." Parallels are trenches dug parallel with the face of the defence which are joined by a communication trench in the form of a "Z"; *Colbrath Journal*, 46.

676 William McGinnis: There is a family legend that the rebels burned William alive in

retaliation for his mother's flight. This contention was brought into question by a report of the following year. See, Col Abraham Wemple to Gen Ten Broeck, 20Sep78, found in *Clinton Papers*, IV, 82-83. Wemple wrote about a Tory raid that destroyed German Flats. He stated, "A man, a son of Mrs Magin who has for some time been deprived of his senses, was burned in a house." This must have been William. If so, he lost his life to loyalist or loyal native actions, not rebel; Co-opting of Sarah: Burleigh, *Kast/McGinnis*, 7-8; Stevens, *Allies*, 1267-68,2299; The cattle: St. Leger Expenses, 221. Item #18 – "An account of cattle delivered for the use of His Majesty's troops at Fort Stanwix... by Dorothy Thompson," 19Aug77. Dorothy was the wife of John.

677 Draper Mss, U11, 202-04.

678 *Colbrath Journal*, 46; Rob Bothwell research. Rob advises that Stiles was 25 at the time. He enlisted on 6Feb77 in Bailey's Regt and served in Capt Darby's Coy. He was from Middlesex, MA, and died 11Jul79; Gansevoort to Gates?, 19Aug77, found in the NYHS, Gates Papers, Mf Reel 3. The Col stated that Stiles was of Col Bailey's Regt. If so, he was part of Badlam's detachment, not Mellon's.

679 No contemporary references for this unrest have been found, so I reluctantly cite – Stone, *Brant*, I, 257. He wrote "some of the officers commenced speaking in whispers of the expediency of saving the garrison"; Benson J. Lossing, *The Pictorial Field-Book of the Revolution or, Illustrations, by Pen and Pencil, of the History, Biography, Scenery, Relics, and Traditions of the War for Independence* (2 vols., New York: Harper & Brothers, 1851) I, 250. "Their ammunition and provisions being much reduced in quantity, some hinted an opinion to their commander that a surrender would be humane policy"; William W. Campbell, 94. He wrote "his provisions daily exhausting; some of his officers, anxious to accept the proffered protection of St. Leger from the fury of the savages by making a timely surrender." If there was no truth to this wavering, it seems odd that three early, "patriotic" historians made note of it.

680 Howard Thomas, 82-83,85; Maria Campbell, 82-84.

681 A photo-reproduction of the original findings dated German Flats, 20Aug77, signed by M. Willett as Judge Advocate, see Swiggett, opposite92.

682 Stevens, *Allies*, 1284. The three Iroquois were held in Albany at the campaign's close.

683 Penrose, *Mohawk Valley*, 253&322. This relationship takes some analysis, but I believe I have it correct.

684 Tryon committee minutes of 5Jun76 and 6Sep77, transcribed in Penrose, *Mohawk Valley*, 79-80,132.

685 Stone, *Brant*, I, No.VIII, xxxviii.

686 *Colbrath Journal*, 47.

687 JA Scott, 296-97. From Burgoyne, *State*.

688 *Colbrath Journal*, 48.

689 NYHS, *Gates Papers*, Mf Reel #3.

690 Report of the Council of War, German Flats, 21Aug77, transcribed in Luzader, 51; Tuscaroras: Their participation was often ignored. Arnold's second letter to Gates of that day omitted them, but the report of the Council of War did not. Likely their nation's junior relationship to the Oneidas led to this frequent oversight; Chief Paul Powless: Draper Mss, 11U, 202-04. Powless, the Oneida chief, was also dispatched from Stanwix as a messenger in this time period. He stole out of the fort at night and travelled to Schenectady to request aid, which suggests that Gansevoort had given up on the upper Valley as a source of relief. Powless may have been a member of this deputation.

Endnotes

691 ibid. Luzader advised that Col Henry Beeckman Livingston was present at the Council of War. If so, he must have ridden on ahead, as Clinton reported that his and Van Cortlandt's Regts had turned about without joining Arnold. See Clinton to the State Council of Safety, 25Aug77, cited in JA Scott, 292.

692 Report of the Council of War, 21Aug77, in Luzader, 51.

693 Mintz, 209. He described Learned as a "plodder."

694 Quotations between endnotes: Arnold to Gates, 21Aug77 found in the NYHS, *Gates Papers*, Mf Reel #3.

695 Many sources claimed that some officers of the 1NY, who had been schoolmates of Walter Butler, successfully interceded to have his death sentence commuted. I concluded that such pleas may have occurred, but it was Schuyler's instruction to send Butler down that saved his life; Fornyea Petition. He wrote that the "Chairman of the County, who was a Humane Man" saved him from death. This must have been Peter S. Deygart. From other evidence, humanity was not Deygart's outstanding feature. Likely, Fornyea's death sentence, like Hanjost's, was a sham.

696 I have not accepted the theories that Hanjost Schuyler was a coarse, uneducated bumpkin with a mental affliction that caused the natives to hold him in awe. A bumpkin or half-wit would not have held the rank of Sjt, nor would he have been chosen for a mission like the Flag. I believe he was personally close to the Indians and they trusted him to speak the truth. Of course, he may have been a rather odd character in looks and/or speech.

697 *Remembrancer 1777*, 445; Claim of Nicholas Schuyler, 17Oct1827 found in the USNA, Records U.S. House of Reps, 21st Congress's committee on Military Pensions, RG233, File No.HR21A-D16.1. Included a deposition by nine witnesses who stated that Hanjost had been sentenced to death; Schuyler family: George Schuyler, 463. Listed the family of Pieter Schuyler and Elizabeth Barbara Herkimer.

698 Nicholas Schuyler's memory: As to Hanjost having been in the Continental service — Roberts, 91,174 shows John Joost and Nicholas Schuyler in Tryon's First Regt and John Joost in the Levies in 1781; George Weaver's memory: MacWethy, 165; Clemency: *Scudder Journal*, 17.

699 Maria Campbell, 84-86; Ken D. Johnson, 308. NYPA R731&372 of Peter P. Bellinger. Peter stated that Arnold took Hanjost Schuyler and his brother prisoner and duped Hanjost into lying to the enemy, using the latter's brother as a hostage to enforce his bargain.

700 Simms, *Frontiersman*, II, 87; George Schuyler, 475.

701 St. Leger to Burgoyne, 27Aug77.

702 Claus to Knox, 16Oct77.

703 *Colbrath Journal*, 48.

704 Deserters: Fernow, XV, State Archives, V.1, 197-209. He listed Cpl Corn'ls Devan and Ptes John O'Neal, Geo Smith and Thos White as deserting on 22Aug77. As no one deserted from Stanwix on the 22nd, I believe they deserted the night before and their names were recorded the next day; *Colbrath Journal*, 48; Enlisted: Cruikshank & Watt, *KRR NY*, App.III. Cornelius Divan was a Cpl in Watts' Coy by year's end and Geo Smith and Thos White served with him as Ptes. These three served the war in the KRR. Divan and White do not appear to have settled in Canada. A Geo Smith settled at CT#3 in 1784. John O'Neal deserted the KRR, but the year is unknown.

705 Stone, *Brant*, I, 257. No original source has been found for this contention, but it is consistent with Gansevoort's other actions.

706 *Colbrath Journal*, 49.

707 *Remembrancer 1777*, 445; Some accounts maintain that Hanjost suborned mem-

bers of this British alliance scouting party into spreading his story and that they were amongst those who arrived at St. Leger's tent during the morning with ever more alarming stories.

708 St. Leger to Burgoyne, 27Aug77.

709 William W. Campbell, 96.

710 There is no indication that anyone got through to Stanwix before the siege was raised. Pixley and Stiles were probably still en route when St. Leger decamped.

711 Claus to Knox, 16Oct77.

712 St. Leger and Claus recalled the sequence of these events differently. I have synthesized both accounts.

713 De Rouville, 228. His derisive poem heaped scorn on St. Leger, but many of his "facts" were patently false or perhaps the product of poetic licence. His opinions also may have been highly coloured by his distaste for St. Leger. Whatever the case, I have been very careful about accepting elements of his diatribe. What is clear from examining de Rouville's poem and von Kreutzbourg's and Rev. Scott's letters, St. Leger had the type of personality that, almost effortlessly, made long-lasting enemies. That a Canadien and a German were particularly offended suggests that St. Leger exhibited ethnocentric behaviour; St. Leger to Burgoyne, 27Aug77.

714 ibid. St. Leger believed these latter messengers were from amongst his closest *allies*.

715 An unsigned letter to Germain, Montreal, 4Sep77 found in the Germain Papers, VI and cited in Graymont, 145.

716 Ken D. Johnson, 547. Deposition of Dennis A. Flanders in NYPA W16396 of Johann Jost Scholl's widow. Flanders noted that the crops were ripe for harvesting before the march to Oriskany. The need would have been substantially greater after the event.

717 *Clinton Papers*, II, 247-48.

718 St. Leger to Burgoyne, 27Aug77.

719 Distances: Hagerty, 95. He provided the distances between the several posts built on the Oneida Carry; Gun ranges: E.B. Hughes, 29-41; Identifying which ruins?: JA Scott, 283.

720 De Rouville, 228. St. Leger's departure was cited as a sign of cowardice by de Rouville.

721 Claus, *Anecdotes of Brant*, 28.

722 Funds: Claus's report of his accounts, 2Dec77, found in NAC, HP, B114, 322 and cited in Kelsay, 208; Dispersion of Brant's men: Stevens, *Allies*, 1463.

723 The two men who carried Anderson's chest and deserted to the enemy were likely John Maddock and John Freeland, who had joined the KRR on 11Aug77 and were noted as prisoners at Stanwix after the siege was raised.

724 De Rouville, 228. He actually suggested that 150 men PLUS the 50 Canadiens were left behind, but that is out of the question, as there were only 132 soldiers of the 34th in the main camp.

725 I have assumed that after the failed experiment to convert the Cohorns into howitzers, the mortar tubes were dismounted from the three-pounder carriages and remounted on their flatbeds in preparation for placement in the new bomb battery. Mortars have a low profile which would allow the construction of a shallow battery position; Tube weight: Smith, *Dictionary*, 118.

726 *Colbrath Journal*, 51. He noted that only one three-pounder carriage was discovered in the camp near the landing on 23Aug; Willett to Gates, 1Sep77, cited in JA Scott, 329. Willett noted the discovery of a three-pounder tube "buried near one of their works." He gave its weight as "1 cwt 3 qrs 10 lbs"; Adrain B. Caruana, *Grasshoppers and Butterflies: The Light 3 Pounders of Pattison and Townshend* (Bloomfield, ON: Museum

Restoration Service, 1979) 5. Stated that the three-pounder Light Infantry gun weighed "1 cwt 3 qrs 16 lbs."

727 *Colbrath Journal*, 49.

728 Arnold to Gates, 23Aug77, transcribed in JA Scott, 288. The General said, "I met an express."

729 Claus, *Anecdotes of Brant*, 28; Norton, 274.

730 Robertaccio research. He advises that the remains of these bateaux may still be seen in the Wood Creek basin at Erie Canal Village, Rome, NY.

731 Mortars abandoned: *Colbrath Journal*, 51; Fuses: Willett to Gates, n.d., cited in Howard Thomas, 88. When Marinus took command in Gansevoort's absence, he advised that no fuses were available for the captured cohorns.

732 *Colbrath Journal*, 51.

733 Jägers' experiences during retreat: *Colbrath Journal*, 51,52; Jäger tactics: I assume that the Vacant Coy followed standard withdrawal tactics, alternately holding various points as its sections retreated down the roadway. For many examples of similar tactics, see Johann Ewald, Robert A. Selig, tr. & David Curtis, annotator, *Treatise on Partisan Warfare, Captain in the Infantry Regiment von Dittfurth in the Service of the Prince of Hesse-Cassel* (Cassel: Johann Jacob Cramer, 1785 – republished, New York: Greenwood Press, 1991); Freyburger's death: *Jaeger Corps' Diary*; List of discharged and missing soldiers, deserters, and those surrendered, from the Princely Hessen-Hanau Jaeger [Chasseur] Corps, from departure from Hanau to 31 March 177? transcribed in Clifford Neal Smith. These names were found in Ms70, Serial No.2 at the Staatsarchiv Marburg, Bestand, Germany. The complete name of the victim was Alexandre Freiburger. See also Watt & Morrison, *Campaign of 1777*, 30.

734 Officers' baggage: Samuel Younglove ; MacKenna: MacMaster, 122. From James Thatcher, *The American Revolution... A Daily Journal*, 88-89; Stevens, *Allies*, 1277. Stevens reviewed MacKenna's later claim and found that his altar silver, bedding, clothing and books had been looted; Blake: NAC, HP, AddMss21875; Natives cause panic: Stone, *Brant*, I, 261.

735 Kirkland to Gordon, n.d. cited in ibid.

736 Orders Group: De Rouville, 228; Wood Creek mouth: St. Leger to Burgoyne, 27Aug77. A march from Old Oneida to the mouth of Wood Ck. would have been readily accomplished.

737 Norton, 274.

738 De Rouville, 228. The Canadien told the tale somewhat differently than St. Leger. He indicated that the main body of bateaux was not reached until the troops arrived at Lake Oneida. This does not make sense, as the creek system was readily navigable as far as the ruins of Fort Bull. De Rouville's obvious desire to paint the picture as black as possible renders all his comments suspect.

739 Various quoted phrases from the *Colbrath Journal*, 49-50.

740 Various quotations from St. Leger to Burgoyne, 27Aug77.

741 Various quotations from Arnold to Gates dated "Mowhawk River, 10 Miles Above Fort Dayton, Aug't 23, 1777, 5 O'clock P.M." cited in JA Scott, 287-88.

742 Arnold clearly had no intention of being caught on the road by Indians and/or Tories.

743 JA Scott, 287-88.

744 Second letter of Arnold to Gates, 23Aug77, cited in ibid.

745 *Colbrath Journal*, 51.

746 Samuel Younglove .

747 *Remembrancer 1777*, 445; In '81, John Lawrence was returned in KRR records as a

deserter on 24Jun78, but this was likely the date that a decision was made regarding his status.

748 *Colbrath Journal*, 54.

749 Lossing, I, 252.

750 These sheets and billets of raw metal weighed an incredible 15,300 pounds (7.65 Tons; 6,940Kg – 7 tonnes).

751 *Jaeger Corps' Diary*. In order to discredit St. Leger, Von Kreutzbourg reported the confusion and panic of the retreat. He stated that the expedition set their tents afire, but this evidence tells us otherwise; As the KRR's tents had been taken or destroyed by Willett's sortie, those left behind belonged to the Regulars, Jägers and Canadiens.

752 *Remembrancer 1777*, 445; *Colbrath Journal*, 51-52; The abandoned clothing was only sufficient for a small company. The musket cartridges represented an issue of 30 rounds for 72 men. On the other hand, 54 wedge tents could house 270 men at the usual ratio of five to a tent.

753 *Scudder Journal*, 18; NYPA R17772 of Abraham & Dorothy Wolleber. A supporting deposition by Elizabeth Shoemaker, noted that Abraham's brothers, John and Dederick were killed at Oriskany and that they "were recognized by their friends who went after the battle to bury the dead"; NYPA R729 of Richard (Hondedrick) Marcus Petrie & Catharine (née Bellinger) Petrie. "His brother and other friends afterwards went to the battle ground to inter him and informed her that they did inter his body." So, some bodies were buried before total decomposition.

754 *Colbrath Journal*, 52. The Lieut combined the events of the 23rd and 24th in his journal.

755 *Willett OB.*. The entry was dated 23Aug.

756 Robertaccio research: Joseph advises that the 6-pounder tubes were recovered from the creek, but not the three-pounder. He theorizes that the two 6-pounder tubes presently displayed at the Crown Point Visitors' Center may be the guns of St. Leger.

757 Arnold to Gates, 28Aug77, transcribed in JA Scott, 290-91.

758 NYHS, Mf Reel #3, *Gates Papers*.

759 As if to prove that the Onondagas had much to worry about, in '79, their castles were the first targets of the Sullivan-Clinton expedition and the attack was mounted from Fort Stanwix.

760 Willett to Gates, 2Sep77, cited in Swiggett, 100; *Gates Papers*. Gave the chief's name as Tewargriate; No record has been found of this chief's visit with St. Leger.

761 Butler to LeMaistre, 14Dec77, transcribed by Smy from NAC, HP, AddMss21756; Butler to LeMaistre, 28Jan78 found in ibid. "By accounts from the Susquehanna River, I am well informed of the rebels having taken prisoner thirty of the Rangers who went from Oneida Lake by leave of Colonel St. Leger. They were to have returned to this place with as many beef cattle as they could drive off. The rebels, as is supposed, got notice of their design and with a party of 200 men surprised and took them with three Indians."

762 St. Leger to Burgoyne, 27Aug77.

763 ? to Gates dated Albany, 25Aug77, transcribed from the*Gates Papers*.

764 Jeptha R. Simms, *Trappers of New York: or, A Biography of Nicholas Stoner and Nathaniel Foster; together with Anecdotes of other Celebrated Hunters and some account of Sir William Johnson and his style of living* (Albany: J. Munsell, 1871 – reprinted, Harbor Hill Books, 1980) 58-60.

765 Morrison, *Livingston*, 7; Pomroy Jones, 361-62. When burial did take place, only the bodies contiguous to the roadway were attended to. Long after, the first folk to settle on the battlefield gathered skeletons and loose bones and put them in a

common grave.

766 Gansevoort to Gates, 12Dec77, transcribed in the *Gansevoort Papers*, 183.

767 Various quotations: Two documents of the Tryon Committee, 25Aug77, transcribed in Penrose, *Mohawk Valley*, 127-30; Cruikshank, *Butler's Rangers*, 42. Within a year, zealous Tryon committeemen had 400 Tory women & children in confinement.

768 Arnold to Gates, German Flats 28Aug77, cited in JA Scott, 291. From the *Gates Papers*.

769 Arrival date: Claus to Knox, 16Oct77; Misconception about St. Leger's force: Von Kreutzbourg to Crown Prince of Hanau, 12Jul77, in *Jaeger Corps' Diary*; Details of and quotations from the Council of War: Von Kreutzbourg to Crown Prince of Hanau, 5Sep77, ibid.

770 This use of the designation "sloop" was likely in the merchant sense – that is, a single masted vessel, fore and aft rigged. A "snow" was a two-masted, square-rigged vessel with a short mast immediately behind the foremast mounting a trysail or spanker.

771 All quotations: St. Leger to Burgoyne, 27Aug77.

772 *Jaeger Corps' Diary*; Stanley, *Horse*, 140.

773 The Return: NAC, WO17/1571(2), 207; Wilhelmy, 265-66. The battalion was comprised of four coys in '77. Added to the Vacant Coy were those of Capts von Franken, von Wittgenstein & von Castendyk. The latter may have led the Col's Coy.

774 Claus to Knox, 16Oct77

775 Guy Johnson to Germain, 11Nov77 & 12Mar78, transcribed in *CHSNY*, VIII, 726-28,740-41. While it is tempting to criticize Guy's performance, it must be recognized that he remained in New York City under the orders of Sir Wm Howe. That he could or should have been more insistent about his utilization is the point I am making.

776 Von Kreutzbourg would have us believe that St. Leger's antipathy or studied indifference was based on ethnic prejudice. However, Hessian Artillery Capt Georg Pausch wrote of St. Leger and the officers and men of the 34th – "A great amount of honor and friendship was demonstrated to us." See, *Pausch Journals*, 31. It was likely that St. Leger's dislike of von Kreutzbourg was of a personal nature, not ethnic.

777 Various quotations: Claus, *Anecdotes of Brant*, 29; Stanley, *Horse*, 139.

778 Various quotations: Garrison Orders at Stanwix in late Aug & early Sep are from *Willett's OB*.

779 Simms, *Frontiersman*, II, 103. Long after the victim's flesh & bones had disappeared, the bayonet remained visible as the expanding tree trunk slowly absorbed it.

780 Kelsay, 140. In his will, Sir William provided for his widow and each of his daughters and sons. In the face of the Committee's resentment, Mary remained at Canajoharie to keep a close eye on her family's real properties. Of her goods & chattels, we have a list found in her petition for losses (Estimate of Losses sustained by Mohawk Indians, State Papers, Canada, Q24, Pt.2, 315-17). A quilted white ball-gown styled in the French mode, 2 pairs of green velvet leggings, 2 scarlet cloaks, silken hose & gloves, 200 hundred silver brooches, 300 silver crosses, 8 hats, a picture, a violin, a set of music books, fine silver service, china, all kinds of bedding, 12 chairs, 3 side-saddles, a wagon, a chaise, a bateau, and plenty of money; Lois M. Huey and Bonnie Pulis, *Molly Brant, A Legacy of Her Own* (Youngstown, NY: Old Fort Niagara Association, 1997) 37&38, 45&46. Gives a complete listing; Quotations: from the testimony of a Child of Molly Brant's, 15Mar1841 cited in ibid, 45&86. From the Hamilton papers, Box 2, folder 12.

781 Helen Caister Robinson, Phyllis R. Blakeley & John N. Grant, eds., "Molly Brant, Mohawk Heroine," *Eleven Exiles, Accounts of Loyalists of the American Revolution* (Toronto: Dundurn Press, 1982) 122. Robinson claimed that Joseph's wife

Catherine was staying with Mary while he was away fighting. Although the article is endnoted, she failed to give a specific source for her contention. As Joseph did not marry Catherine Croghan until '79 (Kelsay, 276), this was clearly not her. If his second wife, thought to have been named Susanna, (ibid, 134) was at Canajoharie, this would help to explain the zealousness of the Oneidas; Claus to Nepean, 8Mar87, cited in Kelsay, 209, found in NAC, CO42/19, 88-89.

782 Affidavits of Martin Dellenback, Elisabeth Haberman, Hendrick S. Moyer, Johannus G. House, Henry Apple, George Herkimer, Hanyost Herkimer, Jacobus Pickett, all dated 20Apr78 and a letter of Jelles Fonda to the commissioners of Ind Affairs, 21Apr78, Penrose, *Indian Affairs*, 125-34; Potter-MacKinnon, 56; Kelsay, 208-09; Graymont, 147.

783 Mrs. Gray: Albany Minutes, I, 839.

784 Stanley, *Horse*, 134.

785 *Clinton Papers*, II, 271fn.

786 Clinton to Hoornbeek, 3Sep77, transcribed in ibid, 272&74.

787 Cruikshank & Watt, *KRR NY*, 21.

788 *Jaeger Corps' Diary*.

789 Stanley, *Horse*, 141; Deserontyon later recalled abandoning Fort Hunter on 8Sep77. David Faux, "The Pro-Patriot Faction Among the Mohawk Indians and the Sale of the New York Lands," *Loyalist Gazette*, Autumn 1980. Taken from the Draper Mss, 14F; Stanley, *Horse*, 141; Cruikshank, *Quinte Mohawks*, 391; Stevens, *Allies*, 1385-86.

790 Claus to Knox, 6Nov77. Claus mentions the complicity of the Oneidas in the sack of Fort Hunter.

791 Details from the claim of John Deserontyon transcribed in Potter-MacKinnon, 67. From NAC, CO42/47, 240; Graymont, 147. She stated, "their white neighbours were only too glad of the opportunity to raise their standard of living at the Mohawks' expense"; Ironically, the Mohawks were vilified in Whig accounts when they took revenge on their "innocent" white neighbours during the May80 raid led by Sir John Johnson.

792 Graymont, 225-29. Little Abraham Tyorsansere and his associate Johannes Schrine Unaquandahoojie were involved in a rebel-motivated peace overture to Niagara in Feb80 and were held in cruel circumstances in the fort's jail.

793 Stuart & Chapel: Stevens, *Allies*, 1387; Communion plate: M. Eleanor Herrington, "Captain John Deserontyou and the Mohawk Settlement at Deseronto," *Bulletin of the Departments of History and Political and Economic Science in Queen's University*, Kingston, Ontario, Canada, No.41 (Nov 1921) 8. Herrington advised that when the Communion plate was brought to Canada, it was divided. Three pieces were retained by the Bay of Quinte settlement and four were given to Grand River. She believed the plate had been buried in '75. I contend this occurred in '77; R.M. Bruce, *The Loyalist Trial* (n.p., n.d.) 63. Has a photograph showing the three pieces of the plate held at the Bay of Quinte; Memorial of John Stuart, 31Dec83, transcribed in ibid, 109-10. From NAC, HP, B215, 96-97. Stuart served as Chaplain to the 2nd Bn, KRR during the war and as Deputy Chaplain to the 34th afterwards. He also maintained his chaplaincy to the Mohawks; Rev John Stuart to Bishop Inglis, 6Jul88, transcribed in ibid, 147. He noted that the plate was in use at the Bay of Quinte settlement.

794 Stanley, *Horse*,78,80,87,97-98,141; Stevens, *Allies*, 1387; Claus, *Anecdotes of Brant*, 28. A year later, Capt John was still in danger of losing his arm due to the wound received at Stanwix. His high level of activity and second wounding in this skirmish speaks to his great courage and remarkable resilience; Hill brothers: This death was

Endnotes

neither Aaron, Isaac nor David, as they served latter in the war. Perhaps, it was John Hill Oteronyente, who had been Brant's companion in England.

795 *Anburey Journal*, 167-69. Offers many observations regarding the Mohawks' lifestyle and manner of war that have a ring of accuracy.

796 Stevens, *Allies*, 1387-88. Stevens' superb analysis of the disintegration of Burgoyne's native contingent is dealt with across several chapters of his work; St. Luc to Burgoyne, 23Oct78 cited in *Hadden's Journal*, 517-37. "This indifference towards the Indians also, who had served in the affair at Bennington, who amounted to 150, disgusted them; many of whom, with their grand Chief, were killed, and of 61 Canadians only 41 remained."

797 Smy transcripts, NYHS, Gates Papers, Box 7.

798 Claus to Knox, 6Nov77.

799 Quotations: Claus to Knox, 16Oct77; Stevens, *Allies*, 1284-85. Stevens cited his usual confusing amalgam of sources for this detail.

800 Quotation: Claus to Haldimand, 5Nov78, transcribed in Penrose, *Indian Affairs*, 169-72. Excellent detail as to why Claus sent Sarah Kast McGinnis on this mission and the superb results of her efforts; Potter-MacKinnon, 108. Sarah McGinnis never received just compensation for her notable efforts. Her treatment was utterly shabby, which was remarkable in view of Claus's strong commendation of her to Haldimand, in which he noted that "she claims no small Merit" in keeping the Six Nations allied to the Crown. This oversight reinforces MacKinnon's thesis on the role and treatment of loyalist women and the historical devaluation of the female in our society. Her comments regarding Sarah McGinnis are particularly poignant.

801 Various quotations: Samuel Younglove.

802 John McDonell (Scotus) to Mathews, 12Dec83 found in HP, AddMss21822. In his account of the *Schoharie* events, he wrote of raising and arming 54 recruits. (for a list of the loyalists and some Indians who participated, see Watt & Morrison, *Campaign of 1777*, 202-12) Many of the recruits were unable or unwilling to join the trek and enlisted in Prov regts later in the war; McDonell's Coy: Muster Rolls of the KRR NY, 21Jan78, found in NAC, WO28/5, 214-20.

803 Capt Mathews to Lernoult, 5Sep77, found in NAC, HP, AddMss21699.

804 Details & quotations from: Samuel Younglove; His use of the word "several" suggested more than two boats. That could mean 9 or more uniform coats were on display, yet the company lost no more than five men during the whole Stanwix phase. Were these spare coats taken from the stolen knapsacks, or was the whole scene a sheer fantasy?

805 Details and quotations: Von Kreutzbourg to the Crown Prince of Hanau, 13Sep77, in the *Jaeger Corps' Diary*.

806 John Enys, Elizabeth Cometti, ed., *The American Journals of Lt John Enys* (Syracuse: The Adirondack Museum and Syracuse Univ. Press, 1976) 91-103. This source contains a wonderful description of the trip up the St. Lawrence River. The reverse trip was extremely fast, but all the more terrifying, due to the vicious rapids that required the aid of native or Canadien pilots and bateauxmen; Loss of bateaux: Petition of Thomas Smith transcribed in Cruikshank, *Petitions*, 330-31.

807 Stevens, *Allies*, 1408.

808 Vallena Munro research. NAC, HP, MG21, B214, AddMss21874, 96-100.

809 Stevens, *Allies*, 1409.

810 ibid, 1407&10.

811 *Smy Transcripts*. Butler to Carleton, Niagara ,14Dec77, transcribed from NAC, HP, AddMss21756. Butler advised that the Oneidas and Tuscaroras successfully ran-

somed the three Iroquois with prisoners taken from Burgoyne's army. Obviously, their motivation was complex.

812 Stevens, *Allies*, 1411. Stevens cited two contemporary journals for 21Sep.

813 Details & quotations: Von Kreutzbourg to the Crown Prince of Hanau, 22Sep77, *Jaeger Corps' Diary*. The deranged Jäger was Friedrich Jaeger, who was dismissed at La Prairie on 22Sep77. See, C.N. Smith.

814 HSGS, II, 41. The editorial text stated that Carleton's tone "grew more petulant and bitter."

815 Quotations from: ibid, 230-31 found in NAC, CO42/36(Q13), 184.

816 K.G. Davies, ed., "The Campaigns of 1777," *Documents of the American Revolution 1770-1783* (Colonial Office Series), Vol.XIV, Transcripts 1777 (Shannon: Irish Univ. Press, 1972) 2-16. In his introduction, Davies offers a very useful and succinct analysis of the Germain-Howe-Burgoyne-Carleton-Clinton-St. Leger relationship.

817 HSGS, II, 41; Lynn, Mary C., ed., Helga Doblin, tr., *The American Revolution, Garrison Life in French Canada and New York, Journal of an Officer in the Prinz Friedrich Regiment, 1776-1783 [Prinz Friedrich]* (Westport, CT and London: Greenwood Press, 1993) 80. Doblin believes this journal was kept by Ensign Julius Friedrich von Hille.

818 Steven, *Allies*, 1347; HSGS, II, 232 found in NAC, CO42/37(Q14), 18-19.

819 The Senecas' recollection of Schuyler's words: Smy Transcripts, NAC, CO42/37.

820 Stevens, *Allies*, 1364. The identity of the three Iroquois envoys has not been found. Stevens was convinced that the principal man was the Onondaga Teaqwanda, as he acted as the native alliance's liaison with British Headquarters in the later war. Stevens apparently was quoting a speech by the Mohawk war captain, Aaron Hill in '79, in which he recalled the council's details. This was likely from AddMss21779, f.19&20.

821 Stevens, *Allies*, 1366.

822 NAC, HP, AddMss21700; Butler's Rangers became the most effective British unit operating in the north. Their creation must be viewed as one of Carleton's most important actions. More than any other regt, BR's constantly took the war to the very doorsteps of the rebels, as far east as New Jersey, south to Virginia and west to the Illinois & Ohio countries.

823 *Smy Transcripts*. Carleton to Burgoyne, 15Sep77, transcribed from NAC, HP, AddMss21699; Rank of Colonel: The see-sawing back and forth of Butler's rank is always confusing. Carleton recognized Butler's militia rank when he referred to him as a colonel.

824 *Smy Transcripts*. Carleton to Butler, 15Sep77, in NAC, HP, AddMss21700.

825 Claus to Knox, 16Oct77. Butler later reported the exchange error and was instructed to credit the government for the excess; In amongst his many large expense items was a tiny charge for tea, sugar and some funds provided to the rebel prisoners, Bellinger and Frey. Morrison research. Rufus Grider Collection, Montgomery County Department of History.

826 *Smy Transcripts*. NAC, HP, AddMss21678.

827 HSGS, II, 41&42.

828 Claus to Knox, 16Oct77.

829 Carleton to Maclean, 21Sep77, cited in Stevens, *Allies*, 1370.

830 Stevens, *Allies*, 1371-72. From HP, AddMss21765, ff.7-8, 48&68.

831 Claus' formal request for payment: Claus to Carleton, 6Oct77, found in the *Claus Papers*, V25, 13-16; The discussion: Claus to Knox, 16Oct77; Due to Carleton's petty machinations, Claus spent years pursuing repayment of his expenditures on behalf of St. Leger's expedition.

832 Stanley, *Horse*, 143. "The Bridge from Batten Kill was broken up, and floated down the

Endnotes

River, and all communication with Canada voluntarily cut off"; Burgoyne's report to the administration of 20Oct77 found in NAC, WO42/37, 286 stated the army "passed the Hudsons river on the 13th and 14th of September" on the "Bridge of Boats."

833 "John Brown and the Dash for Ticonderoga," [Brown's dash] *The Bulletin of the Fort Ticonderoga Museum,* V.II, No.1 (Jan 1930), 37-38; Brown to Lincoln, 10(18?)Sep77, cited in Stone, *Burgoyne & St. Leger,* 349.

834 Lynn, *Prinz Friedrich,* 78-82; Stone, *Burgoyne & St. Leger,* 346-52; Ketchum, *Saratoga,* 376-79. Ketchum advised that the final count of Canadiens taken rose to 119, which agreed with HSGS, II, 41 which stated that more than 100 were captured; Russell P. Bellico, *Sails and Steam in the Mountains, A Maritime and Military History of Lake George and Lake Champlain* (Fleischmanns, NY: Purple Mountain Press, 1992) 180-84. Excellent accounts of the attacks on the posts; *Brown's dash,* passim; Andrew R. Fisher collection. George H. Jepson, *Herrick's Rangers* (Bennington, VT: Hadwen, Inc., 1977) 3, 19. Herrick's men overwhelmed the works on Mount Defiance.

835 *Hadden's Journal,* 117,464-65; After the '77 campaign, Powell held a number of appointments in Canada. He was St. Leger commanding the Montreal district in '78 and in '79-80 commanded the southern district below Montreal at Fort St John's. Powell replaced LtCol Mason Bolton as commander of the 8th Regt and the upper posts in Oct80. See also, Cruikshank & Watt, KRR NY, 22-25,73-74, and Arthur Britton Smith, 105&108.

836 *Brown's dash,* 20; Lynn, *Prinz Friedrich,* 78-79.

837 Brown to Lincoln, 26Sep77, cited in Stone, *Burgoyne & St. Leger,* 351; Lynn, *Prinz Friedrich,* 80-81. The PFR account differed in some details from Brown's.

838 ibid, 82.

839 Ketchum, *Saratoga,* 368&371. He gave the Crown's casualties as 160 dead, 364 wounded and 42 missing for a total of 566. Total U.S. casualties were somewhere between 273-313; Freeman's Farm (or 1st Saratoga) was considered one of the most significant battles fought during the rebellion.

840 Quotations: Respectively by MA Gen John Glover and NH LtCol Henry Dearborn cited in Ketchum, Saratoga, 369.

841 The First Canadian (1CDN) was supported by, and accredited to, NYS. The unit was heavily engaged in both Saratoga battles; Roberts, 60. Shows the unit as a NYS Additional Regt.

842 Ketchum, *Saratoga,* 363-65.

843 ibid, 356-72; Mintz, 187-99; Lossing, *Pictorial Fieldbook,* I, 51-56.

844 William W. Campbell, 100; Morrison, *Fulton County,* 28-30. Capt Abraham Veeder's Coy, Third Regt., joined Gates' army in early Sep77 and fought in both battles at Saratoga. Capt Nicholas Rechtor's Coy, Second Regt, joined Gates in early Sep, fought in both battles and returned home after the surrender; Morrison research. NYPA W2461, widow of William Van Slyke. Van Slyke mustered in Capt Fox's Coy, Second Regt, and went to Stillwater. Served a month under Gen Gates and returned home before the surrender; PA Pension of Benjamin Dickson. Marched under Major Saml Clyde to Saratoga. Returned home before the surrender; "Thirteenth Regt, (Stillwater-Saratoga) Albany County Militia '77," *Stone Arabia Battle Chpt, SAR Newsletter,* Dec 1993. An anonymous writer claimed that the Albany Cty militia "was present in limited numbers at the first battle of Saratoga."

845 Text of Sir Henry Clinton's decoded message, 12Oct77, cited in Ketchum, *Saratoga,* 375. The author gave an analysis of Burgoyne's troubled state of mind and questioned the judgements he made because of Clinton's 'promises'; Mintz, 201. From

the *Riedesel Memoirs* I:160.

846 William L. Stone, tr. *Letters of Brunswick and Hessian Officers During the American Revolution* (Albany: 1891 — facsimile, New York: De Capo Press, 1970) 119.

847 Stevens, *Allies*, 1415.

848 Burgoyne painted too dark a picture, as he later fielded 6,600 men.

849 Stevens, *Allies*, 1415-16. Regardless of the ostensible purpose of this flag, the officer was clearly intended to alarm Burgoyne's army; *Pausch Journal*, 81. He recorded on 21Sep that a picket brought in a prisoner who said that the *feu de joie* and cheering heard the day before marked the capture of Ticonderoga. Pausch thought this an obvious lie. Nonetheless, this entry meant that the Germans had heard about the attack on Ticonderoga several days before the flag brought the information to Burgoyne.

850 Stone, *Orderly Book SJJ*, 98fn. From Burgoyne, *State*.

851 *Pausch Journal*, 82.

852 Secret letter, Burgoyne to Riedesel, 10Sep77, transcribed in *SJJ OB*, 97fn. Stone wrote a sequel to this story – Riedesel ordered three bateaux buried rather than two. His men erected a board inscribed, "Here lies the body of Lieutenant X," but the artifice did not mislead Stark's men and the "graves" were dug up. Later, these bateaux were used by them to cross the Hudson and interdict Burgoyne's rear lines — the ultimate backfire of the plan.

853 HSGS, II, 237. From the NAC, CO42/37, 310. Oddly, this order was dated 19Oct77, long after the movement took place.

854 St. Leger's brevet rank of brigadier general disappeared once he arrived in Burgoyne's sphere of activity. This has led many to conclude that he had assumed the higher rank on his own authority. I believe that contention unlikely, as the grand army's brigadiers were slated to return to their substantive ranks once they joined with Howe's.

855 Powell to Carleton, 27Sep77, found in NAC, CO42/37, 137-38.

856 John McDonell (Scotus) to Maj Mathews, 12Dec83, found in NAC, HP, MG21, B162, V.2, 135. These personal firearms disappeared after being removed during the evacuation. Prior to the 1Bn's disbandment, their owners applied to McDonell for reimbursement, much to his discomfort. How this issue was resolved has not been discovered.

857 Powell to Carleton, 29Sep77, found in NAC, CO42/37, 217.

858 Maclean to Carleton, 30Sep77, found in ibid, 141.

859 Powell to Carleton, 30Sep77, found in ibid, 219.

860 Lynn, *Prinz Friedrich*, 82,94. The Jägers were sent to the advanced camp on 28Sep; *Field Jaeger Corps*, 28-30.

861 Duncan's 1788 petition transcribed in *Loyalist Petitions*, I, 474-75.

862 Stanley, *Horse*, 156-57.

863 ibid, 158; Stone, *Burgoyne and St. Leger*, 48. Stone maintained that the troops were angered with Burgoyne after Freeman's Farm. Other historians claim he maintained their obedience and affection (at least the British) even after their surrender and even after he was paroled to Britain and the comforts of home; When he defaulted on his promise to return to America to join them in their captivity, the "bloom came off the rose."

864 Schermerhorn's attempt failed when he fell ill en route and was captured. Having suffered a year of imprisonment in chains and the loss of all his properties, he died in Jun86 in deep distress and poverty. His wife Elizabeth died two years later. See, Alexander Fraser, ed., *Second Report of the Bureau of Archives for the Province of*

Ontario (2 vols., Toronto: Legislative Assembly of Ontario, 1904 – republished, Baltimore: Genealogical Publishing Co., Inc., 1994) II, 1024-5,1073,1268 and a transcript of Wm Schermerhorn's undated petition to Sir John Johnson in the collection of M. Ross Williams from the Dr. H.C. Burleigh Papers.

865 Stevens, *Allies*, 1422.

866 Powell to Carleton, 10Oct77, found in CO42/37, 234; Sir John's courier: Capt John Jones, of Jessup's King's Loyal Americans. Jones' property lay between Forts George and Edward. Due to his intimate knowledge of the topography and cool courage, he was a most successful courier. Simultaneously, he was serving as the Deputy Barracks Master at Ticonderoga.

867 Powell to Carleton, 11Oct77, found in NAC, CO42/37, 236.

868 H.H. Robertson, unpublished manuscript, "Burgoyne's Loyal Americans, Some notes on Burgoyne's Campaign 1777." AO, H.H.Robertson Papers. His study contained a 16Oct77 return of Gates' army at Saratoga. There were 13,216 "Present fit for duty" and a grand total of 18,624 which included 3,875 "On command." The majority of the latter were from the militia brigades that scoured the surrounding country for British couriers and stragglers.

869 Alex Fraser's Coy of Select Marksmen was composed of picked men from the British regts. The unit was virtually destroyed at Bennington, but, as Burgoyne relied very heavily upon Fraser's coy for scouting and deeds of great daring, it was reconstituted on 2Sep77. See, Stanley, *Horse,* 140. From, "G[eneral]: O[rders]:, Camp at Duar's House." However, these new men, no matter how "active, robust and healthy," could not achieve the efficiency level of the previous complement, which had worked together in the '76 and '77 campaigns. With the great need for men to operate in the woods, the revived coy was immediately employed on the most demanding of missions, along with the Indians, Canadiens and the most combat-efficient loyalist units.

870 Mintz, 207-08.

871 Mintz and Ketchum are quite at variance over what was said and done by Gates and Arnold, but these details have no bearing on St. Leger's story. I refer readers to these two highly detailed and excellent accounts.

872 John R. Cuneo, *The Battles of Saratoga, The Turning of the Tide* (New York: The Macmillan Company, 1967) 88-91. The author offered some interesting views regarding Arnold's role in this action.

873 Mintz, 210-11. Mintz gave the precise strength of 1,845, but failed to quote a source. He assumed they were all Albany County men, which they may have been; Ketchum, *Saratoga,* 397. He gave Ten Broeck's brigade strength as 1,800 and made the observation that this was equal to Burgoyne's force of Brit Regulars; Lossing, *Field Book Revolution,* I, 62, Ward, II, 529 and *Stone Arabia Battle Chpt Newsletter,* Dec 1993. These three sources claimed that the NY brigade strength was 3,000. No sources were cited.

874 Stevens, *Allies*, 1423.

875 Mintz, 212.

876 Stevens, *Allies*, 1473; Cruikshank, *Butler's Rangers*, 39. Cruikshank interpreted Butler's intentions differently, claiming that he had no intention to hold a council at Oswego. Rather, he planned to set off from there and travel to Niagara through Cayuga and Seneca country while recruiting his force and would then depart from Niagara to join Burgoyne.

877 Powell to Carleton, 16Oct77, in NAC, CO42/37, 238; LtCol Francis Van Pfister's Loyal Volunteers joined Burgoyne in Aug77 and fought at Bennington. The Col was

killed in that battle and 107 of his men captured. Various journals of Burgoyne's campaign mention the LV's frequently. See, AO, Ms622, HP, Rl85 (AddMss21827?),114; Leake to Brehm, 4Aug78, found in HP, AddMss21874, 38-39.

878 Gray to Maclean, 16Oct77, found in NAC, CO42/37, 244.

879 *Orders Field Jaeger Corps*, 31.

880 Powell to Maclean, 16Oct77, found in NAC, CO42/37, 248.

881 Lynn, *Prinz Friedrich*, 82.

882 Quotations: MacKay to Le Maistre (Meter), 1Dec77, found in NAC, HP, MG21, B71, 379-80; H. C. Burleigh, *Captain MacKay and the Loyal Volunteers* (Bloomfield: Bayside Publishing Company, 1977) 8. From the HP, letters to the Ministry 1778-81, 134. MacKay was strongly criticized for abandoning the artificers. Carleton, piqued that MacKay had refused to retain command of the Canadien Coy earlier in the year, poisoned the capt's prospects over this event. Consequently in '78, Haldimand did not recognize MacKay as the LV's commandant. Samuel died in '79, having suffered severely from the "exigencies of the service" and left his family in terrible distress. Ironically, Haldimand noted that he had been "an exceeding good soldier," which was certainly true; Cruikshank & Watt, *KRR NY*, 238. His sons Saml and John served in the 2Bn, KRR as Ensigns till the end of war. Saml was 4th senior and John 6th.

883 Powell to Carleton, 19Oct77, found in NAC, CO42/37, 254; Devinnay: NAC, WO28/5, 219. Hugh & John Devinnay were mustered in Duncan's Coy on 24Dec77, having enlisted on 8Nov77. There was no record of their names on the KRR rolls prepared in '81, nor on the list of Casuals prepared that year. (MG21, B158, 208-10) They simply disappeared.

884 Ketchum, *Saratoga*, 410-11; Mrs. General Riedesel, Claus Reuter, tr. & ed., *Letters and Journals Relating to the War of American Independence and the capture of the German Troops at Saratoga* (Toronto: German-Canadian Museum of Applied History, 2001) 94. Reuter translated her words as, "The savages had lost their courage, and they were seen in all directions going home. The slightest reverse of fortune discouraged them, especially if there was nothing to plunder."

885 Stevens, *Allies*, 1431,1439-40. The captured Mohawks were taken to Schuyler at Albany and he resettled them in the Valley. In Jun78, a rescue party of their kin and some Akwesasnes took them to Canada.

886 ibid, 1438.

887 Lynn, *Prinz Friedrich*, 84.

888 HSGS, II, 237-38. Transcribed from NAC, HP, Q15, 201-02.

889 Mary Beacock Fryer, *King's Men, the Soldier Founders of Ontario* (Toronto & Charlottetown: Dundurn Press Limited, 1980) 223; LtCol John Peters, "A Narrative of John Peters, Lieutenant-Colonel in the Queen's Loyal Rangers in Canada Drawn by Himself in a Letter to a Friend in London," *Toronto Globe*, July 16,1877.

890 Lynn, *Prinz Friedrich*, 84-85.

891 *Orders Field Jaeger Corps*, 32-33.

892 Jessups's party: Fryer, *King's Men*, 195; The Convention: After the '77 campaign, Haldimand was burdened by a large number of loyalist soldiers who were "under the convention." (for the Articles of the Convention, see Chidsey, 194-96) When it became obvious that the Cont'l Congress refused to accept the terms Gates had agreed to with Burgoyne, Haldimand considered himself released from this obligation and employed all of the loyalists in active military roles; Munro: A return of Munro's Coy, 25Jun77–24Dec77, found in NAC, WO28/5, 218.

893 Green Mountain Rangers: The Green Mountain Boys were an additional regt of the

New York ContLine. See, Roberts, I, 61; Elizabeth Gray: Lynn, *Prinz Friedrich*, 85. "[T]he wife of an Albany officer from the Royal New York Regt. with her children." As Maj Gray, his wife and two children were quartered at St. John's the following year (a return of 16Jun78. NAC, WO28/10, Pt.1, 110), I have concluded that the subject lady was Elizabeth Gray (neé Low); Sullivan & Flick, *Albany*, I, 838-39. As endnoted previously, a list dated 15Sep77 indicated that Gray's family and many others, including John Munro's, were to be sent to the enemy. Why Mrs. Gray and her children got through, and so many others did not, is a mystery; Snowfall: Lynn, *Prinz Friedrich*, 85.

894 Various quotations: Maclean to Carleton, 1Nov77, found in NAC, CO42/37, 260.

895 Weekly State of the Garrison of Ticonderoga and Mount Independence, 1Nov77, ibid, 284.

896 Haldimand to Clinton, 26May79, transcribed in HSGS, III, 109 from NAC, HP, Q16-1, 111-17. He wrote, "[T]he Hanau Chasseurs are... both by nature and Education Totally unfit for an American War... conspicuous in repeated and considerable Desertions"; Haldimand to Clinton, 1Nov79, transcribed in ibid, 136 from NAC, HP, B147, 113-18. Haldimand wrote that his German troops were, "inactive, indolent, and helpless, and so addicted to desertion that I dare not trust them in any of the Frontier Posts, so that in fact they are more an Incumbrance when there is a scarcity of Provisions than an additional strength."

897 Bolton & Butler to Clinton, Niagara, 23Nov77, transcribed in *CHSNY*, VIII, 741. When the need to support Burgoyne evaporated, Butler and Brant offered to support Clinton on the Hudson. What incredible zeal!; Smy transcript. Butler to Carleton, Niagara ,14Dec77, from NAC, HP, AddMss 21756. Two of the Iroquois taken with the Flag party, and released due to the efforts of the Oneidas and Tuscaroras, visited John Butler at Niagara and advised that his son, Ten Broeck and Bowen had still been in irons when they left Albany; Cruikshank, *Butler's Rangers*, 39.

898 Lynn, *Prinz Friedrich*, 85.

899 Letter from Maj Gray, 22May82, in NAC, WO28/5, 98. Gray stated that "Severals of our Regt. was made Batoemen of when St. Leger went upon his Expedition in the Artilery Boats etc and were employed in the same manner coming Back." They were "Enterd on our Books from May till Nov 5 1777 which Day they Deserted." I have attempted to identify these men. Francis Dubois and Henry Whitemore deserted on 24Oct77, but they had not enlisted in May. Thos Atherton and Thos Thompson deserted on 5Nov77, but neither of them had enlisted in May. Jacob Hoult, Donald McMullen and one of the many John McDonells deserted on 1Nov77 and had enlisted on 6May77. Not much help!

900 *Orders Field Jaeger Corps*, 36.

901 Various quotations and details: Lynn, *Prinz Friedrich*, 86.

902 Don Higginbotham, *The War of American Independence,Military Attitudes, Policies, and Practice, 1763-1789 – Wars of the United States Series* (Don Mills, Ont: Fitzhenry & Whiteside Limited, 1971) 199fn4.

903 Macksey, 144.

904 *Gansevoort Papers*, 178fn.

905 An address by the officers of the 3NY to Col Gansevoort, 12Oct77, transcribed in ibid, 178&179.

906 Gansevoort's reply to his officers, ibid, 179&180.

907 In Congress, 4Oct77, and Hancock to Willett, 5Oct77, transcribed in Wm Willett, 137.

908 Roberts, I, 87.

909 Gansevoort to his wife Catherine, 2&8Nov78, excerpted in Egly, *1NY*, 114.

910 Clinton to Heath, 30Oct80, excerpted in ibid. For additional details on garrison life at Stanwix, see ibid, 116&150.

911 ibid, 156&157.

912 Cochran to Van Cortlandt, 13May81, excerpted in Graymont, 245.

913 Mackesy, 147onwards; Stephen Bonsal, *When the French Were Here, A Narrative of the Sojourn of the French Forces in America, and Their Contribution to the Yorktown Campaign Drawn from Unpublished Reports and Letters of Participants in the National Archives of France and the MS. Division of the Library of Congress* (Garden City, NY: Doubleday, Doran and Company, Inc., 1945) passim. A saccharine sweet account of the French participation.

914 The USS *Oriskany* CVA34 was built in October 1945 and mothballed at the close of hostilities. On 25Sep50, the carrier was re-commissioned for the Korean War and saw service throughout the conflict. She later received a considerable overhaul and served in the Viet Nam War. See <www.geocities.com/Pentagon/Bunker/2272/index.html>; Other Essex class carriers whose names had a Revolutionary War connotation were – Bennington, Bon Homme Richard, Bunker Hill, Franklin, Hancock, Lake Champlain, Lexington, Princeton, Ticonderoga and Valley Forge.

915 *Remembrancer 1777*, 445.

916 St. Leger to Burgoyne, 27Aug77. He said that the rearguard who fled numbered 200. One has to question how St. Leger would know and the number seems very unlikely as it represents the size of an average battalion.

917 Mackenna to Montgolfier, 10Aug77.

918 150 stood the field: Deygart to Albany committee Chairman, 9Aug77, in *Clinton Papers*, II, 203; Willett, Juvinus.

919 Scudder, 18.

920 Benjamin Dickson's PA pension application, S22208. Several details and quotations follow as an indication of Dickson's depth of memory. They suggest that the pre-ciseness of the number he gave as killed and prisoners at Oriskany might have been remembered from accurate records he had kept at the time and which were later lost to posterity. Benjamin stated that he had kept "a small journal in which he had noted several incidents" which he believed had been lost when his house was burned by Indians in Nov77. He may have recorded the number of casualties in this journal and the statistic was burned deep into his wonderful memory. Here are some examples from his pension. He told of being in a detachment in Apr77 sent "to a place near the Delaware River to quell a number of Scotch tories." In Jun77, "Captain Whitakers Company marched with the regiment of Colo. Cox... com-manded by Brig. Genl Herkimer to the mouth of the Unadilla... to make battle, or treat, with one Brandt an Indian educated by Sir William Johnston, who had col-lected about 200 indians and tories 22 miles lower down the river..." In the latter part of July77 with Gen Herkimer went "to within 4 miles of Fort Stanwix, at that time besieged by the British forces under Genl St Leger. An engagement took place between the two armies in which the Americans lost 346 men killed and prisoners. Capt Whitaker's Company however did not reach the ground until after this engagement when his men assisted in taking care of the wounded..." Benjamin was later appointed 1Lieut in Garret Putman's ranging Coy for nine months "and for the greater part... acted as and did the duties of Captain... Putman being sick." While at Ft Herkimer, Benjamin was involved in several skirmishes with the Indians. In two of these, he received "slight flesh wounds, but yet visible; One the right leg by a buck shot, and the other on the left leg by an indian spear." He

recalled being called out in the Spring of '80 to oppose Sir John at Caughnawaga.

921 Morrison Research. NYPA S11471 of George Stine, dated 20Sep1837.

922 NYPA W16645 of Hugh McMaster.

923 NYPA R11960 of Jacob A. Young.

924 NYPA S23644 of John Frank.

925 NYPA R731&732 of Peter P. Bellinger.

926 Claus to Knox, 16Oct77. "They therefore on the 6th marched on, to the number of upwards of 800, with security and carelessness. When within 6 miles of the Fort they were waylayed by our party, surprised, briskly attacked and after a little resistance, repulsed and defeated; leaving upwards of 500 killed on the spot"; de Rouville. His poem stated, "Until at the end more than five hundred remained, but all of these were slain... " In his fn#11, de Rouville stated that the militia had 800 men; *Norton Journal*, 273. Norton noted the rebels lost 500; On the other hand, St. Leger to Burgoyne, 11Aug77, stated "The compleatest Victory was obtained, above 400 lay dead on the Field."

927 Butler to Carleton, 15Aug77.

928 MacKenna to Montgolfier, 10Aug77. He wrote, "attacked 1000 "Bostonnais" (Bostonians)... here were killed two hundred."

929 Fonda to Schenectady Committee, 8Aug77, NYPL, Emmet Col, No.4611.

930 *Clinton Papers*, II, 191-92.

931 William W. Campbell, 12. Note, this page number applies to the third edition of 1880.

932 Stone, *Brant*, I, 242.

933 Pomroy Jones, 348.

934 *Remembrancer 1777*, 394-95.

935 Butler to Carleton, 15Aug77.

936 Claus to Knox, 16Oct77.

937 Claus, *Anecdotes of Brant*, 28.

938 Butler's Rangers Pay Lists. HP, AddMss21765. McGinnes was in Caldwell's Coy; *McGinnis Journal*.

939 Norton, 273.

940 Stanley, *Horse*, 128.

941 1776: NAC, WO28/5, 186-90; 1777: NAC, WO28/5, 211-20; Watt & Morrison, *Campaign of 1777*, 37-65.

942 Capts John Hare Sr. & James Wilson dead. Rangers James Clement dead and David Secord wounded.

943 Penrose, *Indian Affairs*, 125-34.

944 Morrison research. Minutes of the Council of Appointment, NYHS, V.II, 21-22,29-30.

945 Stevens, *Allies*, 1022. Quoting a Mohawk explaining the attitude of the Indians who served under Burgoyne and St. Leger two years after the events of '77.

INDEX

Comments

1. Page entries for "battles," "committees," "congresses," "creeks," "flags," "forts," "Indian nations," "Native castles and towns," and "rivers" are found under those keywords in this index.
2. All military units are found under the keyword "army."
3. A native's affiliation is designated by a two- or three-letter abbreviation after his/her name, eg. De — Delaware; Kah — Kahnawake; Tu — Tuscarora.

A

Adirondack Mountains — 31–32, 168, 170

adjutant — 91, 140, 169

adjutant-general — 74, 206

Adongot [Se] — 95

"Advance," St. Leger's — 110–11, 119, 121, 126–27

agent, *see superintendent*

alarm, *see signals*

Albany, NY — 29, 43, 47, 50, 60–61, 67, 78, 81, 90, 97, 99, 103–04, 107, 122, 131, 133, 142, 189, 201, 206–14, 217–23, 229–32, 262–63, 270–72, 274, 278, 290, 292, 296, **306–07**, 319

Albany Committee, *see committees of safety*

Albany County, *see counties*

"Alert," St. Leger's — 89, 102–05, 108, 110, 134

Allen, Jacob — 190

ambush — 135, 157–**61**–75, 178, 274, 316–17, 320, 322, 325–27

Ament, Evert — 190

America — 21, 26, 33–34, 36, 42, 44, 48, 54, 61, 69, 82, 87, 118, 128, 264, 266, 280, 314–15, 323

ammunition — 36, 65, 68–69, 87, 92, 94, 97, 101, 113, 116, 124, 126, 132–33, 222, 248, 265–66, 272, 280

Ancrum, William — 74, 206–08, 211

Anderson, Joseph — 119, 252–53, 256

Anderson, Samuel — 300

Anglican — 57, 273

Aorsen, Aaron — 104, 120

army

British — 27–28, 32, 45, 49–51, 60, 64, 72, 85, 89, 91, 98, **110**, 111, 114, 196, 233, 238, 246, 267, 276, 289, 294, 298, 302, 307

artillerymen — 37, 51, 72–73, 75, 79, 92–94, 104, 119, 127, 196, 199, **215**, **232**, 247, 249, 252, 254, 258, 266, 280, 295, 309, 320–21

Engineer — 93, 230–31, 294, 309

Marksmen, Coy of — 298–99, 301

8th (King's) Regt — 33, 43, 50,

64, 73, 84, 91–92, 101–02,
109, 111–12, 127, 194,
199, 204, 216, 224, 234,
252–53, 258, 276, 281,
295, 316, 320–21
Light Coy — 73, 91, 111, 113,
191, 276
28th Regt — 69
29th Regt — 32
31st Regt — 58, 294–95
34th Regt — 43, 69, 73–74, 78, 84,
92–94, 101–02, 111–13,
127, 193–94, 199, 224,
252, 254, 258, 277, 280,
287, 295, 316, 320–21
47th Regt — 301
48th Regt — 69
53rd Regt — 287, 95–96, 307
62nd — 289
80th Light Armed Foot — 111
95th Regt — 69
French — 69, 75, 315
German — 27, 51, 72, 289, 298–99,
302, 307
Brunswick — 76, 280, 292, 295,
301, 307, 309
Prinz Friedrich Regt — 287–88,
290, 294, 305, 307, 309
Hesse Hanau
Artillery — 293
Jäger Regt — 85, 89, 101, 104,
158, 160, 234, 265–**66**,
273, 277, 280, 296, 301,
304–05, 309
"Vacant" Coy — 92, 105,
124, 128, 131, 158,
160–**61**, 166, 173–74, **177**,
190, 195, 254, 258,
265–68, 317, 320–21
Provincial — 28, 37, 51, 64, 89, 138,
289
Butler's Rangers — 52, 58,
283–85, 308, 320
King's Royal Regt of New York
(Royal Yorkers) 1st Bn —

32–33, 37, 43–44, 50, 56,
58, 64, 66, 68–79, 84,
92–93, 102–05, 111–12,
119, 125, 128, 131, 155–56,
160, 170, 173, 180–**81**–84,
191, 195, 199, 204, 212,
216, 226, 247, 252–53, 258,
267, 276–77, 280, 287, 296,
300–01, 305, 307–09, 317,
321, 323, 326
Col's Coy — 73, 102, 119,
178, 252
Daly's Coy — 178, 224
Duncan's Coy — 73, 258
Gray's Coy — 178, 224, 252
McD's (Alex) Coy — 68
McD's (Angus) Coy — 73, 178
McD's (Jno) Coy — 110, 276,
294
Watts's Light Coy — 59, 73,
101–02, 127, 134,
155–**56**–58, **161**, 166,
170–71, 174
K's Rl Yorkers 2nd Bn — 33
Loyal Volunteers — 300–02
Quebec Militia — 72–76, 302
de Rouville's Coy — 75, 84,
91–93, 101–02, 104, 110,
119, 128, 131, 212, 321
Queen's Loyal Rangers — 305
Royal Highland Emigrants —
43–44, 75, 267, 278, 292,
294–95, **302**
United States
Continental — 34, 39, 42, 48, 51,
86, 91–92, 95, 103, **113**,
115, 140–41, 152, 169,
171, 188, 205, 216, 220,
227, 240, 242, 249, 276,
289, 315, 318
Northern Army — 88, 92, 118,
205, 232, 240, 278–79,
287, 289–90, 292, 298, 301
Artillery, Lamb's Second Regt,
Walker's Coy — 36,

87–88, 104, 130, 190,
230, 233, 240, 247
Engineers — 34, 60, 62, 81, 309
Massachusetts — 190, 206, 233,
262
Badlam's detach't — 76, 88,
95, 99, 100, 107, 116, 120,
205, 236
Learned's Brigade — 76,
133, 205, 214, 220, 229,
240, 257, 289, 298
Bailey's Regt — 205, 265
Jackson's Regt — 205,
245, 265, 290, 299
Wesson's Regt — 107,
120, 126, 205, 225, 227,
230, 239–40, 265
New Hampshire, Third — 274,
298
New Jersey, Third — 30, 33,
34, 36, 40, 48
New York — 190, 206, 298
1st — 62, 205, 259, 262,
314, 317
2nd — 226
3rd — 60, 62, 86, 113, 120,
126–27, 236, 240, 247,
312–14
1st (Benschoten's) Coy —
120, 189
2nd (DeWitt's) Coy —
62, 90, 116, 120
3rd (Jansen's) Coy — 120
4th (Swartwout's) Coy —
120
5th (Aorson's) Coy — 120
6th (Gregg's) Coy — 120,
225
7th (Tiebout's) Coy — 120
4th — 34, 169, 226
5th – 313
1st Cdn — 222, 263, 265,
289, 299
Green Mount'n Regt — 305
Levies, New York — 313

Militia
colonial — 141–42
Massachusetts — 287
New York — 27, 140–43, 290, 299
Albany County — 27, 30, 149,
205, 212, 214, 290, 322
1st Albany (Alb) Regt — 202
2nd Albany (Schen) Regt –
103, 117, 133, 202, 212
15th Albany (Sch/D'boro)
Regt — 103, 117, 133, 212
Dutchess County — 219
Tryon County — 30, 33, 36, 42,
78, 84–86, 91, 94–95, 103,
113, 115–17, 133, **173**,
197, 208, 219–20, 222–23,
239–40, 242–43, 248, 257,
262, 270, 289, 318
brigade — 27–28, 76, 117,
134, 139–40, 143–57,
159–88, 199, 201, 204,
212, 243, 250, 290, 313,
315–22, 325–27
rangers — 224
1st (Canaj) Regt — 139,
147–48, 154, 157,
159–**61**–63, 168–72, 179,
187–88
1st (Whitaker's) Coy —
147, 186, 188
4th Coy — 169, 198
5th (Dief's) Coy — 184
8th (Brown's/Miller's) Coy
— 147, 226
2nd (Palatine) Regt — 139,
148, 150, 154, 159, **161**,
167, 169, 170, 172, 183
1st (Hess's) Coy – 172
2nd Coy — 150
3rd (Fox's) Coy — 170, 178
5th (Brdbk's) Coy — 145
6th (Rechtor's) Coy —
148–50, 187–88
7th (Howse's) Coy — 145,
167

3rd (Mohawk) Regt — 139,
148, 160–**61**, 164–**65**, 168,
174, 225, 316
1st (Gardinier's) Coy —
148, 168, 178
2nd (Davis's) Coy — 145–46
4th (Visscher's) Coy — 145,
180
5th (Pettingell's) Coy — 147
6th (McMaster's) Coy — 225
Fonda's Exempts — 164
4th (Kingsland/German Flats)
Regt — 42, 139, 148, 159,
161, 168–70, 172, 175,
197, 245
4th (Harter's) Coy — 152
Ittig's Coy — 149
5th (Kortright/Old England)
Regt — 58, 139
Ulster County — 219
Arnold, Benedict — 43, **221**–26, 229,
231–33, 238–50, 256–57,
259–63, 289–90, 298–99,
322–24
artificers — 204, 212, 287, 301–02
artillery, Crown and U.S.
battery — 196, 199, 204, 229, 233,
235, 240–**41**, 252
conductor — 75
gun (solid shot/canister) — 32, 36,
40, 50, 72, 80, 82, 87–89,
101, 117, 121, 124,
126–27, 131, 152–53,
179–80, 189–90, 194, 196,
198, 205, 211, 216,
219–21, 233, 236, 239,
246–47, 249, 253, 257,
260, 265, 272, 294, 297,
300–01, 307, 309, 314–15,
327
carriage — 133, 204, 252–55, 258
Cohorn (shells) — 73, 101, 132–34,
196, 205, 212, **215**,
219–20, 229–30, 236, 246,
252, 254, 256–58, 321

howitzer (mortizer) — 230, **232**,
298
six–pounder — 73, 101, 133, 196,
199, 230, 252, 255, 258,
298
three–pounder — 73, 133, 190,
196, 252, 254, 258, 260
Austin, Charles — 195, 204
axe, *see also hatchet, tomahawk*
Axe Carrier [Se] — 95

B
Badlam, Ezra — 76, 88, 95, 99, 100,
116, 190
baggage — 68, 78–79, 121, 127, 148,
187, 206, 248, 253–54,
257, 294, 305, 309
Bagley, Josiah — 190
Bailey, John — 233, 241
Ball, John — 190
ball, rounds — 66, 68, 69, 87, 94,
101, 103, 114, 126,
162–64, 167–70, 172,
176, 178, 183–85, 196,
199, 203, 216, 235, 252,
258, 273
buck and ball — 170, 253
Barclay, John — 217
bark hut — 92, 195, **251**–52
barn — 127, 131, 216, 273
barracks, troops — 36, 62, 133, 212,
301, 309, 314
bastion — 36, 120, 126–27, 131, 133,
194, 197–**98**, 212, 231,
260
bateau(x) — 36, 40–41, 66, 74–75,
78–79, 102, 104, 114, 119,
124, 126–27, 132, 221,
234, 251–58, 260–61,
265–66, **271**, 276–77, 287,
293–95, 301, **308**–09–**10**
artillery — 132, 253, 308
brigade — 79, 91, 94, 104–**05**, 111,
116, 257, 263
Batten Kill, NY — 298

battles
  Bemis Heights (2nd Saratoga) —
      297–99, 302, **306**
  Bennington — 248, 269, 289, 292,
      305–**06**
  Bunker's (Breed's) Hill — 21, 141
  Freeman's Farm (1st Saratoga) —
      279, 288–89, 295, **306**
  Hubbardton — 289
  Lake George, 1755 — 29, 125
  Oriskany — 43, 155–89, 193, 197,
      199–200–06, 210, 213–14,
      217–18, 220, 223–25, 231,
      239, 243, 246, 250, 259,
      263–64, **306**, 315–23,
      325–27
bayonet — 56, 104, 144, 170–71, 174,
      180, 182–83, 185, 229,
      254, 270, 289
Beating Order — 32, 75, 283, 285
beef/beeves, *see cattle*
Beeler, Jacob — 169
Bellinger, Frederick — 197, 204, 206,
      224
Bellinger, Peter — 139, 148–49,
      152–53, 172, 185, 325
Bellinger, Peter P. — 318
belt, *see wampum*
Bemis Heights, NY — 292
Benschoten, *see Van Benschoten*
Bird, Henry — 111–18, 120–22, 191,
      193–94
birth — 22, 47, 256
blacks — 142–43, 152, 270
Blacksnake Dahgayadoh [Se] — 96,
      114, 122–23, 177, 326
Blake, Charles — 254
Blatcop [One] — 152, 159, 166–67
Bleecker, Leonard — 120, 190
blowdown — 159, **161**, 176, **183**
boats, *see bateau(x)*
Bogardus, Lewis — 190
Bolton, Mason — 64, 71, 281, 285,
      300
bombs, *see artillery, Cohorn*

Boston, MA — 21, 39, 62, 75, 88,
      141, 302
"Bostonians / Bostonnais" — 41, 63,
      83, 318
Bowen, Nancy — 193
Bowen, William Ryer — 224, 238, 264
Bradstreet, John — 29, 62, 133
Brant, Joseph [Mo] — 45–65, 76, 78,
      85, 87, 103–04, 107, 115,
      122, 134, 153, 156–57,
      168, 200, 213, 235–36,
      247, 251, 269–72, 319
Brant, Margaret — 270
Brant, Mary (Molly) [Mo] — 28, 47,
      134, 155, 270–71
Brant, Peggie — 48
Brant's volunteers — 57, 63, 82, 107,
      108, 121, 127, 134, 157,
      159, **161**, 164–**65**, 174,
      272, 317
Bread, Peter [One] — 279
bread, *see provisions*
Breadbake, John — 145
brigade major — 69, 93, 94, 153, 203
Britain — 48, 54, 62, 88, 114, 123,
      137, 207, 238–39, 267,
      280, 314
Brooks, John — 133, 205, 219, 227,
      229, 233, 237, 241, **245**,
      289, 299
Bronk–a–horse [Mo] — 168–69
Brown, John — 287
Buck Island — 73, **77**, 89–93, 101–02,
      104, 106, 220, 276–77,
      300
Burgoyne, John — 21–**22**, 26–27,
      32–33, 36–38, 44–45, 49,
      63, 66–67, 69, 72, 74, 78,
      80, 84, 90, 92, 94, 97, 101,
      118, 125, 141, 200, 206,
      208, 212, 217, 220–21,
      240, 251, 258, 262,
      265–71, 273–74, 278–81,
      284–90, 292–**99**–305,
      310–11, 320–23

Grand Army — 72, 101, 125, 211, 218, 220, 248, 253, 266, 269, 272, 276, 279, 287–88, 292–93, 296–97, 300, 305, 310
  capitulation — 300–03, 308
  "Reflections" — 21
  "Thoughts" — 49–51
Burnett, John — 91
Butler, Catherine — 84, 87
Butler, John — 27–30, 37–38, **52–54**, 57–59, 63, 65, 68, 71–72, 74, 78, 81, 84, 87, 93–99, 105–09, 113–14, 122–24, 134–35, 137, 140, 156–57, 170, 174, 179–**81**, 184, 197, 205–08, 211, 224, 234, 238, 248, 254, 262, 264, 267, 272, 278, 282, 284–85, 300, 307, 318–21, 323–24, 326
Butler, Thomas — 30
Butler, Walter — 74, 109, 224–25, 227, 229, 232–34, 236–38, 243, 256, 274, 289, 322
Byrne, William — 73, 179

C
Caldwell, John 1 — 37, 38, 59, 95
Caldwell, John 2 — 226
camps
  Burgoyne's — 138, 220, 239
  natives' – 191, 193, 195, 198, 200, 208, 210, 233, 269
  St. Leger's — 127, 134, 175, 185, 191–**92**, 202, 224, 226, 234–35, **241**, 245–46, 249–50, 253, 255, 258, 260
  Provincials' — 191, 195, 216, 323
camp followers, *see women*
Campbell, Colin — 292
Campbell, John — 292
Campbell, Samuel — 188
Campbell, William — 319

Canada — 23, 29, 44–46, 50, 60, 62, 69, 76, 118, 130, 139, 142, 179, 186, 200, 221, 234, 269, 274, 286–87, 292, 296, 298, 300, 302, 305
Canada Indians, *see Indian Nations, Seven Nations of Canada*
Canadagaia [Mo] – 273
Canadians (Anglophones) — 179
Canadiens (Francophones) — 32, 37, 51, 74–76, 79, 84–85, 102, 104–05, 113, 196, 212, 263, 267, 280, 287, 301
canister, *see artillery*
Captain Bull (De) — 82, 134
Carleton, Guy — 21, 23, 32–33, 36–38, **43**–47, 49, 52, 53, 56–59, 63–68, 71–76, 80, 84, 89–90, 101, 107–10, 118, 217, 234, 258, 267, 276, 280–87, 294–97, 300–03, 307, 319, 323
cartridges, *see ball, rounds*
Casler, George — 184
Casler, Jacob — 160
cataracts of the St. Lawrence — 77, **79**, 234, **271**, 277
cattle — 84, 88, 93, 101, 201, 225, 235, 262, 274, 308
Caughnawaga, NY — 202, 222, 225
Chambly, QC — 32, 72
Chase, Joshua — 190
chasseurs, *see army, Jägers*
Cherry Valley, NY — 65, 76, **138**, 147
Chimney Point, NY — **291**, 294–95, 301, 307, 309
Church
  Anglican — 28
  of Jesuits (RC) — 33
  Roman Catholic — 129
Clapsaddle, Enos — 42
Claus (Johnson), Ann/Nancy — 124, 125, **249**
Claus, Catherine – 125
Claus, Daniel — 22–28, 37, 44,

66–**67**–68, 71–72, 79–80, 88–89, 92–93, 98, 107–09, 121–26, 130, 134, 137, 140, 197, 200, 217, 224, 234, 238, 246, 248, 251, 267, 272, 274–75, 282–86, 297, 319, 323, 327

Claus, William — 125

Clergis, George — 75, 111

Clerk, Francis — 226

Clinton, George — 82, 223, 226, 250, 264–65, 272, 314, 322–23

Clinton, Sir Henry — 47, 290, 292, 296–97, 307, 311, 323, 327

Clyde, Samuel — 171, 188

Cochran, Robert — 256, 314

Colbrath, William — 104, 197, 205, 229–30

Colden, Cadwallader — 141

Colonel Louis (Atayataghronghta) [Kah] — 152, 166, 279

colours, *see flags*

Collerton, Charles — 101, 104

commissary — 61, 75, 92, 116, 225, 265, 309

Commission, Indian, *see Indian Commission*

committeemen — 29, 33, 94, 98–99, 138, 147, 149, 152, 185, 200, 213, 227, 264, 327

committees of safety — 28, 57

  Albany County — 49, 61, 98, 138, 212

  K'land&G/Flats — 149, 220, 232, 237

  Schenectady — 202

  Schoharie — 133

  Tryon — 29, 33, 41–42, 85, 88, 94, 98–99, 107, 115–16, 133, 136, 213, 220, 222, 231, 264, 324

communion plate — 274

Confederacy, *see Indian Nations, Six Nations*

Congregationalist — 33, 57

Congress

  Continental — 29, 34, 38, 41, 49, 51, 85, 95, 118, 131, 201, 214, 229, 260, 312–13, 315

  NY State — 88, 103, 107, 143, 212–13, 217, 223, 272, 322

Conine, Phillip — 190

Connecticut — **25**, 50, 231

Continental Congress, *see Congress*

corduroy — 157–**61**–**65**–68, 187

Cornplanter [Se] — 96–**98**, 122, 135

corvée — 74, 92, 110, 280

Cortlandt, Pierre — 103

council, state, *see Congress*

councils, native — 22, 39–40, 54, 59, 61, 83, 88, 90–91, 95, 98, 109, 111, 114–15, 117, 122–23, 135, 200, 202, 246, 248–49, 267, 278, 307

counties, New York

  Albany — **25**, **31**, 74, 98, **138**, 139

    Schoharie district — 214, 218

    Rensselaerwyck — 296

  Charlotte — **25**, **31**

  Tryon — **25**, **31**, **35**, 57–58, 76, 88, 94, 98, 103, **138**–39, 173, 175, 218, 221, 227, 238, 243, 265, 313, 322, 324–27

    Canajoharie district — **138**–39

    Kingsland & German Flats district — **31**, **138**–39

    Kortright/Old England district — **138**–39

    Mohawk district — **31**, **138**–40

    Palatine district — **31**, **138**–39, 264

  Ulster — **25**, 57

court martial — 87, 104, 233, 236–38, 256

covenant chain — 63, 84, 96, 108, 122, 281

covert way — 36, 126

Cox, Ebenezer — 82–83, 139, 153, 156, 159–62

Cox, William — 184
creeks
   Canada — **35**, 40, 132, 252, 254, 260
   Fish — **35**, 36, 40, 115, 117, 132
   Oneida — 35–36, 202
   Oriska(ny) — **146**, 150
   Salmon (River) — **35**, 77, 108, 134
   Saquoit — **146**, 150
   Staring — 148
   West Canada — **35, 146**
   Wood — 34–**35**, 40–41, 66, 87, 99, 107, 113, 115–17, 120–22, 126, 131–32, **146**, 217, 249, 251, 253–56, 260, 308
Crofts, William — 73–74, 93
Crouse, Robert — 198
Crown Prince, Hanau — 234, 267, 277
Crown Point, *see forts*
Crown, British — 26, 44, 48, 58, 95, 122–24, 130, 140, 169, 195, 220, 224, 227, 275, 282, 300

D
dam — 36, 133
Daveny, Hugh — 302
Davis, Benjamin — 175
Davis, John James — 145, 185
Dayton, Elias — 30, 34, 36, 39
Deane, James — 81
Deerfield, NY — **146**, 149–50
Demuth, Hans Marcus — 152–53, 189, 201, 213
Denniston, George — 190
deputy agent/superintendent — 23
de Rouville, *see Hertel de Rouville*
Desertonyon, John [Mo] — 79, 86, 88–89, 122, 253, 268, 273–74, 321
deserters — 74, 207, 209, 225, 227, 238, 240, 247–48, 253, 256–58, 298, 301, 309, 313–14, 321
Detroit, QC (MI) — 23, 74

DeWitt, Thomas — 62, 90, 120
Deygart, Peter S. — 147, 201, 213, 217, 231, 237, 270–71, 319, 322–23
Deygart, William — 322
Diamond Is., NY — 288, **291**, 294, 300, 308
Dickson, Benjamin — 318
Diefendorf, Henry 1 — 42, 184
Diefendorf, Henry 2 — 189–90
Dillenbach, William — 42
Dillenback, Andrew — 183
d'Irumberry de Salaberry, Ignace–Michel–Louis–Antoine – **76**
discipline, military — 70–72, 85, 87, 104, 110, 142, 150, 155
dispatch riders, *see express*
districts of counties, *see counties*
Docksteder, Frederick — 275
Docksteder, John — 275
Douw, Volkert — 91
drums/drummers — 69, 93, 104, 120, 126, 190, 205, 230, fifer — 245, 283
   chamade — 205
   doublings — 104
   long roll — 269
   retreat — 69, 93
   reveille — 230
   to arms — 233
   tattoo — 93
   troop — 104
drunk, *see liquor*
Duesler, John — 168
Duncan, Richard — 73, 296
Dutch — 29, 60, 141, 150, 169, 182, 211

E
Eckler, Christopher — 168
Elmer, Ebenezer — 40
Empey family — 143, 226
Empey, Jacob — 144
Empey, Maria — 226–27

Empey, Philip Sr. — 226–27
England/English — 21, 26, 37, 38, 45,
    47–49, 54, 64, 66, 82, 143,
    182, 273, 282, 285, 302
Esopus, NY— 57, 213, 278 *see also*
    Kingston
exempts — 143, 164
express (courier) — 148, 201, 217,
    225, 253, 256–57, 262,
    276, 290, 292, 294, 297,
    301–02

F
Failing, Henry N. — 187
Failing, Jacob J. – 187
Farquharson, John — 75
fieldpieces, *see artillery*
firearms/firelocks, *see muskets*
flags
  British, Grand Union — 57, 58,
      105, 192, 194–96, 301
  camp — 192, 194–96
  Continental — 127, 194
  truce — 128, 130, 204–05–07, 224,
      227, 233–34, 242, 245,
      247, 256, 292, 305
  U.S. Regt'l — 140, 199
Flanders, Henry — 149
flankers — 154, 158, 160, 191
flogging — 58, 85, 87, 104, 238, 243
Fonda, Adam — 319
Fonda, Jelles — 103, 164, 264, 322
Florida, NY — 148
Folts, Hon Jost — 152, 189, 201
Fornyea, Christopher — 224, 238
Forster, George — 33, 38, 73
Fort Hunter, NY — 61
Fort Stanwix Treaty Line — 47, 63,
    65, 139
forts
  Brewerton — 35, 256, 262
  Bull — 40, 81, 102, 133, 255
  Chambly — 27
  Crown Point — 31, 44–46, 50, 78,
      118, 291

Dayton — 31, 34–35–36, 42, 62, 90,
    91, 115–16, 131, **138**, 143,
    145–**46**–48, 168, 186, 188,
    202, 210, 214, 217, 220,
    226–27, 233, 235–36, 240,
    247–48, 257, 263, 274,
    306, 316–17
  Edward — 91, 99, 103, 218, 271,
      273, 293–94, 302, **306**
  Frontenac — 29, 62
  George — **291**, 302, **306**
  Herkimer — **146**
  Miller — 218
  Montgomery — 290, **306**
  Mount Defiance (Sugar Loaf Hill)
      — 287–88, **291**, **304**
  Mount Independence — 94,
      287–**88**, **291**, 296, 301,
      304, 307, 309
  Newport — 36, 40, 81, 126, 251,
      256
  Niagara — 37–38, 43, 49, 52–54,
      57, 59, 64, 68, 71, 74, 78,
      93, **97**, 102, 249, 262,
      266–67, 276, 280–81, 284,
      300, 307
  Ontario/Oswego — 22, 29, 40, 60,
      282
  Oswegatchie — **31**, 33, 38, 73, **77**,
      93, 234, 276–**77**, **306**
  Royal Blockhouse — 35, 41, 120
  St. John's — 32, 48, 62, 75–76,
      280–**81**, 285, 294, 303,
      306–07, 309
  Schuyler, *see Stanwix* — 39
  Schuyler (7 Yrs War) — **35**, **146**,
      150, 188
  Stanwix — **cover,** 33–**35**–36, 39–40,
      54, 60–62, 66, 79, 85–91,
      94, 98–100, 103–05, 109,
      113–17, 120–21, 124,
      126–27, 130–36, **138**, **146**,
      148, 153, 157–59, 180,
      186, 189–**92**–203, 212–22,
      227, 231–36,

239–41–44–65, 267,
269–75, 289, 293, 299,
306, 308, 312–14, 320–21,
323, 325, 327
Ticonderoga — 31, 44, 50, 62, 94,
97–99, 101, 106, 116,
211–12, 248, 279–80, 285,
287–88, 291–92, 294–96,
300–10
Fox, Christopher W. — 170, 172, 178
fraise/freize — 36, 126
Fralick, Valentine — 167
Frank, John — 149, 318
Fraser, Alexander — 298–99, 301–03
France/French(men) — 40, 55, 60,
81, 312, 314–15
treaties w/ United States — 315
Frey, Barent — 153
Frey (Shoemaker), Gertrude — 238
Frey, Hendrick — 153, 203, 231, 264
Frey, John — 153, 197, 203–04, 206,
224, 238, 325
Frey, Philip — 153, 216
Freyburger, Alexandre — 254
fusee/fusil — 171

G
Gahroondenooiya (Lying Nose)
[Ono] — 122
Gansevoort, Leonard — 61, 120
Gansevoort, Peter — 60–62, 81–82,
85–87, 90–92, 100, 107,
113–16, 120, 136, 143,
152–53, 179, 189, 196–97,
206, 209–10, 214, 216,
219, 230, 235–36, 247–48,
253, 256–58, 260, 262,
312–13, 316, 318, 323–24
Gardinier, Jacob — 148, 178, 180–83,
187
Garlock, Adam — 231
Gates, Horatio — 118, 240, 242–43,
250, 257, 260, 262–63,
271, 274, 278–79, 287,
289–90, 295, 297–98

German(y) — 222, 239, 273, 277
German (language) — 124, 164, 173
German Flats, NY — 34–35–36,
39–40, 94, 97, 117, 133,
139, 143, 145–46, 148,
205, 210, 213, 219, 222,
225–27, 231, 237, 242,
257, 281, 314
Germain, Lord George — 26, 45–48,
51, 56, 63, 84, 239,
280–81, 284–85, 323
Glenn, Henry — 221
Glennie, James — 196, 204, 230
grape shot, *see canister*
Gray, Elizabeth — 305
Gray, James — 30, 32, 56, 58–59, 64,
78, 93, 94, 102–03, 271,
300–01, 305
Great Peace (Iroquois) – 150
Gregg, James — 81, 88, 104, 120
Gros, Rev. Johann Daniel — 147
Gummersall, Thomas — 294
guns, *see artillery*
Guy Park — 21–22

H
Half Moon, NY — 217–18, 25
Hamilton, Alexander — 311
Hamilton, William Osborne — 75
Hancock, John — 229
hanger, *see sword*
Hansen, John — 61–62, 116, 212, 225
Hare, John — 56, 79, 89, 102, 108,
113, 115, 185–86
Harper, John Jr. — 58, 82
harvest — 115
hatchet, *see also tomahawk*
hatchet (metaphorical) — 22, 54,
100, 150, 196, 274, 278,
300
Haudenosaunee, *see Indian Nations,
Six Nations Confederacy*
Haunnagwasuke, Cornelius Henry
[One] — 152, 159
hay — 115, 128, 131, 216

Helmer, Adam F. — 152, 189, 201, 212, 218
Helmer, Frederick — 149, 153
Herkimer, Abraham — 84
Herkimer, George — 84, 322
Herkimer, Han Jost — 42, 131, 153, 196, 254, 271, 322
Herkimer, Nicholas — 42, 65, 76, 78, 82–94, 100, 103, 107–08, 115, 117, 133, 143, 148–54, 159–62, 167, 171, 174, 176–77, 179, 183–**84**, 186–89, 196–97, 201–04, 206, 210, 218–20, 222, 231–33, 250, 259, 263, 315–16, 319, 322–27
  death of — 233
  home — **146**, 148, 231
Hertel de Rouville, Jean–Baptiste–Melchior — 75, 131, 212, 221, 231, 255
Hess, John — 172
Highlanders, Scottish — 28, 29, 170, 182
Hildebrand, Phillip — 92, 254
Hill, Mary [Mo] — 39
Hillyer, Nicholas — 68
horse — 147–50, 154, 159–60, 162, 164, 171–72, 186–87, 251, 258, 270, 274, 294, 299, 308
hospital — 273, 280
Howe, Sir William — 45, 47–50, 52, 54, 65–68, 72, 81, 101, 105, 217, 248, 281–82, 292, 311–12, 323
Hoyes, Robert — 193–94, 252
Hubbell, Nathaniel — 34, 60, 92
Hudson Highlands, NY — 67, 312
Hull, William — 233, 237, 289

I

Indian affairs — 21, 37, 39, 57, 86, 93, 125, 142, 229, 267, 272, 274, 277–78, 281, 285

Indian castles and towns
  Akwesasne [Mo] — **31**, 33, 77, 98
  Allegheny — 74, 95
  Canadasaga [Se] — 275
  Canajoharie [Mo] — 42, 47, 57, 61, 63, 83, 87, 107, 123, 134, **138**, 145, 159, 202, 251, 267, 269–70, 273, 322
  Cayuga [Ca] — 54, 270, 275
  Coolateen — 272
  Finger Lakes — 74
  Fort Hunter [Mo] — 30–**31**, 48, 57, 61, 87, 107, 123, 134, **138**, 164, 168, 251, 267–68, 273–74, 302–03, 321
  Ganaghsaraga (Canasaraga) [Tu] — **35**, 53
  Genesee (Chenussio) [Se] — 52, 95, 162
  Grand River — 320
  Kahnawake [Mo] — 77, 91, 116, 166
  Kanawolohale [One] — 33, **35**, 41, 49, 81, 90, 98, 116, 118, **138**, 255
  Lower Castle, *see Fort Hunter*
  Old Onedia, *see Kanawolohale*
  Onondaga [Ono] — 53, 102, 262,
  Oquaga [mixed] — 47–48, 57, 58, 63, 78, 91, 103–04, 115, **138**, 251, 272
  Oriska [One] — **31**, 134, **138**, **146**, 150, 152, 187–89, 201–02, 210, 220, 225–26, 263, 270, 317
  Seneca Lake [Se] — 96, 97
  Skoiyase [Se] — 81
  Tiononderoga, *see Fort Hunter*
  Upper Castle, *see Canajoharie*
Indian Commission, U.S. — 39, 49, 61, 91, 103, 235, 278
Indian council, *see council, native*
Indian Department

Six Nations — 21, 23, 37, 47, 56, 59, 66, 74, 89, 93, **97**, 102, 113, 134, 153, 224, 226, 235, 320

Quebec — 23, 37, 53, 80, 109, 292

Indian Nations

Affiliates of the Six Nations

  Mohicans — 57

  Squakis — 166

Allies of the Six Nations —

  Delawares — 27, 49, 54, 82, 134, 251

  Lakes Nations — 39, 72, 93, 134, 157, 174, 199, 204, 242

    Chippawas — 108

    Ottawas — 108

    Potawatomis — 108

    Wyandots — 23, 108

  Mississaugas — 59, 74, 85, 91, 102, 108, 111–15, 117, 121, 127, 200, 242, **251**, 256

  Western Nations — 39, 275

River Indians, Stockbridges — 39, 279

Six Nations Confederacy — 26, 27, 37–39, 48–49, 53, 55, 57, 60–61, 71, 74, 84, 90, 91, 95–97, 99, 102, 105, 108–09, 111, 116–18, 122, 139, 141, 150, 170, 185, 191, 196, 198, 224, 229, 242, 262, 267, 274–75, 278, 281–82, 320, 327

  Cayugas — **24**, 53, 57, 79, 103–04, 122–23, 134, 157, 160–**61**, 195, 247, 275

  Mohawks — 22, 28, 30, 39, 42, 47–48, 52, 54, 57, 61–63, 76, 82, 84, 87, 107–08, 121–23, 134, 157, 159–**61**, 164, 168, 174, 178, 203, 222, 224, 251, 253, 255, 268–70, 273, 278, 302–03, 317, 322–23

  Oneidas — **24**, 33–34, 39–41, 47, 49, 53–55, 57, 59, 90, 96, 98–99, 103, 115–18, 120, 122, 126, 134, 150–**61**, 166– 67, 187, 191, 196, 199, 218–19, 222, 224–25, 236, 240, 245–47, 249, 253–54, 262, 264, 270, 272–73, 278–79, 300, 314, 317

  Onondagas — **24**, 53, 90, 122, 134, 157, 224, 262, 278, 300

  Senecas — **24**, 39, 51–54, 57, 81, 90, 93, 95–97, 108–09, 113–18, 121–22, 124, 127, 134, 156–57, 160–**61**, 163, 166, 195, 224, 247, 275, 300, 319–20

  Tuscaroras — 34, 39, 53–55, 57, 96, 122, 156, 159, 240, 262, 278–79, 300

Seven Nations of Canada (Canada Indians) — 22–23, 39, 66, 68, 72, 80, 157, 242, 269, 274, 303

  Akwesasnes — 32, 53, 98

  Kahnawakes — 116, 152, 278, 285

  Kanehsatakes — 53, 274, 285

Indian Territory — **24–25**, 35, 47, 61, 77, 139, 270, 272

Indian trade — 39, 54, 65, 72, 88, 102, 122–23, 149, 220, 275, 300

interpreter — 37, 47, 81, 107

Ireland/Irish — 32, 64, 69, 175, 216

Irondequoit Bay, IT (NY) — 74, 93, 95, 105, 109, 123

Iroquois Confederacy, *see Indian Nations, Six Nations*

Ittig, Michael — 264

J

jail (gaol) — 42, 43, 226–27

Jansen, Cornelius — 120, 190, 253

Jemison, Mary [Se] — 124
Jessup, Ebenezer — 44, 45, 305
Jessup, Edward — 305
Johnson, Guy — 21–**23**–28, 33, 37,
        38, 45–53, 57, 66–67, 72,
        105, 140, 147, 149, 153,
        179, 267, 282, 284–85,
        323
Johnson, Mary — 22, 28, 38
Johnson (Watts), Lady Mary (Polly)
        — 30, 44–**46**–47, 66,
        124–25, 191, 300
Johnson, Nancy — 125
Johnson, Quahyocko Brant [Mo] —
        42
Johnson, Sir John — 27–**28**–30,
        32–33, 37, 40–42, 44,
        47–51, 56, 58–59, 64,
        66–67, 69, 75, 78–79, 85,
        89–91, 94, 98, 105, 110,
        113, 124–25, 134–35, 137,
        140, 147, 152, 155–58,
        166, 168–70, 174–75, 178,
        182, 191, 193, 197, 200,
        204, 224, 226–27, 238–39,
        248, 254–55, 265, 276,
        287, 296–97, 300, 302,
        305, 319
Johnson, John Jr. — 44, 125
Johnson, Sir William — 21, 25,
        27–28, 37, 39, 44, 47, 49,
        54, 57, 96, 125, 142, 249
Johnson, William — 125
Johnson Hall — 28, **30**, 48, 125
Johnston, John — 82, 275
Johnston, Robert — 231–33
Johnston, William — 275
Johnstone, Rev. William — 63
Johnstown, NY — **31**, **138**, 147, 179,
        222, 263–64
Jones, John — 297, 300
Jones, Pomroy — 319, 325

K
Kanonraron, Aaron [Mo] – 273

Kayashuta [Se] — 95
"Keepers of the Fire," *see Onondagas*
kettles — 97, 193, 196, 258, 273
Killegrew, Sjt. ? — 94, 197
Kilts, Conrad — 188
King George III — 30, 32, 41–42, 48,
        51, 53–56, 58, 63, 65, 70,
        83, 84, 93, 95–96, 109,
        120, 128, 136–37, 174,
        198, 212, 234, 237–38,
        274, 277, 280, 283, 294,
        296, 302
Kingston, NY — 212–13, 217, 223,
        264, **306**
Kirkland, Rev. Samuel — 33–**34**, 49,
        54–55
Klock, George Jury — 83, 159
Klock, Jacob — 41, 82, 139, 145, 153,
        156, 159–60,
Klock, Jacob Jr. — 150
knives — 32, 97, 166, 172–73

L
Lachine, QC — 66, 68, 69, 73, 74,
        77–79, 91, 277
lakes
    Champlain — **24**, **31**, 33, 36–38,
        43, 46, 78, 97, 221, 265,
        281, **288**, **291**, 293, **304**,
        306
    George — 29, **31**, 287–88, **291**,
        293–95, **306**, 308
    Oneida — **24**, 34, 40–41, **77**,
        114–16, 120, 126, 132,
        254–56, 262
    Ontario — **24**, 38, 41, 50, 74, **77**,
        91, 96, **105**, 276–77, 293,
        306
    Otsego — 139
La Marquisie, Bernard — 60, 62, 81,
        86, 92, 126, 133
Land, Robert — 65
land patents — 44
    Banyar — 58
    Harpersfield — 58, 65

Kingsborough – 179
Kortright — 58
New Stamford — 58
landings
Lake George — 287–88
Lower — 111, 126–27, 131, 190,
219, 250–52
Upper — 190, 194
Langan, Patrick — 66, 89
La Prairie, QC — 27, 32, 266, 279,
306
Lawrence, John — 258
Leake, Robert — 300
Learned, Ebenezer — 76, 217, 220,
241–42, 298–99
Leathers, John — 185
Lernoult, Richard — 59–60, 95, 199,
249, 251, 256, 260, 276
lifeguards — 148, 162
Lipscomb, Richard — 73, 179
liquor — 54, 75, 78, 86, 91, 93, 96,
108, 123, 149, 163,
213–14, 250, 252–54, 256,
258, 263, 275
litters — 186–88, 204, 303
Little Falls, NY — 139, **146**, 148, 188
Little Warriors' Society — 193
Livingston, Henry Beekman — 226
Livingston, James — 222, 263, 289
"Lobsters," *see Army, British*
Long Sault cataract — 102
Lonis, George — 172, 186
Lundy, James — 75, 132, 267, 271

M
McClellan, Thomas — 190
McCrae, Jane — 138, 303, 324
McDonell, Alexander (Aberchalder)
— 64, 68–69
McDonell, Angus — 73
McDonell, (Donald) John Jr. (Scotus)
— 64, 73, 110, 178–82,
184, 252, 276
McDonell, Hugh (Aberchalder) — 64
McDonell, John (Leek) — 64

McDonell, John (Scotus) Sr. — 58,
64, 110, 264, 276, 294
McDonell, Kenneth — 73
McGinnis, George — 173, 235, 275
McGinnis, Richard — 41, 320
McGinnis, Robert — 41
McGinnis, Sarah Kast — 174, 220,
235, 275
McGinnis, William 1 — 41
McGinnis, William 2 — 235
MacKay, Samuel — 301–02
Mackenna, Father John — 124, 215,
254, 316, 318
McKenzie, John — 73, 158, 171
Mackesy, Piers — 311–12
Maclean, Allan — 43, 44, 279, 285,
294–95, 301–02, 307, 309
McMaster, Hugh — 318
Madison, Samuel — 81, 88
Magee, Peter — 190
"Main party," St. Leger's — 104–05,
110, 119, 124–27, 131
Mann, George — 212
marksmen — 111, 131, 133, 162, 164,
166–67, 169, 178, 185,
189, 197–98, 216, 235,
239, 246, 297, *see also,*
Coy of Marksmen
Martin, John — 126
Masonic Lodge — 28, 78
Massachusetts — **25**, 28
Mellon, James — 126, 131, 206, 225,
230, 239
Merckley, William — 167
militia, system of — 141–43
militia, *see army*
Miller, Adam — 182, 184–86
Miller, Jacob — 226
mineshaft — 231, 239
Mohawk Region — 26, 33, 38, 43, 57,
58, 64, 84, 97, 189, 201,
218, 227, 313–14
Montreal, QC — 22, 32–33, 44,
47–49, 56, 58, 64, 67, 69,
71, **77**, 88, 93, 235, 250,

266–67, 279–80, 285–86, 293, **306**

Morrison, James — 318

mortars, *see artillery, Cohorns*

Munro, John — 278, 305

musket(ry) — 30, 32, 56, 72, 83, 93–94, 97, 104–05, 144, 155–56, 163, 166, 168, 171–73, 175–76, 179, 182–83, 186, 194, 197, 207, 229, 239, 247, 252–53, 263, 268–69, 289, 294, 299, 315

mutilation (ritual) — 86, 138, 199

N

navy

French — 55, 315

Royal/Prov'l — 27, 43, 46, 48, 102, 105, 128, 179, 266, 272, 281, 287, 290, 302

U.S. — 43, 221, 315

neutrality, native — 78, 95, 123, 262, 273, 278

New Dorlach, NY — 147, 226

New England(ers) — 21, 41, 116, 118, 131, 217

New Hampshire Grants, NY — 64

New York City — 29, 45, 47–48, 62, 65– 66, 116, 217, 265, 267, 290, 292, **306**, 315

New York Province/State — 21, **24–25**, 29, 32, 45–46, 77, 86, 118, 120, 141, 143, 145, 238, 272, 314

Council of Appointment – 322

Niagara, *see forts*

Nine Mile Point — 114, 121–22

Northern District (Military), NY — 27, 29, 140

Norton, John — 320

O

oath of allegiance — 104, 226

Ojagehte (Fish Carrier) [Ca] — 122

Old Isaac [One] — 49

Old Smoke [Se] — 54, 96, 97, 122, 135, 195, 200

Oneida Carry, the — 34–**35**, 38–40, 62, 79, 81, 121, 131, 178, 314

Onoghsokte, Hill, Isaac [Mo] – 273

Oppenheim, NY — 145

orderly book — 69, 78, 191, 305

Ostrander, Thomas — 190

Oswego (Onondaga) Falls, NY — **35**, 115, 119, 262

Oswego, IT (NY) — 22, 29, **35**, 40–41, 50, 65, **77**, 81, 84–85, 90–91, 98–109, 113–15, 122, 196, 249, 251–52, 265–66, 272, 275, 282, 285, 293–94, 300, 308, 320

Oswegatchie, *see Forts*

Oundiaga [Ono] — 122

oxen — 114, 148, 150, 160, 164–**65**, 270, 308

P

paint (Indians) — 90, 108, 163, 279

Palatine Germans — 64, 143, 182

parade, the — 120, 212

Paris, Isaac — 153, 193, 275–76

Parliament, British — 21, 137

patrol — 40, 111–21, 126, 127, 235, 307

Paulus Hook, NY — 47

Peekskill, NY — 223, 226

Pennsylvania — **24**, **25**, 48, 122

Peters, John — 305

Petrie, William — 172, 232, 236

Pettingell, Samuel — 147

Philadelphia, PA — 67, **306**

Phillips, William — 78

picket

(guard) — 149, 150, 216, 230, 297

(palisade) — 36, 62, 126, 221, 225

pilot — 75, 79

Pine Ridge — 132

pioneering (military) — 131–34, 212
Pixly, Eli — 236, 248
"Place of Sorrows" — 167
Point Clair, QC — 68, 78
Pontiac Uprising — 27, 49, 54
Pool, Hendrick? — 82
Potts, William — 73, 91, 102, 300
powder, gun — 54, 82, 87, 103, 163,
        196, 230, 260, 309,
        314–15
Powell, Henry Watson – 287, 294–95,
        297, 300–01, 303, 307
Powless, Paul [One] — 152, 235–36
Presbyterian, *see Congregationalist*
prisoners — 86, 89, 97, 104, 126, 131,
        150, 172–75, 185–86, 193,
        196–97, 199, 203–04, 229,
        234, 238, 242, 249, 254,
        258, 262, 273–79, 287,
        303, 305, 310, 313,
        316–18, 321, 325
proclamation
  Arnold's — 238–39, 324
  Herkimer's — 100–101, 103, 107,
        139, 144
  Johnson/Claus/Butler — 224,
        227–29, 324
  St. Leger's — 128–30, 224, 227, 324
Provincials, *see army, British*
provisions — 68, 75–78, 86–88,
        92–94, 101–02, 104–05,
        113, 116, 119, 123–4, 126,
        132, 148, 197, 201, 214,
        222, 234, 247, 252,
        256–57, 259, 263–66, 272,
        276–77, 280, 292–94, 296,
        300–01, 307, 321, 327
Putman, Israel — 226

Q
Quackenboss, Abraham – 187
Quackenbush, Abraham — 168, 169
quartermaster — 93, 102, 140, 217,
        269, 271, 294
quartermaster–general — 74, 75, 267

deputy — 74, 92, 221, 295
Quebec City, QC — 27, 63, 67, 110,
        221, 282, 284–85,
        299–303
Quebec Province — 21, **24–25**, 32,
        36, 43–46, 53, 56, 66–67,
        75–76, 179, 280–81, 283,
        285, 305, 309–10
Queen Anne's Chapel — 273

R
rainstorms — 132, 175–76, 190, 219,
        261, 277, 314
Rangers, (Crown) Indian Dept — 27,
        37, 58, 71, 74, 102,
        108–09, 121–22, 131, 134,
        155–58, 160–**61**, 163, 173,
        175, 180, 184–86, 235,
        252–53, 262, 267, 282,
        285, 308, 317, 321, 326
rapids, *see cataracts*
rearguard — 148, 160, 164–**65**, 168,
        188, 190–91, 213, 225,
        280, 317
Rechtor, Nicholas — 148
recruits — 226–27, 239, 276, 296, 300
Red Jacket [Se] — 163
redoubt
  Breymann's — 299
  St. Leger's — **192**, 196, 199, 204,
        241, 253
Regulars, *see army, British*
Reyter, George — 137
rifle(men) — 33, 131, 152, 162, 168,
        198, 236, 254, 258, 265,
        268, 298–99
rivers
  Charlotte — 57, 64, 110, **138**
  Hudson — **24, 31**, 33–34, 44,
        66–67, 232, 250, 279, 286,
        290, 293–94, **306**
  Mohawk — **24, 31**, 33–35, 43, 45, 50,
        58–59, 74, 78–79, 91, 103,
        111, 116, 132–33, **138–39**,
        146, 148–49, 168, 175,

192, 194, 208, 218, 234,
238, **241**, 293, **306**
Oswego — **24**, 35, 119
Richelieu — 281, 293
St. Lawrence — **25**, **31**, 36, 38, 77,
79, 88, 91, 217, 234, 265,
271, 276–77, 279, 293,
306
Salmon, *see creeks*
Susquehanna — 58, **138**–39
roadwork — 91, 131–32, 155, 159
Roof, Johannes — 131, 137
Roff/Roof, John — 231
Royal Blockhouse, *see forts*
Rudyerd, Henry — 93, 231, **288**, **308**
"ruse de guerre" — 180–**81**–82,
243–49, 256

S
Sabbath — 215, 233
sachems — 61, 95, 116, 122, 124, 254,
272, 275
St. Leger, Barry —
frontispiece — 40, 43, 51, 64–67,
69–**70**–76, 80, 84, 89–93,
101–15, 120–21, 124–31,
142–43, 147, 152, 158,
174, 178, 193–200,
204–07, 210, 212, 215–17,
220, 224–25, 230, 234,
239–42, 246–68, 271, 273,
276–82, 285, 287, 289,
292–98, 302, 310–11, 316,
320–24, 326
drinking — 131, 193, 263, 288, 327
sally port — 36, 208, **241**
sally/sallies — 127, 131, 134, 152, 153,
179, 185, 189–94, 199,
207–08, 233, 240, 242,
251, 253–54, 259
Sammons, Frederick — 145, 147
Sammons, Jacob — 180, 182
Sammons, Plat — 225, 227
Sanders, Henry — 184
sap, *see siege trench*

Saratoga, NY — 239, 251, 287, 300,
302, **306**
Savage, Joseph — 87, 104, 190
Saweetoa [Se] — 95
Sayengaraghta, *see Old Smoke*
scalp(ing) — 81, 86, 97, 104, 114,
124, 127, 136, 138, 164,
167, 172–73, 179, 196,
199, 216, 254, 274, 301
Schenectady, NY — 133, 214, 221,
306
Schermerhorn, William — 296
Schoughyowote [Ca] — 79
Schuyler, Elizabeth — 243, 245
Schuyler, Hanjost — 42, 224, 237–38,
243–49, 253, 256, 258,
270, 324
Schuyler, Nicholas — 243, 245
Schuyler, Philip — **29**–30, 33, 36,
39–40, 50–51, 54, 59–60,
64, 76, 78, 81–87, 90–100,
103, 107, 113, 116, 118,
133, 189, 200–01, 205,
210, 214–15, 219–24, 229,
232, 281–82, 300, 323
Schuyler's Corners — 150
Sciawa [Se] — 95
Scotland/Scotsmen — 28, 58, 64, 110,
140–41, 160, 170–71, 182,
227, 301
Scott, Robert — 274
Scott, Thomas — 292
Scott, Rev Thomas — 193
Scotus, *see McDonell, John*
scouting — 40, 56, 58, 85, 90, 99,
104, 108, 111, 117–18,
147, 155, 191, 208, 235,
243, 246–47, 313
Scudder, William — 259, 317
Seeber, Jacob — 169, 188, 204
Seeber, William — 94, 98
Senagena [One] — 152, 159, 166, 188
sentinel/sentry — 133, 189, 197–**98**,
207, 259, 309
Serihowane [Se] — 95

Seven Years War — 29, 48–49, 111, 132, 141, 143, 147, 150, 171, 314

shells, *see artillery, Cohorn*

Sheqwoieseh (Dragging Spear) [Tu] — 122

Shoemaker, Rudolph — 227, 237–38

Shoemaker's tavern — 227–**28**, 237, 289, 321–22

siege
  of Boston — 39
  of Fort St. John's — 48
  of Fort Stanwix — 126–261
  of Quebec — 27

siege trench — 211, 221, 230–31, 235–36, 239, **241**, 246–48, 252–54

signals — 105, 119–20, 126, 152, 158, 189, 296, 309

Singleton, George — 73, 158, 171, 175, 191–92, 205, 258

Sir John Johnson's Corps, *see army, Prov'l, Royal Yorkers*

Sits, Henry — 172

Skenandon [One] — 41, 53

Skenesborough, NY — **291**, 305–**06**

Skinner, Joseph — 68

sluice — 133

Smith, Henry — 162

Snell, John — 188

Snell, Peter — 167

snipers/sniping, *see marksmen*

snow — 303, 307, **310**

Sommers, Peter — 226

sortie, *see sally*

spear, *see spontoon*

Spencer, Edward [One] — 90, 94, 167

Spencer, Henry [One] — 152, 159, 167

Spencer, Thomas [One] — 90, 98–100, 115–16, 152, 154, 159, 167

Sponable, John — 150, 200

spontoon — **113**, 163–64, 168, 180, 182, 208

Spoor, John — 86, 87

Staring, Henry — 149

State Council, *see Congress, NY State*

Stephane, Lenea — 137, 216

Stiles, Ely — 236, 248

Stillwater, NY — 205, 218–19, 229, 232, **306**

Stine, George — 318

Stockwell, Levi — 190, 208, 213, 236

Stone Arabia, NY — **31**, **138**, 143, 226

Stone, William L. — 319, 325

Stuart, Rev. John — 84, 87, 273

superintendent, deputy, Indians (Crown) — 37, 52, 66, 72, 80, 105, 109, 122, 157

superintendent general, Northern Indians (Crown) — 21, 25, 38

superintendent, Western Expedition — 66–**67**, 88, 93, 124, 285

surgeon — 62, 68, 140, 160, 162, 172, 174, 195, 204–07, 231–33, 254, 277

Swartwout, Abraham — 104, 120, 190–91, **244**

sword — 32, 148, 152, 168, 171, 178,184, 203, 268, 313

Sytez, George — 196

T

tactics — 76, 111–**12**, 114, 119, 135, 162–63, 166, 168–72, 174, 180, 242, 259, 269, 289, 299

tailors — 68–69

teamsters — 160, 164–**65**

Teaqwanda [Ono] — 122, 327

Ten Broeck, Abraham — 42, 212, 290, 299

Ten Broeck, Peter — 42, 224, 238, 264, 322

tents — 124, 127, 132, 191–92, 216, 249, 252–53, 255–58, 268, 272, 309

Tewahangaraghkan, Honyery [One]
152, 159, 166, 188,
270–71, 278
Tewahangaraghkan, Honyost [One]
— 152
Teyawarunte [Ono] — 122, 327
Thompson, Alexander – 325
Thompson, Andrew — 235
Thompson, Dorothy — 220, 235
Thompson, Elizabeth — 220, 235
Thompson, Henry — 178
Thompson, Margaretha — 220
Thompson, Samuel — 235
Thompson's trading post — 149, 220
Three Rivers, NY — **35**, 109, 111, 114,
116–17, 124, 127, 134, 150
Tice, Mrs. (Christian) — 48, 264
Tice, Gilbert — 47–49, 65, 102, 108,
128, 130, 285, 302
Ticonderoga, *see forts*
Tiebout, Henry — 104, 120
Timmerman, Henry — 187–88
Tocenando [Se] — 195
tomahawk — 32, 97, 144, 162–64,
166–68, 171, 173–74
Towasguate [Ono] – 262
Towawahgahque (Rail Carrier) [One]
— 122
trade, Indian, *see Indian trade*
treaty, native, *see council, native*
Treaty Line, *see Fort Stanwix Treaty
Line*
Tribes Hill, NY — 224
Trumbull, Jonathon Jr. — 231
Tryon, William — 48
Tryon County, *see counties*
Turtle clan — 97
Tyorsansere Little Abraham [Mo] —
273

U
Unadilla (Tyonadello,) NY — 63, 65,
78, 82, 85, 108, **138**, 153
Unaquandahoojie, Johannes Schrine
[Mo] — 273

uniforms — 32, 59, 64, 68–69, 73, 76,
94, 99, **119**, 140, 143–45,
155, **177**, 180–**81**, 186–87,
197, **232**, 243, 252, 259,
276, 292
United States — 38, 42, 61, 63, 90,
95, 211, 234, 238–39, 274,
276, 315
treaties w/France — 315

V
valley
Mohawk — 21, 26–28, 33–51, 56,
61, 63, 66, 95, 99, 114,
128, 131, **138**, 149, 153,
178–79, 198, 200–02, 205,
211, 215–16, 224–25, 239,
258, 298, 323, 326
Schoharie — 215, 264, 276, 294
van/vanguard — 154, 159–60, 179,
190–91, 263
Van Benschoten, Elias — 120, 190–91
Van Cortlandt, Philip — 226
Van Dyck, Cornelius — 205, 222, 241
Van Eps, Evert — 164
Van Schaick (Gansevoort),
Caty/Catherine — 81, 87,
113, 196, 211, 313
Van Schaick, Goose — 60, 76, 81, 88,
95, 99, 103, 107, 114, 133,
219, 314
Van Vechten, Anthony — 169, 322
Van Vechten, Derick — 186
Veeder, Volkert — 168, 169, 187, 322
victuals, *see provisions*
Visscher, Frederick — 139, 147, 153,
164, 168–69, 172, 187,
225, 322
Visscher, John — 145, 147
Volunteer, Gentleman — 64, 171, 179
Von Hille, Julius — 288, 301, 305,
308–09
Von Kreutzbourg, Carl — 234, 265,
267–68, 272–73, 276–77,
279–80, 304–05

Von Riedesel, Baroness — 302
Von Riedesel, Friedrich Adolph — 293, 297
Vrooman, Peter — 133

W
Waggoner, Joseph — 83, 84
wagons — 124, 132, 148, 155, 159–60, 164, 175–76, 187, 204, 221, 248, 252–53, 258, 273, 287, 321, 327
Wakarantharaus, *see Powless*
Walrath, Garret — 172
Walroth, Henry J. — 169, 174, 193, 199, 204
Walter, George — 167, 183
wampum belt/string — 48, 53, 90, 117, 123, 193, 195, 275
war axe, *see hatchet*
war belt, *see wampum*
War Captain — 41, 96, 97, 122–**24**, 135, 152, 157–59, 162, 174, 195, 200, 214, 246–47, 249, 255, 268, 270, 275, 319–20
  rogue — 108
Washington, George — 40, 48, 54, 141, 226, 232, 311, 314
watch, pocket — 173, 187
water supply — 217, **241**
Watson Powell, *see Powell*
Watts, Margaret — 47
Watts, Stephen — 58, 59, 73, 111, 156–58, 171, 180, 184–85, 187, 196, 204, 213
Weaver, George M. — 245
Wesson, James — 115, 210, 214, 219, 227, 236–37, 241
Whitaker, Thomas — 27, 186, 188

Wilkinson, Richard — 119
Willett, Marinus — 62, 126–27, 189–**92**, 203, 206–10, 217, 220, 231, 233, 236, 241–43, 246, 262, 269, 313, 316, 318, 322, 325
  letter to troops — 208–10
  sally, Aug 6 — 189–**92**–94, 196, 252–53, 267, 275, 316, 319, 323
  sally, Aug 8 — 208–14
William of Canajoharie [Mo] — 57, 82, 178, 213
Willson, James — 102, 108, 113, 121, 186
Wolf Clan — 53, 97
women
  followers — 30, 98, 125, 249, 281
  garrison — 114, 136–38, 196, 230, 246, 256
  inhabitants (Loy) — 42, 48, 131, 139, 203, 264, 276, 307
  inhabitants (Whig) — 53, 65, 100, 188, 207
  native — 47, 82, 93, 96, 123, 193–95, 224, 251, 270–71, 274–75, 278, 282, 302–03
Woodruff, Hunloke — 62, 207
Wraxall, Peter — 142

Y
York City, *see New York City*
Young, Andrew — 204, 212
Young, Jacob A. — 318
Younglove, Moses — 160, 172–75, 198, 254, 275–77

Z
Zimmerman, John — 188